The Emergence of Monasticism

The Emergence of Monasticism

From the Desert Fathers
to the
Early Middle Ages

Marilyn Dunn

Blackwell Publishing

© 2000, 2003 by Marilyn Dunn

BLACKWELL PUBLISHING
350 Main Street, Malden, MA 02148-5018, USA
9600 Garsington Road, Oxford OX4 2DQ, UK
550 Swanston Street, Carlton, Victoria 3053, Australia

First published 2000 by Blackwell Publishers Ltd, a Blackwell Publishing company
First published in paperback 2003

2   2007

Library of Congress Cataloging-in-Publication Data

Dunn, Marilyn.
   The emergence of monasticism: from the Desert Fathers to the early Middle Ages / Marilyn Dunn.
     p. cm.
   Includes bibliographical references and index.
   ISBN 978-0-631-13463-3 (hardcover: alk. paper)—ISBN 978-1-4051-0641-2 (paperback)
   1. Monastic and religious life—History—Early church, ca. 30–600. I. Title.

BR195.M65 D86 2001
271'.009'015—dc21   00-057905

A catalogue record for this title is available from the British Library.

Set in 10.5 on 12 pt Galliard
by Kolam Information Services Pvt. Ltd., Pondicherry, India

For further information on
Blackwell Publishing, visit our website:
http://www.blackwellpublishing.com

Contents

Preface

Early monastic history is a uniquely complex subject. No other area of history potentially covers so many disciplines and areas, intellectual and geographical. It can extend itself over the study of history (political, religious, social and economic), theology, liturgy, archaeology, philosophy, religious studies, gender studies, sociology and anthropology. The widely differing methodologies and approaches which exist may be sampled across the great range of journals in which it is possible to read about monastic issues from *Revue Bénédictine* and *Studia Monastica* on one hand, through periodicals such as the *Journal of Early Christian History* and *Semeia*, to *Annales* on the other. Yet for all the great weight of interpretation which can be brought to bear on monastic history, there still exists a major divide between those who are perceived as 'monastic historians' and other historians and theorists, a gulf which separates those whose approach is primarily textual and liturgical from those who work with, in and from other disciplines. This book represents, as far as is possible within the obvious constraints of a chronological framework, a first attempt to examine monasticism in the light of the great variety of relevant approaches. Its working title was 'Out of the Desert' – a title by which I had hoped not only to pay tribute to the nuanced and compelling ideas which are emerging from the study of Egyptian monasticism but also to indicate that the book follows the broad trajectory of the most important aspects of monastic development from the fourth to the seventh centuries rather than being an exhaustive or region-by-region survey.

One of the primary problems for the historian working in this field is the nature of monastic literature itself. A large part of the purpose of monastic texts is to look back to earlier days of monasticism and beyond that the Bible. The constant repetition of sections taken from earlier works is one of the most noticeable features of monastic writing – especially monastic rules

– in which the search for perfection was always accompanied by the perception of earlier wisdom and the desire to maintain orthodox tradition. It is, perhaps, easier to see where each piece of writing stands in monastic tradition than to see where it is going in terms of monastic development. Here, I have attempted to place such writings in context. Some areas have proved or will prove controversial, but I have always maintained that history moves forward by debate and dialectic and hope that it may be conducted in an open and civilized manner.

I would like to express thanks to those who have helped and supported me in writing this book. To Tony Goodman, for suggesting I write it in the first place and to John Davey for commissioning it. To a number of colleagues and friends in a variety of disciplines, particularly Donald Bullough, Thomas Clancy, Gary Dickson, Judith George, Richard Rose and Alex Woolf, for advice, discussion, encouragement and criticism. None of them should be blamed for any view expressed here. To Craig Fraser and Penny Galloway for practical help as well as moral support. To many students for asking difficult questions and generally keeping me on my toes. To the staff of a number of libraries, particularly those of Glasgow and Edinburgh University Libraries, New College Library, Edinburgh and the Bodleian Library, Oxford.

My greatest debt is to Michael Baron, who has sustained me over the years in writing this, providing constant encouragement and assistance, and to whom the book is dedicated.

MD

Abbreviations

AB	*Analecta Bollandiana*
Annales ESC	*Annales. Économies. Sociétés. Civilisations.*
CC	*Corpus Christianorum*
CSEL	*Corpus Scriptorum Ecclesiae Latinae*
EHR	*Ecclesiastical History Review*
JECS	*Journal of Early Christian Studies*
JEH	*Journal of Ecclesiastical History*
JMH	*Journal of Medieval History*
JRH	*Journal of Religious History*
JRS	*Journal of Roman Studies*
JTS	*Journal of Theological Studies*
PG	Migne, *Patrologia Graeca*
PL	Migne, *Patrologia Latina*
RAM	*Revue d'Ascétique et de Mystique*
RB	*Revue Bénédictine*
REAug	*Revue des Études Augustiniennes*
RHR	*Revue de l'Histoire des Religions*
RM	*Revue Mabillon*
SC	*Sources Chrétiennes*
SM	*Studia Monastica*
TADMO	McLaughlin T.P., *Les Très Ancien Droit Monastique de l' Occident* Archives de la France Monastique, vol. XXXVIII (Ligugé – Paris, 1935).
TRHS	*Transactions of the Royal Historical Society*
VC	*Vigiliae Christianae*
ZKG	*Zeitschrift für Kirchengeschichte*

1

The Emergence of Christian Eremitism

In 324 an Egyptian villager named Aurelius Isidorus of Karanis was attacked by two enraged neighbours, Pamounis and Harpalos, when he turned their cow, which was eating his crops, off his land. In a written complaint to the local government official, dated June 6, he describes how he was set about so violently that

> if I had not obtained help from Antony, a deacon, and Isaac, a monk (*monachos*), they would probably have finished me off altogether.[1]

The casual nature of Aurelius' reference to 'Isaac, a monk' – a man whose testimony would weigh equally with that of a deacon – in a formal document, suggests that by 324 the *monachos* or monk was a recognized fixture on the scene in the *khora*, the inhabited countryside of Roman Egypt. Tradition has long fixed the emergence of Egyptian monasticism around this period. On the other hand, the papyrus' brief reference raises even more questions than it answers. How, when and why did Christian monasticism originate and why had it become an institution well known, by the 320s, in rural Egypt?

The appearance in the Christian church of individuals or communities strictly separated from the world and devoted to a life of religious contemplation or service is a phenomenon which historians have long sought to explain. Older rationalizations of the rise of monasticism have included the suggestion that it was a response to the imperial adoption of Christianity in the fourth century,[2] a call to return to the values of Christian martyrdom[3] or a result of a widespread and deep-seated anxiety.[4] It has been suggested that Christian monasticism might simply be a continuation of the Jewish ascetic tradition represented by groups such as the Essenes and *Therapeutae* and of the communal traditions of early

Christian groups imitating the way of life of the Apostles.[5] Others have argued that the origins of Christian monasticism might in part have been located in an economic crisis in third- and fourth-century Egypt: the same Greek word *anachoresis* was used to designate both flight from tax obligations and the increasingly common phenomenon of retreat to a solitary religious life. Papyri containing questions to be put to oracles at this period frequently asked 'Shall I become a fugitive?' and this had led to the conjecture that many farmers, impelled originally by the harsh reality of tax obligations, fled society and took up a life of religion based on the 'hard sayings' of Christ.[6] However, the nature and extent of the crisis is now debated: it is impossible, for example, to quantify the number of farmers and villagers who 'fled' and the papyri suggest that their destination was neither the desert nor the religious life but another village, where they were followed by demands either from imperial officials or from their fellow villagers for their return.

The *Life of Antony*

Recent analyses of the origins of monasticism have focused on the career and letters of the first monk about whom we know in any detail, an Egyptian named Antony, who died about 356 CE. A heroic desert ascetic, Antony is regarded as a paradigm of the early monastic movement and his *Life*, composed a year after his death by Athanasius, bishop of Alexandria,[7] with its narratives of Antony's heroic struggles against the temptation and demons which beset him, has provided inspiration for centuries for writers, artists and musicians. It tells the story of Antony's withdrawal from the world in the latter part of the third century to lead a religious life and his retreat to the uninhabited desert (in the region of Karanis) in about 305. According to Athanasius, Antony was a comparatively wealthy young Christian farmer whose parents had left him three hundred *arourae* of very fertile land. The inspiration which led him to become a monk was that of the Gospels:

> he considered while he walked how the apostles, forsaking everything, followed the Saviour, and how in *Acts* some sold what they possessed and took the proceeds and placed them at the feet of the apostles for distribution among those in need and what great hope is stored up for such people in heaven. He went into the church pondering these things and just then it happened that the Gospel was being read and he heard the Lord saying to the rich man, *If you would be perfect, go, sell what you possess and give to the poor and you will have treasure in heaven* ...[8]

Having voluntarily given away his possessions to embark on a life of religious poverty, Antony's career then follows a trajectory which leads him to become a hermit, moving further and further away from human society. Initially, he apprentices himself to an old man and takes advice from others who are living ascetic lives in the neighbourhood of their villages. He then retreats to the tombs on the fringes of his village. At the age of thirty-five, he abandons the inhabited zone of Egypt altogether and retires to the desert. There he remains for another twenty years, growing stronger in his asceticism, finally retreating to an 'inner mountain' where he is able to live undisturbed in total solitude. The desert is crucial to this vision of monasticism: far removed from the activities of humans it enables Antony to pursue his life of solitary perfection largely undisturbed by worldly cares. Acknowledged by all to be the primary haunt of demons, the desert was also the backdrop to a continuation of Antony's titanic struggles against the demons who had regularly assailed him since he first embarked on a life of asceticism. Antony's constant prayer and intense asceticism – he ate and drank very little – led to a spiritual transformation mirrored in the unaltered state of his body after nearly twenty years in a deserted fortress:

> His body had maintained its former condition. Neither fat from lack of exercise nor emaciated from fasting and combat with demons . . .[9]

The *Life of Antony* created a picture of early monasticism in which the ideals of dispossession, solitude, and personal austerity were paramount and in which the desert became the locus of true religion. Though Athanasius mentions the existence of others leading a life of religion in the neighbourhood of their villages, whose advice Antony initially follows,[10] he makes Antony the real founder of Christian monasticism as his fame as ascetic and thaumaturge spreads and many hasten to imitate his example:

> and so from then on there were monasteries in the mountains and the desert was made a city by monks, who left their own people and registered themselves for citizenship in the heavens.[11]

The *Letters* of St Antony

> My beloved in the Lord, know yourselves! Those who know themselves know their time and are not moved by diverse tongues.[12]

An important source, until recently neglected, for the aims of early monasticism are the seven letters which Antony composed or dictated for the benefit of others aiming to lead a religious life similar to his own. They reflect the extent of his influence in what was clearly a growing

Egyptian monastic movement: six contain very similar teachings, suggesting that they were sent to six different groups of monks. The first reads as if it were intended as an introduction for beginners in the ascetic life. It dwells on the need for repentance and purification and on the effects of the 'spirit of repentance' on spirit, mind and body. It enumerates repentance of the spirit, mind and of every member of the body: eyes, tongue, hand, belly, 'what is below the belly' and lastly the feet. Repentance, guided by the spirit, will 'restore' man to his original spiritual, rational essence.[13] For Antony, the life of an ascetic or *monachos* was a constant struggle for self-knowledge, self-purification and through these, the return of the soul to unity with God, in whose image it was created. According to Antony, true knowledge – *gnosis* – is a return to one's original state and once this is achieved the individual may aspire eventually to union with God.[14]

Antony's letters make no reference to his retreat into the desert: instead, they provide a theoretical and theological basis for the ascetic life which he led there and which others wished to embrace. His ideas are broadly based on the teachings of the great third-century Alexandrian theologian Origen, who himself had been greatly influenced by Platonic thinking. According to his cosmology, before the creation of the world all rational beings had originally been equal and had chosen by their own actions whether they were to be saved or damned. Souls were originally spiritual beings or intelligences which had enjoyed a pre-existence in which they had exercised free will and grown cold in charity. As a result, they had fallen away from God and – depending on the extent of this self-willed alienation – become either angels, human souls or devils: the condition of a child at birth depended on the extent of the willed alienation of its soul from God as a spiritual being in the pre-existence. Origen proposed a trichotomic anthropology in which each human is divided into body (*soma*) or flesh (*sarx*), soul (*psyche*) and spirit (*pneuma*). The body had been good in its first essence, but had become a place of confinement and correction for the soul. In its fall, the pre-existent *nous* or intelligence had grown cold and become the soul: as a result of its alienation from God, the *nous*, seat of participation in God's image had become associated with the area sometimes known as 'the soul of all flesh' and therefore with all the phantasms and desires which trouble the body. In Origenist anthropology angels and demons war over the soul. Origen believed that the religious celibate whose *nous* of its own free will chose to be illuminated by the Holy Spirit could achieve a spiritual union with God in a recreation of the state which Adam had found himself before the Fall. In such conditions, it was possible for the soul to ascend once again to be unified with the God from which it had fallen away. The study of and contemplation of scripture played a fundamental part in his concept of spiritual progress.[15]

Antony's ascetic thinking fits into an Origenist framework of the soul's alienation from and return to God. He expounds an Origenist history of the creation:

> Not only at one time did God visit his creatures but from the foundation of the world, whenever any have come to the creator of all by the law of his covenant implanted in them, God is present with each one of these in his bounty and grace by his Spirit. But in the case of those rational natures in which that covenant grew cold and their intellectual perception died so that they were no longer able to know themselves according to their first condition, concerning them I say that they became altogether irrational and worshipped the creation rather than the Creator.[16]

In his first letter, he claims that:

> [the Holy Spirit] sets them a rule for how to repent in their bodies and souls until he has taught them the way to return to God their creator.[17]

In the same letter, he also refers to the important role of the mind, Plato's and Origen's *nous*, which will play an important part in the process of purifying the soul for ascent to God

Antony also stresses the soteriological role of Christ. Through the 'written law', the commandments given to Moses, but applicable to the whole of humankind, humanity was given a second chance to achieve redemption and return to its original nature from which it had fallen through persistent sin. When this, too, failed, humanity was given a third chance to redeem itself, though the coming of Christ to earth. Jesus had taken on himself the form of man – in everything except sin – to ensure the salvation of humankind. Antony understands the *parousia*, the presence of Christ, in both its historical sense and also in a spiritual sense. He interprets the Bible not just as history but as a spiritual, eternal message. For him, the presence of Christ and his teaching will restore the unity shattered by man's sinfulness and fall, creating communion with Christ through the receiving of the 'Spirit of Adoption'. Yet while it is possible for the individual to purify the body and receive knowledge of the 'Spirit of Adoption', lasting achievement of the vision of God is possible only after death has freed the soul from the body.[18]

Antony's combination of Origenist and Biblical inspiration reflects the penetration of the *khora*, the cultivated countryside surrounding the towns and villages along the length of the Nile not only by Christianity but by the theological and philosophical ideas which were the intellectual currency of Alexandria in the third century. Paradoxically, the spread of Christianity into the countryside may have been fostered by the Decian persecution of the church in the mid third century when Bishop Dionysius of Alexandria was exiled to Libya, while many of his clergy were sentenced to deportation to the region of Mareotis and ordinary Christians, both men and women, were sent to the mines of Upper Egypt. Religious teachers who also understood both Greek and Coptic moved amongst the rural population in the late third century and the first Coptic Christian teacher and scholar of whom we know by name, Hieracas of Leontopolis in the Nile Delta,[19] taught an Origenist version of Christianity at the beginning of the fourth century. Social and economic factors also encouraged the spread of ideas from Alexandria. Distinctions between urbanized Greeks and wealthier Coptic farmers were to an extent elided. Even if many of the wealthier Copts could not write Greek they could understand it and versions of Platonic and Origenist belief could begin to filter into the smaller Egyptian towns and from there to the *khora*. The ability of Antony and other ascetics to read the complex works of Origen and Plato has been questioned – but a wide range of religious and secular literature was read in the provinces and it was quite possible that they absorbed Origenist or Platonic ideas in a diluted or second-hand form.[20]

Asceticism

Modern shorthand for many of the religious movements of the time including monasticism labels them not only 'world-rejecting' but also claims that they involved a radical 'rejection of the body'.[21] This is probably misleading as the anthropology advanced by Origen himself as well as by many other Christian groups depended on a sophisticated view of an intricate relationship between body and soul. When called upon to explicate the difficult Biblical text, 'The soul of all flesh is blood', Origen interpreted the creation of Adam to mean that there were two levels of being: a spiritual Adam made in the image of God and a hylic or fleshly Adam. The body, it is true, might be regarded as a tomb or prison for the soul; but even this understanding was based on the premise that *within* the human body was real evidence of the divine in this world, in the shape of the soul; and that the body, container of the soul, was the vessel in which divine and material converged. From this premise – influenced by the Stoic linking of body and soul – a transformational asceticism could emerge.[22]

Asceticism is usually defined in negative terms – often as a rejection of sex, or food or both but might more productively be seen also as a discipline or collectivity of disciplines which aim at the transformation of the self and the construction of a new one. Framed in opposition to the dominant society around it, asceticism is not to be understood merely as a process of rejection but also as one involving not only the construction of a self but also of a new set of social relations or understandings.[23] The most common form of asceticism practised in later antiquity was based on sexual abstinence: renunciation of sex was seen as a means of cutting the individual's links with the lower, material existence and therefore as the basis for self-transformation, leading to attainment of a more spiritual plane of existence. Such ascetic practices, though far from universal, were widespread. In Egypt at the end of the fourth century, Hieracas, who taught amongst the Copts of the Nile Delta, preached that the married would not enter heaven.[24] The third- and fourth-century Christian church in Syria was radically encratite (from the Greek *enkrateia*, continence) as some of its members maintained that it was a sexual act which had caused the loss of the Spirit and that sexuality was really part of the animal world. The *ihidaya* or celibate was regarded as a member of an elite.[25] Emphasis on sexual renunciation might involve not so much a simple rejection of marriage so much as its radical reconceptualizing: many within the Syrian church believed that it was possible to recapture the Holy Spirit by maintaining chastity *within* marriage. The *Acts of Thomas*, a text of Syrian origin, describes a young couple who do not consummate their marriage in 'filthy intercourse', but instead dedicate themselves to Christ.[26] Other writings suggest a more complete rejection of marriage and emphasis on single celibacy. The similarly-named *Gospel of Thomas* – another text from a Syrian background surviving in a Coptic codex of the fourth century which may have been read by monks – proposes a goal of radical self-transformation. Jesus tells his disciples that they will enter the kingdom:

> When you make the two one, and when you make the inside like the outside and the outside like the inside and the above like the below and when you make the male and the female one and the same, so that the male be not male nor the female, female; and you fashion eyes in place of an eye and a hand in place of a hand and a foot in place of a foot and a likeness in place of a likeness . . .[27]

As posited by this text, the ascetic programme leads to the forging of a completely new identity – in which the body is transformed and the individual is genderless, consistent and singular. Singularity is emphasized in a number of sayings throughout the text: for example, 'a person cannot ride two horses or serve two masters'. Singularity brings prizes not granted to others:

> Many are standing at the door, but it is the solitary who will enter the bridal chamber.[28]

Obscure though this statement might appear to be, its sense is that the singular – a person whose existence has been transformed by an ascetic regime – will be rewarded by a new reality or realities: the ascent of his or her soul to achieve union with God. In his letters, Antony himself proposes a singularity in the sense of the uniting of soul and body when he writes that:

> [The Holy Spirit] also gives them control over their souls and bodies in order that both may be sanctified and inherit together.[29]

and he sees this control being achieved through fasting, vigils and celibacy:

> First through many fasts and vigils, through the exertion and the exercises of the body, cutting of all the fruits of the flesh.[30]

The Coptic word used in the fourth-century manuscript of the *Gospel of Thomas* in translation of the original Syriac *iḥidaya* is *monachos*. Thus the word which Athanasius uses of Antony and which we would translate as 'monk' might partly be understood in terms of its connotations of oneness and unity of being, denoting those who had embarked on an ascetic programme and achieved self-transformation as outlined in Antony's own letters.

Anachoresis

The term *monachos* has further connotations, associated with the root *monos*, which can imply solitary as well as single. Where the Antony of Athanasius' *Life* differs from the married celibate of the early Syrian church, or the celibates of groups such as that which formed around the Coptic teacher Hieracas in Egypt, is in his extreme *anachoresis* by which he physically removes himself further and further from human society and habitation.[31] Antony's letters make no allusion to this aspect of his own life, perhaps because for him this was only a preliminary to the theology and scheme of self-transformation which he wished to teach. Athanasius claims that others had already begun to make a less dramatic version of this gesture:

> there were not yet many monasteries in Egypt and no monk knew at all the great desert, but each of those wishing to give attention to his own life disciplined himself in isolation not far from his own village.[32]

Individual renunciants – 'apotactics' – celibates who had adopted a distinctive style of dress and lived in community houses as well as syneisakts, women who lived a life of chastity under the spiritual direction of clerics, had long been a feature on the scene in both Alexandria and smaller towns even in the early fourth century; but the *monachos* as exemplified by Antony and even by those who had retreated to the edge of their villages, was an individual who was more decisively removed from society, deliberately standing outside all social connections as far as possible.[33] The *Life of Antony* does not give any direct explanation for the rise of this new development, but does imply that it led to a more disciplined ascesis and suggests that not only *anachoresis* but also renunciation of all property, a process not necessarily undergone by all apotactics, was necessary for true monasticism. Athanasius thus lays much greater stress on the features which distinguished its hero from earlier ascetics than those which he shared in common with other types of renunciants.

Athanasius does not entirely neglect the transformational aspect of his hero's life – he not only refers to Antony's sparse diet but also observes how his body remained unchanged after twenty years of fasting and contemplation.[34] The *Life* also contains many echoes of Antony's own theology. Athanasius has Antony reflect that

the ascetic must always acquire knowledge of his own life.[35]

Antony's idea that virtue is implanted within the soul is also accurately reflected in the *Life*.[36] But in his overall picture of Antony's career, Athanasius gives prominence to Antony's removal from society and his abandonment of money and possessions rather than the theology and detailed ascetic practice of the *Letters*. In doing so, he defines early monasticism not by those elements which locate Antony firmly within the already existing tradition of celibacy and limited withdrawal from society but by Antony's inspiration by the words of the gospel, his renunciation of his property and the distance which he places between himself and society.

Varieties of Early Asceticism

The paradigm of monasticism which Athanasius chooses to present through his *Life of Antony* was partly shaped by developments in theology and church organization which took place in his own lifetime. Athanasius' career was dominated by his struggle against the recently-developed theology of Arianism, which he perceived as undermining belief in the divinity of Christ. He was exiled no less than five times from his diocese of Alexandria for his opposition to this belief by a rival Arian hierarchy and the emperor who favoured them.[37] One of his main purposes in writing the *Life* was to hold up Antony as an icon of the anti-Arian orthodoxy which he had struggled to maintain since becoming bishop of Alexandria in 328. Antony's fourth letter actually condemns Arius as the founder of the doctrine which had opened up 'an un-healable wound' in the church[38] and Athanasius is happy to credit Antony with a prominent role in the anti-Arian struggle. Throughout the *Life*, Antony demonstrates his acceptance of Athanasius' Christology: when, for example, he is attacked by demons, which in Athanasius' view were manifestations of the human fear of death, he repulses them by making the sign of the cross, which in his own theology represented Christ's victory over death.[39] In explicitly attributing Antony's miraculous powers to Christ and in portraying Antony as unlettered, Athanasius advances a model of Christ-centred religion and natural, as opposed to learned or philosophical, wisdom.[40]

Athanasius had spent part of the first six years of his episcopate and his third period of exile amongst desert monastic circles which had grown up over the previous four decades or so. His self-imposed task in his narrative is to incorporate an already existing movement, by definition opposed to the current norms of society, into the official church. The *Life* attempts both to reach out to the growing monastic movement in Egypt – and also to one which was just beginning to develop in the West – and to underpin the powers of his own hierarchy. Crucially, although Athanasius in general did not particularly favour the cult of relics, which as *loci* of spiritual power possessed the potential to fragment episcopal control of the church, the *Life* claims that the Athanasian hierarchy was custodian of three out of four 'relics' left by Antony – a cloak and two sheepskins – so that it became guardian of his posthumous charisma.[41] Athanasius also sought to promote Antony's style of monasticism as the most acceptable form of asceticism within his church. In his schema of Antony's retreat, he does not allude even obliquely to the older style of ascetics who remained in cities and towns. To him, such individuals, living in their own houses, and groups might encourage the type of unlicensed and dangerous speculation which had produced Arianism.[42] Athanasius had already attempted to gather virgins and female ascetics, who were probably amongst the first Christian ascetics in Alexandria into safe and controllable groups (see pp. 51–2 below). Followers of Hieracas were to be found in small groups in Alexandria itself – much to the discomfiture of Athanasius, who opposed their belief that the kingdom of heaven was open *only* to the chaste. Athanasius' attempts to make the desert attractive to others and his suggestion that a life of asceticism conducted there would bring freedom both from the burdens of riches and of taxation, was an attempt to ensure the continuance of an episcopally-directed asceticism within an orthodox church.[43] Athanasius also used the *Life* to send a message to ascetic and monastic movements outside his control. Antony is made to reject both the Arians – who had claimed him as one of their own – and the Melitians. The latter group, with its alternative church hierarchy which had existed before Athanasius became bishop of Alexandria and which had formed an alliance with the Arians in upper Egypt, also generated its own monks and, in time, monasteries.[44]

Differing Cosmologies, Parallel Movements

Asceticism and even a monastic life-style were not confined to the more obviously Christian groups in fourth-century Egypt. Manichaean missionaries had arrived in Egypt about CE 270, offering a world-myth which gave an answer to the question which seems to have troubled so many at the time: if God is good why is there evil in the world? Its founder, Mani, offered the solution that, as man was rooted in both darkness and light he could not be saved entirely; however, according to his teaching, Jesus controlled a mechanism for distilling the light from within all humankind. When this was finally accomplished the universe would burn and all light would be refined and restored to the realm of light.[45] Manichaeism, although equipped with a Jesus-soteriology which differed radically from that of Pauline Christianity, had features in common with the many varieties of Christianity which circulated in the third and fourth centuries (and was regarded by some as a Christian heresy).[46] Mani had originally been a member of the Jewish–Christian sect of the Elkasites, but left it to develop the dualistic teaching of Marcion and the concept of the docetic Christ, common to a number of Christian groups of the era.[47]

The vision of a descending, spiritual saviour was incorporated into a series of related belief-systems which emphasized the utter transcendence of a supreme god and at the same time interposed an intermediate level of being or beings between the transcendent god and the cosmos. These beings included an evil demiurge who had created the earth. Such ideas were characteristic of the range of beliefs generally labelled as 'gnostic' (but better described as Biblical-demiurgic), many of which attributed a soteriological role to Christ as the bringer to earth of a saving 'gnosis' or knowledge.[48] Paralleling the Manichaean idea of light imprisoned in humanity, the idea that the world itself was the creation of a lower and malevolent demiurge or series of powers provided an answer to the problems of theodicy and the existence of evil on earth, while the belief that Christ – often seen by these groups as a spirit who did not possess a human body – had brought with him a hidden *gnosis* or knowledge offered the vista of redemption to the initiate.

Although Origen had evolved many of his theories and arguments to counter what he believed to be the determinism, fatalism, the lack of belief in God as creator of the world and what he saw as the false gnosis of the Christian-demiurgics, the influence of Platonism led to schematic resemblances between his speculations and their beliefs. Plato's technical vocabulary could be adapted to a variety of purposes – hermetic,

Manichaean, Christian-demiurgic or Origenist.[49] Manichaeism, demiurgic belief and Origenist theology – high or popular – all broadly affirmed in their different ways the grossness of the material world and the possibility of the ascent of the soul to God. All would develop the idea that this could be achieved through transformational asceticism.[50] Both the Christian demiurgics and Antony taught a *gnosis* – even if they meant rather different things by it. Christian-demiurgic groups existed in Alexandria and possibly elsewhere in Egypt, while the *mānistānān*, shelters for the Manichaean 'elect', resemble the orthodox communal monasteries which began to develop from the 320s onwards. Athanasius' emphasis on the distinctive and orthodox nature of Antony's asceticism represents a conscious attempt to minimize any superficial or programmatic resemblances between it and that of the demiurgics and Manichaeans.[51]

The Image of Monasticism

Ultimately, Athanasius was remarkably successful in creating an enduring association between monasticism and the desert, an association subsequently maintained in slightly later monastic literature such as the *Apophthegmata Patrum* and the *History of the Monks in Egypt*. *Anachoresis*[52] was identified by Athanasius with complete withdrawal to the desert, a picture which influenced many later presentations of monasticism at the expense of its other manifestations. His tracing of Antony's retreat, from his village to the tombs outside it, then to his 'outer' and finally to an even more remote 'inner' mountain in the great desert may, with its positive valuation of 'inner' (as in the Inner Mountain), in many respects be a symbolic journey based on Antony's own corporeal or spiritual experiences.[53] It nevertheless became a classic trajectory of the monastic life reinforcing in the minds of readers and listeners the ancient polarization between Desert and City – even though many hermitages and monasteries would grow up in the neighbourhood of towns and cities and even inside cities.[54] His propaganda was successful in influencing later writers who give the impression that the only true monks were either hermits, like Antony, or those who lived in large organized communities such as that of the Pachomians (see chapter 2, in this volume) which had begun to appear from the 320s on in Upper Egypt. In the 380s, a westerner, St Jerome, would divide monastic life into three groups – hermits, cenobites who lived in communal monasteries, and finally *remnuoth*, who seem to be apotactics in the older sense of the word. Jerome had no hesitation in disparaging this last group:

> The third class is that which they call *remnuoth*, a very inferior and despised type ... They dwell together by twos and threes, not many more, and live

according to their own will and independently. They contribute to a common fund part of their earnings, that they may have a general store of food. But they live for the most part in cities and fortified towns...[55]

A variant on this picture was produced in the early fifth century West by John Cassian who wrote of cenobites, hermits, 'sarabaites' and a fourth unnamed category of 'bad' monks; this in turn would influence the later Benedictine *Rule*. Such categorizations obscure the fact that Egyptian asceticism had originally covered a broad spectrum of life-styles and that not all ascetic groups required their members to renounce all property. The latter development was mainly pioneered by large formally-organized communities such as that of Pachomius in Upper Egypt. The *Life* is silent about the rise of the communal Pachomian monasteries as they were not a source of particular concern to Athanasius at the time of its composition.[56]

The Growth of the Eremitic Movement

Athanasius contributed to the development of the image of the holy man as exemplar, an image which would be replicated many times as the monastic movement grew. He claimed that Antony inspired so many others by his example that he turned the desert into a city for monks, who 'registered themselves for citizenship of the heavens'.[57] A cluster of hermits settled on Antony's mountain and an important 'desert' monastic settlement began to grow on the 'Mount' of Nitria – the abrupt, cliff-like formation and desert strip which marks the frontier between the edge of the desert and the alluvial Nile valley – close to the village of Pernoudj and less than nine miles from the episcopal town of Hermopolis Parva (Damanhur). The first hermit to settle there, in about 315, was Amoun, who was swiftly joined by others.[58] Although Antony had found refuge from visitors and imitators in his 'inner mountain', aspirants to an ascetic life-style tended to congregate in ever-growing colonies around famous ascetics. The transmission of ascetic ideas initially depended on a culture of word and example rather than on any written instruction – Antony's letters appear to be the exception and even these were designed to be read aloud to a group – and Egyptian eremitic monasticism was never an entirely solitary affair. Antony himself received visitors and seems to have supervised monks in the region of Arsinoë.[59] Amoun had not originally been able to discourage imitators who settled near him, following his example, although he eventually retreated to a site about 12 Roman miles further south. This in turn developed into another famous group of monastic dwelling known as Kellia – literally, 'the cells'. Another famous colony of hermit-monks grew up at a more remote site 52 Roman miles from Nitria at Scetis (the Greek version of the Coptic name Shiêt). Known now as the Wadi' n Natrun, this 'desert' site was situated by springs on the margin of a natron 'lake': the sources speak of a marsh and palm trees which provided the ascetics who settled in the area with raw materials from which they wove baskets. Other hermit settlements could be found elsewhere in the Nile Delta at Diolcos and Panephysis, at Kalamon and the Mount of Porphyry in the Eastern Desert, and at Arsinoë in the Fayyum. Some settlements – such as those further south at Oxyrhyncus and Antinoë in the Thebaid – were near towns and cities: Palladius, author of the *Lausiac History* claims that amongst the twelve hundred ascetics in the neighbourhood of Antinoë, there were not only communal monasteries but 'anchorites who have shut themselves up in caves'.[60] The *History of the Monks in Egypt*, written in the 390s, made the – exaggerated – claim that there was 'no town in Egypt or the Thebaid' which was not surrounded by hermitages 'as if by walls'.[61]

The dwellings of the earliest desert hermits were cells which, according to the sources, they usually built for themselves from mud bricks: the cell of a new arrival might be built in a day. The cells were often more numerous and extensive than might be imagined; Amoun is said to have constructed two domed cells on the 'Mount'[62] while the great Macarius constructed four in different parts of the 'desert'. Two were small and without windows, for use during the penitential seasons of Lent; one was so cramped that he could scarcely stretch his legs; and in the fourth he received visitors.[63] The cells of the famous anchorites who had practised asceticism for many years might be situated within an individual compound and furnished with all necessities, even a well. More junior monks lived in improvised shelters or caves or, in some areas, in ancient tombs cut from the rock. Hermit colonies such as Kellia or Esna in Upper Egypt constructed a church for communal worship on Sundays, but the main religious exercise of the monks consisted of *hesychia* – solitary prayer, recitation of the psalms and meditation in their cells – which would clear their mind of distractions and bring them nearer to God.[64]

The basis of daily monastic life which developed amongst the hermits was a round of meditation on the scriptures (*melete*), psalmody and manual labour. Normally, monks worked at weaving and plaiting their mats and baskets while meditating in their cells. As well as providing the means for supporting their meagre needs in food and clothing, work was seen as a way of achieving the ideal of unceasing prayer. When Apa Lucius was visited by a group of religious who refused to work he explained that:

> By working and praying all day long, I can complete around sixteen baskets. I give away two of these to any beggar who comes to my door. I

make my living from the rest. And the man who receives the gift of two baskets prays for me... That is how, by God's grace, I manage to pray without ceasing.[65]

The rapid growth of the monastic movement may be gauged from the claim by Palladius, author of the *Lausiac History*, that there were, towards the end of the fourth century, no fewer than five thousand monks on the mount of Nitria alone. Even allowing for some characteristic exaggeration on Palladius' part, it is clear that Nitria was by then a large and flourishing organization with its own identity and supportive infrastructures:

On the mountain live some five thousand men with different modes of life, each living in accordance with his own powers and wishes so that it is allowed to live alone or with another or with a number of others. There are seven bakeries in the mountain which serve the needs of both these and also of the anchorites of the great desert, six hundred in all... In the mountain of Nitria there is a great church by which stand three palm trees each with a whip suspended from it. One is intended for the solitaries who transgress, one for robbers if any pass that way and one for chance comers... Next to the church is a guest-house where they receive the stranger who has arrived until he goes away of his own accord, without limit of time, even if he remains two or three years... In this mountain there also live doctors and confectioners. And they use wine and wine is on sale. All these men work with their hands at linen-manufacture so that all are self-supporting. And indeed at the ninth hour it is possible to stand and hear how the strains of psalmody rise from each habitation so that one believes that one is high above the world in Paradise. They occupy the church only on Saturday and Sunday. There are eight priests who serve the church in which, so long as the senior priest lives, no one else celebrates or preaches or gives decisions...[66]

This description shows that while the monks of Nitria lived alone or in small groups, they formed part of a larger whole which acknowledged its group identity both by keeping the same hours at psalmody as well as in the communal worship – the *synaxis* – on the 'holy nights' of Saturday and Sunday. It also functioned as a group – or number of groups – as ascetics employed an *oikonomos* or steward to sell their crafts and organize their supplies.[67] Scetis and Kellia each developed a *xenodocheion* for the reception of visitors and the care of the sick.[68] The *History of the Monks in Egypt* even claims that the desert monks provided food relief for the village poor and for the poor of Alexandria – but as this text was composed in a milieu where the charitable monastic orientation advocated by Basil of Cæsarea (see pp. 36–8 below) was known, it is not necessarily reliable.[69]

Techniques of Bodily Control

The teaching of the 'old men' or 'fathers' of the desert aimed to reproduce what they themselves had laboriously learned over many years: the subduing of the body so that the soul might be freed from the passions and united with God. They worked in the same theological and spiritual framework as Antony, combining a fundamental principle of distinction between 'soul' and 'body' with the acknowledgement that they went hand in hand and were not dualistically separated. In the monastic body, eikonic and hylic bodies merged with Adam's body from the narrative of the Fall. Knowledge about body and soul and their creation appears to have been taught as part of the higher realms of monastic instruction and presented the monk's body as a battleground between warring armies of demons and angels. Only by control of his *nous* or mind, the most critical of all the faculties, could the monk hope to turn his soul towards God. Thus he had first to battle to master the bodily urges for food and sex which risked separating his soul from the divine.

The first step in avoiding sexuality was bodily removal to the alternative society of the hermit colonies, safe from contact with the corrupting world: John of Lycopolis taught that even the most perfect could not succeed if they remained close to villages. Women and even children were recognized by the fathers as constituting a possible focus of sexual temptation: according to Athanasius, one of the phantasms sent by the demons to tempt Antony took on the shape of a boy.[70] But even though the monks of fourth-century Egypt sought to avoid sexual intercourse and sexual temptation in the first place by fleeing the world, there still remained the fact of sexual desire which could not be tamed immediately or even after many years. Palladius was told by Apa Pachon that he had spent forty years in his cell and had been 'tempted' all the time. The 'old men' of Egypt devoted much effort to the taming of thoughts about sex, the demons of lust and fornication.[71] These might manifest themselves as visions of a sexual nature, as masturbation, or as 'movements of the flesh', erections and emissions during dreams, phenomena which were considered and debated with great attention. There were various methods of restraining erections and emissions, such as fatiguing oneself through work. But there seems to have been general agreement, based on Greek medical theory, that the primary method of overcoming thoughts of sex was through control of food intake.[72] Antony taught that the soul might consent to such 'movements' (which were, however, without passion) or that they might be caused by demons or by nourishment.[73] The monks of Egypt followed a variety of diets – some, for instance, allowed the consumption of wine, others did not. But all seem to have agreed that the monastic diet should not include meat. The body was thought to contain four humours, blood, black bile, yellow bile and phlegm, which in turn produced other humours such as semen. The 'drier' the body was, the less semen it would produce. Meat was seen as a primary source of moist humours and therefore banned from the monastic diet altogether (and sleep, also seen as 'moistening', could be reduced by periods of prayer during the night). The medical writer Oribasius taught that moisture in the body might be dried out by salty or 'dry' foods or foods which relaxed the digestion – lentils, salted olives, grapes, prunes, salt itself, brine and vinegar. Chick-peas were permitted but only if roasted to dry them out: coarse bread, made with bran, was considered drying. Another theory held that the body burned with innate heat and that to cool this down, one should eat only raw, cold food. Mythologizers of desert monasticism attributed astonishing austerity in diet to the monks. Writing in the fifth century John Cassian claimed that their diet included salt fish, a herb called cherlock, small salt fish, olives, bread – and only one vegetable, the leek – and that a 'feast' held by some of the most prominent ascetics consisted of a Roman pound of bread each, accompanied by a drop of oil, five roast chick-peas, three olives, two prunes and a dried fruit. Drastic calorific reduction alone is capable of producing impotence and Cassian seems to suggest that an individual could achieve almost perfect chastity by living on two loaves of bread a day, drinking little and depriving himself of sleep.[74] The *History of the Monks in Egypt* claimed that some monks never ate bread or fruit but only endives.[75]

The Gift of the Word and the Renunciation of Self-Will

Monks visiting Antony asked him to:

Speak a word to us: how may we be saved?[76]

The spiritual life of the hermits of Egypt was not, as accounts of colonies such as Nitria show, conducted in utter solitude but depended on the passing on of wisdom from 'elders' to younger or less experienced ascetics, a system of personal example and instruction by which the charisms of word, manner of life or miraculous powers[77] would be passed on from one generation of ascetics to the next. Eventually the sayings of the most famous fathers were set down in collections such as the *Apophthegmata Patrum*, the *Sayings of the Fathers*, in which their wisdom was crystallized for the edification of the many and the benefit of future generations.[78]

The 'gift of the word' may not have been possessed by all monks, but it was recognized that some displayed particularly great faculties of inspiration and teaching. The words of the elder – the 'Apa' or 'Father' – compelled attention and obedience from his immediate disciples and such 'fathers' demanded that their disciples were obedient to their words and learned the complete renunciation of their own will. Poemen claimed that:

> The will of man is a wall of bronze between himself and God and a stone of stumbling. When a man renounces it, he is saying to himself, 'By my God, I can leap over the wall'.[79]

The desire to avoid the sin of pride meant that even famous fathers might, out of humility, give spiritual guidance only reluctantly, deferring instead to other, older monks:

> They used to say that if anyone came to Apa Poemen, he sent them to Apa Anoub first, because he was older in years. But Apa Anoub used to say to them, 'Go to my brother Poemen, because he has the gift of the word'.[80]

When asked for a 'word', Apa Or, a man of profound simplicity and humility, instructed Apa Sisoes to follow him in everything he did, adding that in his own opinion he was inferior to all men.[81] Only under the guidance of the word of an elder, could progress be made, slowly, imperceptibly, in the spiritual life. John, known as 'the Dwarf', was sent by his Apa to water a dry twig many miles away every day. According to one version of the story, his obedience was rewarded when after three years the twig blossomed; but in another, after the end of a year, the elder merely pulled it out of the ground and threw it away.[82] The greatest monks had themselves achieved a level of self-abnegation and endurance leading to total detachment and tranquillity. Apa Or's own obedience was so complete that his disciple, Athre, could demonstrate it to another monk, Sisoes:

> He [Athre] took the fish, intentionally cooked some of it badly and offered it to the old man who ate it without saying anything. So he said to him, 'Is it good, old man?' And he replied, 'It is very good.' Afterwards he brought him a little that was very good and said to him, 'Old man, I have spoiled it.' And he said to him, 'Yes, you have spoiled it a little.'[83]

The apa–disciple relationship established obedience as the fundamental monastic virtue: only by the complete relinquishing of the will might spiritual progress be made. The gradual and difficult nature of this progress and the heights of ascetic power which might be reached after many years of self-discipline and detachment are encapsulated in the story of the visit made by Apa Lot to Apa Joseph. Lot asked:

'Apa, as far as I can I say my little office, I fast a little, I pray and meditate, I live in peace and as far as I can, I purify my thoughts. What else can I do?' The old man stood up and stretched his hands towards heaven. His fingers became like ten lamps of fire and he said to him, 'If you will, you can become all flame'.[84]

Hermits and Society

Although they had withdrawn from society, the first monks could not avoid it altogether. They had renounced society to achieve mastery of their bodies, self-transformation and the creation of an alternative reality: but the perceived power which stemmed from their renunciation attracted crowds of the faithful eager for the cures, advice and mediation which they could perform through their spiritual powers and charisma.[85] The advice of John of Lycopolis, the most famous of the hermits of the Thebaid, was sought by generals and he was said to have predicted the death of emperors. Visitors were not always welcome; even during a period when he had decided to remain totally incommunicado, Antony was pestered by a military officer who wished him to exorcise his daughter who was possessed by a demon. Such demands, according to Athanasius, eventually drove Antony to his 'Inner Mountain', perhaps a metaphor for his retreat into a more concentrated state of contemplation.[86] But as the fame of the most prominent monks grew, visitors began to arrive from great distances and even from overseas: Apa Arsenius turned away a 'virgin of senatorial rank' who had come all the way from Rome with the harsh words:

I pray God to take the remembrance of you from my heart.[87]

Arsenius was concerned lest others – especially women – should beat a path to his door. Nevertheless, the reception of visitors soon became one of the signs of ascetic achievement and even solitaries made preparations, such as keeping a blanket for their use, to receive them. And a genre of ascetic literature detailing visits, real or imaginary, to the most prominent holy men and monastic groups grew up – the *Lausiac History* of Palladius and, more importantly for the West, the *Conferences* of John Cassian. One of these, the *History of the Monks in Egypt*, written by a monk but directed as much to a non-monastic as a monastic audience, provides us with an incomparably vivid affirmation of the asceticism and powers of the most prominent Egyptian monks at the end of the fourth century. Revealingly, it is couched in the shape of a travelogue, ending with a litany of the dire tribulations encountered on a tour of the abodes of the most famous monks and monastic groupings of the era, which heightens the sense of

awe surrounding the men who are its destinations.[88] The ascetics themselves have become living monuments, objects of veneration and fascina-
tion presented as the acme of Biblical, ascetic and thaumaturgical culture
in the picturesque 'otherness' of a mythicised Egypt. The practice of
pilgrimage to Egyptian ascetics and to the Egyptian and Syrian deserts
antedated the account by several decades – visitors from the western parts
of the Empire had begun arriving as least as early as the 370s to experience ascetic life for themselves or to visit famous holy men. And while
ascetics became the objects of pilgrimage and veneration, monks also
began to settle at holy places and shrines which contained the relics of
saints or by the sites of former pagan temples which had been Christianized, such as the Serapeion at Alexandria.[89]

Ascetic behaviour itself is performative by nature and some of monasticism's most complex interactions with non-ascetic society, such as the
numerous dramas of exorcism performed by Antony and other spiritual
athletes, created a bridge between Christians and pagans, offering a
powerful demonstration of the truths of the new religion. Belief in
demons was universal – the major difference between pagan and Christian
demonology being that pagans believed in both good and evil demons,
while for Christians they were entirely evil. Origenist belief as exemplified
in Antony's sixth letter to his monks characterized demons as souls which
had wilfully alienated themselves from God by their own free will: for
Antony they could inhabit human bodies causing thoughts of pride,
weariness, levity and depression. While Athanasius' account of a sermon
given by Antony to his monks shares this idea, rather than dwell on their
attacks on the mind he emphasizes their nightmarish external aspect,
providing the *Life*'s inspiration for artists and writers for centuries to
come.[90] This may have been closer to some aspects of popular belief than
Antony's own more austere view. But belief in the power of demons to
inhabit human bodies was shared by all and this suffused rituals of
exorcism, in which the exorcist took on the part of the community, re-
establishing the correct boundaries between clean and unclean, with their
drama.

Through the spiritual gifts of exceptional ascetics, tangible benefits
might accrue not just to individuals but also to entire communities or
regions. Abba Theon, who had lived as a hermit for thirty years,

> was held to be clairvoyant by the people of those parts. A crowd of sick
> people went out to see him every day, and, laying his hand on them
> through the window [of his cell], he would send them away cured.[91]

The charisma and self-marginalization of the hermit increased his
power as intermediary and intercessor in the eyes of non-ascetic society.
Egyptian monasticism influenced the rise of similar developments in Syria

where the remarkably performative withdrawal from society of Symeon Stylites, who lived on top of a pillar outside Antioch for several decades in the fifth century, served to attract a stream of pilgrims from the city and the surrounding countryside. Known to the local villagers as 'the lion', Symeon was the most charismatic of all the 'holy men' who served as protectors and arbitrators in the village communities of fifth-century Syria, where they fulfilled the role of patron in a period where rural societies lacked any real sense of community or leadership.[92] The engagement of holy men of the Egyptian desert with nearby rural communities also took place on a more mundane level, as they hired lay servants and agents to bring them supplies or to sell their handicrafts or produce; some monks even hired themselves out as agricultural labourers at harvest-time.[93]

The discernment of some of the most prominent ascetics quickly led the church hierarchy to attempt to promote them to positions of responsibility outside the monastic movement. John Cassian would later claim that monks were warned not only to flee women, the source of sexual temptation, but also bishops who would wrench them from their lives of contemplative quiet by ordaining them priest. One of the most famous pieces of desert folklore concerns the Kelliot Apa Ammonius, who cut off his own ear in order to avoid ordination and when still threatened with the prospect of becoming a bishop, threatened to cut out his tongue;[94] but some of his close associates seem to have accepted non-monastic responsibilities without undue trauma. Another of the 'Tall Brothers' of Kellia, Dioscouros, was made bishop of Hermopolis Parva in 391 (and therefore became reponsible for the monks of Nitria), while Eusebius and Euthymios served the patriarch of Alexandria as *oikonomoi* or stewards.

Theology in the Desert: Evagrius of Pontus

The monastic colonies of the Egyptian desert may have sheltered a number of heterodox ascetics and even Manichaeans who lived undetected amongst more orthodox Christian monastic and clerical groups: in the late fourth century Timothy Ailouros, the bishop of Alexandria, 'allowed' monks and clerics to eat meat on Sundays – a remarkable ruling, given normal monastic dietary theory – in order to detect the Manichaeans to whom meat was completely forbidden.[95] Evagrius of Pontus, formerly a cleric of Constantinople who lived as a monk in Kellia from 384 until his death in 399, warned both monks and nuns against the insidious propaganda of those who taught a 'false *gnosis*', whom he claimed he had encountered in the desert itself. His *Sentences to a Virgin* indicate the nature of the demiurgic and docetist doctrines which he wished them to avoid – but he gives no clues as to who propagated such teachings. Evagrius himself was the most notable monastic theorist of the fourth century. In his youth he had been a disciple of Basil of Cæsarea and Gregory of Nazianzus, from whom he had learned about the writings of Origen; he also studied with the 'Tall Brothers' of Kellia. An ascetic writer of great distinction, Evagrius produced, as well as his *Sentences* for monks and nuns, a number of important works: *Antirrhetikos, Of the Eight Evil Thoughts, On Prayer*, and the trilogy *Praktikos, Gnostikos* and *Kephalaia Gnostica*.[96]

Evagrius' main achievement was to teach and set down in writing a systematized theory of asceticism. He frequently wrote in the gnomic form of short, individual sentences and often in the form of imperatives developed by the Stoics: each was designed to be meditated on and internalized. Evagrius followed in the general tradition of Origen and Clement of Alexandria, who were themselves often indebted not only to the Stoic but also to the Platonic and Aristotelian traditions. According to him, the summit of achievement for the *nous monachos*, the monastic intellect which had subdued all passions, is *gnosis* or knowledge of God. The first steps of the religious life begin with the contemplation of God through contemplation of his creation: the final step is contemplation of God himself. For the beginnings of *gnosis* to dawn, Evagrius insists, the soul must be purged and refined through a constant vigilance and examination of thoughts and exercise of the virtues. The fear of God strengthens faith, which is in turn strengthened by abstinence (*enkrateia*). Abstinence is made unshakeable by perseverance and hope, and from these is born the absence of passion (*apatheia*) whose offspring is charity (*agape*). Charity is the doorstep to natural knowledge which is followed by 'theology' and supreme beatitude. Once the 'health of the soul' has been achieved through *praktike, hesychia* commences, leading to the achievement of perfect charity which itself gradually melts into *gnosis* or knowledge of God.

While the intellectual influences of Clement and Origen are apparent in Evagrius' overall schema, he is closest to the fathers of the Egyptian desert when he discusses the fundamentals of *praktike* – the examination and discovery of the 'thoughts' (*logismoi*) which must be purged to make the soul healthy. His characterization of thoughts is overwhelmingly hostile: they are mostly negative and evil and inspired by demons. But if he is close here to the simple monks of the desert, the intellectual once again asserts himself in the identification of the Eight Evil Thoughts which are the basis of all evil ideas. He repeats these in more than one of his works and they almost inevitably follow the same sequence – gluttony, fornication, avarice, sadness, anger, *accedia*, vainglory and pride. His classification of the faults and their remedies was based on a tripartite division of the soul into passionate or concupiscent, irascible and rational parts and perhaps also on Galen's medical theory of curing by opposites. Fasting restrains lust. Love – 'charity' – counters avarice and depression. Anger requires several antidotes – gentleness, compassion and charity. *Accedia* (listlessness) demands tears, perseverance and constant vigilance; while vainglory and pride require both humility and the sobering remembrance of past failure. Once the eight evil thoughts are vanquished, the achievement of *apatheia*, passionlessness or 'impassibility', releases the *nous* or intellect of the monk to the highest state known on earth – contemplation of, and union with, God.

Evagrius' undertaking was not a mere mechanical reduction of eremitic asceticism to a dry intellectual schema. He was a valued teacher whose pupils prized his gentleness and his spiritual gifts, while his letters reflect his great capacity for friendship. Such were his charisma and powers of discernment that Theophilus, patriarch of Alexandria attempted – without success – to appoint him bishop of Thmuis. Evagrius' *gnosis* was not an intellectual knowledge but rather the fruit of *praktike*, itself a result of the operation of individual free will and the grace of God. While his treatise on prayer took a stand against a material picture of God, he came to believe that the soul was illuminated during prayer. Troubled by the question, after many years of intensive ascesis, of the origin of this light, he travelled south to the Thebaid to consult the renowned hermit John of Lycopolis. John could not say whether the light was of human or divine origin, but added that the soul could not be illuminated in prayer without the grace of God. Evagrius himself eventually came to the conclusion that when the condition of *apatheia* was reached then the soul's own light would begin to show, as a prelude to its being bathed in the light of the Holy Trinity, of the Saviour who is the Son of the un-seeable Father.

Evagrius died in 399, just before bishop Theophilus of Alexandria expelled several hundred monks from Nitria and Scetis, allegedly for following the teachings of Origen and denying that God could be visualized in human form.[97] The real reasons behind this extraordinary action, however, were almost certainly political as Theophilus himself had formerly been an Origenist and had even campaigned against the idea of a God in human form.[98] His real targets were Eusebius and Euthymios, two of the 'Tall Brothers', who had served him as *oikonomoi* in Alexandria but who had exposed corruption in his administration of the church. Ironically, one consequence of the expulsion of the monks, who settled temporarily in Palestine before being readmitted to Egypt in 403, was the strengthening of Origenist ideas there. The reputation of Evagrius – never mentioned by Theophilus in his accusations of Origenism – seems to have diminished in neither the Egyptian church (though the great monastic leader Shenoute later worried about his teaching on prayer and his supposedly symbolic interpretation of the Lord's Supper) nor that of Palestine, where his *Sentences to Monks* and *Sentences to a*

Virgin were written for the communities of monks and nuns on the Mount of Olives headed by his western friends Melania and Rufinus. Rufinus, who left the Holy Land for Italy in 397, translated a number of Evagrius' works into Latin and Evagrius would also figure prominently in his Latin version of the *History of the Monks in Egypt*.[99] But the later association of *apatheia* in the west with the doctrines of Pelagianism and the reaction of the greatest western theologians of their days against the latter meant that Evagrius' theoretical work would be largely sidelined as monastic life there followed a different pattern of development.[100] Evagrius' most enduring legacy to western religious life would be his concept of the eight 'evil thoughts' which reached the West through the writings of John Cassian and eventually evolved into the Seven Deadly Sins.

2

The Development of Communal Life

Amongst the pioneers of communal asceticism in Egypt may have been the Manichaeans. Their founder Mani was influenced both by Buddhism and by the Jewish–Christian Elkasites, a sect possibly inspired by the ascetic Jewish community of the Essenes at Qumran. Regarded by the pagan author Alexander of Lycopolis as a Christian heresy, Manichaeism developed *mānistānān*, communal buildings resembling those discovered at Qumran, in which their elect gathered to pray and eat.[1] The Melitians, who had split off from the Alexandrian hierarchy in the early fourth century, not only had their own hierarchy of bishops and priests, but also developed their own monasteries possibly from as early as the 320s.[2] However the founder of orthodox cenobitism – from the Greek *koinos bios* meaning common life – was Pachomius. In his monasteries (*cenobia*), monks lived in a highly regulated fashion, eating and sleeping in common refectories and dormitories and meeting in church at more regular intervals than their eremitic counterparts.

Pachomian Literature

The history of Pachomius' early ascetic life and monastic intentions is obscured by the complex and still unclear nature of the relationship between the early texts associated with his communities or *koinonia*. Pachomius himself left only letters and perhaps two 'instructions' though even his authorship of the latter remains debated.[3] Several *Lives* of Pachomius exist, in the Coptic dialects of Sahidic and Bohairic, in Greek and in Arabic. Not only is the relationship between the *Lives* a complicated one of interdependence, but each represents a different viewpoint, analysis or stage in the history of Pachomian monasticism.[4]

No one text has primary authority: the earliest version of the Coptic tradition is not original, while shared oral traditions lie behind all the early *Lives*. Like his contemporary Antony, Pachomius has been the victim of revisionist hagiography. The later *Greek Life*, like the Latin version of the *Life of Antony*, became the means by which the knowledge of its subject spread outside Egypt. Even before that knowledge left Egypt, it had already been moulded to some extent by monastic ideas characteristic of Lower Egypt and by the Alexandrian hierarchy, with which the *koinonia* was associated under Pachomius' successors. The *Paralipomena*, a series of anecdotes concerning Pachomius, contains a condemnation of Origenism and the *Letter of Ammon* has Pachomius recount how he rejected various heretical groups who had tried to ensnare him. Similar problems exist for the monastic instructions composed by Pachomius and his immediate successors, the *Precepts, Precepts and Institutes, Precepts and Judgements* and the *Precepts and Laws*.[5] The questions of their authorship, the order in which they were composed, and the relationship between what Pachomius and his successors actually wrote or dictated and the texts eventually rendered into Latin in 404 by St Jerome have all been debated, though it is now clear that the *Lives* should be used to explicate the contents of the rules and not vice versa.

Pachomian *koinonia*

The *Lives* indicate that Pachomius, the son of a pagan family – his name denotes a dedication to the God Khnoum – had served in the Roman army. Moved and inspired by the friendly and charitable treatment he had received at the hands of Christians when a soldier, he converted to Christianity on his discharge from the army. At first he attempted to serve others, following the example of the Christians who had helped him; next, he adopted a more obviously ascetic life, attaching himself to an older hermit, Palamon. Eventually he left Palamon, whom he still continued to visit, and beginning to gather followers of his own, set up a communal monastery, probably at some time in the 320s.[6] This first communal foundation was at Tabennese in the Thebaid, but in the twenty years in which he functioned as its head – he died in 346 or possibly 347 – other houses grew up creating what became the Pachomian federation of communities. As well as Tabennese itself these included Šeneset-Chenoboskion where he had first led an ascetic life, Phbow and further south Phnoum; to the west Thbew and Thmoušons, while further north, in the district of Panopolis (Smin) lay Tse, Tkahšmin and Tsmine. There were two female communities, one at Phbow, the other at Tabennese itself.

Why should Pachomius, who was initially involved in the eremitic style of monasticism which had developed in Egypt, have turned to a more fully communal mode of monastic expression? Could he have been influenced by the example of Manichaean or Melitian communities?[7] The *Lives* of Pachomius themselves contain conflicting messages about his religious objectives. In one version, he promises, while still a soldier, to serve all humanity; however, the *Bohairic Life* has Pachomius assert that the 'service of the sick in the villages is no work for a monk' while in a sermon he explicitly elevates the values of mutual charity and obedience above those of eremitism:

> the brothers who are the lowliest in the *koinonia*, who did not give themselves up to great practices and to an excessive ascesis but walk simply in the purity of their bodies and according to the established rules with obedience and obligingness... In the view of people who live as anchorites, their way of life does not seem perfect and they are looked on as the lowliest. [They] will be found perfect in the law of Christ because of their steadfastness. They practise exercises in all submissiveness according to God. They are also far superior to those who live as anchorites for they walk in the obligingness of the Apostle.[8]

By contrast, the *First Sahidic Life* suggests a slow evolution from eremitism into cenobitism, claiming that Pachomius was instructed in a vision to 'serve mankind' and 'to fashion the souls of men so as to present them pure to God' and hinting at not only at a charitable orientation but also at a specific teaching role in a monastic context.[9] The monks who joined Pachomius pooled all their resources for food and for themselves and any visitors and eventually a fully communal organization emerged, one in which all monks would

> bind themselves in a perfect *koinonia* like that of the believers which Acts describes: 'They were one heart and one soul'.[10]

The idea of *koinonia*, distinctive to the Pachomian monastic movement, denotes something held in common. The idea of mutual support in the religious life implicit in this term – and in the *Life*'s use of the text from Acts – suggests that one of the chief strengths of the movement founded by Pachomius was the way in which its monks, among them many recent converts like Pachomius himself, could sustain one another in their ascesis.

Pachomian Beliefs

Close study of the Pachomian literature suggests that Pachomius, like Antony, was the recipient of Christian teaching filtering out of

Alexandria. One of the principal influences on his teaching was probably the *Shepherd* of Hermas, an early work with connections to Judaic as well as Christian thought, which had influenced Origen himself and which taught a non-demiurgic *gnosis* – albeit in a simple and practical form, stressing the need to drive out the bad thoughts which spoil the good ones. Pachomius taught not only that the soul might be attacked by demons, but also that demons might implant *logismoi* or 'thoughts', not necessarily always evil in themselves, but which required to be carefully checked in case they did indeed prove to be of diabolical origin.[11] Knowledge of self would come out of this process of examination of thoughts; but the possibility of the vision of God sprang not just from the purity of heart which came from self-examination, but also from one's correct conduct towards one's fellow monks.

To what extent Pachomius accepted or understood the more theoretical aspects of Origenist teaching is unclear as later texts tended to attribute to him an anti-Origenist stance absent in earlier ones. The *Greek Life*, for instance, acquits him of Origenism by affirming that he believed in the resurrection of the body – but this affirmation is not present in the earlier *Bohairic Life*,[12] and one fragment of the *First Sahidic Life of Pachomius* might suggest that he held an Origenist view of the body as a garment of skins as it records that he wore a hairshirt round his loins.[13] But whatever the nature of Pachomius' beliefs about body and soul and the nature of the resurrection, the *koinonia* seems to have existed in a state of permanent expectation of the Second Coming of Christ. The *Regulations of Horsiesios* instruct the heads of communities that they will render an account before God, a theme later repeated, thanks to St Jerome's translation, in the *Rule* of St Benedict, but which here must be put in the context of belief that the Day of Judgement would soon dawn.

Historians have long debated the existence of a 'gnostic' element in Pachomian monasticism. The Nag Hammadi Codices were found near the town of that name by an Egyptian villager in 1945. This collection of thirteen papyrus manuscripts includes the *Apocryphon of John* and forty-three other works, most of which have been classified up until now as 'gnostic'. Also present are selections from the gnomic wisdom-text, the *Sentences of Sextus* and a much-altered Coptic version of an extract from Plato's *Republic* dealing with the tripartite nature of the soul. The collection as a whole is ascetic in nature, illuminating the questions of the transformation of the self and the ascent of the soul.[14] It was found only a few miles from Tabennese, Phbow and Šeneset and the question arose of whether it originally belonged to or had been read by Pachomian monks.[15] A multitude of questions still surrounds the codices and the exact circumstances in which they were buried or hidden in a town rubbish heap,[16] but if the texts are regarded as an ascetic rather than as a 'gnostic' collection they begin to look less problematical. If monks did indeed read these writings, they did not necessarily share in their demiurgic cosmology and mythology or even use them – as has been suggested – for heresiological purposes: they may simply have been interested in their ascetic content. There are, however, other mysterious dimensions to Pachomian monasticism. Pachomius' letters of spiritual exhortation contain a mystical alphabet, a code understood only by himself and his followers (though another famous Egyptian monastic leader, Shenoute of Atripe, claimed some knowledge of it). Alphabet mysticism – though of a different nature – is also found in the Nag Hammadi codices. Pachomius' alphabet code, however, should probably be viewed as part of the monastic *gnosis* which he taught, rather than as evidence of any demiurgic belief on his part.

Life in the *koinonia*

How did the communities of the *koinonia* succeed in achieving monastic ascesis together with meditation, prayer, psalmody and manual labour in the context of formally organized communities? To earlier generations of historians the Pachomian *koinonia* appeared as nothing less than a 'monstrous' and regimented system of labour camps, its houses reminiscent of the army barracks with which Pachomius would have been familiar in his days as a soldier in the Roman army, its spiritual values subordinated to relentless agricultural and craft production.[17] This impression may partly have been created by Palladius' later description of the communities:

> Some come in at the sixth hour and eat, others at the seventh, others at the eight, others at the ninth, others at the eleventh, others in the late evening, others every other day... So is it also with their work. One works on the land as a labourer, another in the garden., another at the forge, another in the bakery, another in the carpenter's shop, another in the fuller's shop, another in the tannery, another in the shoemaker's shop. Another in the scriptorium, another weaving the young reeds. And they learn all the scriptures by heart.[18]

As a visitor to Egypt, Palladius never went further south than Šmin in Upper Egypt and his information on the Pachomians was second-hand and sometimes inaccurate. His description of the crafts practised by the *koinonia* contains the only reference to the existence of tanneries, while he also retails the picturesque tale of how Pachomius was given his rule of life by an angel, a story possibly gleaned from the later *Lives*.[19] Jerome's introduction to his Latin rendering of the rules associated with the Pachomian *koinonia*,[20] texts which largely post-date Pachomius himself, also gives an overwhelming impression of a rigidly-organized group. He claims that within each monastery monks were divided up into individual houses according to the trade they practised, a development which can only have come with the expansion of economic activities. Jerome, though, had even less contact with Pachomian monasticism than did Palladius: he elevates an annual administrative meeting of the heads of houses into a spiritual as well as a business gathering.

The reality of the early *koinonia* was probably much less regimented than suggested by either Palladius or Jerome. Equipment and materials were distributed by the official whom the latter calls the *hebdomadarius*: some monks practised crafts, others were engaged in agriculture. The structures of the *koinonia*'s hierarchy were relatively simple: there were superiors, house-masters and their deputies, and all monks took it in order to cook and serve their brethren food. Later regulations refer to supervisors in charge of the bakery, of irrigation and of farming. Most of the monks appear to have been Egyptian peasants, some of them very recent converts to Christianity, but several – including Pachomius' successor Theodore – belonged to the Greek elite.[21] Jerome's claim that the order of seniority within each community was decided by the individual's date of entry to it is supported by the regulations themselves. These also specify that admission to the community was not to be automatic. The origins of monastic probation may be found in the provisions which state that anyone aspiring to join the *koinonia* must show that they are not a runaway slave or a criminal, that they can not only renounce possessions and parents but also support monastic discipline. No private property was permitted, not even the tweezers needed to remove thorns from a monk's bare feet: the total renunciation of property, which Athanasius highlights as a particular feature of Antony's ascesis, was put on a more formal basis by the Pachomian communities when they made willingness to renounce property part of the conditions of admission.[22]

Monks lived in cells which might house two or three individuals, grouped or built in 'houses' of twenty or so. Each house was governed by an *oikiakos* or house-master (Latin: *praepositus*): a large section of the *Precepts and Institutes* is devoted to regulating the behaviour of this key official and a whole series of Biblical curses is heaped on the head of the *oikiakos* who proves to be unsuitable.[23] Pachomius' own charisma was so great that he could let a younger monk show him a better way to plait rushes into a mat without considering this instruction a threat to his authority:

> After the young brother had taught him, he sat down to work again with joy because he had vanquished the sin of pride.[24]

However, after his death of plague in 346/7 the community was beset by problems of succession and leadership when the elders in the community seem to have resented being governed by one younger than themselves; these problems were compounded by moves towards commercial expansion.[25] Tendencies towards the revolt against the head of the *koinonia* were solved by moving abbots between monasteries on a regular basis.[26] All these circumstances favoured the setting down of rules and regulations partly attributed to Pachomius but in reality largely or entirely composed by his successors.[27]

In community, monastic psalmody now took on a more formal aspect than in the hermit-groups of Nitria and Scetis. While Pachomian monks – who were expected to learn to read – could spend part of the night working and meditating, they also took part in a communal midday and evening service which, like that of the hermits, was made up of psalms, prayers and prostrations: a major part of it, however, consisted of the monks' listening in silence to a passage of scripture recited by one monk standing in the church ambo, while the rest of the congregation worked in silence at plaiting mats or baskets. The daily Scripture readings were replaced by psalms on Sundays.[28] The liturgical tradition established by the *koinonia* may have been largely communal but was still recognizably a meditative one. However, while liturgical practice was to a large extent largely communal in nature, food asceticism was a matter for the individual monk: Pachomius is said to have insisted that a generous measure of cooked food was placed on the refectory tables every day so that the brothers might have the possibility of deciding individually to abstain. He does not appear to have imposed his own fasting practices upon the community as a norm,[29] and even abandoned the usual monastic practice of avoiding meat when he ordered a kid to be cooked and served to a sick brother.[30]

Pachomian monks had withdrawn from secular society to live in a redefined ascetic society – but even this, as the Pachomian literature reveals, could still harbour sexual, social and disciplinary problems. *The Precepts and Judgements* aim to discourage complaints, slander, 'murmuring' or disobedience.[31] The *Greek Life* lays great stress on the importance of obedience, through a Biblical text which would be repeated by other monastic authors such as Basil of Cæsarea:

> The Lord says, I have come down from heaven not to do my own will but to do the will of the one who sent me.[32]

In a community, the problems of sexual temptation, always a burden for the hermit-monk, now became acute. A precisely-measured social space is created around each monk in order to avoid the contact which may turn the mind and body to sexual thoughts or actions; monks always keep a forearm's length between them.[33] The need to avoid bodily contact, immodest behaviour or sexual activity recurs in a number of instructions: in the 'assembly', monks are instructed to sit modestly with their garments covering their knees.[34] Bathing is strictly regulated as is the oiling of the bodies of the sick.[35] Anyone found seeking out the company of boys or playing with them is to be warned.[36] A distance is maintained between the male and female sections of the Pachomian communities. The only monks allowed to visit the two women's communities are those who have female relations there and female visitors are treated with honour but kept at a distance.[37]

Koinonia, Villages and Cities

As Pachomian monasticism developed, its relationship to non-ascetic society became more complex. Pachomian monks had renounced all property and withdrawn from society to perfect their souls – but as economic units, Pachomian monasteries interacted with the society around them. Recent research has demonstrated that the Pachomian group of monasteries were mostly not 'desert' creations. Instead, they were situated in or near villages, often abandoned, but sometimes still inhabited. Pachomius supposedly created Tabennese after being led to the deserted village of that name by a vision – but in reality, villages abandoned or partly vacated because of tax burdens or plague offered an ideal opportunity to house a community. The acceptance of Pachomian monasteries by villagers may well spring from the fact that the monks occupied previously deserted land – on which, crucially, they could afford to pay taxes, unlike the peasants who had fled to other villages to avoid the tax-collector. As time went on the monasteries acquired more and more land[38] and their rules reflect the development of farming: the *Regulations of Horsiesios*, one of Pachomius' successors, include detailed instructions on irrigation. Like the other Pachomian monasteries, with the possible exceptions of Phnoum, thought to have been in the desert, Tabennese enjoyed a location near the Nile: not only was it placed in fertile land, but the Nile offered transport and access to markets for its goods. The fact that the Nile was used for transport explains the spread of the Pachomian *koinonia* over a distance of a hundred and seventy-five kilometres, between the towns of Šmin (Panopolis) in the north and Sne (Latopolis) in the south. Far from being a desert phenomenon, Pachomian monasticism was based on an association with villages, towns, the Nile and the fertile land around it.

Urban and Suburban Monastic Communities

In the late fourth century, the Pachomian *koinonia* continued its expansion with the foundation of the famous community of Metanoeite-Canopos near Alexandria, perhaps on the site of the former pagan shrine of the Serapeion. A circle of monasteries began to grow up around Alexandria from the late fourth century onwards. Similar phenomena also occurred in smaller cities and towns: although Egyptian monks – both hermits and those living in community – attempted to live as far as possible by the work of their own hands, all had need from time to time of alms and donations and these were easier to obtain in or near a town or city than in the desert, where only the most famous communities or hermit-groups were the objects of sustained pilgrimage. Alexandria also contained monasteries which developed attached *xenodocheia*, shelters or hospices for monks and pilgrims which would have involved monks in some interaction with society and which added the concept of the service of others to their monastic ascesis.[39]

Shenoute of Atripe

If the reputation of the *koinonia* may have dimmed after Pachomius' death[40] – though the attention paid to it by visitors and commentators such as Palladius and Jerome suggests the contrary – other houses, partly inspired by the Pachomian example but not part of the *koinonia*, had already grown up. Among these were the White and Red Monasteries, created around the mid-fourth century in the desert near Šmin, in an area which already housed four Pachomian communities. The desert location of both houses may signal a wish to indicate a greater austerity than that of the *koinonia*, although the White Monastery was near the 'deserted' village of Atripe which may not have been entirely depopulated.[41] In around 383–5 Shenoute, the nephew of the founder of the White Monastery, became its head.[42] Under his leadership – he is supposed to have died aged well over one hundred in 466 – this community became the chief monastic centre of Upper Egypt, supposedly housing two thousand and two hundred monks and also a community of eighteen hundred nuns. A holy man of immense charisma with acutely developed powers of discernment and 'clairvoyance', the ability to see into the hearts of others, Shenoute functioned as patron and even provider for the villages of the area. His *Life* records his concern for the poor and oppressed and he is credited with miracles in which he multiplied grain and bread. Shenoute would also prove to be a ruthless force in the struggle against paganism, and a fierce opponent of demiurgic belief and some aspects of Evagrian Origenism, while he is also regarded as the founder of Monophysite monasticism. As a centre of the Monophysite faith and focus of opposition to the Chalcedonian hierarchy in the fifth century, the White Monastery would become a pastoral centre for the Christian laity in a way in which the Pachomian monasteries did not. Its church, with a western narthex sheltering penitents and catechumens, appears to have been open to the local populace on Saturdays and Sundays and to have exercised a semi-parochial function.[43] And while Pachomius had demanded that anyone wishing to join the monastic community should show that they could support monastic discipline, it was Shenoute who enforced a period of probation which lasted two or three months. He introduced the concept of the monastic vow, whereby anyone entering the community had to swear not to steal, lie or defile his body.[44] Although a giant in the Egyptian monastic world who left a corpus of letters and sermons behind him, the fact that he wrote in Coptic (though he was able to read Greek) together with the absence of a Greek or Latin *Life*, ultimately limited Shenoute's reputation to Egypt itself.

Basil of Caesarea

> He reconciled most excellently and united the solitary and community life. These had been in many respects at variance with each other and rife with dissension, while neither of them was in absolute and unalloyed possession of good and evil; the one being rather more calm and settled tending to union with God, yet not free from pride, inasmuch as its virtue lies beyond testing or comparison; the other which is more orientated towards practical service, being not free from the tendency to turbulence ... he brought them together and united them, in order that the contemplative spirit might not be cut off from society nor should the active life be unaffected by the contemplative.[45]

This was the judgement of his friend and contemporary Gregory of Nazianzus on the ascetic and monastic achievement of St Basil of Caesarea. As Gregory's eulogy makes clear Basil (*c*.330–*c*.378) was not the founder of ascetic life in his region. Fourth-century Asia Minor was home to a wide variety of ascetic movements – Apotactics, Encratites, Montanists, Messalians, Euchites and Eustathians – all of which were characterised by a rejection of material goods or sexual activity. It is this background which Gregory discreetly evokes when he writes of the tendency of the communal life in the region towards 'turbulence'.

Prominent amongst the ascetic groups which flourished in Asia Minor was the one led by Eustathius of Sebaste. His followers – women as well as men – had adopted a radical asceticism of a free-wheeling pre-monastic type which eventually led them into trouble with the church authorities: at the Council of Gangra (340s/50s) they were accused of condemning marriage while failing to maintain chastity themselves, denouncing the ownership of goods, organizing private conventicles, admitting runaway slaves to their society, dressing distinctively, allowing women members to dress as men and cut their hair, eating and fasting at different times from the rest of the church and 'despising' married priests. Early in his career, Basil was greatly influenced by his sister Macrina, who had been inspired by the example of Eustathius to turn her family home into an ascetic colony; he himself became Eustathius' friend. Eustathius – who does not actually seem to have been amongst those excommunicated at Gangra – was made bishop of Sebaste and continued to exercise an important influence on Basil, who regarded him as a great teacher, for nearly two decades.

In his youth, Basil had studied in Cæsarea, Constantinople and Athens, spending six years there before returning to Asia Minor. He had also seen for himself – probably in 356 or 357 – the monastic life of Egypt, Palestine, Syria and Mesopotamia. In the late 350s, following the death of his brother Naucratius who had followed Macrina in becoming an ascetic, he himself attempted to lead a 'philosophic' life along with his friend Gregory of Nazianzus. In a rural retreat in Pontus – which Gregory described with some feeling as a 'rat-hole' – they studied the works of Origen who would exercise a great influence on their theology, compiling the *Philokalia* from his writings. Basil's vocabulary sometimes indicates that he shared in a broadly Christian Origenist or Platonist tradition.[46] He writes that when he arrived in Pontus it was his intention to overcome the passions of desire, fear, anger and grief:[47]

> The mind (*nous*) . . . withdraws within itself, and of its own accord ascends to the contemplation of God. Then when it is illuminated without and within by that glory, it becomes forgetful even of its own nature.[48]

He also describes the desire for God, possessed naturally by each individual and sown in everyone from the beginning of their life.[49]

In 357 Basil was ordained a priest and from his retreat in Pontus he began to engage more with the life of the organised church. In 365, he settled in Cæsarea in Cappadocia and in 370, he became its bishop. Following Eustathius' episcopal example, he founded a hospice for the poor: this, in time, was expanded into the famous *Basileiados* – a 'new city' of buildings which cared for the afflicted and destitute as well as housing the bishop and clergy. But in 373 he broke with Eustathius as a result of the debate on the nature of Christ triggered by the Arian controversy.

After this point Basil regarded Eustathius as a wolf in sheep's clothing and began to condemn his type of asceticism He set himself up as the arbiter of ascetic life in Asia Minor, commissioning the tract *De Virginitate* from Gregory of Nyssa and using his influence to create ascetic communities which were obedient to his church hierarchy and in which men and women would be separated. After their break, he wrote to Eustathius emphasizing that his inspiration had come from the gospels and already-established monasticism:

> Reading the Gospel and realising that the basic prerequisites for human completion are the renunciation of one's fortune, giving to the poor and retiring from all wordly cares and affections. I searched to find someone else who felt the way I did, so that together we could overcome the adversities of human life. And I found many in Alexandria and the rest of Egypt and others in Palestine and Coele-Syria and Mesopotamia.[50]

He had, he wrote, been unwilling to listen to accusations about Eustathius' teaching – but he had been deceived. Despite Basil's attempt to partially rewrite his own ascetic history, there is little doubt that Eustathius had exercised a major influence on him. While monasteries in Egypt had developed *xenodocheia*, originally for the shelter of travelling monks and pilgrims, Basil's desire to combine monasticism with charity owes much to Eustathius' radical social teachings and his establishment of a *ptochotropheion* or centre for poor-relief at Sebaste.

The Longer and Shorter Rules

Basil's principal monastic writings are the texts known as the *Longer* and *Shorter Rules*. These collections of precepts in question-and-answer form – Basil himself never called them rules – appear to have evolved in several stages. The *Longer Rules* are prefaced with an address to a group of Christians who had gathered to escape the outside world for one evening only, a more exclusively 'monastic' character only emerging in the revisions and extensions of the work which Basil later produced, and even more so in the Latin adaptation of an early stage of the compilation made after his death by Rufinus of Aquileia.[51] However, although the *Rules* are full of moral teaching which has application to the ascetic Christian layperson, they also include questions and answers which suggest that, as time wore on, Basil had also begun to write for formal monastic communities, for example when he discusses the usefulness of a communal life, admission, probation, profession and the admission of children.[52]

Property and the Monastery as a Source of Charity

The foundation of Basil's monastic teaching in the totality of his *Longer* and *Shorter Rules* lies in Scripture which he constantly cites, and in the commandments of God to which he constantly refers. The foundation of the charitable monastic life which he envisages is Matthew 22: 36–9:

> Master what is the great commandment according to the law?
> Jesus said unto him, Thou shalt love the Lord thy God with all thy heart and with all thy soul and with all thy mind.
> This is the first and great commandment.
> And the second is like unto it, Thou shalt love thy neighbour as thyself.[53]

Basil was profoundly affected by this gospel injunction and used scripture to argue that almsgiving brings forgiveness of sins. On entry to the monastery, the individual should liquidate his or her goods and give away these funds as charity over a period of time. He quotes Christ's injunction to

> Sell all your goods and give to the poor and you will have treasure in heaven.[54]

Possession of property within the community runs contrary to the testimony of Acts

> where it is written that not one of them said that any of the things which he possessed was his own.[55]

There are ascetic as well as charitable reasons for rejecting wealth. Involvement with material possessions hinders the monk from the achievement of total impassivity and detachment from the world, from the prospect of the spiritual refashioning of the self.

Since the renunciation of wealth for charitable purposes is fundamental to his vision of monasticism, Basil spends a good deal of time on the mechanics of this process. If the community member could not draw up a list of his property and dispose of it himself, he was to leave this task to a responsible person, presumably in the first instance the superior of the community. 'Unjust' relatives must not allowed to keep back a member's property and Basil was prepared to allow individuals to go to law to prevent such sacrilege being committed.[56] He was also realistic enough to see that it might be difficult for community members to disentangle property completely from that of their families, so families were encouraged to hand over any income from property they retained.[57] Although it is clear that Basil expected a substantial number of recruits to his monastic life to come from the propertied classes, he was also conscious that not every community would have such income and worried lest this become a source of shame to the poor while the better-off became inflated with pride. He therefore stipulated that any such income should be given by the members' relatives to the local bishop for distribution as alms, rather than be handed over directly to the ascetic group.[58]

Not only did Basil wish community members to give their income away as charity: he also disapproved of gifts to the community from members' relatives. While he left it up to individual community heads to decide whether to accept these or not, he himself is very doubtful about the propriety of receiving them, believing that they both affected the group's reputation and caused problems within it. But he conceded the right of heads to decide for themselves what to do and even permitted the steward to consider whether donors should be rewarded in any way (though he regarded this last question as decidedly worldly).[59] Basil's aim was to see religious communities both supporting themselves and raising income for charity from manual work and he specifically recommends the trades of agriculture, building, shoemaking, carpentry and metalworking as suitable for members of a religious community to practise. In prescribing work for monasteries, he wrote in conscious opposition to radical ascetic groups such as the Messalians or Euchites, who thought manual work irreconcilable with a life of prayer. Basil believed that it was possible to follow two apostolic commands – to 'pray without ceasing' and to 'work night and day' and that

> we must not treat the ideal of piety as an excuse for idleness or a means of escaping toil.[60]

Community members must work both to provide their own subsistence and for charitable purposes:

> it is God's will that we should nourish the hungry, give the thirsty to drink, clothe the naked.[61]

And work also has another purpose, representing both ascetic effort and an opportunity to practise the virtue of endurance in a way pleasing to God.[62]

Community

Basil was firmly committed to the values of the common life:

> I recognise that the life of a number lived in common is useful in many ways. To begin with, none of us is self-sufficient ... But apart from this, the fashion of the love of Christ does not allow us to look at each his own good. For 'love', we read 'seeketh not its own'. Now the solitary life has one aim, the service of the needs of the individual. But this is plainly in conflict with the law of love which the apostle fulfilled when he sought not

his own advantage, but that of the many which might be saved . . . Secondly in such separation the man will not even recongise his defects readily, not having anyone to reprove him and set him right with kindness and compassion.[63]

Basil also believed that the working of the Holy Spirit in one individual passed over to the rest of the community: his vision of the religious life was based on the image of a fully integrated Christian community, dwelling in perfect harmony in the service of God. This did not imply that he believed in a religious democracy; but at the same time, his superior is not the autocratic abbot of later monastic history. Instead, he is the head of the community by virtue of his spiritual gifts and should he slip from the high standards expected of him he may be admonished by the 'pre-eminent' among the brethren.[64]

Basil insisted that a Christian community should be governed by scriptural commands: he writes that if one of the community believes the superior to be acting contrary to them, he should be allowed to raise his doubts. While he is clear that the primary monastic virtue is that of obedience 'unto death', like that of Christ himself, it is the gospel which is the ultimate law in his community and to this even the superior must be subject.[65] Acutely conscious of the importance of proper authority which draws its basis from the spiritual accomplishments of the superior, Basil nevertheless emphasizes that the superior must also balance authority with the practise of a Christ-like humility and compassion for his brethren:

> Let meekness of character and lowliness of heart characterise the superior. For if the Lord was not ashamed of ministering to his own bond-servants, but was willing to be a servant of the earth and the clay which he had made and fashioned into man . . . what must we do to our equals that we may be deemed to have attained the imitation of him? This one thing, then, is essential in the superior. Further he must be compassionate, showing long-suffering to those who through inexperience fall short in their duty, not passing sins over in silence but meekly bearing with the restive, applying remedies to them all with kindness and delicate adjustment. He must be able to find out the proper method of cure for each fault, not rebuking harshly, but administering and correcting with meekness . . .[66]

In Basil's thought, humility was, paradoxically, the badge of authority: the way in which the superior was expected to be capable of blending both qualities as he ministered to his community reflects the expectation that he would be imbued with the charisma conferred by obedience to the teaching of the gospels, and the achievement of a true life in the spirit.

According to Basil, the superior was doctor of the soul:

As for one who shows hesitation in obeying the commandments of the Lord, in the first instance all should sympathise with him as a sick member of the body and the superior should try to cure his infirmity by his private admonitions; but if he perseveres in disobedience then the superior must correct him sharply before all the brethren and apply methods of healing by every method of exhortation. But if after much admonition he is still unabashed and shows no improvement in his conduct, he becomes his own destroyer as the saying is and with many tears and lamentations, but nevertheless firmly as a corrupted and utterly useless member, we must cut him away from the body, after the practice of doctors...[67]

The idea of private reproof is related to Basil's insistence that

All things, even the secrets of the heart, are to be revealed to the superior.[68]

By the 'superior', Basil means here not just the head of the community but a whole class of brothers advanced both in years and in spiritual gifts to whom all other members of the community must make a full account of their thoughts – just as the hermits of Egypt subjected their thoughts to the scrutiny of older and more experienced fathers. Confession of every thought – and even of every event which takes place on a journey if an individual is sent outside the community – is to be made to these seniors. Basil affirms that a skilled observer sees sin in a man as a doctor sees disease and that confession is made to 'doctors of the soul' or 'to those who are entrusted with the mysteries of God'. The latter represents the only suggestion in the rules that such confessions might perhaps be made to a priest rather than simply to seniors. For Basil such confessions are medicinal in their purpose:

Let the superior employ corrective methods on the afflicted after the example of doctors, not being angry with the sick but fighting the disease. Let him face the illness and by more laborious regime if necessary, cure the soul's sickness. For example, he will cure vainglory by ordering practices of humility; idle speech by silence; excessive sleep by watchings with prayer; bodily idleness by labour; unseemly eating by deprivation of food; murmuring by separation, so that none of the brethren chooses to work with the offender, nor to let his work go in with that of the rest, as we said above, unless he appears to be cured of his vice by unreserved penitence.[69]

Members of the Basilian Community

Unlike the radical group led by Eustathius, in Basil's monasteries, men and women lived together but were separated. Whereas the Egyptian ascetics and communities had regarded the presence of boys as a possible

source of sexual temptation,[70] Basil took the first steps in the system-
atizing of the practice of child oblation when he wrote that children old
enough to be educated and brought up in the fear of God may be
admitted to monasteries in obedience to Christ's command:

Suffer the children to come unto me.[71]

Parents were to hand over their children to the community before
witnesses. The final version of the *Longer Rules* includes a detailed set
of regulations for the admission of and upbringing of children, who are to
live in a separate part of the community from adults; although they pray
at the same times, they follow a separate timetable and eat separately.
They are to be educated, though some may be set to learn crafts from
adults. Basil is anxious that those old enough to join the community
permanently are left to do so without coercion, so they are given time to
consider this step. Adults too undergo a period of testing and probation
and Basil sets down detailed discussions of how slaves or married persons
aspiring to be part of the community should be received.

The Significance of Basil's Writings

There are relatively few references to Basil's own monasteries apart from
his original foundation at Annesi, yet he occupies an important place in
monastic history. He set down in writing a theory of communal life based
firmly on the idea of active charity towards others. With this charitable
orientation he combined the more traditional monastic emphasis on
anachoresis and detachment from earthly things. Gregory of Nazianzus'
assessment of Basil's activity highlights this orientation towards 'practical
service' and the way in which he managed to blend it with a more
contemplative asceticism usually associated with the eremitic life.
(Whether Gregory's claim that he also founded hermitages near his
monasteries is another matter as Basil's emphasis on the common life is
accompanied by a negative or at best ambivalent attitude to the solitary
one.) His *Rules* brought to monastic life a move towards moderation in
matters of diet and ascesis, ruling simply that the one criterion for self-
control is abstinence from anything which might lead the soul into a
destructive pleasure.[72] This moderate monastic 'practical' life, with its
tradition of service to others, was a version of monasticism which would
prove very attractive to some of the aristocratic monks and bishops of the
fifth-century West, while Basil's teachings on confession and obedience
would exercise a long-lasting influence on monastic thought.

3

Women in Early Monasticism

Christianity sent out an ambivalent message to its female adherents. On one hand, Paul had proclaimed that:

> There is neither male nor female, neither bond nor free; for ye are all one in Christ Jesus...[1]

while on the other the first epistle to Timothy – not a genuine Pauline work but one which gained canonical status – enjoined women to 'learn in silence in all subjection'.[2] An important sect of the of the second century, the Montanists, was led by two female prophets, Priscilla and Maximilla,[3] but in more conservative and mainstream forms of Christianity, women were unable to advance beyond the rank of deaconess, a position created to preserve the modesty of adult females at baptism.[4] In general, women were perceived in both Christian and non-Christian society as intellectually and physically inferior, disadvantaged by their bodies and by a suspect sexuality. Older taboos surrounding menstruation and the physical processes of reproduction found their way into many varieties of Christianity, perhaps reinforced in the fourth century as the number of converts dramatically increased. Menstruating women, regarded as polluted, often felt constrained by social pressures from participating in the Eucharist, even though a number of church synods from the third to the late fourth century encouraged them to overcome this hesitation.[5] For those Christians who accepted the Genesis version of creation, it was woman, in the person of Eve, who was responsible for the Fall: personifying pride or concupiscence (as well as being its object) she gave the fruit of temptation to her husband. The North African theologian Tertullian (c.160–c.225) regarded woman as the 'devil's gateway'.[6] Alternative mythologies did not necessarily paint a more positive picture as the female was often identified with matter and chaos: in the cosmology of the Sethian demiurgics, it was Wisdom, a female aeon, who caused a disturbance in the *pleroma* by rushing towards the light of her divine parent, and as a consequence, brought forth Ialdabaoth, the evil creator of this world. The demiurgic-Christian Valentinians visualized the ultimate God as embracing both genders but consisting of a male principle and mere female consort. Such beliefs and assumptions could penetrate the most rarified heights of theology: Origen, though he did not deem the soul to be gendered, classified the mind (*nous*) as masculine and sense-perception (*æsthesis*) as feminine.[7]

Transcendence or Transformation of Gender

While popular beliefs and even higher theology often transmitted the view of the female as weak, intellectually inferior and polluted, other beliefs could contradict or circumvent these stereotypes. Although Origen had identified the higher faculty of mind or *nous* as male, his theory of the alienation of souls from God led him to regard bodily characteristics such as gender as transient or temporary. The present body along with the spirit would be transformed throughout the ages and would lose its sexual characteristics in part of the great cycle of *apocatastasis*, in which all souls – and transfigured bodies – would return to God at the end of time.[8] The sexual nature of the body and sexual differences were evanescent, disappearing as each body and soul underwent a process of transformation, which would continue after death. In Origen's vast aeonic perspective, gender differences melted into comparative insignificance.

Not all theologians of the Early Church reflected the dominant patriarchy by constructing a male God: the Cappadocians, Gregory of Nyssa and Gregory of Nazianzus, taught that there was no gender in the Godhead. Such views, when taken together with a view of the soul which held that God and humankind are ontologically linked, had important consequences for their view of gender. Gregory of Nazianzus finds differences of body but not of soul between men and women.[9] He refuses to blame Eve disproportionately for the Fall, while Gregory of Nyssa's *Life* of his sister Macrina – who had created an ascetic community including her brother Peter and possibly other men as well – decisively rules out any link between woman and the sexual or the irrational side of human nature, declaring that:

> In this case it was a woman who provided us with our subject; if indeed she should be styled woman, for I do not know whether it is fitting to designate her by her sex, who so surpassed her sex.[10]

By 'surpassing her sex' Gregory did not mean that Macrina became more like a man, rather that she had transcended human nature to live an angelic life.[11] Gregory was not only influenced by Origen but had the highest regard for the achievements of his sister, mother and grandmother, all prominent figures in Christian life in their area. Gender, he held, was bodily and temporary, assigned by God along with the body and passions in order to preserve the soul, which would eventually return to its maker. Another Cappadocian writer, Basil, bishop of Ancyra between 336 and 358, composed a treaty of virginity, noteworthy not least because it often reflects his earlier medical training. He believed that female virgins dedicated to a life of religion

> have a female body, but they repress the appearance of their body through ascesis and become, through their virtue, like men, to whom they are already created equal in their soul.[12]

Another strand of opinion, influenced by the dominant patriarchy, held that even if the female was to be identified with sinfulness and weakness, her faults could be transcended and she could become male.[13] The *Gospel of Thomas*, one of the texts found in the Nag Hammadi Codices, postulates female to male transformation as an ideal:

> Simon Peter said to them, 'Let Mary leave us for women are not worthy of life'.
>
> Jesus said, 'I myself shall lead her in order to make her male, so that she too may become a living spirit. For every woman who will make herself male will enter the kingdom of heaven.'[14]

A symbolic gender transformation appears in the *Apocryphal Acts of the Apostles*, a second-century text which tells the story of Thecla, a young female disciple of Paul to whom he gives the right to preach and baptise. Thecla puts on male clothing and cuts her hair like a man's – a transvestism associated with her baptism and a symbol of her taking on of Christ.[15]

However, many within the church could not accept that it was possible for individuals to free themselves entirely from the body's demands and lead entirely spiritual lives. In this, they were led by the highly influential North African theologian Tertullian. Strongly influenced by the Stoic concept of the body and soul as a unified organism, Tertullian considered that it was impossible for any mere human unilaterally to declare him or herself liberated from the demands of the flesh. Tertullian condemned the narrative of Paul and Thecla as an abusive text. Some of his most powerful writing is contained in his treatise *On the Veiling of Virgins* in which he criticizes the actions of a group of Carthaginian girls who had dedicated themselves to chastity and appeared unveiled in church. While their radical declaration of virginity had been greeted with admiring enthusiasm by many of the Carthaginian Christian community, Tertullian recoiled from an action which he saw as both dangerous and self-deluding, arguing that they could not, as they went about unveiled, rise above the need for modesty and sexual shame.[16]

Informal Ascetic Groups

The belief that women could become 'male' or that gender was temporary meant in practice that in some ascetic groups and sects men and women mixed freely, convinced that the temptations of the flesh were either irrelevant or could be overcome by spiritual achievement. In the late third or early fourth century, the Copt Hieracas preached continence and virginity to both male and female followers in the Nile Delta, while in fourth-century Asia Minor, Eustathius of Sebaste led an encratite group of men and women. Eustathius and his followers condemned marriage and married priests, while the women dressed as men and cut their hair short, in symbolic rejection of physical gender. In fourth-century Alexandria, a number of wealthy and literate young women vowed themselves to lives of virginity and continence. Some lived as *agapetes*, syneisakts or *subintroductae* in chaste 'spiritual marriage' with men or under the guidance of priests in arrangements based in one way or another on a familial structure.[17] Later in the fourth century, a former slave called Sisinnius founded a 'brotherhood' of men and women. According to the *Lausiac History*:

> By his grave manner of life he drove out whatever masculine lusts there were in himself and by self-discipline he curbed the feminine element in the women, so that the words of Scripture were fulfilled, 'In Christ Jesus, there is neither male nor female'.[18]

Women in the Desert

Could women aspire to be the ascetic counterparts of the monks of the Egyptian desert? The hermit monks had removed themselves to the desert in order to cut off any contact with society; women were classed as the primary source of distraction and temptation which might bring a monk to ruin. Yet there is evidence that some women ascetics succeeded in living in this harsh and predominantly masculine environment. Amma ('mother') Theodora lived somewhere outside Alexandria (possibly Nitria, Kellia or Scetis) while Amma Sarah lived in the desert of Pelusium. Sayings attributed to both women and to Syncletica appear in the *Apophthegmata*[19] where Theodora deals with the question of the demon of *accedia*, that destructive spirit of boredom which so preoccupied Evagrius. The question arises of who taught them in the first place. Were they former syneisakts or members of urban ascetic groups who had then embarked on *anachoresis*? Had they been amongst the visitors who ventured into the hermit colonies to learn from the greatest teachers – and if so where did they stay? Yet question-marks hang over the beginning of these women's careers rather than their development.[20] Advanced in ascesis, Sarah could confront a challenge from hostile male ascetics on grounds of gender so successfully that her reply passed into the *Apophthegmata*:

> Two old men, great anchorites, came to the district of Pelusium to visit her. When they arrived, one said to the other, 'Let us humiliate this old woman'. So they said to her, 'Be careful not to become conceited thinking to yourself: Look how anchorites are coming to see me, a mere woman', But Amma Sarah said to them, 'According to nature I am a woman but not according to my thoughts'.[21]

Once power in ascesis and the total annihilation of femininity was achieved, these women attained the same status as men. The fact that their sayings are recorded in the *Apophthegmata* betokens respect, admiration and the likelihood that they were visited and consulted by males. Theodora seems to have maintained contact with bishop Theophilus of Alexandria.

Women's Communities

The Pachomian communities, with their more formal communal basis, adopted a slightly different perspective where women were concerned. Pachomius had to face the problem with which many other male ascetics, including Antony, had been confronted: the problem of the care of sisters and other female relations when the males of the family entered a monastery. The first female Pachomian foundation was headed by his sister and regulations on visits suggest that other monks had relatives in female houses. But the Pachomians were acutely sensitive to what they perceived as the dangers of sexuality even in single-sex houses and there was apparently no question of setting up communities where men and women might mix.[22]

Asceticism and the Women of the Roman Aristocracy

From the 350s on a number of women of the Roman aristocracy, attracted by reports of Egyptian desert monasticism, began to embrace the ascetic life. In 352/3 Marcellina, sister of the future Bishop Ambrose of Milan, was publicly veiled as a virgin by the pope and lived in ascetic retreat in her mother's house. The conversion of the aristocrat Marcella, one of the *gens Caeonia*, occurred around 355, when her husband died.[23] The death of a husband or father was a significant event in the lives of ascetically inclined female aristocrats, as they had little legal autonomy as wives or daughters. Sometimes married off at an early age – even before the legal age of consent – women had very limited rights and a large number of duties within the confines of family and married life. A woman could not act for herself in court. Laws regarding marriage were largely framed to protect property and upper-class marriages were undertaken for the advantage of the two family groups concerned, to gain property or perhaps to cement political alliances. There were more upper-class women than men and therefore a widow might be expected to remarry in order to support the political or economic ambitions of her own *familia*, under whose control she ultimately remained, however many marriages she might make. Though some Roman writers attempted to construct a picture of mutual support in marriage, the wife was largely encouraged to remain entirely dependent on her husband. For a man of the upper classes, the ideal of marriage was regarded as a civic duty, a microcosm of the civil order; for a woman, in practice, it merely imposed another degree of subjection in addition to that already exacted by her family.[24]

However, it was possible for some widows to evade family obligations. When Marcella decided to follow an ascetic lifestyle, she briskly refused her mother's plans for her to remarry and handed over all control of possessions to her mother. She dressed simply and ate plainly associating only with her mother and others who had followed her example, seeing monks and clergy – the only men with whom she ever spoke – solely in company. Other aristocratic widows in Marcella's mould were her friend Paula, who lived in Rome as an ascetic for five years before leaving for Egypt and settling in the Holy Land, and Melania the Elder. A member of the *gens Antonia*, a noble Spanish family, Melania married around 356, but had lost two of her three sons and found herself a widow by the age of twenty-two. This was the decisive moment in her life. Handing over her surviving son to the guardianship of the Praetorian Prefect she left Rome in 372 for Egypt, seeking out the most prominent Nitrian ascetics. Another widow, Fabiola, a twice-married member of the *gens Fabia*, dedicated herself to the religious life in public one Easter in front of the Pope and the entire assembled congregation at the Lateran basilica.[25]

As well as these formidable widows, a number of virgins took up the religious life. These included Paula's own daughters Blesilla, who became part of Marcella's circle, and Julia Eustochium. Marcella's friends also included Asella who, according to St Jerome's didactic and not necessarily trustworthy account of her life, had been dedicated to a life of virginity by her family at a young age. Probably also under the influence of Marcella, Irene, sister of Pope Damasus (366–85) vowed herself to a life of virginity, but died before she reached the age of twenty. An aristocratic widow, Lea, acted as 'mother' to a group of virgins.

Jerome

Marcella, Paula and Melania were educated and now independent women; but even freed from the constraints of family life and expectations, they still felt the need for spiritual guidance and, in particular, a higher level of education so that they might study Scripture. They could only obtain this from men. The first males who formed part of the spiritual circles of these powerful women were not of their own high rank, but provincial intellectual clerics such as Jerome and his friend Rufinus who became their advisers and teachers. Born in Illyria *c.*331, Jerome arrived in Rome in 382, commanding an impressive intellectual and spiritual reputation.[26] Now a man in his fifties, he had lived in the East for a number of years and had several writings and translations to his credit, though he had not as yet carried out the great biblical translations which made his name. At this stage in his career he was an exegete, often dependent on and enthusiastic about the work of Origen.[27] He had personal experience of eastern monasticism: inspired by the *Life of Antony*, he had lived in the Syrian desert as a hermit – not a happy experience as his neighbours regarded him as an outsider and heretic.[28] Yet this does not seem to have deterred him from continuing to lead and advocate a life of Christian asceticism.

In 382, Jerome became secretary to Pope Damasus and was quickly recruited as scriptural teacher and spiritual adviser to Marcella, Paula and their circles. It was Marcella who first took the initiative in seeking out Jerome as a teacher,[29] proving a determined task-mistress, as she constantly plied him with questions to which he sat up until the small hours replying. Paula and Eustochium also demanded translations, commentaries and guidance, particularly where their own study of the Bible and Hebrew was concerned: Paula apparently took a more sophisticated allegorical view of texts than did Marcella, but in the early fifth century Marcella would lead the assault in Rome on Origenist doctrine, to which Jerome was by then opposed, to his satisfaction.

Jerome visited the households of these women and became their close associate, teacher and confidant, demanding great ascetic commitment from the younger members of the group. At the same time he castigated ascetics and Christians who did not share his views in such biting terms that pagans rushed to read his most damning strictures.[30] Such behaviour made him unpopular with many of his co-religionists, an unpopularity which was further exacerbated by the sudden death of Paula's daughter Blesilla in 384. A young and lively widow she had, following an illness, turned to a life of asceticism under Jerome's spiritual direction, fasting and mortifying herself until, after a few months, she was dead. Romans were horrified when her mother fainted at her funeral and Jerome was widely blamed for her death. Shortly afterwards, his patron Pope Damasus also died. For some time, Jerome had already considered leaving Rome: now a charge, perhaps relating to his relationship with Paula, was brought against him. He seems to have been asked to withdraw from Rome and in 385 he and Paula, accompanied by her other daughter Eustochium, departed separately for the East.

Melania and Paula in the East

Was Paula forced to abandon Rome because of her association with Jerome and the death of her daughter? Perhaps, but the pull of both the Holy Land and Egypt on the women who had studied Scripture, read the *Life of Antony* or listened to tales of desert asceticism so eagerly had swiftly become apparent. Although Marcella remained as a house-ascetic in Rome, Melania the Elder had already departed for Egypt in 372/3. Paula herself met up with Jerome again in either Cyprus or Antioch and together they embarked on a pilgrimage tour of the Holy Land before visiting Egypt. Paula may even have wished to found a convent of her own near Nitria, where she visited all the most prominent monastic leaders of the day[31] and had to be persuaded by Jerome to join him in the Holy Land. They were not the first prominent western ascetics to make their homes there. After leaving Egypt, Melania and at some point her own spiritual advisor, Jerome's friend Rufinus, had settled on the Mount of Olives – where, it was believed, Christ would come to earth for a second time – founding their own associated communities of monks and nuns around 379–80. (Several years later, they were visited by Evagrius of Pontus, at that stage a cleric running away from an unhappy love affair: it was Melania who persuaded him to visit the ascetics of Egypt, thus launching him on the last stage of his spiritual odyssey.) In 385, Paula and Jerome stayed for a time with Melania and Rufinus before founding their own monasteries at Bethlehem.

The ascetic life lived by both groups in the Holy Land was exacting. Melania herself observed the most extreme personal austerity: when at the age of sixty she revisited Egypt she took a travelling companion to task for washing and resting on a rug:

Be sure of this, be sure of it, that I am in the sixtieth year of my life and except for the tips of my fingers neither my feet nor my face nor any one of my limbs have touched water, although I am a victim to various ailments and the doctors try to force me. I have not consented to make the customary concessions to the flesh, never in my travels have I rested on a bed or used a litter.[32]

The communities of Melania and Rufinus were given spiritual precepts – the *Sentences to Monks* and *Sentences to a Virgin* – by Evagrius, who urged them to avoid false *gnosis*, to exercise restraint in food, drink and speech, to achieve *apatheia* and unite their souls with God. In the eulogy which he wrote on Paula's death, Jerome painted an idealized portrait of life in Paula's community. Eustochium and Paula and a group of nuns dressed plainly, lived simply, without any private property and sang six offices of psalms every day. Paula prevented the nuns from quarrelling, stealing or paying too much attention to their appearance (like Melania, she did not believe that cleanliness was next to godliness) and prescribed extra fasts for those troubled by sexual desires. Paula and Eustochium both humbled themselves by performing household tasks and serving the plain food on which the nuns lived.[33]

Despite their ascetic regimes and desire for the self-marginalization which led them to embrace the ascetic life in the first place, neither Paula nor Melania could quite dissociate themselves from their aristocratic background. In Paula's convent, while all the nuns dressed identically, they were divided into three groups, on the basis, Jerome implies, of social class.[34] Both women spent their lives using their position or giving away their wealth in support of the monastic movement. When Melania first arrived in Egypt, she went straight from Alexandria to Nitria and deposited three hundred pounds of silver in a precious casket at the feet of the venerable Apa Pambo – who, as she ruefully told Palladius later, promptly delivered a stinging rebuke for her pride when she attempted to solicit thanks for the gift.[35] She sustained the pro-Nicene party in Egypt on death of Athanasius[36] and when Theophilus expelled the Origenist monks from Nitria and they fled to Palestine, where the authorities forbade them any assistance, it was Melania who brought food to them, disguised as a slave. Arrested by the local governor, who was ignorant of her true identity, she rounded on him, instantly reassuming part of her old identity with all the imperious disdain of a *grande dame* accustomed to deference on account of her rank and declaring:

For my part, I am So-and-so's daughter and So-and-so's wife, but I am Christ's slave. And do not despise the cheapness of my clothing, for I am able to exalt myself if I like and you cannot terrify me in this way or take any of my goods.[37]

She encouraged her granddaughter to follow her example: Melania the Younger succeeded in persuading her husband, to whom she had been married against her will at an early age, to agree to a celibate marriage, selling off vast family estates, some of them as far away as Britain, to support the church and monasticism.[38] Paula died in 404, having given away all her vast fortune in support of churches, monasteries and charity and leaving Jerome's community which had depended on her support with severe financial problems.

Palladius – an Origenist who had studied with Evagrius at Kellia – devotes about one-third of the stories in his *Lausiac History* to female ascetics and communities and singles out the achievements of these great ladies who had devoted themselves to an ascetic life and works of charity. He puts their attainments on a par with those of men:

> It is necessary also to mention in my book certain women with manly qualities, to whom God apportioned labours equal to those of men, lest any should pretend that women are too feeble to practise virtue perfectly.[39]

He writes admiringly of Melania the Elder that she perused

> every writing of the ancient commentators, including three million lines of Origen and two-and-a half million lines of Gregory, Stephen, Pierius, Basil and other standard writers. Nor did she read them once only and casually, but she laboriously went through each book seven or eight times.[40]

Palladius claims that Melania had been saved from 'knowledge falsely so called' – probably the docetic and demiurgic beliefs against which Evagrius campaigned[41] – and may even suggest that she wished to reunite the intellectual part of her soul, the *logistikos*, with God:

> thanks to the grace of these books ... elevated by kindly hopes she made herself a spiritual bird and journeyed to Christ.[42]

He also hints that Paula had once nurtured similar aspirations. He observes darkly that:

> She was hindered by a certain Jerome from Dalmatia. For though she was able to surpass all, having great abilities, he hindered her by his own jealousy having induced her to serve his own plan.[43]

Separation

Many in the post-Nicene church acquiesced either in notions of female impurity or a view of the body similar to that of Tertullian and attempted to disband any groups of ascetics which included both women and men. In Egypt, Athanasius exerted himself in the attempt to reduce the class of vowed virgins to an submissive and ancillary arm of the Alexandrian church. He defined Christian virgins as those who renounced the possibility of a worldly marriage and dedicated themselves to the idea of a marriage with Christ, possibly even subscribing to a written vow of chastity. He endeavoured to direct syneisakts,[44] those living in 'spiritual marriages' or under the direction of priests, either into communities which he could control or into their family household, subject to the authority of their families. He did not believe that men and women could lead spiritual lives together without sexual distraction: in 'spiritual marriages', he argued, the virgin's attention was divided between her male companion and Christ. Instead, she should abandon other men and enter into dependence on Christ alone in reflection of her status as Bride of Christ. Some of his thinking would influence others in the fourth century, notably Ambrose of Milan.

Similar attitudes can be found in the *Panarion* of Bishop Epiphanius of Salamis which denounced an ascetic leader named Aerius, alleging that under the influence of Arianism he had led a large following of men and women away from urban and even rural society and challenged the authority of the bishop. Eustathius of Sebaste also found himself condemned in the 340s or 50s by the Council of Gangra for allowing the sexes to mix in his ascetic group and for allowing women to deny 'male power over their heads', to cut their hair and to 'become men'. When Basil of Cæsarea came to create his own monasteries, as a bishop he bowed to conventional thinking. Despite his previous friendship with Eustathius, despite the religious influence of his sister, mother and grandmother, and despite the views of his brother Gregory of Nyssa on the non-gendered nature of the soul, his women's and men's groups were strictly segregated.[45] The socially conservative Basil[46] used his influence to create ascetic communities obedient to his church hierarchy in which men and women were separated. He commissioned the tract *On Virginity* from Gregory of Nyssa who promoted the idea that the best form of ascesis was that controlled by Basil himself. Typically, the more otherworldly Gregory (who was nevertheless the only one of the Cappadocian Fathers ever to have married) lists groups of anarchic ascetics but tends to see the best in them, believing that many have merely gone astray from originally good intentions.[47]

It is noticeable that even in the already-segregated Pachomian *koinonia*, there is evidence that enclosure of women and their separation from men became more strict with the passage of time. Despite the existence of written rules, an additional male supervisor was appointed for the women[48] and even more complete segregation enforced. The *Lives* of Pachomius record supervised visits by monks to relatives in the female houses, where they are not allowed to eat or drink[49] and there are no visits by women to the male community, suggesting that enclosure was stricter for women than men. Male visits to the female house to carry out any work were – in theory at least – surrounded by an increasing number of restrictions.[50] Palladius may exaggerate the strict separation of the male and female communities:

> the women are on the far side of the river, the men opposite them … So, when a virgin dies, the brethren, having crossed in a ferry boat, with palm leaves and olive branches, take the body across, singing the psalms the while and bury it in their own cemetery. But apart from the priest and the deacon no man goes across to the women's monastery, and they only on Sunday.[51]

In the same chapter, he tells of the despair and suicide of a Tabennesiot nun who was persecuted by her sisters when she accidentally spoke to a man who presented himself at the gates, together with the suicide of her accuser. This may be a legend, but if so it is one which testifies eloquently to the Pachomian *koinonia's* reputation for strict separation of the sexes. Comparison of the *Bohairic Life* and *First Greek Life* in fact shows that Tabennese's funerary practices gradually evolved to minimize the female role and the possibilities for male–female contact and that it is likely that in this latter respect Palladius was giving an accurate account of their state in the late fourth century.[52] Shenoute similarly paid lip-service to the notion that the same crown had been prepared for both men and women who persevered, but in practice the female communities of his congregation were subject to his authority and supervised by a senior monk.[53]

Although the *Apophthegmata* privileged the sayings of the great Amma Theodora along with those attributed to Sarah and Syncletica as pearls of desert wisdom, some of the legendary *Lives* of Egyptian and Syrian female monastic saints impose their own distorting message on the asceticism of their subjects.[54] The presence of Syrian female ascetics in the desert was regarded as a danger to their male counterparts and they were required to wear the veil, while the accounts of saints such as Mary of Egypt and Pelagia dwell on their past as prostitutes – temptresses whose condition is ineluctably linked to their bodily state until, in both *Lives,* the sinning female is rescued through the agency of a male religious figure. Even so, beneath the gloss of stereotype, some fragmentary sketches of women seeking gender transformation may be glimpsed. Mary is found naked in the desert, scarcely recognizable as a human being: her body is burned black by the sun, her white hair cut short like a man's. In the desert, she has transcended gender – only, in the narrative, to become conscious of it once more at the approach of a male. Pelagia ends her days in a monastery in the guise of a eunuch, a being beyond both masculinity and femininity.

Enclosed Virginity

By the late fourth century, it was becoming clear that acceptance of the possibilities of gender transcendence or transformation, which had hovered so tantalisingly before some ascetic women for a century or two, was becoming increasingly undermined by the view of woman as weak and polluted and by a pessimistic view of the human condition similar to those advanced by Tertullian and the other great North African theologian, Cyprian (d.258).[55] For religious communities, segregation of the sexes and enclosure were becoming the norm. Jerome's Letter 22, written to Eustochium in 384 when he was at the height of his influence in Rome and spiritual director to Paula and her group, is a savage polemic on the subject, designed to be circulated amongst the Roman elite. In it, he openly attacks religious groups in which men and women mingled freely.

Described by one modern scholar as 'the greatest slander of women since Juvenal's sixth satire,'[56] Letter 22 presents Jerome's view of how monastic life should properly be lived together with a lengthy and bitingly vicious satire on the conduct of ascetic groups in contemporary Rome. Jerome uses Egyptian monasticism to define his parameters: in Egypt there are genuine hermits and cenobites but also undisciplined groups of *remnuoth* – he prides himself on his knowledge of the Coptic word – living in cities and following no fixed rule. Such *remnuoth*, Jerome claims, were common in Italy and he makes it clear that he has nothing but contempt for them. He paints a savagely caricatured portrait of such ascetic groups in Rome, seeking to expose asceticism in which men and women associate freely as delusion or, more often, downright pretence. Rome, he claims, is full of clergy who had been ordained simply in order to gain freer access to women. His greatest contempt is reserved for the so-called female ascetics whose motives he sees as either sublimation – rich widows with their fine clothes and retinues of eunuchs, fawned on by clergy, 'retiring, after a questionable supper, to dream of the Apostles' – or a cloak for sexual misconduct in the cases of the impure 'virgins' who sin, claiming that 'to the pure all is pure,' and then abort the consequences of their lust.

At the heart of this vicious attack lies Jerome's theory of sexuality. Resonating from the deepest recesses of his being in a way in which no amount of reading of Origen had been able to stifle was his conviction that the demands and temptations of the flesh were inescapable and that anyone who attempted to deny them was at best self-deluding, at worst a liar. Men and women could not mix freely without the serpent of sexuality rearing its head: and he knew from his own bitter experience the power of the flesh. In the same letter, he describes to Eustochium his stay as a hermit in the Syrian desert, where, despite constant self-mortification and fasting he had been assailed by acute sexual fantasies:

> though in my fear of Hell, I had condemned myself to this prison house, where my only companions were scorpions and wild beasts, I often found myself surrounded by bands of dancing girls. My face was pale with fasting, but though my limbs were cold as ice, my mind was burning with desire and the fires of lust kept bubbling up before me, while my flesh was as good as dead.

In this last sentence, as Jerome seeks to convey to Eustochium from his own lived experience his certainty that the human will and restraint of the body alone cannot purify the mind, he shows the distance which already existed between his asceticism and that of the desert fathers of Egypt. His later *Life of Hilarion* rehearses the same scenario. Even his earlier *Life of Paul the First Hermit*, composed in the late 370s after his stay in Syria, had already hinted at a possible ascetic crisis. In this work, the startling presence of a mythical centaur, human in its upper parts, animal in its lower, may be read as a symbol of Jerome's view of the desert as a place where the spiritual struggles to free itself from the sexual or more simply as a metaphor for the semi-bestial nature of the human condition.[57] He counsels Eustochium to study not only the writings of his own patron Pope Damasus, but the works of those resolutely non-transformational ascetics, Tertullian and Cyprian.

If Jerome himself had, after fasting and mortification of his body, experienced the phantasms of desire; if Saint Paul had begged after prison, beatings and torments to be released from the 'body of death', how much more, he argued, must a young girl like Eustochium, used to the sensations of easy living, be prone to sexual temptations and longings. The solution to this problem was simple: she must remain, as far as possible, enclosed and stay away from corrupting society. Jerome demands that Eustochium should have only other dedicated virgins for company, should keep as far as possible to her room, fast and mortify her flesh, avoiding wine and rich foods both of which can stimulate sexual desire, filling her days and nights with prayer at set hours and Bible reading. In other words, she should become an enclosed virginal nun.[58]

Letter 22 constantly reveals Jerome's preoccupation with the physical: in describing the loss of virginity by women *in their souls* he resorts to the grossest of physical metaphors drawn from Scripture – such women will be found opening their legs to all who pass by. In describing Eustochium's enclosed existence, he characterizes her as a Bride of Christ: her domestic sequestration in her room is articulated by Jerome as the presence of the Bride in the bridal chamber of the Song of Songs.[59] There, undefiled, she will wait for her lover:

> When sleep overcomes you, he will come behind the wall, will thrust his
> hand through the aperture and will caress your belly; and you will start up
> all trembling and will cry, 'I am wounded with love'.

This 'figuration of asceticism in terms of linguistic metaphors of desire'[60]
shows Jerome still struggling with his own physical nature. So physical are
his metaphors that he can even – in Rufinus' view blasphemously –
congratulate Paula, the mother of this particular Bride of Christ, as *socrus
Dei* – God's mother-in-law.

Jerome's focusing on virginity and his insistence that Eustochium
should take the Virgin Mary as her example had been foreshadowed a
few years earlier by Ambrose, bishop of Milan, whose writings on virginity
Jerome praises in Letter 22. Ambrose's own sister, Marcellina, had been
the first to respond to reports of eastern asceticism by taking the veil as a
consecrated virgin in the 350s and in the 350s he began to recruit female
virgins for his church. His homiletic work *On Virgins* offered the virgin
willing to dedicate herself to Christ a heavenly Bridegroom far superior to
any earthly husband with whom her parents might provide her.[61] This
appeal, directed to young women of marriageable age (previously, the
church had usually admitted only women over forty to the rank of consecrated virgin) enraged aristocratic Milanese families who considered it
their right to marry off daughters as the interests of the *gens* and property
strategies dictated. Ambrose replied to their protests with a series of
sermons which became the work *On Virginity* in which he implored the
aristocracy not to 'keep the children back from Christ'[62] and exploited the
nuptial imagery of the Song of Songs – though it is, perhaps, clearer from
his imagery than from Jerome's that the union about to take place is
between the *soul* of the virgin and Christ. Both Ambrose and Jerome
would contribute to the development of the doctrine of the perpetual
virginity of the Virgin Mary – a doctrine which greatly reinforced the idea
of the superiority of virgins and celibates. Indeed, Jerome had argued in
Letter 22 that the only good of marriage was that it produced more
virgins and claimed that their reward in heaven would be a hundred-
fold, while those of the widowed and married, defiled by sexuality,
would be only sixty-and thirty-fold respectively. Such ideas, vigorously
but unsuccessfully combated in the 380s and 90s by figures such as
Helvidius and Jovinian, gradually gained acceptance in the church.[63]

Monastic Enclosure and Monastic Rules

In works written after the notorious Letter 22, including his commentaries on Ephesians and Galatians written about 387, Jerome would flatter
and perhaps placate his own circle, who had decisively renounced their

femininity, upholding the idea that women could transcend their gender and become 'male'.[64] But in view of his stinging denunciation of informal ascetic groups in which men and women mixed (and which he would echo years later in his Letter 125), it is not surprising that when he and Paula finally settled in Bethlehem, they broke with their previously more informal association by living in separate religious communities. Melania and Rufinus had already anticipated them by creating twin communities on the Mount of Olives, an indication of the trend towards separation of the sexes and the institution of segregated communities. Paula only permitted her nuns to leave the convent to go to mass in the neighbouring church and did not even allow eunuchs – beings who defied gender categorization – as servants.[65] In the fifth century, Melania the Younger (whose southern Italian and Sicilian female communities – separate from that of her husband – included eunuchs)[66] ruled that the nuns of her grandmother's foundation on the Mount of Olives were never to have contact with any man. The convent was supported entirely from its patroness' wealth and even had its own water supply, so that there was no need for its members to go outside.[67]

Strict enclosure and the status of Bride of Christ, awaiting her Bridegroom, would become the norm for nuns in the West by the fifth century. However, two monastic rules for women composed in the latter years of the fourth did not entirely fit what were becoming the prevailing trends. In the West in the 390s Augustine of Hippo composed a rule for monks and is believed to have given the same text – addressing women in exactly the same fashion as men – to a community of women.[68] The rule itself deals realistically and charitably with the problems of sexual temptation and does not impose strict enclosure, allowing nuns, like monks, to leave the convent to go not just to church but also – in groups – to the public baths. Is the feminine transcription of the rule really by Augustine himself or by an anonymous adapter? It has been dated by those who accept its authenticity, to a decade or so after Augustine's conversion, a point when the memory of his beloved mother Monica was still vivid in his mind. And while many of Augustine's writings have been characterized as adumbrating a masculine God and a Christ who does not represent women,[69] one of his letters suggests that he foresaw a point where female ascetics would not require male tutelage any more. It is also possible that for a time Augustine may have shared the views of the Cappadocians on the spiritual equality of women;[70] and in the 390s he did not worry so much about the burdens of sexuality or Original Sin with which he would later become preoccupied. He writes to and of mature ascetic women as if they are male,[71] and if such passages are not expert flattery, they lend support to the thesis that the *Rule* could quite possibly have been given to female ascetics.

One of the most intriguing of all monastic texts, composed a little earlier than Augustine's monastic rule is the *Sentences to a Virgin* of Evagrius of Pontus.[72] This short series of precepts for the ascetic life, which has its male counterpart in Evagrius' *Sentences to Monks*, was written for a deaconess, Severa, who was a member of Melania's community on the Mount of Olives. The noticeable differences between this and the masculine rule have suggested that Evagrius, despite his Origenist background and the fact that he had been a pupil of Gregory of Nazianzus, took a gendered view of the religious life and believed that women were intellectually and spiritually incapable of attaining the same heights as men. Instead, Evagrius refers to the virgin as 'Bride of Christ' and to the marriage of her soul with Christ. The chastity of her flesh will be acceptable to Christ and the virgin will see, hear and touch her Bridegroom.

The complexities of this text await full analysis. While there are no references in the *Sentences to a Virgin* to *gnosis* or to the 'evil thoughts' which afflict the higher or intellectual part of the soul, Evagrius does affirm that a virgin's soul may be 'illuminated' – a highly significant statement in the context of Evagrius' mysticism of light, implying the highest spiritual achievement in terms of transformational asceticism. Reference to 'illumination' would seem to put the spiritual capabilities of women on a par with those of men. Evagrius' avoidance of the term *gnosis* may spring not so much from a fundamentally gendered view of religious attainment but from his awareness of the religious controversies of the time. In the *Sentences*, Evagrius attempts to combine the concept of the union of the soul with God, fundamental to his theology, with the development of a discourse of the virgin as the Bride of Christ which was not only pioneered in the West by Ambrose and Jerome, but had eastern antecedents in Methodius of Olympus and Athanasius.[73]

4

The Meaning of Asceticism

The earliest ascetic movements of which we know in the West antedate the development of Egyptian monasticism or the arrival of any version of the *Life of Antony* in the West. Varieties of transformational asceticism were practised by western Christians as early as the second century. In Rome, Justin Martyr records the existence of men and women who had been disciples of Christ from an early age and who had lived together in chastity for many years. The Valentinian sect also flourished in Rome in the second century, while around the middle of the third century, a Roman priest named Novatian, the author of a tract entitled *On the Good of Chastity*, periodically withdrew from his duties to lead an ascetic life.[1]

Eastern Influence on Western Monasticism

The influence of the monasticism of the Egyptian desert first began to be felt in the West in the 340s. The first formal ascetic community in Italy was probably created by Bishop Eusebius of Vercelli (344–71), who had spent some time in exile in Egypt as a result of his involvement in the Arian controversy. A former Roman cleric who had dedicated himself to a life of chastity, Eusebius did not found a monastery as such but was the first bishop in the West to impose chastity and community life on his clergy. By the 370s, however, there were monasteries of men or women in a number of Italian cities including Milan and Rome itself. Valerian, bishop of Aquileia, organized his clergy on ascetic lines and his successor, Chromatius, created what Jerome would call 'a choir of the blessed' – an ascetic group centering around Chromatius himself. In Milan, Ambrose either founded or encouraged the growth of monastic communities as well as presiding over the public veiling of women who had dedicated themselves to a life of virginity.[2] At Emona (Ljubljana) Jerome knew both a monk named Antony and a group of nuns.[3] Knowledge of monastic life had also reached Gaul. St Hilary of Poitiers was exiled from his diocese in 353 and spent four years in Phrygia in the eastern part of the empire. There, he attended the council of Seleuceia in 359, a council at which Eustathius of Sebaste was also present, and he visited Constantinople shortly after – as did both Eustathius and Basil of Cæsarea.[4]

The two periods of exile spent by Athanasius in the West – at Trier between 335 and 336 and Rome between 339 and 346 – were at one time thought to have inspired monastic life in the West, but knowledge of his *Life of Antony* exercised a much more significant influence on the development of monasticism. At Trier, the imperial capital, in the late 360s or early 370s, Jerome and his friend Bonosus had taken the decision to adopt a strict ascetic ideal, probably influenced by the *Life*.[5] About ten years later, St Augustine's friend Ponticianus gave details of a similar experience in the same city. Augustine describes this incident in his *Confessions*:

> [Ponticianus] began to tell... the story of Antony the Egyptian monk, whose name was held in high honour by Your servants, although Alypius and I had never heard it until then... After this he went on to tell us of the groups of monks in the monasteries... There was a monastery at Milan also, outside the walls, full of good brethren under the care of Ambrose, but we knew nothing of this either... Eventually he told us of the time when he and three of his companions were at Trier. One afternoon, when the Emperor was watching the games in the circus, they went out to stroll... near the city walls. They became separated into two groups, Ponticianus and one of the others remaining together, while the other two went off by themselves. As they wandered on, the second pair came to a house which was the home of some servants of yours, men poor in spirit, to whom the kingdom of heaven belongs. In the house, they found a book containing the *Life of Antony*. One of them began to read it and was so fascinated and thrilled by the story that even before he had finished reading, he conceived the idea of taking upon himself the same kind of life and abandoning his career in the world – both he and his friend were officials in the service of the state – in order to become your servant...[6]

This story testifies to the influence of Latin translations of the *Life of Antony* in the West – Jerome's friend Evagrius of Antioch produced a free version between 362 and 373 and in 374 after visiting Evagrius, Jerome went to live in the semi-desert in Chalcis amongst the hermits of Syria.[7]

While intellectuals such as Jerome and his friend Rufinus felt the attractions of asceticism and monasticism, the ascetic life appears to have spread relatively slowly among the males of the Roman aristocracy.

Womanly influence may have been a less powerful factor in producing conversions than is sometimes thought: the husband of only one of the women with whom Jerome corresponded is known to have renounced Roman paganism and it is not even clear that this was prompted by his wife. The rise of asceticism and monasticism were not greeted with enthusiasm by all: the death of Blesilla had shocked upper-class Romans and Jerome had left Rome in disgrace. Not all ascetics were regarded as genuine: many were thought of as a fakes and hypocrites.[8] Married Christians resented the manner in which propagandists such as Jerome and Ambrose promoted virginity and Jovinian and the writer known as Ambrosiaster spoke for many others when they asserted that married persons and married priests were invested with the same dignity and worth as their virgin counterparts. Jerome's notorious pamphlet *Against Jovinian*, in which he castigated marriage and particularly remarriage, was withdrawn from circulation by one of his own friends, who correctly estimated its offensive potential.[9]

Suspicion of asceticism and monasticism was also born of financial considerations. Many members of the Roman aristocracy were naturally alarmed when they saw the dissolution of great patrimonies as a result of their owners' decisions to take up lives of Christian asceticism. In 400 Melania the Elder, then aged sixty, was forced to return to Italy from Egypt to back her granddaughter's decision to live as a married celibate and also to persuade her own son and his wife, as well as a niece and her husband, to embrace the ascetic life and permit the young couple to give away their vast properties. 'In doing so,' commented Palladius:

> She fought with beasts in the shape of all their senators and their wives who tried to prevent her in view of [similar] renunciation of the world on the part of other senatorial houses.[10]

But some upper-class males did become ascetics and monks. In several cases, adverse life incidents and the sudden experience of a sense of loss verging on anomie contributed to producing a profound life change. Pammachius, described by Jerome as 'the first amongst the monks of the first city', became an ascetic after the death of his wife, one of Paula's daughters.[11] In the case of the Gallic aristocrat Sulpicius Severus, his decision to abandon a successful career for the monastic life in the 390s may have been precipitated by the death of his wife as well as by the example of Martin of Tours, whose *Life* he would write. The ascetic career of Sulpicius' friend Paulus Meropius Paulinus, an aristocrat who became first a monk and later bishop of Nola, began only after the death of his son in the 390s.[12] And in northern Gaul, a number of aristocrats began to join the monastic movement, attracted by the miracles and charisma of Martin of Tours.

Martin of Tours – the first western monk-bishop

The first western monk to become a bishop was Martin of Tours, a protégé of St Hilary of Poitiers.[13] Born in Pannonia and brought up in northern Italy, Martin (d. 397) was not an aristocrat but a former Roman soldier who became bishop of Tours in Gaul by popular acclamation. After leaving the army, he had found a mentor in Hilary, bishop of Poitiers and was made an exorcist in his diocese. When Hilary was exiled at the end of 356 for his opposition to Arianism, Martin embarked on a series of wanderings to Hungary, then the Balkans and Milan, finally settling on the island of Gallinara off the Ligurian coast. Perhaps, on Hilary's orders, he was waging a campaign against Arianism – this would account for his settling outside Milan in a *monasterium* during the reign of the Arian bishop Auxentius and his hermit life on the island of Gallinara might have been enforced, a result of exile by the Milanese authorities. When Hilary returned from the East, where he had had the opportunity to learn about the ascetics of Asia Minor, Martin installed himself at a 'hermitage', Ligugé, just outside the city. It was on account of his miraculous powers, reckoned 'truly apostolic' by the citizens of Tours and other neighbouring towns that he was enticed out of this hermitage and consented to become bishop of Tours in 371.

Martin was a surprising and uncomfortable recruit to the Gallic episcopate which was highly aristocratic in composition and at this juncture not remotely ascetic in orientation. His fellow-bishops were married and his ascetic lifestyle presented a challenge to its standards and practices. One of Jerome's most vicious polemics, *Against Vigilantius*,[14] was directed against a Gallic presbyter who had defended the status of married clerics and resisted the ordination of ascetics and celibates to clerical office. Vigilantius did no more than represent the feelings of many in the Gallic church who supported its old-established tradition of married clergy and bishops. Sulpicius makes clear that Martins' appointment as bishop of Tours had many episcopal opponents. To his counterparts, the unlettered former soldier manifestly lacked the cultured *civilitas*, the urbane values which they represented. Martin, however, was a figure with whom the peasants of the rural Touraine could identify. As the frontiers of the Roman Empire began to give way under barbarian pressure and German incursions across the Touraine led to the slaughter of its inhabitants and the destruction or abandonment of many settlements, Martin, simply clad in a rough cloak, strode across his diocese, preaching, healing, exorcising and destroying pagan shrines.

Almost immediately after his consecration, Martin founded another hermitage, a few miles outside his episcopal city of Tours. Sulpicius gives few details of any ascetic practices followed by Martin or of his spiritual goals. Sulpicius' own background was aristocratic and the monastery which he himself would create on his family estates, while partly inspired by Martin, appears to have been an aristocratic and cultured foundation. His mother-in-law Bassula lived an ascetic life nearby. In writing about Martin, Sulpicius constantly utilized his own classical education and culture and attempted to present asceticism in an acceptable light to those who shared his cultural background. In the *Life*, Martin's monasticism is at first presented as arduous and semi-eremitic but Sulpicius also endeavours to show his monastic group in another light. Eighty disciples join him, living in caves and huts near his own cell by the banks of the Loire in what at first appears to be a loosely organized hermit group, resembling those of the East. Although Martin was not popular amongst aristocratic bishops, Sulpicius suggests that he had no difficulty in attracting monks from the upper classes – his disciples are presented as coming from cultivated and wealthy social circles:

> What is all the more remarkable is that many of them were said to be nobles who, having been brought up quite differently, schooled themselves to bear with this humbling and demanding life.[15]

The economic basis of this life may possibly have come from the revenues of the church of Tours; but Sulpicius echoes the words of Acts 4:32-4 in claiming that the community pooled the resources of its well-born members:

> No-one possessed anything of his own there; they made everything over to common ownership.[16]

This meant that at Marmoutier, as the monastery would become known, ascetic life was not too arduous. Whatever Martin's own background, his followers were still permitted some of the cultivated *otium* of the upper classes of the later Roman Empire and were not expected to soil their hands in manual labour as did eastern monks. The *Life* suggests that peasants performed the heavier tasks needed to maintain the community, while the younger monks only copied manuscripts. What little Sulpicius does tell us about Martin's own ascetic practices – generally prayer, vigils and fasting – are not presented as part of either the unceasing rhythm of settled communal routine or the minute self-observation and infinitesimally slow progress towards self-purification of the Fathers of the Egyptian desert. Rather, we are treated to several vignettes of the purposeful preparations of a spiritual athlete limbering up for combat with the devil.[17] Although Sulpicius in the *Life* carries on a dialogue with the values and practices of eastern monasticism, it is clear that Martin is a very different – and in Sulpicius' eyes – superior figure.

Although Martin was succeeded as bishop by one of his former clerical opponents, Sulpicius claims that his prestige was so great that a number of Marmoutier's monks also went on to become bishops themselves. One of these was Heros of Arles, who possibly disseminated knowledge of monasticism in the south of Gaul before his ejection from his see in 412. In the early part of the fifth century a number of bishops from that area began to show an interest in monastic life and attempted to find out how monasteries should be organised. In northern Gaul, Martin himself had found one episcopal supporter for the ascetic movement in Biship Victricius of Rouen who consecrated virgins and founded monasteries in his own diocese.

The First Western Monastic Rule

The first western monastic rule was composed by another monk who became a bishop, St Augustine of Hippo.[18] His history could not be more different from that of Martin. Born in North Africa, the son of a Christian mother and a father who was originally a pagan but later converted to Christianity, Augustine had become a follower of Manichaeism at the age of eighteen. He abandoned Manichaesm after nine years and in Milan, where he taught rhetoric, he was attracted to neo-Platonism, which initially provided him with some non-Manichaean answers to the problem of evil. He also listened to the eloquent sermons of Ambrose and, reluctantly, he found himself drawn to their message. Ambrose's overcoming of Augustine's intellectual objections to Christianity led him to become a catechumen in the Catholic church. After a mystical experience in 386, Augustine finally converted to Christianity in 387.

Augustine became not just a Christian, but a Christian ascetic. The first did not imply the second: there were many ordinary married Christians and Christian monasticism was still a new development in the West, often regarded with hostility or suspicion. However, Augustine, who had earlier lived with a concubine, whom he had dismissed in order to marry a woman of his own class, gave up thoughts of marriage altogether. The major influences on his decision to embrace asceticism were Ambrose, a notable advocate of virginity and Christian chastity, and the *Life of Antony* which Ponticianus had brought to his notice. Now, with his conversion and that of his friend Alypius, the little commune of friends with which he and his mother lived was transmuted into an overtly Christian ascetic group.

After his return to his native North Africa several years later, probably in 397, when he was made bishop of Hippo, Augustine produced a rule for a monastic community. It has been debated whether this rule was addressed to monks or to an episcopal clerical community, such as those established by Eusebius at Vercelli or Valentinian and Chromatius at Aquileia, but there seem no good reason not to regard it as a monastic rule.[19] It reflects Augustine's past, being strongly tinged by neo-Platonism, with its idea of the movement of the soul towards the One:

> to have one heart and soul seeking God.

But it also takes as it model the community of the Apostles and the earliest Christians:

> Do not call anything your own;
> possess everything in common.
> . . .
> For you read in the Acts of the Apostles:
> 'They possessed everything in common', and
> 'Distribution was made to each
> in proportion to one's need.'

The description of the Apostolic community in Acts was, according to Athanasius, one of the biblical texts which inspired Antony,[20] but Athanasius stresses distribution to those in need rather than the possession of goods in common. However, Augustine was deeply influenced by the experience of living a religious life in a community of friends.

There is a considerable distance between Augustine's monasticism and that of Egypt. His vision of asceticism is coloured not by an Origenist idea of self-transformation but by the Gospel message of renunciation and his own experiences. In his commentary on Psalm 132 (composed *c.* 407), Augustine would give a definition of 'monk', interpreting part of the root of the word *monachus* (*monos* = one) as the unity of heart and soul described in Acts (rather than in the sense of the 'singularity' of early transformational and monastic texts):

> '*monos*', that is 'one alone' is correct usage for those who live together in such as way as to make one person, so that they really possess, as the Scriptures say, 'one heart and one soul' – many bodies but not many souls, many bodies but not many hearts.

The community which Augustine describes in his rule is one held together largely by the bonds of mutual love and friendship and where the superior of the community (who in any case is subject to the overall authority of a priest)

> shall willingly embrace discipline and instil fear.
> While both are necessary, he shall strive, nevertheless,
> to be loved by you rather than feared, mindful always
> that he will be accountable to God for you.

This last phrase would be echoed in the sixth century in the *Rule* of Benedict of Nursia.

Augustine evidently expected that the community would attract recruits of widely differing social status and he warned those from poor backgrounds not to become inflated with pride, while the rich were not to congratulate themselves for providing much of the community's common substance. He believed that a religious community should be united by the bonds of mutual love rather than be governed by a hierarchy of officials and through obedience before love. His *Rule* names no officials other than the superior and the priest: he mentions those responsible for food, clothing and books, but gives them no special title and prescribes that they serve their brothers without grumbling. The community not only had an oratory, but also took part in church or cathedral services – presumably the celebration of the Eucharist. Monks might wash their clothing either in the monastery itself or at a laundry. The advice of a physician is to be followed on personal hygiene and should he prescribe it, monks are to go to the public baths, without grumbling – though never on their own.

In the final chapter of the *Rule*, Augustine mentions the element which makes contemplation and mutual charity possible – the element of grace:

> The Lord grant you the grace
> to observe these precepts with love
> as lovers of spiritual beauty,
> exuding the fragrance of Christ
> in the goodness of your lives;
> you are no longer slaves under the law,
> but a people living in freedom under grace.[21]

In later years, he would defend with increasing vehemence the necessity of God's grace to accomplish anything and even at this relatively early stage in his career, he invokes its centrality to the monastic life.

Augustine is thought to have adapted the *Rule* for a convent of women (see p. 57 above). Another, shorter legislative text, the so-called *Ordo Monasterii* (sometimes known as the *Regula Secunda*), has also been attributed to him: in the sixth century Bishop Cæsarius of Arles used it alongside the *Rule* (confusingly also known as the *Regula Tertia*) when he wrote his own monastic rule and it is explicitly attributed to Augustine in a seventh-century manuscript where it also appears alongside the *Rule*. This brief rule shares Augustine's emphasis on the apostolic life and contains instructions for psalmody which suggest that its liturgy originated in northern Italy, where Augustine first converted to Christianity and asceticism.[22] Like the *Rule*, it lays stress on the apostolic model of ascetic life, while opening with the Gospel injunction to love of God and neighbour (Matthew 22: 37–40), a quotation used by Augustine throughout many of his other writings.

Contrasting Approaches to the Monastic Life

The most influential writers on asceticism and monasticism in the West would turn out to be Jerome and Augustine, who, as well as being ascetics were respectively the greatest exegete and greatest theologian of their day. Both men's understanding of asceticism and the religious life differed in many crucial respects from that of Origenists and seekers after self-transformation. Both had been inspired in the first place by the *Life of Antony*, a work which did not present Antony's Origenist theory of monastic life so much as its results, stressing his inspiration by the Gospel and his adoption of voluntary poverty. As a result of its inspiration, Jerome had lived for two or three years in the Syrian desert in the 370s, but the extent to which he understood the true nature of Syrian or Egyptian monasticism is questionable.[23] While he learned some Syriac, he spent much of his time studying Hebrew and eventually fell out with his monastic neighbours because of his refusal to involve himself in schisms in the local church and in Trinitarian controversies. His *Life of Paul the First Hermit*, a work composed shortly after his stay in the desert, does not paint a picture of the monk as transformational ascetic, but is a highly coloured picture of a fictitious hermit of the Thebaid whose retreat, according to Jerome, predated that of Antony and whom, he claimed, Antony venerated.[24] Paul's eremiticism is painted as a personal response to the Decian persecution of the church. In the *Life* Jerome alludes briefly to the asceticism of the monks of the Syrian desert – one who lived as a recluse for thirty years on coarse barley bread and muddy water, another who ate only five dried figs a day while living in an old cistern – but makes no reference there or in any other parts of the text to objectives such as 'knowledge', 'singularity' or union of the soul with God which appear so frequently in eastern writings. The aspect of this type of monasticism which he appears to come closest to understanding, apart from the dispossession and *anachoresis* which feature in the *Life of Antony*, is that of the food asceticism which was designed to suppress sexuality, but this was based on widely-known medical theory. And by his own admission in his highly-coloured account to Eustochium (see pp. 54–6 above) his mortification of his own flesh had proved unequal to dispelling fantasies of sex. No one, Letter 22 had seemed to suggest, could be entirely liberated from sexuality: St Paul himself, Jerome reminded Eustochium, had begged to be liberated from the 'body of death'. Jerome's own intense physicality increased the original gap which existed between his understanding of monasticism and the ascetics of fourth-century Egypt and Syria.[25] Augustine was similarly distanced. Although his experiences of friendship and communal life had led him to emphasize the same text from Acts as the Pachomian *koinonia*, there is no suggestion that he practised the type of transformational asceticism of earlier ascetic groups or of the Egyptians: indeed his rejection of his past as a Manichaean 'auditor' could have prejudiced him against this genre of beliefs and practises. Instead, as a convert and a bishop, he invoked the transforming power of the grace of God.

Jerome had, of course, read Origen, but in an exegetical and not a monastic context, scanning and using the works of the earlier theologian when writing his own commentaries. Boundlessly enthusiastic for the master's work, he even cribbed from it in places[26] and in 383 went so far as to express the view that all who had condemned him were 'mad dogs'.[27] However, much that Origen had written had been speculative, originally designed to combat the various heterodox currents of the third century, principally demiurgic belief and Marcionism. Now, in a post-Nicene church which sought definition and uniformity of doctrine, some of these theories might be misread as certainties. There were critics of Origen in Rome and since the 370s, the fanatical Bishop Epiphanius of Salamis had been conducting a campaign against the 'heresies' which he perceived in Origen's writings. Although he was his friend, Jerome, less expert as a theologian than as an exegete, appears to have been unaware for many years that anything was amiss, until in the early 390s Epiphanius brought the matter forcibly to his attention in a dispute which began as a matter of ecclesiastical politics and personal alliances.[28] In a breach of the rights of John, Bishop of Jerusalem, Epiphanius had consecrated Jerome's younger brother Paulinian as priest, in order to allow him to celebrate mass in Jerome's own community in Bethlehem (also under John's jurisdiction). Epiphanius then attempted to set things to rights, adding to his letter a detailed list of the heresies of Origen, which he invited John to condemn. This letter was never answered. The dispute escalated and in 397 Jerome, in a savage polemical work *Against John of Jerusalem*, condemned John's 'Origenist' teaching on matters such as the resurrection body. Since 393, under Epiphanius' influence, he had begun to turn against his former hero and he spent nearly two decades pursuing the errors of Origenism wherever he thought he found them (though sometimes, with characteristic perversity, laying himself open to accusations of Origenism, by recommending uncontroversial sections of his work).

What were the consequences of this change of heart for monasticism? Initially, it caused a split between Jerome and Rufinus, his childhood friend and spiritual adviser to Melania. As head of the monastery on the Mount of Olives, Rufinus sided with his bishop. There were deeper reasons, too, behind his backing of John: the dispute revealed the very real gulf between Rufinus' spiritual orientation and that of Jerome.

Rufinus and Melania were friends of Evagrius of Pontus, who had even written rules for their monasteries enshrining the notions of *apatheia* and *gnosis*: in other words, they embraced the version of transformational asceticism which had its roots in Origenist thought and which was based on ideas such as the pre-existence of souls as well as the gender-less resurrection body. Though Rufinus was reconciled with Jerome in 397, perhaps through the mediation of Melania, in the same year he left Jerusalem and returned to the West. There, in order to counter the attacks of Epiphanius, Jerome and others on Origen, he set about the project of translating Origen's work for the benefit of a Latin audience, convinced that if the public could read his genuine and uninterpolated works, such as *On First Principles*, they would soon see that the great third-century theologian was no heretic.

The debate which then intensified as Rufinus went about his work of translation was not about asceticism or monasticism as such,[29] but it touched on matters fundamental to Origenist asceticism and once again revealed the extent of the gap between Jerome and the Origenists. Jerome protested that Origen's notion of the resurrection body denied that body's sexual characteristics, thus implying the irrelevance of gender differences on earth.[30] Here, as in Letter 22, Jerome revealed his view that, whatever he may have written in the interim about the possibility of women becoming male, gender and sexuality were realities which could not be denied or transcended.

Eastern Texts in Western Translation

It may not have been until the expulsion of the Origenist monks from Nitria in 400 by Theophilus of Alexandria and their arrival in Palestine that Jerome fully realized the connection between Origenism and the monasticism of Lower Egypt. In 404, after his patron Paula died, leaving him in charge of a monastery and strapped for cash, he set about translating the Pachomian rules with the evident intention of using them for his community.[31] Apart from the fact that the routine of craft occupations outlined there might help put his monastery on a firm economic footing, these rules had another great advantage in his mind: he stated his conviction that no 'heresy', by which he undoubtedly meant the Origenism of the monks of Nitria, Scetis and Kellia, had ever contaminated the Pachomian *koinonia*.

Rufinus' arrival in the West in 397 had the additional effect of bringing into circulation in Latin a number of important works of eastern monasticism. He translated for his friend Ursacius, head of the Italian monastery of Pinetum, an early (and incomplete) version of Basil's *Longer* and *Shorter Rules*, which he urged him to circulate.[32] In doing so, he transformed Basil's introductory discourse to a group of Christians living in the world into one directed to a monastic community, thus obscuring the way in which the original text slides from addressing a wider audience into a discourse to a more closed ascetic community. Rufinus opens his adaptation and translation of Basil's *Rules* with the commandments which Basil regarded as the fundamentals of communal monastic life:

Love God with your whole heart and soul,

and

Love your neighbour as yourself.

This is a more positive and outward-looking conception of the monastic life than that of the Egyptian Origenist hermits, who placed great emphasis on the more negative stripping away of personal desires. Yet he also writes of *theoria*, the knowledge by which we can perceive and contemplate the glory and magnificence of God – a close counterpart of Evagrian Origenist teachings; while Basil's whole approach concentrates on the fulfilment of evangelical counsels, rather than on the internalized process of contemplation and deconstruction of the personality, Rufinus' selections often focus on faults. But he also preserves Basil's juxtaposition of some of these faults with their opposing good qualities and he places near the beginning of his translation the idea that the correction of the errant soul is like the care of a sick child by a parent or doctor. In organizational terms, Rufinus passed on a pared-down version of Basil's already rather sketchy structures. Basil proved popular and in subsequent years at least one version of the complete Basilian rules was circulating in the West in Latin translation.

Another monastic text translated by Rufinus, the *History of the Monks in Egypt*, is overtly Origenist in tone. This work purported to be a record of a journey down the Nile made by seven monks of the Mount of Olives monastery in 394 to visit some of the most notable of the Desert Fathers.[33] Rufinus altered the original work to expand on Evagrian Origenist perspectives at several points. Thus in the section describing the teaching of John of Lycopolis, he substitutes for the original a discourse concentrating on the vice of arrogance and some characteristically Evagrian teaching on prayer. The fact that he also deals with the question of anthropomorphism and the close parallels between some parts of this addition and his translations of the Basilian rule and Origen's *Peri Archon* suggest that Rufinus' Latin version of the *History* should be dated to about 397–8. On the image of God, John is made to declare that:

if ... we stand before God with a pure heart and free from all the passions and vices we have mentioned, we can insofar as this is possible, see even

God and as we pray the eyes of our heart are turned towards him and we see that which is invisible with the spirit and not with the flesh: this is a learning of the mind and not of the flesh. For no-one can suppose that he can behold the being of God in itself, but he shapes for himself some kind of appearance or image in his heart in some corporeal likeness.[34]

Rufinus himself had probably never visited Lycopolis: during his stay in Egypt he had been based in Alexandria and it is unlikely that he ventured further south than Nitria and Kellia. This section, which almost certainly represents his own views rather than John's authentic teaching, was bound to attract unfavourable attention from anti-Origenists as time went on. Rufinus was also responsible for the Latin versions of Evagrius' *Sentences* for his and Melania's communities, though these were probably made before his return to the West.

Pelagianism and the Crisis of Asceticism

It was not until as late as 415 that Jerome finally turned on Evagrius as an Origenist, denouncing his work as a basis for monastic life. In a letter in which he also takes a vicious sideswipe at Melania the Elder, raging that her name 'bears witness to the blackness of her wickedness', Jerome attacks the Evagrian concept of *apatheia* – to claim that one could achieve this, he sneers, one would have to be either God or a stone.[35] His vehemence sprang partly from the fact that a new 'heresy' was attracting his attention. In the second decade of the fifth century, the Irish or British lawyer Pelagius arrived in Rome and became the leader of an ascetic group: he and his followers appeared to claim that a baptized Christian could live, if she or he so willed, without sin. This doctrine of *impeccantia* or sinlessness looked to Jerome, from his monastery in Bethlehem, suspiciously like a new version of Origenist *apatheia* rearing its ugly head. Jerome maintained that Pelagius claimed to have overcome sexual temptation entirely through the exercise of free will and claimed that:

> I alone ... am not held down in Adam's grip. Other poor fellows who have not heard my words may live shut up in cells and, without so much as seeing a woman, may remain still tormented by desire. As for me, though surrounded by droves of women, I fell not the slightest tingle of concupiscence ... By the power of my own free will, I bear wherever I go the conquering sign of Christ.[36]

The spread of Pelagianism amongst the Roman elite alarmed not just Jerome but also Augustine of Hippo who deplored what he held to be to be the excessive belief of the Pelagians in the potentiality for good of the human will. Just as Jerome felt that no one could be without sin as

sexuality and the human condition could not be denied, so Augustine
worried that this ascetic group was denying the necessity of God's grace –
fundamental to his own conception of monasticism – and over-emphas-
izing what could be accomplished by human free will alone. Moreover,
the Pelagians also seemed to deny Original Sin and opposed his own ideas
on predestination. For them, to accept the notion of predestination was
to introduce the concept of fate into Christianity by the back door, while
doctrines of grace were little more than an excuse to abandon responsibility for one's own actions. Pelagius was moved to great indignation,
when early in the 400s he read the plea to God contained in Book Ten of
Augustine's *Confessions*:

> Give me the grace to do what you command, and command what you
> will.[37]

This seemed to him to downgrade free will. Yet while optimistic about
the potentialities of the human will, he also demanded a good deal of it,
believing that every Christian should attempt to keep all of God's commandments. Augustine, by contrast, took a severe view of the ultimate
fate of sinful humankind, but believed in the transforming power of
divine grace for the redemption of sinners.

By the 390s, it had become clear that Augustine's own conception of
monasticism had been based on the idea of the grace of God:

> you are no longer slaves under the law,
> but a people living in freedom under grace.[38]

Now, in the wake of the controversy caused by Pelagius' ascetic teachings,
questions of grace and free will were being defined with an increasing
degree of sharpness which had not been found necessary by earlier
theologians. Augustine developed the belief not only in the need for
the enabling grace of God but also for his cooperative grace – the idea
that God not only enabled human choices and actions but also that
nothing further could be accomplished without his continuing help.[39]
A direct challenge to the Pelagian movement, the evolution of this
doctrine also confronted those who practised transformational asceticism,
as it implied that transformation could only be achieved with the cooperative grace of God. Transformational ascetics had not denied the
need for God's grace: Evagrius saw his *praktike* as a joint operation of
grace and free will.[40] But this did not make a fine distinction between
different types of grace as diagnosed by Augustine. All who had believed
in Evagrian or Origenist-derived monastic teachings now faced being
discredited on two grounds. They not only ran the risk of being classed,
in the eyes of influential figures such as Jerome and Augustine, as followers

of the 'heretical' Origen, but also of being identified with the Pelagians, anathematized at the Council of Carthage in 418. Conscious of the way in which Augustine's doctrine of predestination seemed both to remove any human initiative from the process of salvation and invalidate the idea of a monastic life where ascetic discipline would lead to growth towards God, one western follower of Evagrius of Pontus rose to the challenge and created a version of monastic theology designed to reply to Augustine. In doing so, he attempted to construct a 'third way' in which it was clear that both grace and human effort played a role in the transformation of the individual.

John Cassian and the Re-fashioning of Evagrian Asceticism

Between about 420 and 430, John Cassian composed two works about the monastic life: the *Institutes* and the *Conferences*.[41] Cassian's own early background is something of a mystery, but he was probably a native of Dacia, which would account for the fact that he could read both Greek and Latin.[42] He tells us that he had been a monk first in Bethlehem, before travelling to Egypt. He appears in the historical record in the *Dialogues* of Palladius along with a friend, Germanus, as one of the foreigners ordained or promoted by John Chrysostom, bishop of Constantinople. Although there is no direct evidence to confirm this, it is generally assumed that he and Germanus, like Palladius, were refugees fleeing Egypt in Theophilus' anti-Origenist purge of 399–400: Cassian himself refers to the 'anthropomorphite' crisis of 399 in his writings.[43] Cassian later visited Rome, possibly in an attempt to win support for John Chrysostom, when the latter was deposed from his see, may have visited Antioch, and finally settled at Marseilles in southern Gaul before 420. Marseilles was a diocese ruled by an ascetically-inclined bishop, Proculus, and there tradition claims that Cassian founded two monasteries, one for men and the other for women.[44]

In southern Gaul, Cassian became part of an influential monastic and episcopal network. Both *Institutes* and *Conferences* were planned to assist the process of monastic foundation which was now gradually getting under way in the area, backed by some local bishops who had themselves perhaps been influenced by Martin of Tours' protégé, Heros of Arles. It was clear that the predominant mode of monasticism in southern Gaul was going to be cenobitic: Jerome's characterization of urban ascetics as undisciplined and dangerous *remnuoth* would lead him to the conclusion by 415 that the only legitimate monastic lifestyles were eremitism and cenobitism – of the two, as far as the episcopate was concerned, cenobitism represented the more controllable entity.[45] The *Institutes* are dedicated to Bishop Castor of Apt, who was keen to found monastic communities in his own diocese which so far lacked any, while the dedicatees of the *Conferences* are Castor's brother Leontius, Bishop of Fréjus, Helladius, an ascetic who became a bishop, and Honoratus and Eucherius, the founder and guiding spirit of the great southern Gallic monastery of Lérins (see chapter 5, in this volume), and another group of monks who lived on the Stoechades, a group of islands near Marseilles.

Superficially, nothing could be simpler. Cassian would assist the bishops and other monastic founders of southern Gaul by bringing them the benefit of his Palestinian and Egyptian monastic experience. But how extensive was that? It has been recognized since the 1930s that Cassian was a follower of Evagrian theology: Books Five to Twelve of his *Institutes* deal with Evagrius' eight 'evil thoughts' or, as he puts it 'principal faults' and this, together with the circumstance of his ordination along with Palladius by Chrysostom, has suggested that he was one of the victims of Theophilus' anti-Origenist activities. Beyond this, his knowledge of Egyptian monasticism was, in reality, limited. The monastic practices described in the first four books of the *Institutes* refer not only to the monasteries of Egypt and also sometimes to Palestine, where he had indeed lived in a community for a time, but even to Cappadocia and Mesopotamia. These sections of the *Institutes* have proved a minefield for historians of eastern monasticism, especially as part of the text as we know it today has probably been interpolated.[46] In Books Two and Four, Cassian makes a number of references to Tabennese or the Thebaid when dealing with liturgy and admission – thus creating an impression of familiarity with communal monasticism. On close examination, this first impression dissolves: his remarks on the liturgy claim that he is describing rites followed 'throughout the whole of Egypt and the Thebaid' – a dubious concept, given the variety of monastic practice in Egypt[47] – and while his admission procedures resemble those of the Pachomians they are not identical. A third reference to the silence of the Pachomians at mealtimes is something he could have learned from Jerome's translation of the Pachomian rules and he mentions both Basil's *Rules* and Jerome's translations in his preface. Some of his knowledge of the East may have even been picked up in Gaul itself: Cassian never, for instance, visited Cappadocia and yet he recommends reading at mealtimes on the pattern of Chapter 180 of Basil's *Shorter Rules*, a section not translated by Rufinus, but possibly known in southern Gaul as other, fuller translations of Basil began to circulate there.[48] It looks as though Cassian solved the problem of a comparative lack of first-hand knowledge of communal monasticism by cobbling together information from a variety of written sources which could be read in the West and which he had probably used when founding his own communities in southern Gaul.

Similarly, the *Conferences* are far from straightforward works. They take the form of twenty-four lengthy discourses on the eremitic life and spiritual achievement supposedly delivered by a number of desert fathers in the presence of Cassian and his friend Germanus as they made a tour of the hermitages of Scetis, Diolcos and Panephysis.[49] Cassian never mentions either Kellia or Evagrius, the single most important influence on his theology – this is generally held to be because of his awareness that Evagrius was now a controversial name in the West.[50] Some of the fifteen names he cites as speakers – including seven monks of Scetis – appear to be those of well-known ascetics, but others are obscure figures.[51] Some parts of the *Conferences* – such as Abba Serapion's exposure of a monk's false humility in *Conference Eighteen* – contain material also found in the *Apophthegmata Patrum* and Cassian can also be shown to have used the *History of the Monks in Egypt* as well as Evagrius of Antioch's Latin version of the *Life of Antony*.[52] The *Conferences* represent not the unadulterated teaching of Lower Egyptian monasticism – which had, in any case, been shaken to its roots by the crisis of 399–403 – but an elaborate construct in which Cassian seeks to present his own particular view of the monastic life, its goals and its end. Together, *Institutes* and *Conferences* represent a most carefully crafted picture: it is generally acknowledged that when Cassian was writing the first, he was already planning the second and although he claims that the *Institutes* deal with the cenobitic life and the *Conferences* with the eremitic, they have an essential unity: in general, the *Institutes* may be said to deal with outer observances, the *Conferences* with the inner person. While later readers such as Benedict of Nursia may have understood from reading Cassian's *Conferences Eighteen* and *Nineteen* that the hermit life was technically superior to that of the community, taken together these conferences make it quite clear that he considered the cenobium the best way of life for the majority, as it guarantees a solid religious formation. As a cenobitic founder himself, Cassian required community members to be aware of his full spiritual programme, which embraced the development of the soul as well as outward discipline and observances. And both sets of texts contained passages – Book Twelve of the *Institutes* and *Conferences Twelve, Thirteen* and *Twenty-Three* – which were vehicles which he used to counter Augustine's and Jerome's views on grace, free will and sin.

Grace and Free Will

It used generally to be held that Cassian composed his highly significant *Thirteenth Conference* at some point after 425, when the relationship between grace and free will was the burning theological topic of the moment, possibly as late as 426–7 when Augustine wrote his treatises, *On Free Will and Grace* and *On Rebuke and Correction*. However, these were the product of a debate between Augustine and the monks of Hadrumetum in North Africa, and it is now thought that *Conference Thirteen* was probably composed before the debate reached its climax. In *Conference Thirteen*, Cassian proposes an understanding of the relationship between grace and free will which builds on his earlier statements in Book Twelve of the *Institutes*, where he had taught in Chapter 13 that:

> The divine gift is never made as payment for our own work or for human effort, but is granted by God's mercy to those who long for it.

In Chapter 14, he adds:

> I do not say this as if I were making human effort void, trying to dissuade anyone from a purpose of industrious work, in fact observe that it is the consistent opinion of the Fathers, not just my own, that we cannot attain perfection without this effort; yet, of itself, without the grace of God, it is incapable of bringing us to our goal.

In *Conference Thirteen*, Apa Chaeremon maintains once more that there is a delicate balance between grace and free will: but here he also seeks to move further towards the Augustinian position on grace, emphasizing the role of God in originating the will to do good:

> it is clear that the origin not only of good acts but even of good thought is in God. He both inspires in us the beginnings of a holy will and grants the ability and the opportunity to bring to fulfilment the things that we rightly desire.[53]

Later in the *Conference*, Cassian emphasizes the manner in which divine providence both precedes and accompanies effort.[54]

Cassian tries very hard to show that an ascetic life which depends on the idea of spiritual progress also acknowledges the need for divine grace. In his view of the monastic life this cooperation of grace, which strikes a spark of good in the human heart, combines with individual effort to move towards virtue. Yet he concedes that however greatly the will may be drawn towards virtue, it is inhibited by what he refers to as 'the flesh',[55] and he acknowledges in *Conference Twenty Three* that no one is without sin. Just as *Conference Thirteen* takes up a position with regard to Augustinian and Pelagian views on what can be achieved through free will, so this conference seeks to deal with the Pelagian idea of living without sin. Cassian castigates the latter notion as a snare and delusion: no one is free of sin, and those who maintain the contrary are blind to the sins and faults which remain within them.[56] Cassian, in fact, took a less pessimistic view of the Fall of Adam and Original Sin than did Augustine: he held that Adam did not entirely lose his prelapsarian knowledge of good and also that Christ had redeemed humankind from the bargain Adam had made with the devil. In this, he is closer to the Greek Fathers of the Church: while they did evolve a doctrine of Adam's original Fall and our inheritance of the consequences of the Fall, they were much less explicit over mankind's inheritance of sin as a result of the Fall than was Augustine. Nevertheless where the major ascetic controversy of the day is concerned, Cassian had attempted to protect his version of monasticism by trying to show, as far as he could, that it did not differ from the position of Augustine and Jerome. At the same time, however, he maintains older ideas of signs or stages of spiritual progress – the stages of humility in *Institutes* Book 4, 39, and the indicators of sexual purity laid down by Chaeremon in *Conference Twelve* (see below) – thus recognizing the value of setting aims and goals for moral and spiritual progress in a way which Augustine's monastic rule does not.[57]

Cassian also had another problem to overcome: the fact than much of his spiritual doctrine depended on that of Evagrius, an Origenist whose concept of *apatheia* had, in 415, been specifically singled out by Jerome for criticism. Here, he obviously thought that discretion was the better part of valour. In order to pass on without censure the monastic teaching which had inspired him, he avoided mentioning Evagrius' name altogether and changed or translated some of his key vocabulary. But his changes do not just reflect a desire to conceal Evagrian thought. Cassian – whose own lengthy and discursive writing style stands in complete contrast to the stark, gnomic form often adopted by Evagrius – adapted and developed his source for theological and didactic reasons. Thus, in his hands, the tricky notion of *apatheia* becomes the less controversial (and less technical) 'purity of heart', nevertheless preserving the Evagrian idea that it was the gateway to something more significant.[58] He retains Evagrius' idea of the eight 'evil thoughts', though in Books Five to Twelve of the *Institutes* they begin to transform into more generally applicable terms by becoming the eight 'principal vices' and would eventually transmute into the familiar Seven Deadly Sins. In *Conference Fourteen* he uses the Greek terms *praktike* and *theoretike*, closely related to Evagrius' ideas of the *praktikos* and *gnostikos*, but now in relation to biblical study and contemplation. Elsewhere, he renders *praktike* as *actualis disciplina* (active discipline) or *actualis vita* (active life) or *actualis conversatio* (active way of life). He uses *theoretike* several times, but generally prefers the Latin term *contemplatio* or, in *Conference Fourteen* when dealing with study of the Bible, 'spiritual knowledge'. The Evagrian and Origenist concept of union of the soul with God is discreetly developed in the way in which Cassian suggests that prayer and contemplation may provide a window on to 'beatitude'.[59] In *Conference Ten* he perhaps comes nearest to admitting any involvement with controversial views, when he gives a highly biased, and only partial, account of the 'anthropomorphite' controversy.[60] In *Conference Three* he interweaves the concept of 'three calls', which he may have drawn from Antony's first letter and 'three renunciations' which is not a repetition but an adaptation of part of Evagrius' *Kephalaia Gnostica*.[61] His teaching on 'fiery prayer' does not even appear to be purely Evagrian in background, but to owe a great deal to a knowledge of the Messalian sect, although it is not clear where or when in his travels in the East he had acquired this knowledge.

Cassian has been credited with composing the most extended western treatment of male monastic sexuality. In *Conference Twelve*, Apa Chæremon is made to describe a series of signs by which the monk may know that he is making progress in avoiding the sins of the flesh.[62] The first degree of purity is that the monk is not seized by 'carnal impulses'; the second that he does not dwell on voluptuous thoughts – if such thoughts arise he can control them and stop thinking about them; the third that he is not moved, even slightly, by desire when he sees a woman; the fourth that he does not experience, when asleep, any 'movement of the flesh' – even the most innocent.[63] The fifth step is reached when the monk can read or hear a discourse involving the idea of human procreation without allowing his mind to be touched by the remotest thought of sexual pleasure. The sixth and final stage is reached when the monk's sleep is not even troubled by visions of seductive women. We may not, declares Chæremon, think such illusions to be a sin, but they are an indication that lustful thoughts still lurk in the depths of our being. Once this stage has been reached with the help of God's grace, according to Chæremon, the individual is on a level of purity with a few celebrated monks. The problems of orgasmic dreams and nocturnal emissions are also dealt within Book Six of the *Institutes* and *Conference Twenty-two*. Antony had believed that it was possible for a chaste monk to experience emissions occasionally without there being any cause for concern, and Cassian also concedes that emissions may occur without there being any evidence of impure thoughts.[64] But the monk cannot decide this for himself. Following the doctrine of obedience which Cassian lays down in *Conference Nineteen*, in which the cenobitic monk must give up self-will entirely, he must explain his situation to his superiors, answer their questions and await their judgement on his moral state.

The Legacy of Cassian

Cassian found that there still remained other facets of eastern monasticism to be adapted and moderated to suit western tastes. The heroic asceticism of the desert, the extreme austerity in sleep, dress and food practised by the monks of Egypt as relayed by texts such as *Life of Antony* and the *History of the Monks in Egypt*, astonished and even intimidated some western readers. Sulpicius Severus made a Gaul protest, when confronted with the meagre diet of Egyptian ascetics, that Gauls were not angels and could not be expected to live on these rations.[65] Though Cassian could not resist dwelling lovingly on the way in which the Egyptians made use of dry or uncooked food and had as their greatest delicacies leeks, the herb cherlock, salt, olives and sardines, this was not prescribed as an actual menu.[66] While he thought that a very restricted diet of two loaves a day and reduction in sleep would – with the help of divine grace – show whether perfect chastity could be achieved,[67] in general, he identifies dietary austerity as a lack of obvious gluttony. He may also have been influenced by the differences between the Gallic and Egyptian climate, which also led him to make concessions when it came to clothing:

> For our cold winters would not allow us to make do with slippers or tunics or a single frock, whereas wearing a tight hood or a sheepskin would only make onlookers laugh...[68]

No doubt to the dismay of some of the bishops and ascetics who were dedicatees of his writings, Cassian was a severe critic of the Gallic monasteries which had already been established. Only with great reluctance, did he admit that it might be acceptable to set up a monastery near one's kin; but if that were done, he ruled that the monks should support themselves by the work of their hands rather than live off family wealth. In common with Basil and Pachomius, he insisted on self-support through manual labour.[69] This was a criticism of the Gallic monasticism associated with Martin of Tours and even of that of Lérins, the home of two of his dedicatees, where the monks did no manual work. Cassian was also highly critical of developments in the Gallic liturgy. We learn from his writings that in Gaul a daily round of monastic liturgy had developed which consisted of the offices of Nocturns, Lauds, Terce, Sext, Nones and Vespers and that a vigil was held on Friday nights. Cassian campaigns against the length of the liturgy in some of the Gallic offices, by telling a version of the story of the 'Rule of the Angel'. One account of this appears in the *Lausiac History* of Palladius, where an angel is said to have visited Pachomius and instructed him and his communities to

> pray twelve prayers each day and twelve prayers at the nightly vigils...and to add to each prayer a psalm.[70]

This story was originally written as an explanation of the origins of the ceaseless prayer and meditation of the Pachomian monks. However,

Cassian retells it in a very different setting – that of the apostolic community founded by St Mark – and applies the angel's instructions to a daily prayer-ritual of psalms chanted to God. The community had been arguing amongst itself over the length of the daily communal: some had suggested that at least fifty psalms should be recited each day. The angel sings twelve psalms – followed by an alleluia – and vanishes.[71] Deconstructed, Cassian's story may be read as a criticism of the length of the Gallic liturgies of his time. Although he had never set foot in the cenobia of Upper Egypt, he nevertheless insisted that

> throughout the whole of Egypt and the Thebaid, the number of psalms is fixed at twelve both at Vespers and the night vigils.[72]

Whether he ever succeeded in restraining the Gallic tendency towards over-long offices is not clear.

In *Conference Fourteen* Cassian bequeathed an important legacy to the West in and beyond the monastic life in the shape of his idea of spiritual knowledge. Apa Nesteros, who gives the conference, not only states that *praktike* is to be found amongst cenobites as well as solitaries, but extends it to seculars as well as monks. This discussion follows on the two which deal with grace and on one level is a continuation of them. In it, Nesteros identifies contemplative or spiritual knowledge with the understanding of Scripture. This is to be understood on two levels – historical and spiritual. Nesteros explains that historical sense relates to the knowledge of the past, while tropology is a moral explanation about the correct life, allegory deals with the prefiguration of further mysteries (by events in the life of Christ, or by the church or the sacraments) and anagogy reveals 'even more sublime and sacred heavenly secrets'; he also claims that there is a mere rhetorical slickness which passes for spiritual knowledge, but that real spiritual knowledge stems from true holiness. Thus Cassian transmitted an essentially Origenist method of Biblical study to the West in *Conference Fourteen*, in fact, an attractive and attainable objective to late Roman elites – the goal of a spiritual knowledge which was based on the reading of scripture.

Despite the richness of his teaching and his attempts to find common ground with the school of thought represented by Augustine and Jerome, Cassian fell foul of Augustine's Gallic ally, Prosper of Aquitaine, who thought that he took far too optimistic a view of the human potential for good. His position was, however, supported in southern Gaul by many influential writers: Vincent of Lérins and Faustus, third head of Lérins and later bishop of Riez, both attacked hard-line Augustinian concepts of grace and free will and their theology came to predominate in southern Gaul in the late fifth century. But Augustinian views triumphed in the sixth, and Cassian was stigmatized as a 'semi-

Pelagian' with dubious views on free will. With the defeat of Origenism, Pelagianism and even 'semi-Pelagianism', no-one developed his minute examination of bodily mechanisms and sexual desires. But his works were widely read and his influence in monastic circles was still considerable. His own designation of sarabaites[73] – Jerome's *remnuoth* – as an inferior and 'bad' type of monk effectively cut off western monasticism from any memory of free-wheeling pre-monastic Christian groups with their varieties of transformational asceticism. In the sixth century Benedict of Nursia, grasping the importance of obedience to a superior, would take up his description of hermits and cenobites as the higher forms of the monastic life, while stigmatizing sarabaites. Benedict would conclude his own highly pragmatic and simple rule by recommending Cassian along with Basil and the *Lives of the Fathers*: for him these works contained the higher spiritual truths of the monastic life. About the same period, Cassiodorus would also prescribe him for his monks – though with a warning about his views on grace. Gregory of Tours sent copies of Cassian's works to hermits, and in Ireland in the 590s the praise-poem written on the death of Colum Cille of Iona testifies to the saint's love for his writings. And at the end of the sixth century no less an authority than Pope Gregory the Great in his *Morals on Job* would base his classification of the Seven Deadly Sins on the Evagrian system of 'eight evil thoughts', relayed to the West in the *Institutes* as the 'eight principal vices', thus assuring Cassian at least a footnote in the wider history of European culture.

5

The Evolution of Monasticism in the West

The Aristocratic Monastery: Lérins

The most famous monastery in southern Gaul was Lérins, created on an island off Cannes in the early fifth century. Its founders were a Gallo-Roman nobleman, Honoratus and his associate Caprasius together with Eucherius who had originally settled on the neighbouring island of Lero with his wife Galla. In the early 420s, Honoratus persuaded his young relative Hilarius, the son of a prefect of Gaul, to join him there. About 425 or 426 the community was also joined by Hilarius' brothers-in-law Lupus and Vincentius of Toul. Around the same time, Maximus of Riez who had for a long time 'served Christ in secular garb' and his protégé the Breton or Briton Faustus arrived on the island. In 431 Eucherius persuaded his relation Valerianus (probably the son of the praetorian prefect of Gaul) to take up the monastic life at Lérins. The aristocratic Salvian, a childhood friend of Honoratus, whose moralistic writings condemned not only the exploitation of the lower classes by the powerful but also what he saw as the headlong rush to destruction of the whole of society, left his wife and daughter to lead a religious life at Lérins.[1] The political upheavals which took place in Gaul and the Roman world in the mid-420s, when some of Lérins' most important figures joined the community suggest that part of the attractions of the religious life lay in the fact that it was a refuge from political perils. In a decade which saw the usurpation of the imperial office, the murder of a prefect of Arles, the restoration of Valentinus, the Visigothic attacks on Arles, and even the murder of Bishop Patroclus of Arles in 426, Lérins – the 'hermitage' – may initially have appeared as a secure refuge from the violence of the outside world.

Many of the aristocrats who arrived at Lérins in times of crisis soon became bishops. If the aristocratic leadership of Lérins had initially been drawn to the religious life partly out of feelings of insecurity, these feelings must have begun to fade somewhat as imperial restoration in Gaul got under way and they could now resume more conventional aristocratic careers by becoming bishops. Lérins' remarkable role as a nursery of bishops in the fifth century underlines the elite nature of the community. The western aristocracy had already replaced older aristocratic ideals of public service in, for example, the magistrature, by the ideal of public service through the episcopate; and in the early years of Lérins, a monastic training became part of the *curriculum vitae* of a number of episcopal aristocrats. Honoratus, Salvian, Vincentius and Faustus of Riez were all ordained as clergymen and were therefore easily promoted to episcopal rank. Lupus left Lérins ostensibly to dispose of his property but was prevailed upon to become bishop of Troyes and never returned. Honoratus became bishop of Arles – with the support of influential aristocrats – in 426 or 427. His hagiographer, Hilarius, succeeded him. Eucherius became bishop of Lyon between 427 and 443. Salonius, Eucherius' son, ruled over the diocese of Geneva; Veranus, his other son presided over Vence. Maximus and Faustus were successively bishops of Riez and Theodore of Fréjus. And other monks of Lérins would also become bishops of Tarentaise and Cimiez.[2] Lérins would thus influence dioceses and the development of monasticism on the Rhône–Saône axis as far north as the Jura and even, indirectly, Britain and Ireland.

The influence of Cassian, who had dedicated the second set of his *Conferences* to Eucherius and Honoratus, on the literary development of Lérins was considerable. Many of the first generation – some accompanied by their sons – who arrived at Lérins and went on to become bishops were middle-aged men who had received the secular education appropriate to the aristocracy. They grasped Cassian's identification of contemplation with scriptural study as an encouragement to transfer the skills they had learned as part of their secular education to the writing of sermons and the study of theology and scripture. Lérins soon became the most important cultural centre in Gaul, producing not only *In Praise of the Hermitage*, the *Life of Honoratus* and the theological writings of the 'semi-Pelagian' school, but a variety of other texts including the moralistic writings of Salvian. Lerinese abbots and bishops cultivated the classical art of letter-writing. *The Life of Honoratus* insists that his letters were so tender that they should be kept not just in scriptoria or libraries but in 'the coffer of the heart itself'.[3] The sermons of Hilarius of Arles reflect a rhetorical training; Hilarius also composed poetry. Writing to his relative Valerianus, a man of the highest rank, to warn him against the 'philosophy' of the secular world and encourage him to convert to the ascetic life, Eucherius reveals his education in pagan as well as Christian letters. Faustus of Riez had read Virgil, Juvenal and possibly other pagan authors. An exegetical tract by Salonius, bishop of Geneva, is considered to be influenced by his father Eucherius' rhetoric. Such accomplishments have even led to the suggestion that Lérins possessed a good library and that its monks were not ashamed of their classical culture.[4]

If some aspects of Cassian's teaching appealed to the aristocratic monks of Lérins, the *Life of Honoratus* suggests that there were also elements in Basil's *Rules* with which the early community there could identify. It describes Honoratus' activities within the community as a caring superior, echoing Basil's view of one who serves the community as well as ruling over it.[5] Honoratus is credited with profound knowledge of the souls of his monks,[6] as well as with the concept of correction of or reprimand for faults,[7] and is opposed to excess or ostentatious self-denial.[8] The main traits which Honoratus demands of his monks are obedience and humility, both of which are important to Basil as well as to Cassian. It also claims that, as superior, Honoratus taught love of God and of one's neighbour – the fundamental tenet of Basil's *Rules*.[9] Where the monastery's relations with the outside world are concerned, the *Life* makes the specific claim that Honoratus entrusted a network of helpers with the distribution of alms outside the monastery on his behalf, thus in one way fulfilling Basil's idea of the monastery as a source of charity,[10] although there is no suggestion that the monks of this predominantly aristocratic community practised crafts or manual labour as both Basil and Cassian recommend. All this and more[11] in Hilarius' picture of Honoratus suggests that at Lérins acquaintance with Basil's writings went even beyond the contents of Rufinus' translation and that the works of Basil were known in the West independently of Rufinus by 420–425.[12]

The 'Jura Fathers'

Other Gallic monasteries may have resented the wealth and influence of Lérins. The *Lives of the Fathers of Jura*, composed in eastern France in the early sixth century reflects the existence of conscious opposition to Lérins. They tell the story of how Romanus, head of one of the Jura monasteries, attempted to resist the attempts of Bishop Hilarius of Arles – a former monk of Lérins – to control his monasteries by ordaining him priest.[13] The Jura *Lives* paint a picture of a western monasticism which is very gradually moving away from the models of the first half of the fifth century. Though the 'fathers' – Romanus, Lupicinus and Eugendus – were of high rank, their *Lives* point out that they practised austerity and that their communities – Condat and Lausinne – took in poor as well as rich, practised manual labour and followed the full common life. All this contrasts with, and may represent criticism of, Lérins. In the *Life* of Lupicinus, his care for the spiritual welfare of his monks conforms to the Basilian pattern where the abbot acts as the physician of souls; but there are also hints of a move towards the composition of an independent rule of life for the monasteries. The *Lives* tell us that Eugendus refused to follow 'oriental archimandrites' after the monks' individual cells were destroyed in a fire at the beginning of the sixth century and instituted a fuller common life with an individual dormitory, the first recorded instance of a monastic dormitory in the West.[14] The concluding sections of his *Life* reveal that the rules of Basil and Pachomius (wrongly identified as a Syrian) and the writings of Cassian were read daily and suggests that that the monks also knew of the 'institutions...of the holy fathers of Lérins'; but it also affirms that they had a rule of their own. The *Lives* promise an exposition of this rule, but it never appears – unless the texts of the *Lives* are to be read as a rule of sorts.[15]

The Evolution of Early Western Monastic *Rules*

The practice of creating written rules for the guidance of monastic communities gradually developed in the West. The first western religious rules composed after Augustine's are known collectively as the *Rules of the Fathers* and were written in the fifth and possibly early sixth centuries. They consist of five separate but closely-related texts: the *Rule of the Four Fathers*, the *Second Rule of the Fathers*, the *Rule of Macarius*, the *Third Rule of the Fathers* and the *Oriental Rule*.[16] The titles of all the rules reflect the influence of the written representations of the East on the West and the first three even present themselves as the record of a meeting of eastern monastic leaders. In the *Rule of the Fathers*, the speakers are identified as Serapion, Macarius, Paphnutius and another Macarius, some of the most famous names in Egyptian monasticism, but in reality only borrowed to lend authority to what are, in fact, western cenobitic rules. Though it uses Egyptian names, the earliest of the group, *Rule of the Four Fathers*, opens with an inauthentic evocation of

> the desolation of the desert and the terror of various monsters [which] do not permit the brothers to live singly.[17]

This short series of rules reflects the increasing institutionalisation of the monastic life and the fact that it was felt necessary to set down practical instructions in writing. The influence of the rules of Basil and also of Pachomius in Jerome's translation is clear. The 'fathers' of the first rule prescribe that all brothers should obey one superior, whom they describe by the phrase *is qui praeest* – he who presides, the term used in Rufinus' translation of Basil.[18] The only other officials mentioned are the brother who looks after the cellar, the guardian of the community's moveable property and a second in rank, whose duties are never actually specified and who might just possibly be the cellarer himself.[19] In the *Second Rule of the Fathers*, the head of the community is known by the term *praepositus*, a term familiar from Jerome's version of the Pachomian rules.[20] In the *Rule of Macarius*, (attributed to 'Macarius who had under his order five thousand monks') a number of sections taken from Jerome's version of the Pachomian text call the superior *praepositus* – but elsewhere, the superior is referred to as abbot and has a *praepositus* as his second in command.[21] The *Third Rule of the Fathers* mentions an abbot and prior.[22] The most detailed of all, the *Oriental Rule*, sets up a much more elaborate hierarchy of officials, comparable to those found in sixth-century rules: an abbot, prior, two senior monks, appointed after consulting the community, a cellarer, gardener, doorkeeper and weekly servers.[23] The rules reflect a period of change and consolidation in western cenobitic life from apparently tentative beginnings – though this may be a literary convention to establish the authenticity of the 'conference' – to a point where the superior is known as an abbot and may have a large number of subordinate officials to help him govern his cenobium.

As the cenobitic organization outlined in the rules becomes more elaborate, the list of the qualities expected of the monks themselves becomes longer. The *Rule of the Four Fathers* mainly stresses the need for obedience. The *Rule of Macarius* begins with the 'horizontal' links of charity and love which hold the community together in addition to the 'vertical' ties of obedience. The *Oriental Rule* contains very lengthy discussions of the special qualities needed by the abbot and prior. So much authority is now concentrated in their hands that it is essential that men of the right calibre are chosen. The authoritarian structures of the *Oriental Rule* where the abbot, though aided by a prior and senior monks

shall freely make decisions on all matters within the monastery[24]

look forward to those of the sixth-century *Rule* of Benedict of Nursia, where, despite the existence of mechanisms for consultation, the control of the abbot is complete.

Detailed procedures for admission to a community develop. The *Rule of the Four Fathers* imposes a week's delay on a poor man (who might be attempting to better his lot) but spares the rich (who are giving up their wealthy life-style) this indignity.[25] The monastery thus appears as a place of relative prosperity – but it is also the case that recruits may also give some goods or property to the community. The instructions of the *Rule of Macarius* are more detailed, specifying that if a recruit brings property it has to be placed in front of the brothers before being accepted. In a phrase which was taken up in the sixth-century Benedictine *Rule*, the entrant is to understand that he shall not from that hour be the judge, not only of the property that he brought but even of himself...[26]

although there also appears to be a three-day cooling-off period in which the new brother can leave. There are sections on the reception of clerics and guests and on the punishment of wrongdoers. The daily round of offices and prayer is never described in any detail: it is simply presented in the *Second Rule* as being well-established, though there are sections on behaviour in church. Psalmody plays an important part in the offices (though they are also described as 'prayer'). The monks take it in turn to sing the psalms in order of seniority. *The Second Rule of the Fathers* lays down the principle later adapted by Benedict:

> Nothing ought to come before prayer.[27]

The *Rule of the Four Fathers* and the *Second Rule of the Fathers* prescribe reading and meditation until the third hour: the monks then work until the ninth hour when they eat.[28] This is in contrast to Martin of Tours' monastery and the early years at Lérins where manual labour does not seem to have been the norm. The *Oriental Rule* suggests a similar time-table,[29] but in the *Rule of Macarius* and the *Third Rule of the Fathers* the period of meditation only lasts until the second hour.[30]

In the *Rule of Macarius* the theme of behaviour within the monastery is prominent:

> Mutually striving after most perfect obedience, let them be peace-loving, gentle, moderate, not proud, not abusive, not murmurers, not scoffers, not talkative, not presumptuous, not self indulgent, but pleasing to God, whose Christ they serve. Neither pursuing blasphemy nor contradicting anyone let them not be slow in compliance, but ready for prayer, perfect in humility, girded in obedience, alert during vigils, happy while fasting.[31]

The *Third Rule of the Fathers* repeats earlier prohibitions against receiving monks from other monasteries but also seems to suggest that monks may wish to join the community for which it was written because it is stricter. Other original legislation covers punishments for theft, and reveals that clerics may reside in the monastery. Women are forbidden to enter the monastery and monks may not frequent nunneries. The *Third Rule* insists that the abbot is not allowed to keep any property back for himself. If he defies this ruling, he is to be brought to the attention of the local bishop and if he does not amend after being chastised by the bishop he is to be deposed. This is the first acknowledgement in any of this series of rules of relations between a monastery and the diocese in which it is situated, suggesting a date of composition after the Council of Chalcedon in 451 (see below). At the same time, both the *Third Rule* and *Oriental Rule* focus more on the figure of the abbot than do the earlier rules in the group, a development which would lead towards the emergence of the abbot as the pivotal figure in the sixth-century Benedictine *Rule*.

Problems of Location

Some of these rules have been identified as the 'institutes of Lérins' referred to in the *Lives of the Fathers of Jura* or the institutes composed (under the influence of Lérins) at Condat for Agaune.[32] In the 470s, Sidonius Apollinaris, bishop of Clermont, brought a monk from Lérins to act as head of a monastery there and rule it according to the 'statutes' of Lérins or Grigny. But there is no general agreement amongst those in favour of a Lérins identification as to their date of composition. While one suggestion places the *Rule of the Four Fathers* in the period 400–40 CE others believe that it developed there more gradually from the arrival of Honoratus (and crystallizing around his *dicta*), only taking final shape in its present 'conciliar' form during the rule of the third Abbot, Faustus, at some point after 456 but before 462. Depending on which of these points of view is accepted, the *Second Rule of the Fathers* could therefore have been codified either around 427 – or have crystallized from the 420s onwards. The *Rule of Macarius* might possibly have been composed after Faustus became bishop of Arles in 462 – and be almost contemporary with the *Regula Orientalis*. However, the *Regula Orientalis* has also been dated to the end of the fifth century and the *Third Rule of the Fathers* placed as late as the 530s.[33]

Not all authorities even agree that these rules were used at Lérins or believe that the monastery, in its early days, required any written rule.[34] Suggestions that the *Rule of Macarius* is linked with Lérins are based on a much later source, the *Life of John of Réomé*, composed in 659.[35] This recounts the saint's stay in Lérins, but does not specifically say that he followed the rule there. It only makes him instruct his monks according to this rule after his return from the island monastery.[36] Despite fifth-century references to 'statutes' and 'institutes' of Lérins, such writings, if they existed, may have been brief in nature. The little information which we possess suggests that the influence of Cassian, Basil and Jerome on Lérins was still strong at the end of the century. There are echoes of Cassian's teaching in the *Monita*, a brief work of spiritual instruction ascribed to Abbot Porcarius (485–490).[37] Porcarius' pupil Cæsarius, later (502–542) bishop of Arles, echoes Cassian (and sometimes Basil and Pachomius) in the initial sections of the rule which he composed for nuns.[38] The continuing importance of the writings of Cassian and Basil at Lérins is also suggested by the way in which knowledge of these rules spread. The *Monastic Rule* of Columbanus indicates that principal influences on Irish monasticism in the late sixth century were the writings of Cassian, Basil and Jerome: knowledge of their work may have reached Ireland, either directly from Lérins or perhaps through Auxerre, as early as the fifth century.

Monastic Development in the *Rules* of the Fathers

Although the *Rules of the Fathers* are based partly on Cassian and Basil, there are indications that they were composed for a centre or centres with different priorities from those of Lérins. Hilarius' picture of a caring, Basilian abbot who taught the love of God and of neighbour is not repeated in the *Rules*. They do not portray a monastery which acts as a charitable centre for the Christian community at large. While the *Rule of Macarius* opens by repeating the first Gospel commandment (Matthew 22: 37) on which Basil bases his vision of the spiritual life:

Thou shalt love the Lord thy God with all thy heart and with all thy soul and with all thy mind,

there is no sign of the second (Matthew 22: 39):

Thou shalt love they neighbour as thyself.

Similarly, some passages are very close to Cassian, but there is no reference either to his ideas on spiritual training or to the higher level of contemplation as scriptural study, outlined in *Conference Fourteen*, which is dedicated to Honoratus and Eucherius. Manual work – not practised in the early days of Lérins – is mentioned in the earliest of the series of rules.

The *Rules of the Fathers* could have been composed for monasteries headed by less charismatic or less influential leaders than the abbots of Lérins. Many of the Basilian elements lacking in the *Rules* are those which stem from the aristocratic or charismatic nature of leadership – the solicitude and care which Basil expected the head of a community to exercise and which Honoratus evidently took up with zest, were appropriate forms of asceticism for a high-status leader to exercise. Such virtues ensured the pastoral care of the community, but also represented an exercise in humility and charity for its head – an exercise which may have been risky for an abbot of lower social standing or spiritual achievement to undertake. Continual care and consideration for those under one's authority requires either aristocratic self-confidence or (in the case of the less well-born) personal charisma – or both. The *Rules of the Fathers*, equipped with a false Egyptian provenance to enhance their authority and a less 'theological' stress on obedience than either Cassian or Basil, provide increasing support for the less charismatic leader, as the hierarchy of monks with specific duties in the community expands and the distance between the abbot and his monks is also increased.

As the stratification of the monastery becomes more apparent in these rules, so too does the severing of its ties with the outside world. The charitable function in society envisaged by Basil disappears, suggesting that they were composed for monasteries less prosperous than Lérins, where the initial distribution of charity appears to have come from the wealth of its own recruits and not from manual work. There may be some validity in older theories which suggested that the *Rules* took shape from 465–470 onwards elsewhere in southern Gaul or – more plausibly – in Italy, where some of them were known to Benedict of Nursia in the sixth century. An important clue to their origins may lie in the fact that the *Rules'* quotations from the psalms are taken from the Roman rather than the Gallican psalter, suggesting a central or southern Italian place of composition rather than one in Gaul or Northern Italy.[39]

The Changing Shape of Monastic Life

Many minor monasteries were created throughout Gaul and Italy throughout the fifth century, as the result of personal devotion or asceticism, small and informal communities where no rule would have been required. House and villa 'monasteries' sprang up as aristocrats or the prosperous took to a life of religion and turned their own homes into religious retreats for family and friends.[40] Some time after his appointment as bishop of Clermont Ferrand in 469, the Gallic aristocrat Sidonius Apollinaris visited an old acquaintance, Maximus, and found him leading a changed life. Maximus now ate sparingly, had grown his beard long and dressed very simply. His villa was furnished with goat-hair hangings, hard couches and simple three-legged stools – not the sort of furnishings normally found in the villa of a former Palatine official. Sidonius' first thought was that he must have converted to a life of Christian asceticism and become a monk. In fact, Maximus had been coerced into accepting ordination as a priest, but it is clear that Sidonius associated his austere life-style with that of the house monastery. The numbers of such 'monasteries' are impossible to quantify and many of them must have disappeared when their founder died.

Holy Places and the Cult of Saints – another locus for monasticism

One religious phenomenon which was to have a marked effect on the evolution of monasticism was the rise of the cult of holy places and relics.

It was a short leap from belief in the intercession of the saints in heaven to belief in the miraculous powers of the bodies in their tombs below. From the third century, the slow sanctification of the Christian year began as calendars of saint's days were gradually built up, in celebration of the birth, martyrdom or solemn translation of the martyrs' bodies from extra-urban cemeteries to urban churches and basilicas. The ascetic Bishop Victricius of Rouen, who welcomed the relics of Italian martyrs to his diocese in northern Gaul, enunciated a theology of relics when he declared that the visible physical remains, the 'blood and dust' of the saint's body opened the 'eyes of the heart' to the *praesentia*, the living presence of the saint.[41]

Ascetics were swift to associate themselves with the devotion to holy places and relics and monastic communities now grew up beside holy sites and basilicas housing the relics of saints. There were well-established connections between the monks of the Judaean desert and Jerusalem: some monks even 'withdrew' to the holy city itself, seeking out the spiritual benefits to be gained by proximity to the holiest of holies. By the 380s, monastic cells were found beside the Holy Selpulchre itself. The *Pilgrimage of Egeria* reveals, in the 380s, the participation of monks and nuns in the liturgy sung at the Holy Sepulchre. There were also connections between Egyptian monasticism and the Holy Land: Melania the Elder together with Rufinus presided over monastic establishments near the Holy Sepulchre while Jerome and Paula settled at Bethlehem.

In the West, the possibilities for fusing monastic life with the cult of relics is illustrated by the career of Paulinus of Nola[42] who came to regard St Felix of Nola as his spiritual patron. He retired to the shrine of St Felix at Cimitile near Nola in Southern Italy, where he created his own monastic community centred round a shrine which was open to pilgrims. As well as the body of Felix, Paulinus also treasured relics of John the Baptist, the apostles Andrew and Thomas, St Luke and the martyrs Gervasius and Protasius (sent to him by Ambrose), Vitalis, Agricola, Proclus and Euphemia, tangible reminders of a presence which watched over the living and who would intercede for his soul before God either when he died, or at the Last Judgement. Paulinus' friend and Martin of Tours' biographer, Sulpicius Severus, also created a shrine in his family monastery around the tomb of a man whom he regarded as a saint – Clarus, an aristocratic priest who had set up his own monastery near Marmoutier. The *Life of Eugendus*, one of the 'Jura Fathers', records that his monks travelled to Rome and brought back relics of the Apostles, which were enshrined in the monastic church.[43] Cassian's own monastery for men at Marseilles was built at the site of a third-century necropolis and beside the shrine of St Victor on the rocks above the port.[44]

Basilical Monasteries in Gaul and Italy

Whether Cassian's monastery for men should be counted as 'basilical' is unclear: although it was situated next to a shrine, it was not necessarily formally attached to it. At the same time, the class of monk whose main function was the singing of the liturgy in churches open to the public grew. In fifth-century Gaul, large basilicas were constructed over the tombs or relics of a number of saints and were served either by clergy or by monks from a linked monastery who chanted a liturgy in the basilica at regular hours of the day. The first major church of this kind in Gaul was St Martin's in Tours, staffed by clergy. The second major basilical monastery to be set up in Gaul in the liturgical service of a saint was at Paris, founded according to Gregory of Tours over the tomb of St Denis, by St Genovefa.[45] There, liturgical service provided by monks created a solemn and decorous succession of offices which effectively invoked the intercession of the saint in heaven on behalf of the pilgrims to his church. The most famous example of a liturgically-orientated monastery in the period is that of St Maurice at Agaune founded in 515 at the burial place of the martyrs of the Theban legion. Originally a martyrial cult site colonized by two ascetics, Agaune was turned into a liturgical monastery by the Burgundian prince Sigismund on the advice of Bishop Maximus of Geneva and with the support of Bishop Avitus of Vienne. In 524, Agaune would also house the body of Sigismund, the first martyr-king of the early medieval period. Despite Roman prohibitions against burial within cities, bishops, kings and aristocrats began to have themselves buried *ad sanctos*, as near to the tombs of the saints as possible in the hope of gaining merit by proximity to such powerful sources of spiritual power.[46] Later in the sixth century the Frankish ruler Chlothar I built a church to the powerful intercessor St Médard at Soissons, while Guntram was the patron of St Marcel at Chalon. In the seventh century Dagobert I would richly endow St Denis (royal burials there began when an infant son of Chilperic I – also named Dagobert – was interred there in 580). There were also royal burials in St Geneviève and St Denis, Paris.[47] The Merovingian rulers buried in these churches hoped to ensure the intercession of saints through performance of the liturgy by the monks whose monasteries were attached to the churches: both St Marcel and St Denis would adopt the solemn perpetual chant of Agaune (see below) as a suitable liturgy for the burial place of kings. The creation of such basilical monasteries marks a departure from the concept of the monastery as the extension of and setting for the personal asceticism of its founder: instead, such houses represented the desire to invoke the protection of the saints for the living and the dead and to commemorate the departed.

In Rome, monks sang part of the round of liturgy at the great basilicas.[48] The earliest reference to a monastery associated with a Roman basilica comes from a source which claims that Pope Sixtus (432–440) had founded a *monasterium in catacumbas* – a monastery at the catacombs, beside the basilica of St Sebastian on the Appian way. Pope Leo the Great (440–461) founded the oldest of the three basilical monasteries which surrounded St Peter's by the early middle ages and Pope Hilarius (461–8) added a monastery (possibly later known as St Stephen's) to the Laurentian basilica outside the city walls. Roman monks assisted the clergy of the major basilicas, the Lateran, St Peter's the Liberian basilica (Santa Maria Maggiore) and St Paul.[49]

The monks of basilical monasteries in Italy and Gaul did not live the type of common life practised in the stricter monasteries. They were materially supported by the diocese and the monks did not have to perform manual work. In view of his belief in manual work, it seems unlikely that Cassian's Marseilles monastery for men – built in the period *c.*420–440 – was originally conceived on such lines. The claims made in the *Lives of the Fathers of Jura* that the monasteries of Romanus, Lupicinus and Eugendus worked and practised the full common life may represent a veiled criticism of not only of wealthy monasteries but even of those whose primary function was liturgical and who had moved away from the primitive ideals of monastic poverty and self-sufficiency.[50]

The Liturgy of the Monasteries and Basilicas

The growth of the cult of saints and relics also helped to bring changes to the monastic liturgy. In the fourth century, the hermits of Lower Egypt had ruminated continually on the psalms in their cells as they wove their palm-leaf or rush mats. The only episode approaching anything like a formal daily period of psalmody occurred before the main meal taken each day in the monk's cell:

> And indeed, at the ninth hour, it is possible to stand and hear how the strains of psalmody rise from each habitation so that one believes that one is high above the world in paradise.[51]

Monks worked at weaving and plaiting their mats and baskets while meditating in their cells: indeed, work might be seen as a way of achieving the ideal of unceasing prayer. When Apa Lucius was visited by a group of religious who refused to work he explained that:

> By working and praying all day long, I can complete around sixteen baskets. I give away two of these to any beggar who comes to my door. I

make my living from the rest. And the man who receives the gift of two baskets prays for me.... That is how, by God's grace, I manage to pray without ceasing.[52]

Only on Saturday and Sundays were psalms sung communally in church. The Pachomians, living in highly organized cenobia, had communal morning and evening services, but these offices largely consisted of the monks' listening in silence to readings.[53] This meditative tradition, in which the monk turned over each word of psalm or scripture in his mind, scrutinizing and weighing its innermost meaning in search of illumination, was the foundation of the spiritual life of the monks of Egypt. There was little difference between the spirit in which the ceaseless prayer of their daily existence was performed and that of the two formalized and communal offices, which were still centred around meditation.

A greater formalization of monastic psalmody took place in Cappadocia in the third quarter of the fourth century when Basil of Cæsarea felt the need to demonstrate to some of the more radical Christian contemplative groups, such as the Messalians, that it was possible to combine work and prayer. He therefore adopted the idea of a monastic day which incorporated the 'little hours' of Terce, Sext and Nones – as well as morning and night time offices and an additional morning office.[54] Basil must have drawn much of his inspiration for his fixed periods of psalmody from the office of the public churches. In the Holy Land monks and virgins took part in the public liturgy of the major shrines: the *Pilgrimage of Egeria* reveals that at Jerusalem around 385 the monks and laity who attended their churches at the most sacred sites of Christendom observed nightly Vigils, dawn hymns (which would become Matins or Lauds), Sext, Nones and Vespers (or Lucernaria).[55] At the convent in Bethlehem, at which he stayed in the late fourth century, there were, according to Cassian, five offices – one at dawn, Terce, Sext, Nones and Vespers – suggesting that the fact of communal life and the proximity of the Bethlehem monastery to holy places had contributed to extending and formalizing the office.

Possibly the oldest surviving instructions for a western liturgy are to be found in the *Ordo Monasterii* attributed to Augustine. These liturgical instructions themselves had been ascribed to Augustine's friend Alypius bishop of Thagaste, who had spent some time in the Holy Land. This attribution has, however, been questioned on linguistic grounds and in liturgical terms and there are differences between the instructions laid out in this short rule and what Cassian tells us about Bethlehem.[56] And some of the liturgy's features point to a different genesis. There is a very marked differentiation between the length of the night offices of winter, autumn and spring and summer, suggesting that it may have originated in more northerly latitudes, where there are greater variations in the length of the night between summer and winter. It is possible that it was based on the liturgy of the public churches of Milan where Augustine first converted to Christianity and the monastic life.

The Gallic customs to which Cassian had so much objected in the 420s – multiplicity of offices and lengthy psalmody – may have arisen in part from the communal nature of many western monasteries, from the presence of relics in monastic churches and may also have been encouraged by the growth of basilical monasteries. Even in the case of those monastic churches where the public was not usually admitted to venerate relics, the presence of the holy would have encouraged a more solemn and elaborate liturgy. Cassian tried hard to restrict the number of psalms in the office, but it is not clear how successful he was. Perhaps Lérins followed his ideas for a time. In the eighth century, an anonymous text, the *Ratio de cursus qui fuerunt eius auctores*, would claim that the Irish had received their *cursus* or liturgy *via* Lérins.[57] An anonymous Irish monastic rule of the seventh century contains instructions which closely resemble that of Cassian, while Columbanus' liturgy also has discernible links to Cassian,[58] suggesting the possibility that the liturgy Ireland originally received from Lérins might have been based on Cassian's. Against this, it has to be acknowledged that in the first part of the sixth century, Bishop Cæsarius of Arles who had trained at Lérins, set down a *cursus* which he claimed was 'for the most part' based on that of Lérins which contains a higher number of offices and psalms than Cassian would have thought proper, as well as a number of hymns, which play no part in Cassian's liturgical scheme.[59] It is still not clear whether the *Ratio de cursus* is entirely unreliable; or whether the liturgy of Lérins originally based on Cassian's ideas was transmitted to Ireland before being expanded considerably later in the the fifth century; or whether Cæsarius himself made considerable alterations to the Lérins liturgy when he set down his rule for nuns.

While even non-basilical monasteries may have developed more elaborate liturgies than Cassian thought desirable, the basilical churches moved furthest of all away from the older and simpler liturgical forms which he had attempted to popularise.[60] The liturgy performed at Agaune was highly exotic, based on that of the monastery of the 'Sleepless Ones' in Constantinople which first appears at the end of the fifth century. In this system of 'perpetual praise' (*laus perennis*), the monks of Agaune were divided into a number of *turmae* or groups who took it in turns to sing the liturgy so that it could be continued both day and night. The original *turmae* were drawn from the monks of already-existing monasteries, probably including a group drawn from the Jura communities. In the Roman basilicas, the office took on characteristics associated with other public churches such as the cathedrals, by, for example, using the so-called 'Laudate' psalms (Psalms 148–50) in the office of Lauds. Such moves represented one of the earliest breaks with the meditative monastic tradition of the *psalterium currens* which involved a continual cyclical recitation of the psalms from the first to the hundred and fiftieth, commencing over again from the beginning when the end had been reached. Such unceasing repetition helped the monk to learn the psalter as well as providing food for meditation, but was less attractive for the public admitted to some of the offices and so the practice of assigning set psalms to some offices was instituted. In the late fifth or early sixth century, the monks of the Roman basilicas began to say all the psalms over the course of a week: this involved some repetition, but was not, by early monastic standards, a heavy liturgical load.

Monks, Clergy and Monasteries in Ecclesiastical Law

The growth of monasticism in the Roman Empire is reflected in the fact that at the Council of Chalcedon in 451, all monasteries had been declared subject to the authority of the bishop of the diocese in which they were situated and his permission was required for any new foundation – he was empowered to check that it was adequately funded.[61] The same council decided that monks who were clerics – monks ordained to serve the eucharistic needs of their monasteries – remained under episcopal control but at this stage its canons were little-known or poorly-observed in the west. In Gaul, the Council of Arles of 455 had resolved a conflict between Faustus, abbot of Lérins, and his diocesan which limited the bishop's powers in the monastery. While the latter controlled the monks who were clerics, he could not introduce strangers or exercise his ministry in the monastery without the abbot's permission and all lay monks – the majority of the community – were the responsibility of the abbot alone.[62] Gallic councils of the early sixth century aimed to limit the enthusiasm of founders and tried to have monasteries established only near towns so that they could be supervised easily. They also legislated against alienation of monasteries' property by abbots – though bishops themselves seemed able to control the appointment of abbots and even to take advantage of vacancies to acquire monastic property.

One of the major problems which would develop as monasteries built their own churches was that of two competing jurisdictions within the monastery. As the bishop controlled clerics, monks who had been ordained might be thought to come under his jurisdiction rather than that of the abbot, whose authority might therefore be undermined. The preferred solution to this problem from the mid-sixth century onwards for ordinary monasteries was to ordain a single monk to serve mass – other clerics could only reside in monasteries as visitors or as penitents.

Monks for their part were not allowed to encroach on clerical privileges. The places where monastic and clerical status became confused was in basilical monasteries: there some monks may have been ordained, while some of the clergy may have shared the common life of monks. When writing about the shrine of Agaune in the later sixth century Bishop Gregory of Tours appears to use the terms monks and clerics interchangeably and it is often not clear exactly which group he means.[63] At an early stage Agaune had obtained an exemption from episcopal intervention on the same lines as that granted to Lérins, probably because the potential confusion between monastic and clerical status threatened to undermine the abbot's control. But generally on the continent distinctions between monks and clerics were strictly observed. This applied even in terms of appearance: most monks shaved their heads, though the Irish would shave the front, keeping their hair at the back – but the *corona* or circular tonsure on the crown of the head was reserved for clerics.[64] While in secular law a monk was to some extent assimilated to the clerical state in that he was exempt from certain laws and ecclesiastical law forbade him to involve himself in worldly affairs, the ordinary monk did not enjoy clerical privileges. On the peripheries of Christianity, however, monasteries could serve as bases from which a number of bishops sought to convert pagans and non-Catholics. In the late fourth century, Bishop Victricius of Rouen may have used monasteries as mission-stations on the edge of his diocese.[65] In the fifth, St Severinus, the 'Apostle of Austria', was told in a vision to leave his hermitage to found a monastery near a city – and when he attempted to leave this foundation, he was accused of denying his presence to his peoples.[66] Clearly this monastery functioned as a pastoral centre – even if only in the sense that it was used as a base for preaching and baptism. Another example of a monastery as pastoral centre associated with a bishop was Dumio in sixth-century Portugal, from which Bishop Martin of Braga attempted to convert the Suevic kings from Arianism and the people of rural Portugal from paganism or Priscillianism,[67] while earlier in the century British monks such as Samson and Paul Aurelian founded monasteries in Brittany which became the centres of dioceses. Such developments were characteristic of the periphery and not of areas where there were fully organized dioceses. In the fifth century Pope Leo I put monks on the same plane as the laity when he forbade both groups to preach[68] and in Italy – above all in Rome[69] – monks did not take on parochial duties.

By the sixth century, monasticism was a much more diverse, yet in many ways more institutionalized phenomenon than it had been at the end of the fourth. Through the work of Cassian, contemplation had become identified with scriptural reading and study and thanks to the influence of Lérins, Gallic bishops were often now promoters of monasticism rather than its opponents. A monastery might take any one of a number of forms ranging from a small household or villa monastery, perhaps existing only as long as the lifetime of its founder, to a monastery with a hospice attached or to a federation of a number of houses. The development of the cult of holy places and relics and the emergence of basilical monasteries helped bring about changes in the monastic liturgy – though the most extensive of these were confined to the basilical monasteries themselves – while the liturgical function of these houses meant the abandonment of ideals of manual labour and common life. To the traditional alternatives of disposing of property before entry to a monastery or giving all one's goods to the poor, the possibility of donating them to the community was now formally recognized. Monasteries were now legally brought under the supervision of the bishop, while the composition of a number of monastic rules reflects an increasing trend, in some houses or groups of houses, towards institutionalization, with the development of a hierarchy of officials with specific duties and tasks inside the monastery and an increasing emphasis on the person and powers of the abbot. At the same time, older monastic works – Basil, Jerome and Cassian – continued to be read for both spiritual and practical direction and there were probably many smaller monasteries still run largely according to the directions of their founder or abbot.

Cæsarius of Arles and Female Intercessory Monasticism

One of the most remarkable monastic experiments of the sixth century was the creation of a monastery for women where the life of the nuns was mainly devoted to liturgical intercession. To achieve this, two opposing ideas which grew up in the fifth century had to be amalgamated: the concept of the liturgical service of a public church by monks, and the growing idea that women's communities should not only be separated from those of men but also strictly enclosed. The trend towards enclosure of larger female communities which began in the fourth century continued in the fifth in the monasteries founded by the Jura Fathers in fifth-century Gaul. These communities included an enclosed female house at Baume-les-Dames: once admitted and professed, the nuns only left the house when they were buried.[70] While accepting the trend towards female enclosure, Cæsarius also used female monasticism alongside the common life for the clergy as an integral part of his programme for forging a Christian community under his own leadership. On his arrival at Arles, inspired by the African rhetor and disciple of Augustine, Julianus Pomerius, he had organized his clergy to live an ascetic common life as part of his household. They were to perform divine service in the cathedral church of St Etienne – not just Lauds and Vespers, but also the minor hours of Terce, Sext and Nones which would normally have been said within the episcopal residence. They thus brought the divine service to the laity, creating one of the instruments through which, along with his own preaching, Cæsarius hoped to consolidate the Christian community of Arles. A female community – conveniently headed by his own sister and, on her death, his niece – was also to take its place in this overall design: though unusual, this was practicable, as at this period liturgical intercession was still mainly based on psalmody and prayer rather than, as later, the celebration of masses and private masses, actions open only to men. By founding a new nunnery, to be controlled by himself and members of his own family, Cæsarius aimed to create a bulwark of intercession for himself and his city of Arles: a community of virgins whose prayers and praise would rise like incense to heaven and protect both himself and his flock.[71]

Cæsarius' first attempts to establish a female community met with disaster. It was originally constructed outside the city walls, probably on the Roman cemetery of Alyscamps, near the holy site of the tomb of St Genesius, but was destroyed by the incursion of the Franks and Burgundians in 508. A new house was consecrated in 512, now situated safely inside the city walls – near their south-east corner, beside an older basilica, which had formerly served as Arles' cathedral and incorporating older buildings which were adapted to the needs of the nunnery.[72] Cæsarius took every measure possible to guarantee the success and financial independence of his nunnery: he even alienated church property to obtain revenues for the nuns. He sought papal confirmation of his course of actions – which were approved reluctantly by Pope Hormisdas, who suggested that in future the buyers of church property should make donations directly to the nunnery. Despite his reservations about Cæsarius' actions, Hormisdas also ruled, as Cæsarius had asked, that none of the bishop's successors should appropriate any power for themselves in the convent, in effect giving the nuns the sort of exemption granted to Lérins and the major basilicas. The only rights they are to have are those of visitation 'in the pious exercise of their pastoral responsibilities'. Seven local bishops added their assent to Hormisdas' provisions. Though Cæsarius as a celibate could not rely on family to look after his precious foundation's interests after he died (and after the deaths of his sister, niece and his nephew, Teridius, who was also a cleric) he succeeded in ring-fencing his nunnery about with protective legislation which would ensure its continuance after all their deaths.[73]

The *Rule* of Cæsarius of Arles

For this foundation Cæsarius thought it necessary to compile a new rule.[74] It is indicative of the changes which had overtaken monastic life since its early days that he writes in terms of gender difference rather than of the equality of minds or souls:

> Because there are evidently many differences in customs between monasteries of women and men, we have made a choice, from many, of a few prescriptions by which you may live together, old and young, a life according to the rule and may strive to fulfil spiritually the observances which are specially adapted to your sex...[75]

His *Rule for Virgins* divides into five sections. The first sets down regulations for admission and practice based on Cassian and those of Lérins where he himself had trained as a monk. A second section is partly based on the *Rules* ascribed to St Augustine of Hippo: Julianus Pomerius had introduced him to the works of Augustine and Cæsarius uses excerpts from the *Regula Tertia*. It has been suggested that he was not familiar with the feminine version of Augustine's *Rule*, and that he himself translated parts of the masculine version into female terms, adding parts of the so-called *Ordo Monasterii* ascribed to Augustine.[76] The 'Augustinian' sections of the *Rule* lay down the spiritual basis of a community's life – the Gospel precept that all was to be held in common and no one should possess any private property. The third section of the rule contains Cæsarius' own ideas; a fourth is the so-called *Recapitulation* in which he goes over and confirms or revises what he has set down already, while the fifth consists of regulations for fasting and liturgy based on those of Lérins.

Enclosure

Cæsarius kept strictly to the parameters for female religious life which had been constructed from the late fourth century onwards. Nuns are Brides of Christ:

> consecrated virgins, souls vowed to God, who await the coming of the Lord with lighted lamps and a tranquil conscience...[77]

and as such are 'worthy of profound veneration'; at the same time they are strictly enclosed. While in his *Rule for Monks* he simply states that:

> Women are never to enter the monastery, because it is a sequestered place[78]

nuns are kept under the strictest enclosure. Once the nuns of St Jean had undergone a period of probation and formally entered the religious life, they were not permitted to leave the community ever again. Cæsarius closed up connecting doors between the buildings which housed the nunnery and the old cathedral complex next door. The nuns' link to the outside world was through an official who lived near the house and was chosen by them, their *provisor* or steward. He was one of the very few men permitted to enter the interior of the house:

> Above all, to protect your reputation, do not let any man into the interior of the monastery and the oratories, except for the bishop and the provisor, the priest, deacon, sub-deacon and one or two lectors, of suitable age and manner of life, to celebrate mass at times. Whenever it is necessary to mend the roof, construct doors or windows or make some repairs of this sort, there shall enter with the *provisor* only the craftsmen and their slaves needed to carry out the work – and not even these latter without the knowledge and permission of the mother [abbess]...[79]

While clergy had to be brought into the house to serve mass, younger clergymen were effectively excluded from the convent buildings. The *provisor* himself was not normally permitted to enter the interior of the house unless accompanied by the abbess or other 'very reliable' witness, while the nuns were instructed to guard each other's modesty in his presence. Cæsarius developed Augustine's prohibitions of receiving of illicit letters from men and gifts from outsiders.[80] Contacts with the outside world could only be made through the *salutatorium* or parlour where the abbess, accompanied, as befitting her dignity by two or three members of the community, might receive visitors.[81] The nuns were forbidden to organize banquets for the bishop and local clergy or to take in sewing or laundry, all characterized by Cæsarius as secular occupations and as such unsuitable for consecrated virgins. The only work permitted was the weaving of woollen cloth for their own clothes.[82] Whether even the abbess herself could ever leave the monastic enclosure is doubtful – a regulation referring to her dining *extra congregatione* probably refers to her dining apart from her nuns, privately, rather than outside the nunnery.[83] In a letter to the nuns, Cæsarius declared that

> a soul chaste and consecrated to God should not have constant association with externs, even with her relatives, whether they coming to her or she going to them; lest she hear what is not proper or say what is not fitting or see what could be injurious to chastity.[84]

But his regulations often reflect the impossibility of cutting off all contacts with the outside world – especially as he wished his nunnery to play a significant role in the city. While he excludes even laywomen from the interior of the nunnery (doubtless believing that they would bring secular morals – or the lack of them – into the community), some laypeople were permitted to enter the convent *salutatorium* or parlour where conversation between nuns and their visiting relations could be strictly monitored by the *formaria* (see below) or another senior nun.

The Monastic Community

The daily round of the nuns of St Jean was ruled first and foremost by their liturgical obligation, while the remainder of their time was also suffused by Scripture and prayer. Cæsarius instructs that all are to learn to read and to listen to readings from the Scriptures at mealtimes. Between the second and the ninth hour, the nuns are to work in silence, but are also reminded of the Gospel commandment to 'Pray without ceasing'.[85] Cæsarius' own word-picture of the community meditating tranquilly on the word of God while one of their number reads to them as they spin and weave in harmony leads him naturally into quotation from Augustine's *Regula Tertia*:

> You are to have one heart and soul in God; possess everything in common: for it is read in the Acts of the Apostles 'They possessed everything in common' and 'Distribution was made to each in proportion to each one's need'.[86]

Cæsarius himself eventually uses the term abbess – literally 'female father' – for his superior, but does not give his abbess the sweeping powers with which, a few years later, Benedict of Nursia would arm the head of community. Instead he invokes co-operation with her as 'mother':

> Let all obey the mother after God; let all defer to the prioress.[87]

At the same time, Cæsarius does adapt Augustine's ideas about the correction of delinquent youngsters by older community members, using this instead as a description of the abbess's officials' powers over other members of the community. The community which he is legislating for is a much more structured one than that visualized by Augustine. This is probably due not only to the elaboration of monastic organization which had taken place over the preceding century but also to the size of the nunnery – said to be home to as many as 200 nuns by the time of Cæsarius' death. To assist her the abbess could now call on a second-in-command, the prioress or *praeposita*, and also the *primiceria* or *formaria*. It is not entirely clear whether these two are in fact the same: the *formaria* is senior enough to supervise the meeting between the nuns and their families in the *salutatorium*. She was probably also responsible for the education or instruction of the nuns – or at least was in charge of the novices. The function of the *primiceria* may have been that of choir-mistress, an important role in a community where the liturgy took up such a considerable part of the nuns' day. There were other lesser officials: a *canavaria*, in charge of the wine-cellar (a post only found in Cæsarius and in later rules based on his); a sister in charge of the *lanipendium*, where the wool which the nuns wove was kept; a *regestoraria*, who looked after the convent's money and was in charge of storing clothing and other essentials. There was a nun whose special duty was to care for the sick. The *posticiariae* or portresses were entrusted with guarding the *posticium*, not the main gate to the convent through which, at 'opportune times', important visitors were admitted, but a lesser, side or back door through which the everyday business of the convent was transacted, its material needs were supplied and probably also the door at which charity was distributed to the poor.[88]

The main division in the community, apart from that between ordinary nuns and officials or *seniores*, was between adults and children. Cæsarius was prepared to accept girls as young as six into the community, where they would be instructed in obedience and learn to read (though he forbids the nuns to take in other pupils).[89] The fact that Cæsarius' concern with the regulation of oblation is shared by Benedict of Nursia (see pp. 122–3 below) is another valuable clue to the development of the practice since the fourth century. Basil, whose rule was disseminated in translation in the West, had allowed not only orphans but also other young people to join his communities with the consent of their parents.[90] However, the longer version of his rules reveals that children lived in a separate part of the monastery and Basil would write elsewhere that he thought that the ages of sixteen or seventeen was a suitable age for girls' vows of chastity: he did not assume that children could make permanent commitments in such matters. Both he and Jerome had been aware that even at an early stage in the history of Christian monasticism, there were parents who sent their less marriageable daughters into female communities with a small dowry. As monasteries became familiar features of society, this practice must have become more general.[91] The community of St Jean of Arles in Cæsarius' day may therefore have included members who were not only of different ages but who had very different attitudes towards the highly enclosed society in which they now found themselves confined. In an attempt to maintain unity and harmony, Cæsarius attempted to create a simplicity and uniformity of dress and display in the nunnery which would avoid creating a luxurious atmosphere and smooth out social distinctions between the nuns. Clothing is to be plain, a natural white; no embroideries are permitted (except when the abbess permits, and merely on small towels and facecloths) and bedding is also to be plain. Only silver is to be used in the church plate. No one is permitted to keep a slave.[92] While Cæsarius worries about the prospect of nuns secretly receiving supplies of wine, he also imposes on the abbess the duty of procuring good wine, especially for the ill and those of more refined upbringing.[93] His main concern, however, seems to be that the nuns do not forget their status as holy virgins and offer each other insults and harsh words.[94]

Property, Disappropriation and the Abduction of Nuns

One area of potential weakness in Cæsarius' regulations lay in his views on renunciation of property. Individual disappropriation was a sign of submission to the values of the community. But although he is clear about this principle, the different sections of the *Rule* itself contain a variety of confusing instructions for the shedding of property. Chapter 5 announces that the nuns are to dispose of all property – by charter of deed or sale – and places no actual restriction on the choice of recipient. Nothing is said about the disposal of any profits made from a sale. In fact, Cæsarius' letter to nuns, *Vereor*, written before the *Rule*, makes his own attitude quite clear. He places the struggle for mastery of the desire for wealth alongside the struggle for renunciation of worldly voluptuousness and criticizes nuns who gave the greater part of their goods to their rich families and not to the poor.[95] But the *Rule* itself does not make explicit the latter point. Even greater ambiguity surrounds the property of those who are offered to the nunnery as children. Children who enter the community are required to draw up documents of renunciation either when they reach the age of majority or when they gain control of their parents' property.[96] Doubtless Cæsarius envisaged a simple process whereby they would make over their property to the nunnery once they were old enough to do so. He does not seem to have taken into account either the divisive nature of these arrangements – which allowed some members of the community to retain possessions, even if they could not legally enjoy them – or possibilities that discontented oblates might try to take possession of their inheritance and leave once they came of age or even be abducted and married by men hoping to increase their wealth or social standing. Some reluctant nuns might even connive at their own abduction. Church councils had tried to stop this practice: in 538 the Council of Orleans excommunicated as adulteresses vowed and veiled virgins who consented to live with their ravishers, while in 567 the Council of Tours had to remind laymen that under Roman law the penalty for rape and subsequent marriage of consecrated virgins had been death.[97]

The *Recapitulation*

The *Recapitulation* which Cæsarius added to his *Rule* in the 530s bears vivid testimony to his obsession with his ideal community and the anxieties and practical dilemmas which had beset him since its re-foundation some twenty years earlier. He worries that bishops, with abbesses, in the future may attempt to alter or despoil his cherished creation and even permits measured resistance to this. He is still sensitive to what he perceives as the dangers of contact with the outside world, forbidding the nuns to break strict enclosure and repeating that they are to dispose of any personal property and are not to entertain even bishops. The difficulty of running a community which includes a number of women who do not necessarily have a strong vocation is made plain in his reiteration of regulations against the manufacture of luxuries and personal adornment such as the wearing of purple and fur trimmings. One clause in particular adds a new dimension to these instructions:

> Head-dresses are not to be any higher than the line I have marked on the wall in ink.[98]

The *Recapitulation* reflects the problems which Cæsarius faced in attempting to maintain a distance between the community and the society of which it was very much a part. While insisting on strict enclosure Cæsarius had allotted a semi-public role to his nuns as they sang the liturgy: their performance of the office was divided between two of the three churches attached to the nunnery and the public may therefore have been admitted to see, or at least been able to hear, parts of it.[99]

Liturgy and Intercession

In the last part of his *Rule* Cæsarius laid down for his nuns a complex liturgy, based upon that of Lérins, but also including elements borrowed from the cathedral office. The nuns sang the night office or Nocturns, Lauds/Matins, Terce, Sext, Nones, the evening office of Lucernaria ('lamplighting') or Vespers and a later one called Duodecima ('at the twelfth hour'). On Saturdays, Sundays and major festivals, the office of Prime followed Matins. Prime appears to be a new office, which Cæsarius was introducing only tentatively in the 530s.[100] On Saturdays the nuns kept a long vigil. During the longer winter nights, between the beginning of October and Easter, 'second nocturns' and readings were added to the night office, more than doubling its length, while Cæsarius' individual offices are also longer than Cassian would have thought proper. While

Cassian's only contained psalmody, prayer, a small number of readings and alleluias, Cæsarius also includes hymns, some antiphonal psalmody, readings, and *capitella* (concluding psalm-verses). The public would have been able to hear and perhaps even see the nuns sing part of the office of Matins and Vespers in their 'exterior oratory'.[101]

The trend towards an increasingly intercessory type of monasticism was propelled to some extent by the turbulent times through which Cæsarius and his city lived. By the time he composed the final version of his *Rule*, Arles had been ruled by both Visigoths and Ostrogoths. The political situation in Arles would change once again in 536 when it came under Frankish authority. But Cæsarius was not only concerned with prayers for safety in this life: the opening of his *Rule* reveals the constant anxiety about judgement and the afterlife which also informed his preaching and teaching. His sermons emphasized the terrors of the Last Judgement which for many, he insisted, would lead to eternal fire. He recommended that preachers exhort their flocks on the reality of hell-fire and he himself harangued the sinful telling them that they would find themselves in Tartarus, excluded from the light of heaven. This rhetoric of fear deployed in many sermons is, however, mitigated to some extent by his classification of sins as less or more severe, teaching that the former could be purged by the fire of the Last Judgement.[102] Even so, thoughts of judgement were never far from his mind and Cæsarius believed that the prayers of his nuns would protect his flock and help his soul into heaven. He also took revolutionary measures to create a shrine attached to the nunnery: the nuns were buried in the centre of the triple church which adjoined it. One of the earliest instances in Gaul of burials inside a city, such arrangements reflect Cæsarius' desire to Christianize the topography of Arles, by disregarding Roman prohibitions on burials inside the walls. Ranged in rows in the floor of the basilica of St Marie, the nuns' tombs would serve as a holy shrine for the Christian population of Arles, who were permitted to enter this outer part of the nunnery complex. Cæsarius' very last act to confirm its status was to have himself buried in the basilica of St Marie – once more underlining its importance as a cult centre for the city.[103]

Cæsarius' design for female intercessory monasticism was plundered by his successors for their own purposes. In late 536, two years after he produced the final version of his *Rule* for women, Arles was handed over from Ostrogothic to Frankish rule. Bishop Aurelian of Arles (546–551) was the appointee of the Frankish King Childebert and bishop and king joined together to found a monastery for men and another for women in Arles itself, probably in 547. The existence of two new houses, richly endowed by the king, must have diminished its importance and prestige in the city. Ultimately, Aurelian favoured male over female intercession – the male monastery received the relics of the apostles and of a number of saints – Genesius, Hilary (probably Hilary of Poitiers), Martin of Tours – and even the body of Cæsarius himself, removed from its tomb in the nunnery. After the creation of this new basilica, Cæsaria, abbess of St Jean, commissioned the writing of the *Life* of her uncle in an attempt to recoup for her nunnery some of the position which it had inevitably lost as a result of these events. Later in the sixth century, Aurelian's male monastery even acquired a portion of the cross – and in the seventh, it was the centre of a confraternity, a society set up to pray for the souls of Aurelian and his successors as bishop of Arles, its founder, King Childebert, Queen Ultrogotha and all associated with the basilica, including pilgrims.[104] Although it cannot be dated exactly, this is the earliest surviving western agreement of confraternity with a monastery. Aurelian used Cæsarius' *Rule for Nuns* as the basis for his own rules for both nuns and monks: he has less strict views on probation and admission than does Cæsarius, does not apply Cæsarius' strict rules of enclosure to the monks, and openly states that the public are admitted to watch the nuns sing parts of their liturgy.[105]

Female Monasticism in Sixth-Century Gaul

By the late sixth century there were female houses in all the main cities of central Gaul – at Amiens, Autun, Auxerre, Chartres, Poitiers, Sens and Tours (where there were two). A number of women's communities such as St Pierre-le-Vif at Sens and Ingitrude's community in the courtyard of St Martin at Tours, were founded beside basilicas.[106] The writings of Bishop Gregory of Tours mention a number of holy women and even record a rumour that two virgins had gone to live as hermits on a hill near Tours – though Gregory's evident astonishment at this reflects the danger in which such unprotected women were thought to be.[107] Not all the inmates of Frankish convents were willing converts to the religious life: many must have been child oblates. In addition, the ruling Merovingian dynasty's support for monasticism brought mixed consequences. Kings not only founded or endowed basilical monasteries to ensure prayers for their souls but also began to use religious houses as places of confinement for rival males and as dumping-grounds for unwanted or unmarriageable daughters. Gregory records that King Gunthram imprisoned his widowed sister-in-law in St Jean of Arles and that one of King Charibert's daughters, Berthefled, had eventually walked out of a convent where she had done little more for several years than eat and sleep, showing no interest whatsoever in the religious life. The destructive potential inherent in the combination of Frankish dynastic politics and monastic life came to a head in the revolt of the nuns of the convent of Holy Cross, Poitiers, in 590.

Radegund, Queen and Nun

The nunnery of Holy Cross was the creation of the remarkable Queen Radegund, at one time wife to the Frankish King Chlothar.[108] A Thurigi-nan princess, she had been captured along with her brother after the battle of Berscheidungen on the Unstrut in 531 and brought up by her captor, Clothar, until she reached marriageable age. She was educated in both the catholic faith and in Latin and was sufficiently proficient in the latter to write a poem about the Thuriginan war, in which she had been taken prisoner. Married to Clothar as a teenager, she never had any children: over a period of fifteen years she watched as he took up with a variety of other wives or concubines until one produced a son. Instead, she led a quasi-religious life even when married. She dedicated herself and her *morgengabe*, which included the *villae* of Athies, Saix and Peronne, to religious and charitable work, endowing hospitals and hospices. After Radegund learned that Clothar had, around 550, ordered the murder of her brother, she abandoned the court and took the decisive step of per-suading Bishop Médard of Noyon to consecrate her a deaconess. She left Noyon and retired to Saix, where she led a life of ascetic austerity for several years. Despite her husband's initial attempts to reclaim her, she succeeded in gathering a community around her and established her convent in Poitiers by 561 and another monastery of clerics outside the city where the nuns were buried. It is possible that as Clothar saw his own death approaching, he even resigned himself to assisting the foundation of the house where his holy queen, more nun than wife, might live out her widowhood in a cell attached to her convent. (Radegund never ruled over her house herself but instead installed a woman named Agnes, whom she came to regard as her spiritual daughter, as abbess.) Though she founded her convent with the support of Bishop Pientius, Radegund's relations with his succesor, Maroveus, became probematic when, in 569 she acquired a relic of the Holy Cross for her foundation from the Eastern Emperor,[109] and he refused to preside over the installation of this potent relic in the convent. Gregory of Tours suggests that it was because of Maroveus' hostility that Radegund obtained Cæsarius' *Rule for Virgins*, with its admonitions to resist episcopal interference, for the community.[110]

Not only does Gregory of Tours write about Radegund,[111] but she was also the subject of two full-scale hagiographies, one by the Italian poet – and later bishop – Venantius Fortunatus, who had been her friend for many years, the other by Baudonivia, one of the nuns of the community which she had founded.[112] Each stresses different aspects of her life and sanctity, but both paint a picture typical of many portrayals of female saints of an early conversion to a life of religion. The type of religious activity she carried out in her youth was, according to Fortunatus, a sort of deaconess service while his picture of her married life to Clothar stresses her humility and her desire to live the life of a nun while she was still married to the king:

> At night, when she lay with her prince she would ask leave to rise and leave the chamber to relieve nature. Then she would prostrate herself in prayer under a hair cloak by the privy so long as the cold pierced her through and only her spirit was warm...Because of this, people said that the King had yoked himself to a *monacha* rather than a queen.

This desire for a strict ascetic life was eventually fulfilled when she left her husband altogether, and settled first at Saix, where she could care for the poor and sick and mortify her own flesh by a strict diet.

Both Baudonivia and Fortunatus stress Radegund's charity and unceasing work for the poor and sick. Fortuntatus emphasizes her extreme bodily mortifications (in addition to wearing a hair shirt): once in Lent, she bound her body with iron circlets and chains; on another occasion, she heated up a brass plate made in the sign of the cross and branded herself with it; and she once forced herself to carry a basin full of hot coals. The unsettling nature of this asceticism on the existence of the nuns of the community can only be guessed at. But his poetry gives a rather different picture of Radegund's life in Radegund's convent, where he seems to have been invited to delightful supper-parties and shared with its founder a love of literature and learning. Baudonivia, by contrast, produces a text which stresses Radegund's energy and fidelity in intercession, prayer and charity towards pilgrims. This not only serves to emphasize her continuing role in Frankish royal politics but also presents a picture of feminine values of intercession and peacemaking as well humility in domestic tasks around the nunnery – a representation of asceticism and sanctity which contrasts with the ideal of the 'manly' women characteristic of the earliest days of monasticism.

The forces which tore Holy Cross apart three years after Radegund's death were a result of social tensions produced by the presence of a number of more or less unwilling Merovingian princesses in the convent. Holy Cross was home to at least three members of the ruling family – Constantina, Basina and Chrodechildis. Basina, who was a daughter of king Chilperic, had been placed in the convent in about 580 and in 584 had remained there, with Radegund's support, when her father had attempted to marry her off to a Visigothic prince, while Chrodechildis was (or, according to Gregory, claimed to be) a daughter of King Charibert. Both women led about forty nuns out of the convent in the winter of 590. Bishop Gregory off Tours, whose own niece Justina proved a loyal second-in-command to Abbess Leubovera, was involved in the negotations surrounding the revolt and gives a vivid account of its course.

Chrodechildis and Basina acquired a band of followers who, according to Gregory, committed murder and mayhem: they also made a series of lurid accusations against the abbess – that she kept a man in the convent whose duty was to sleep with her, that she had men castrated, that she held engagement parties in the nunnery, had made altar-cloths into clothes, and that she played backgammon. They also complained that their food was poor and that others had used their bathroom. When Leubovera successfully defended herself against such charges in front of a bishops' tribunal, they went to the King alleging that she had plotted against him. Once again, they met with no success.[113]

The events at Holy Cross paint an unedifying picture of high-status female monasticism in the most prestigious nunnery in late-sixth century Francia. A number of nuns had no real vocation for the religious life and others may originally have been oblates: Gregory of Tours records – as if it were inevitable – that once enclosure had been breached some accepted offers of marriage while others became pregnant. The real gist of Chrodechildis' and Basina's complaints against their abbess stemmed from their consciousness of the difference in rank between them. They complained that the non-royal Leubovera had treated them like low-born serving women instead of the daughters of kings: unwilling or lukewarm participants in the religious life, neither could altogether forget her secular status, though Basina in the end agreed to return to Holy Cross and accept the authority of the abbess. Chrodechildis, however, was allowed to retire to an estate, where she could, at last, be mistress of her own existence – if not abbess of Holy Cross, a position for which she undoubtedly considered herself well qualified on account of her birth. Her conduct of the rebellion suggests that had circumstances been different, she might have proved a capable leader. She had marshalled help from among the workers on the nunnery's estates and while her accusations against the abbess were not believed, she showed considerable deftness by choosing at one point retreat to the church of St Hilary, temporarily rejecting the protection of the relic of the cross for that of a different celestial patron and suggesting that she did not wish to fall into the trap of antagonizing the local bishop. Though Chrodechildis was ultimately frustrated in her campaigns to dislodge the abbess, a form of monasticism would soon emerge in northern Francia and England in which religious and aristocratic aims – already prefigured in Baudonivia's portrayal of Radegund's royal sanctity – were more harmoniously combined. In the seventh century aristocratic – and in England, royal – women took their place at the head of great estate-monasteries and played an important role in both religious and political life.

6

The *Rule* of St Benedict
and its Italian Setting

Italian Monasticism in the Early Sixth Century

By the sixth-century, monasteries could be found throughout the length of the Italian peninsula. In Rome, the basilical monasteries provided liturgical service at the major churches, while at the opposite end of the ascetic scale, a few aristocratic women continued to follow the fashion first established in the fourth century, living in retreat within their own houses. The majority of monasteries, however, were communities of men or women dedicated simply to a round of prayer and contemplation and could be found both inside and outside the cities.[1] Little is known about most of these foundations which seem to have been conventional religious houses, owing their existence to a founder's piety. Monks did not take on parochial duties.[2] The canons of the Council of Chalcedon (451), which included the ruling that monasteries were under the ultimate control of the local bishop, were applied sporadically by popes from the 520s onwards but only systematically by Gregory I (590–604).[3]

In the first decades of the sixth century and possibly for much longer, it seems likely that Italian monasticism was still largely guided by the works of Augustine, Basil and Cassian. The latter were probably used selectively and eclectically: not all members of religious communities would have found it desirable to work or to give their wealth to charity as Cassian or Basil would have wished, instead preferring to lead inward-looking lives of quiet contemplation; though in Sicily an otherwise unknown *vir inluster*, Saturninus, created a *xenodochium* or hospice for the poor in association with a monastery dedicated to St John at Catania.[4] One example of an eclectic approach to earlier monastic writings and rules is to be found in the career of Fulgentius (467–533), Bishop of Ruspe in North Africa, who had been a member of several monastic communities and the founder of several more. A member of a senatorial family, Fulgentius converted to the monastic life after reading Augustine's commentary on Psalm 36. A convinced Augustinian in theological terms, Fulgentius used the monastic rule of Augustine, possibly as the basis of organized clerical life, but also appears to have been heavily influenced by the ascetic works of Basil and Cassian. Exiled twice to Sardinia by Thrasamund, the Arian ruler of Vandal North Africa, he founded two communities there, one for monks and clerics and another for monks[5] and, through his belief in the importance of writing as a means of ascetic and pastoral praxis, influenced a number of his Italian contemporaries.

Eugippius and the Question of his *Rule*

Cassian's identification of contemplation with scriptural study continued to be particularly attractive to intellectually-inclined aristocrats with extensive financial or landed resources at their disposal. One of Fulgentius' correspondents was Eugippius, head of the community centred around the shrine of St Severinus at *Castellum Lucullanum* (now Pizzofalcone, Naples), which played an important role in the aristocratic religious culture of the early sixth century. Eugippius had contacts at the highest levels of society: he corresponded not only with Fulgentius but also with Proba, the daughter of the senator Symmachus and sister-in-law of the philosopher and politician Boethius, who had become a consecrated virgin in the early sixth century and who also corresponded with Fulgentius. Other members of this circle included the learned monk Dionysius Exiguus, who refashioned the method of calculating the date of Easter and translated the *Life of Pachomius* into Latin; and the deacon Paschasius, a prominent member of the Laurentian faction, partisans of the eastern empire in Rome. Lucullanum was a monastery with a scriptorium attached to it and from this scriptorium manuscripts were despatched to members of Eugippius' circle, including Fulgentius, when his Sardinian foundation lacked books. Eugippius, author of the *Life of St Severinus*, was a fervent admirer of the works of Augustine; and Proba – a noble Roman lady who lived as an ascetic in her own home and whose extensive library he had used – was the dedicatee of his great compilation of excerpts from Augustine's works.[6]

The *Rule* Attributed to Eugippius

The inspiration behind the work of Fulgentius and Eugippius was provided by the writings of Basil, Cassian and Augustine. In the seventh century, however, Isidore of Seville in his *De viris illustribus* would claim that

Eugippius had also composed his own rule for the community of Lucullanum.[7] Since the 1970s, this *Regula Eugipii* has been identified with a compilation of extracts from well-known monastic texts, opening with the Augustinian *Ordo Monasterii* and *Regula Tertia*: these are followed by a series of extracts from Basil, Pachomius, Cassian, Jerome's Letter 125, the *Rule of the Four Fathers*, a text known as the *Sentences of Novatus* and a rule known under the title of the *Regula Magistri* or *Rule of the Master.*[8]

It is principally the presence of the two rules associated with Augustine – which appear in their entirety and are distinguished from the extracts from other rules that follow – which has suggested to some that the sequence as a whole is to be identified with the rule composed by Eugippius, who compiled a lengthy series of extracts from Augustine's works.[9] But there are no definitive signs that it originated in Lucullanum. While there are references to the copying of manuscripts by *scribtores [sic]*, the content of many of the extracts points to a community where the monks also practised crafts and were in charge of implements: it quotes from Basil on work and the custody of vessels and tools and mentions the possible entry of pilgrims into an area of the monastery where crafts are practised. Scholars were only able to identify this compilation rule with Eugippius' composition after one of the rules excerpted in it, the so-called *Rule of the Master*, was re-dated to the first half of the sixth century. Previously, this rule had been viewed as a later work based on the *Rule* of Benedict of Nursia. The *Rule of the Master*, however, shows many signs of Irish influence and I have suggested that, rather than being seen as a predecessor of Benedict's *Rule*, it should be associated with the advent of Columbanian monasticism in seventh-century Italy. Its derivative, the so-called *Rule of Eugippius*, probably comes from one of Bobbio's dependent small monasteries or *cellae* which were also agricultural and pastoral centres (see below pp. 184–6).

Cassiodorus: the monastery as guardian of literary culture

At some time after 550, Cassiodorus Senator (480/90–580), who had formerly occupied some of the highest offices of state and who had no heir to inherit his lands, created his own learned retreat, a monastic community with a hermitage attached to it on his family estates at Vivarium in southern Italy.[10] In the early 530s, as Praetorian Prefect and in association with Pope Agapetus, he had planned the foundation of a Christian university at Rome so that the enthusiasm for secular learning which he perceived around him would be channelled instead into scriptural and religious studies. This ambitious project was wrecked by the beginning of the Justinianic wars of reconquest and the death of Agapetus. Between the 530s and 550s Italy was shaken by turmoil of the

Gothic Wars: with the displacement of the senatorial class, the study of letters as a whole went into steep decline and theological investigation dwindled into revision. Vivarium itself housed a library and scriptorium based on those parts of Cassiodorus' original library which had survived the wars of re-conquest and also on books which he had purchased from as far away as Africa. For his monks Cassiodorus prescribed the reading first of secular and then of religious texts: his monastic testament consists not of a rule but of the two books of the *Institutions of Divine and Human Readings*. This desire to preserve religious knowledge and, in its service, secular learning, was influenced by Augustine's *De Doctrina Christiana*,[11] but may also reveal a consciousness of the disappearance of knowledge and the implications of its disappearance for religion. Cassiodorus wrote his *Institutions* in simple language as introductions for his monks to theology and the liberal arts. Book Two, probably composed first, consists of an introduction to the Seven Liberal Arts. Book One introduces the study of the Bible, of the four accepted synods of the universal church and of the work of a range of theologians, Eugippius, and Dionysius Exiguus, before proceeding to cosmography, grammar and punctuation, medicine and eventually even spelling. As well as admonitions to his monks and abbots, and a section on prayer, Cassiodorus inserts a chapter instructing that those too simple to read philosophical writings should cultivate the gardens and work the fields and orchards – though characteristically he cannot resist appending a bibliography on gardening, bee-keeping and agriculture.

Though he counselled his monks to read Cassian with caution, because of his views of grace and free will, Cassiodorus was, in effect, taking emergency measures to ensure that Cassian's monastic programme could survive.

Benedict of Nursia: the *Rule* as programme for monasticism

It has been suggested that the *Rule of the Four Fathers* was composed in Italy[12] and although this is by no means certain, the tradition represented by this rule and the group associated with it was known to Benedict of Nursia, the founder of the abbey of Monte Cassino in Southern Italy, who composed his own monastic rule around the middle of the century. Although it demonstrates familiarity with a wide range of monastic and religious literature, including Basil, pseudo-Basil, Cassian, Augustine, some of the Pachomian texts, Jerome, the *Vitae Patrum*, the *Sentences of Sextus*, the *Didache* and the writings of Cyprian (as well as more popular works such as the *Passio Juliani*) and some of the *Rules of the Fathers*,[13] Benedict's *Rule* is in some ways the inheritor of this tradition. It represents, as they do, an attempt to set out basic structures for communal life. It does not embody the learned and literary monasticism of Lérins or of

Cassiodorus – there is no reference to a scriptorium in the *Rule*, although a library is mentioned and monks are expected to be able to read.[14] Rather, it often attempts to simplify and distil monastic teaching.

However, where Benedict's *Rule* diverges sharply from earlier western monastic rules – as opposed to Cassian's writings – is in its programmatic nature: it uses Cassian's discussion of the different types of monks as a platform for its author's views on the current state of monasticism.[15] Both this programmatic nature and sophistication of approach are most clearly thrown into relief in a comparison with the *Rule for Virgins* of Benedict's contemporary Cæsarius of Arles, an *ad hoc* affair compiled over a number of years and containing a recapitulation in which he feels compelled to restate his major points.

Benedict's *Rule* opens with a summons to the individual monk to listen and to obey – *obaudire* and *obedire*:

> Listen, o son, to the precepts of your master and incline the ear of your heart. Receive willingly and carry out effectively your loving father's advice, that by the labour of obedience you may return to him from whom you had departed by the sin of disobedience.[16]

This is followed by a clear statement of the relative merits of a number of monastic lifestyles based on Cassian's discussion of them in *Conference Eighteen*. Cassian wrote of cenobites, hermits, sarabaites and a fourth unnamed type of monk who becomes a hermit without adequate prior formation in the community. For Benedict, cenobites are the *fortissimum genus*, the strongest type of monk, because they have learned obedience by submitting to the discipline of an abbot and a rule: no one should venture on the eremitic life without a proper training in a community. Here, Benedict is in agreement with Cassian. But this firm statement of the need for cenobitic life at the beginning of a monastic rule appears to stem from an overriding concern about the breakdown of communal life. He has already stressed the need for obedience in his prologue. In Chapter One, he pares Cassian's two complaints about 'sarabaites' – their tendency to hoard money and their unwillingness to accept authority – down to the latter alone. These are monks who

> Not having been tested . . . by any rule or by the lessons of experience, are as soft and yielding as lead . . . They live in twos or threes or even singly, without their shepherd, in their own sheepfolds and not in the Lord's.[17]

For Cassian's fourth, unnamed type of bad monk, Benedict substitutes the 'gyrovagues', chronically disobedient and, in the monastic sense, unstable, wandering about from monastery to monastery, and province to province, effectively outside any authority and discipline. 'The miserable conduct of all these people,' he observes icily, 'is better passed over in silence than spoken about.' It is clear that he wished to characterize instability and lack of discipline as the major monastic evils of his time.

How are stability and discipline to be achieved? In his prologue Benedict has already stressed several times the importance of good works as well as faith,[18] but it is a measure of the limited nature of his initial expectations of his recruits that part of Chapter Four's list of 'Tools of Good Works' is a list of virtues which could often be applied to Christians in general. While it opens with Basil's favourite monastic injunction to love God and neighbour, this is followed by prohibitions against stealing, murder and adultery. Benedict carefully presents the monastic life in the most homely of terms as a 'spiritual craft' which must be be worked at day and night and of the monastery as a 'workshop' where that craft is practised. He reminds the monk that the Divinity watches over all his actions. He is

> To fear the Day of Judgement.
> To dread hell.
> To desire eternal love with all spiritual longing.
> To keep death daily before one's eyes.
> To keep constant guard over the actions of one's life.
> To know for certain that God sees one everywhere.[19]

Benedict also refers to control of thoughts by confession:

> When evil thoughts come into one's heart, to dash them at once on the rock of Christ and to manifest them to one's spiritual father.[20]

The idea of confession of 'secret sins' of thought to a spiritual father emerges again in the course of the *Rule*: Benedict's monastery is one in the tradition of Cassian where no impure thought should go undetected. But at the same time Benedict states in the Prologue to the *Rule* that he hopes to avoid instituting anything harsh or burdensome,[21] and in the final chapter he writes that it is a

> little rule for beginners,[22]

claiming that he is aiming only at modest spiritual objectives:

> we may show that we have attained some degree of virtue and the rudiments of monastic life.[23]

The summit of perfection is to be found not in his own work but in the Bible, the writings of the fathers and the *Conferences* of the Fathers and the *Institutes* and their *Lives* and also the *Rule* of our holy father Basil: what else are they but tools of virtue for good-living and obedient monks?[24]

The Cardinal Virtues

The rule uses the term *conversatio*, not in its older sense, which was closely linked to *conversio* (conversion), but now to suggest the spiritual development, the entire life and conduct of the monks.[25] Benedict bases his idea of monastic life not just on the avoidance of sin, but on the cultivation of virtues appropriate to the communal life – obedience, silence and humility. He instructs monks to shape their own lives in community by constant practice of the three.

Benedict's version of the traditional monastic virtue of obedience is obedience 'without delay': monks must be prepared to obey their superior unhesitatingly, avoiding the indiscipline or 'murmuring' which monastic writers regarded as antipathetic to the spirit of monastic life.[26] A later chapter in the *Rule* reveals just how complete this obedience is to be, when it decrees that monks are to obey even impossible orders. Here Benedict appears to be close to Cassian whose *Institutes* decree that monks should attempt even the impossible. and who tells the story of the heroic obedience of John of Lycopolis. For an entire year, John walked several miles every day to water a dry stick planted in the ground at his apa's command – only to have his spiritual teacher finally tear it out of the soil when it refused to flower. Following both Basil's genuine writings and the pseudo-Basilian *Admonition to a Spiritual Son*, Benedict then allows the monk to explain to his superior the impossibility of the task, allowing the latter to judge whether or not to continue with the order. However, after this apparent relaxation of early monastic severity, Benedict once again subjects the monk to the will of the superior, ruling that if the latter repeats the order, the monk must attempt to carry it out, trusting in the help of God to be able to accomplish it.[27] Joined to obedience are Benedict's emphases on silence (Chapter Six) and humility (Chapter Seven). The role of the monk is to be silent and to learn from his superior:

> For it becometh the master to speak and to teach; but it befits the disciple to be silent and to listen.[28]

Rule, Abbot and Prior

As well as demanding complete obedience from the monk, Benedict also sees the need for firm government within the monastery. The supreme authority in the community is the *Rule* itself:

> In all things therefore let all follow the *Rule* as a master, nor let anyone
> rashly depart from it . . . the abbot himself . . . should do all things in the fear
> of God and in observance of the Rule . . .[29]

Within these constraints, power is almost entirely concentrated in the
abbot's hands. Early western monastic rules had not found it necessary to
describe and underline his authority so clearly: even the *Regula Orientalis*
did so in a much briefer and less sophisticated fashion. Benedict, however,
devotes two chapters to his position, one at the beginning of the *Rule*,
the other towards the end as if he realized that he had to clarify his powers
and duties even further, describing his role as that of father and teacher
and making him responsible to God on the Day of Judgement for
all the souls in his care.[30] The *Rule for Virgins* of Benedict's contemporary Cæsarius of Arles had followed Augustine in vacillating between
statements of the abbess's authority and pleas for cooperation with her
and her subordinates, while at the same time maintaining Augustine's
potentially disruptive social distinctions among the nuns. Cæsarius wrote
as a bishop and must have believed that he would step in – within the
limits set by the rule, which together with his will, aimed to prevent
future bishops from destroying his creation – if there was any real threat
to the abbess or the good running of the convent. Benedict, on the other
hand, inserts in his *Rule* a full description of the abbot's authority and
powers, substituting an explicit link between his person and that of Christ
for any unwritten assumptions of personal charisma or well-intentioned
exhortations to cooperation:

> For he is believed to be the representative of Christ in the monastery, being
> called by a name of his according to the words of the Apostle: 'Ye have
> received a spirit of adoption of sons, whereby we cry "Abba-Father".'[31]

Reinforcement of the abbot's authority extends beyond statements of his
spiritual standing. Benedict's *Rule* creates a strictly hierarchical and
tightly-controlled community in which any possible threat to the abbot's
authority is, as far as possible, removed. So great are the powers which
Benedict gives to the abbot that he has to remind him to exercise them
responsibly:

> Therefore, when anyone has received the name of abbot, he ought to rule
> his disciples with a twofold teaching, displaying all goodness and holiness
> by deeds and words, but by deeds rather than words.
> Let him not make any distinction of persons in the monastery . . .[32]

He repeats such warnings in Chapter 64 of the *Rule* after the section
describing the election of the abbot. Such reminders apart, Benedict
allows the abbot, within the constraints of the *Rule*, great freedom of

action, most noticeably in his instructions concerning consultation with the community on matters of importance. That the issue of consultation is raised at all might suggest a more liberal and egalitarian spirit on Benedict's part than on that of either Cæsarius or of the author of the *Oriental Rule*,[33] but Benedict only mentions the process in order to subject it entirely to the abbot. While he may confer with the senior brethren on routine matters, he is only compelled to assemble and consult the entire community on major questions: Benedict states quite clearly that he need *not* accept the advice he is given. He describes the process of general consultation in such a way as to avoid any suggestion that a junior member of the community might possess wisdom or insight superior to that of the abbot. When this occurs, according to Benedict, it is a gift from God and should not be an occasion for opposition to the abbot's authority:

> Now the reason we have said that all should be called to counsel is that God often reveals what is better to the younger. Let the brethren give their advice with all deference and humility, nor venture to defend their opinions obstinately but let the decision depend rather on the abbot's judgement, so that when he has decided what is the better course, all may obey.[34]

Benedict similarly attempts to neutralize any threat to the abbot from his second-in-command, the prior. The author of the *Regula Orientalis* appears to have shared in a growing concern about the behaviour of this important official, as he inserted in his rule a long passage taken from Pachomius describing the qualities that a good prior should possess and the faults which he should avoid.[35] Benedict's fears focus more specifically on the possible threat posed by the existence of a prior to the abbot's own supremacy: he discusses the office of prior only in Chapter Sixty-five of the rule and expresses grave reservations about such an official:

> It frequently happens that the appointment of a prior gives rise to serious scandals in monasteries. For there are men puffed up by an evil spirit of pride who regard themselves as equal to the abbot, and arrogating to themselves tyrannical power, foster troubles and dissensions in the community.[36]

He concedes very reluctantly that an abbot might appoint a prior and even then lays down directions for his correction, removal and expulsion should he prove unsatisfactory. The abbot's power over the prior is to some extent increased by the fact that in a large community he may also bypass him by exercising day-to-day control of the community through two subordinate officials, the deans, each responsible for the conduct of ten monks: but if they over-reach themselves, they too may be removed.[37] Priests, who might be thought to represent another sort of authority, that of the secular clergy and bishop, are admitted only reluctantly and have to agree to submit to the full discipline of the rule, should they wish to remain as part of the community.[38]

Benedict's *Rule* lends the abbot more support than any of his predecessors – and many of his successors. Such reliance on written regulation reflects a lack of belief in the existence or effectiveness of personal charisma as a bond holding the community together under abbatial authority. While Pachomius' charisma had been so great that he could unhesitatingly sit down beside a young monk who volunteered to teach him a better way to weave or plait without any thought of losing face, Benedict underlines heavily the teaching that a younger brother's good advice is an occasional gift from God which is in no way detrimental to abbatial authority. This concentration on the person and powers of the abbot leads naturally to a fear of the prior absent in Benedict's contemporaries – and indeed most of his successors (the exception being the *Rule of the Master*, which avoids appointing one altogether). The extent of Benedict's emphasis on such questions suggests strongly that he writes from personal experience and was acutely conscious of the absence of strong support for the leader of the community in earlier rules.

The Bonds of Community

The *Rule* often emphasizes the cultivation of individual virtues and *conversatio* rather than the bonds which hold the community together. Benedict does not take as the basis of his monks' life in community either the description of the Jerusalem community used by both Augustine and Basil: this is only referred to in Chapters Thirty-three and Thirty-four when he discusses whether a monk may have any property of his own or not. (The Basilian injunction to love of God and neighbour only makes its way into his text at the head of chapter four's list of 'Good Works'.) Throughout the bulk of the rule, Benedict's view of community relations emerges as a predominantly vertical one. Monks are to obey each other – not just when carrying out the orders of the abbot or his officials – but in all other matters where juniors are to obey their seniors

in all love and diligence.[39]

But in the following chapter – the penultimate in the rule – it is possible to see a recognition of the important fraternal bonds of mutual charity and love which should hold any community together:

Let them practise fraternal charity with a pure love.[40]

The Members of the Community

After the abbot and prior, the most important official in the monastery is the cellarer who is 'in charge of everything' – care of the sick, of children, of guests, of the poor and of the monks' allowance of food; in a large community he may have assistants.[41] Benedict also allows the abbot to appoint monks to look after the monastery's tools, clothing and other property.[42] One of the closing chapters of the *Rule* is devoted to the porters or door-keepers, who control relations between the monastery and the outside world: the chief porter is to be an elderly and trustworthy monk.[43]

Benedict also tackles the general question of seniority. Here at first he appears to follow well-established practice. In the fourth century, Jerome had described the Pachomian monastic tradition in which the order in which the monks walked, sat, intoned psalms, were served food at table and took communion was based on the date of entrance to the community. This is also Benedict's criterion of seniority. But once again, the powers of the abbot could cut through this entire structure to promote worthy individuals, demote the unworthy and admit those already consecrated as monks to whatever place in the hierarchy he deemed appropriate.[44] Benedict also considers the threat posed to the authority of the abbot and other officials by monks who are consecrated priests. Writing in a period before it became customary for a high proportion of monks to take priestly orders, Benedict simply comments that should the abbot desire to appoint a priest or deacon, he should have a suitable monk ordained, though he is concerned that a person who has been ordained may therefore consider himself superior to others:

> Let the one who is ordained be aware of self-exaltation or pride; and let him not do anything other than what is commanded him by the abbot knowing that he is so much the more subject to the discipline of the rule... Let him always keep the place which he received on entering the monastery, except in his duties at the altar or in case the choice of the community and the will of the abbot should promote him for the worthiness of his life...[45]

Children, the elderly, the sick (who are allowed baths and meat), and craftsmen are all dealt with as separate groups in the monastery at different points in the *Rule*.[46] Those who are able to practise crafts are allowed to do so provided they undertake them 'in all humility'.[47] Juniors are to respect seniors and seniors to love juniors.[48] But Benedict, though allowing the very young and the old to eat before the set times for meals, takes a stern attitude towards boys in general who are

> to be kept under discipline at all times and by everyone.[49]

Admission

Any adult wishing to join the community has his seriousness of purpose tested and obstacles placed in his way. He undergoes a whole year's probation and has the entire *Rule* read to him on no less than three occasions during this period so that he has a complete understanding of what he is undertaking. Only after the year's probation, during which he is lodged in a special novices' house under the watchful eye of a senior monk, is he allowed to swear *stabilitas* (stability), *conversatio morum* (proper monastic conduct) and *oboedientia* (obedience) and to place on the altar his petition for admission to the community, while reciting the verse '*Suscipe me*', which is solemnly repeated three times by the whole community. His clothes are taken from him and replaced by the monastic habit. If he possesses any property he may either give it beforehand to the poor or make it over to the monastery by formal donation, retaining nothing for himself. From then on, warns Benedict, he will not have control even over his own body. His petition is kept by the monastery – along with the monk's secular clothes, which are returned to him if he is for any reason expelled from the house.[50]

While Benedict is scrupulous in ensuring that adults enter the community with a full understanding of what they are committing themselves to, his attitude to children 'offered' by their parents is very different.[51] Benedict's instructions for the reception of children into the monastic community are inspired by Basil, but are much more precise. While Basil merely stipulated that children should be handed over to the community in the presence of witnesses, Benedict describes a formal ceremony of oblation in which the child's hand and a petition of acceptance are wrapped in the altar cloth in front of witnesses. Like Basil, he does not specify a minimum age for admission and he writes of very young boys being offered to the community by their parents. In Benedict's eyes such children have no rights and no loophole is to be left open whereby they might be able to leave the community on coming of age. Well-to-do parents are to promise in the petition that they will never tempt their son to leave the monastery by leaving him any property; they may, however, donate property to the monastery 'for their advantage' through a deed of gift, reserving the income to themselves if they wish. This is the strictest and most final version of oblation yet devised, possibly inspired by experience of runaways, with the child at the centre of the ceremony a completely passive figure. Basil had allowed the child the opportunity, on reaching maturity, to follow his own will and leave the house; Cæsarius of Arles had no successful solution to the problem of nuns who might leave the community when they came of age and inherited. Benedict's legislation is much more successful at preserving the stability of the community: no one technically owns property or has the possibility of any future access to it and he thus avoids social division or the temptation to quit monastic life to take up an inheritance. The whole schema may have been too radical even for the late sixth and seventh centuries. None of the rules of that later period, which were to a large extent based on Benedict's, describe his ritual of oblation or even anything comparable – though we know that the practice of offering children to the religious life continued. And even with the adoption of the Benedictine *Rule* in the Carolingian Empire in the early ninth century, the reforming council of 817 decreed that the ceremony of oblation was to be followed by confirmation when the oblate had reached the age of understanding.[52] Benedict's measures for the immediate and final acceptance of children contrast with the caution which he displays when it comes to adult postulants. But by the two very different sets of instructions he hopes to achieve the same thing: that once admitted to his community, an individual only leaves it by death or expulsion.

Discipline

Benedict maintains the abbot's authority and discipline within the monastery by forbidding individual monks to speak out for each other and by a total denial of the individual will. As well as prescribing obedience, silence and humility at the beginning of his *Rule*, he lays down carefully thought-out disciplinary procedures in which the level of punishment is determined by the level of the monk's maturity and understanding.[53] Boys and adolescents are punished by fasts and beatings. An adult found to be 'obstinate, disobedient, proud, murmuring or habitually transgressing the holy *Rule*' is to be admonished twice in private by seniors. Then if he refuses to amend, his punishment becomes public: he is banned first from eating with the community and then from going into church with them. Obstinate refusal to amend may incur beating or expulsion from the community. The latter is a last resort: the abbot and community are to pray for the offender to repent before his actual expulsion and Benedict allows an expelled monk to repent and return to the community – where he is automatically reduced to the most junior rank – not once but three times, before he is banished forever. Benedict's approach, in which he compares the role of the abbot to that of a doctor, is ultimately inspired by Basil who thought that the superior should first attempt to cure the 'infirmity' of disobedience first by private admonitions, then public warnings and 'every method of exhortations'. Benedict knew more than just Rufinus' translation of an early version of Basil's *Longer* and *Shorter Rules*: his view that the abbot, like a doctor, should use all possible remedies on an erring and recalcitrant monk and only finally cut him off – 'amputate' – him from the community (on the basis of I Corinthians 1:23) clearly finds its general basis in the medical imagery which Basil uses in relation to sin and a closer parallel in *Longer Rule* 47: there, quoting the same Biblical text, Basil determines that a recalcitrant brother is as a last resort to be expelled from the community. Finally, Basil advocates that the unrepentant sinner be

> as a corrupted and utterly useless member cut away from the body after the practice of doctors.[54]

Benedict counsels the

> medicine of the Holy Scriptures and last of all the cautery of excommunication . . .

> But if he be not healed even in this way, then let the abbot use the knife of amputation.[55]

The use of expulsion as the ultimate sanction goes back to earlier monastic writings – Augustine and Cassian as well as Basil – but Benedict, characteristically, now places it in an elaborate and thorough set of disciplinary procedures.

The Monastery and the Outside World

Benedict takes care to ensure that the inhabitants of the monastery are cut off from the outside world as far as possible. This trend is also visible in the *Rule of Paul and Stephen*, an Italian rule of a slightly later date,[56] but Benedict devotes a great deal of attention to the topic and appoints not only a doorkeeper but an assistant to control contacts with the exterior. He allows his abbot the prerogative of dining apart from the monks with any guests or pilgrims who might arrive at the monastery gates. While he states that Christ himself is received in the monastery when the guest arrives he claims, at the same time, that he does not want the monks' routine to be disturbed by their arrival at all hours of day and night. This leads to a degree of segregation which effectively (and conveniently) leaves the abbot in control of all contact with outsiders: he has a special kitchen set aside for himself and visitors, with two brothers who serve there for a whole year; and there is also a special lodging for guests. Only the abbot may speak freely with visitors: a monk addressed by guests may not speak without his permission. All such measures seek not only to maintain the independence of the community but also to reinforce the abbot's power and the discipline of the monks.[57] Benedict recommends that the store house, a bakehouse, a garden and a mill, all places where ordinary monks might perform a variety of everyday tasks, are placed within a monastic enclosure wherever possible,

> so that the monks may not be compelled to wander outside it, for that is not expedient for their souls.[58]

Benedict also attempts to limit episcopal interference in the affairs of the community. When it comes to providing the eucharist for the monks, Benedict's preferred solution is that the abbot himself should choose one of his own monks and have him ordained priest.[59] The *Rule* accords with some aspects of Justinian's Novel 123, 34 of 546 in its instructions for the election of the abbot who may be chosen by the 'better part' of the community.[60] Only if the community's choice proves to be an unwise one is the bishop – together with the abbots of the diocese or even its laity – empowered to replace the unworthy choice with a 'worthy steward'.[61] This is the only occasion on which Benedict positively invites outside interference in the affairs of the monastery. While monks may sometimes be sent out on business, contacts with the outside world appear to be very carefully regulated: they are not allowed to discuss what they have seen and heard while away from the community under threat of punishment.

Work and Resources

The rule appears to follow the traditional monastic teaching which regards manual work principally as a means of avoiding idleness, the 'enemy of the soul'. However, its economic importance emerges when Benedict even modifies the timetable of the offices to accommodate it. Monks are to work in winter from the office of Terce (at the third hour) until Nones (at the ninth) and in summer early in the morning and later in the afternoon, so that when the day is at its hottest, they are able to take a siesta or read. Thus Terce is said at the second hour in winter and the fourth in summer and monks who are working far from the church are excused attendance at the offices. Benedict's priorities suggest that he thought the agricultural work of monks might well be crucial to the monastery's survival:

> if the circumstances of the place or their poverty require them to gather the harvest themselves, let them not be discontented; for then are they truly monks when they live by the labour of their hands like our fathers and the apostles. Yet let all things be done in moderation on account of the faint-hearted.[62]

Other monastic rules composed around the same era – the Italian *Rule of Paul and Stephen* and the French *Rule of Tarn* – also indicate that the monks are involved in agriculture, as opposed to gardening and domestic tasks:[63] such instructions suggest that all three rules were composed for monasteries with comparatively limited resources where lay labourers were not necessarily available to work the land as they were at Vivarium. Benedict's instructions on the reception of child oblates reveal that he expects substantial bequests for their upkeep from their parents.

Benedict also envisages within the monastic enclosure the existence of workshops producing goods made by monks who had mastered crafts. He allows artisans to work at their craft provided they do so 'in all humility' and also provided that the monastery charges a little less for their wares than laymen would ask. Once again he stops short of further explanations, so we can only speculate as to what these goods were (possibly the metalwork, carpentry or shoes that Basil recommends monasteries produce) or how they were sold by the monks who managed this business. Benedict doubtless intended only that his monks make enough to help support their own basic requirements of food and clothing. The age of great monastic estates had not yet arrived and there is no sense here of the further evolution of a corporate monastic identity: the abbot is responsible for all tools and goods belonging to the house.[64]

Diet

In conformity with the monastic tradition originating with the Pachomian communities of Egypt, the monks take turns at another kind of work, the preparation and serving of food.[65] Benedict's directions for the diet of the monks allow them two cooked dishes at every meal and a third of fruit or young vegetables if available.[66] Each monk is allowed a pound of bread a day and a *hemina* of wine, probably about three-quarters of a litre of wine, although the use of alcohol is conceded only reluctantly:

> We do indeed read that wine is no drink for monks; but since nowadays monks cannot be persuaded of this, let us at least agree upon this and drink temperately...But when the circumstances of the place are such that the aforesaid measure cannot be had, but much less or even none at all, then let the monks who dwell there bless God, and not murmur.[67]

The *Rule* nevertheless leaves the abbot free to allow more wine or food should circumstances require, for instance at harvest-time, although they should not eat too much or drink to satiety. The sick 'who are very weak' are allowed to eat meat and the diet of the youngest boys is to be less than that of their elders.[68]

Reading

As well as regulating the monks' diet and the timing of their meals, the *Rule* also insists – like other rules – that a part of the day is spent in reading. In winter, a time early in the day is set apart for this, whereas in the heat of summer, the monks may read in the middle of the day. During Lent the monks read (under supervision) in the morning until the third hour of the day, drawing codices from the library; and after supper on days when two meals are served or after Vespers on fast days, works which contain a distillation of the highest spiritual values, such as Cassian's *Conferences* or the *Lives of the Fathers* are read to them.[69]

The *Rule* and its Background

Internal evidence suggests that the *Rule* was produced in 546 or slightly later, perhaps even after 554:[70] thus it was created towards the end of, or just after, the catastrophic Justinianic reconquest of Italy. Many of the major engagements of this war were sieges, conducted far away from Benedict's monastery at Monte Cassino, but in the latter stages of the war, East Roman, Gothic and Frankish troops all swept through Campania.[71] It is tempting to conclude that in a period of dislocation caused by war, Benedict may have seen normal disciplinary problems exacerbated in some monasteries, with vagabond monks abandoning their communities and wandering across the countryside. He might therefore have felt impelled to create a rule which would reinforce the monastic ideals of stability and discipline. But this may not be a legitimate reading of the text. The difficulties in assessing the extent of the possible influence of the war on Benedict are illustrated by the debate over his knowledge and application of Justinianic law relating to monasteries. Some of the *Rule*'s provisions appear to coincide with Justinian's laws regarding monasteries: but if there is an application of Justinianic law, it is a patchy one. This is held by some commentators to reflect the difficulties of communication with the eastern capital due to the disruption of war. However, another interpretation suggests that the resemblances stem from the fact that both Justinian and Benedict were inheritors of the same tradition.[72] It may, similarly, be more helpful to regard Benedict's general outlook as his response, in the light of his own monastic experiences, to the cenobitic tradition rather than to the prevailing social conditions.

Whatever the circumstances of its genesis, the *Rule* represents a solution to the problems of monastic instability and disobedience, reinforcing the bonds of community life by a strengthening of the powers of the abbot, an insistence on absolute obedience and a severing, as far as possible, of contacts with the secular world. The thoroughness with which Benedict executed his project created the most comprehensive monastic rule to emerge from the West. The *Rule of Tarn*, the *Rule of Ferreol* and the *Rule of Paul and Stephen*, composed in south-east Gaul and Italy and probably of slightly later date, are patchwork affairs showing heavy dependence on Basil, Cassian and Augustine or on Cæsarius' work: none of these rules is as comprehensive or as well organized as Benedict's.[73] Many features of the *Rule* would recommend it, either in part or as a whole, to future users. It focused on the person and powers of the abbot and provided ample support for his authority. It was designed for rural monasteries – and from the seventh century until the thirteenth, the vast majority of monasteries would be founded in the countryside. The *Rule's* combination of theoretical simplicity with practical detail would guarantee its survival and use for centuries to come. Excerpted and adapted in the so-called 'mixed rules' of the seventh century and promoted in its entirety by the Carolingian dynasty in the eighth- and ninth-century Empire, Benedict's work would eventually become the most widely-used rule in the medieval West.

Benedict and the Master

Although Benedict's *Rule* demonstrates a wide knowledge of monastic and ascetic writings, from the 1930s onwards it came to be viewed by many as a derivative of the *Rule of the Master* – a work supposedly composed in the 520s–30s.[74] For centuries, it had been assumed that this work was a later adaptation of Benedict's *Rule*, but gradually the idea developed that the reverse was true and that Benedict had made extensive use of the anonymous Master's work, taking from it many of his most important ideas and a good deal of his wording. It was argued that *Rule of the Master* was composed in southern Italy, where Benedict, the founder of Monte Cassino, would have had easy access to it. However, the *Rule of the Master* contains a liturgy where the content of the night office is modulated to take into account a very noticeable variation between the length of winter and summer nights. I have previously suggested that this alone provides a substantial clue to the very different geographical backgrounds of the two rules and that this combines with other evidence to indicate that the *Rule of the Master* is a product of a more northerly region and a later stage of monastic development, when Irish monks had arrived on the continent and settled at Bobbio in Liguria (see pp. 182–4 below). As a whole, the Master's *Rule*, approximately four times the length of Benedict's, is a fascinating but often digressive adaptation of Benedict's for a single monastery, compiled by an adapter who clearly saw the value of detailed instruction and delighted in elaboration.

It does not appear to perceive or share the concerns about the general state of monastic life which motivated Benedict to create his monastic programme: instead, it modifies Benedict's opening appeal to hear and obey, instead inserting a commentary on the Lord's Prayer. The gyrovagues, a source of major concern to Benedict as a symptom of the monastic instability which he seeks to resist, are reduced to the status of troublesome and greedy monastic visitors, who perform prodigies of gourmandizing before departing to eat, drink and sleep the day away at the next monastery.[75]

The Benedictine Liturgy

Many unresolved questions still surround the Benedictine *Rule*. It is possible that Benedict extended the text after it was first written: as it has come down to us, the last seven chapters, which deal largely with questions of discipline, obedience and relations between monks, look as if they may have been additions to an original text.[76] As it stands, it appears to be addressed to more than one monastery – but were these the dozen or so houses in southern Italy traditionally associated with Benedict (see below), for which no certain evidence exists, or for houses in very different geographical locations as its instructions on clothing and climate suggest?[77] The earliest surviving manuscript of the *Rule* comes from eighth-century England, so it is not impossible that the text was added to.[78] In addition, questions might be raised about the liturgical instructions of the *Rule* (Chapters Eight to Eighteen) which appear to be based on the liturgy of the major public churches of Rome. In the late fifth or perhaps the early sixth century the Roman basilicas had abandoned their traditional psalmody (the *ordo romanus vetus*), which had been based on the same principle as that of the monasteries. Now they began to sing the psalter over the course of a week (the *psalterium per hebdomadam*) and certain psalms were allocated to certain offices: for example, Psalms 4, 90 and 133 were always recited at the office of Compline.[79] Chapter Eighteen of the *Rule* produces a variant on this system assigning various psalms to individual offices: while conceding that the actual disposition of the psalms may be altered by a successor, it is careful to specify that the entire psalter must be recited in a week because

> we read that our holy fathers fulfilled in a single day what I pray that we lukewarm monks may perform in a whole week.[80]

Although even the more strictly contemplative monastic tradition had absorbed some elements of the cathedral office – the office of Lauds, for instance – this liturgy is exceptional in its resemblance to the offices of the public churches served by monks. It incorporates hymns and readings, like those of Cæsarius and Aurelian of Arles, as well as prescribing the office of Prime on a daily basis. However neither Cæsarius nor Aurelian nor other, later, monastic rules go as far as the Roman basilicas and the Benedictine *Rule* in tampering with the traditional monastic idea of the *psalterium currens*. All this is at odds with the picture of monastic life given in the other sections of the *Rule* which depict a rural monastery or monasteries in which contacts with the outside world are kept to a minimum. Why should this be coupled with the intercessory liturgical style typical of the public basilicas of Rome? There are a number of possible solutions to this problem. The first is that Benedict had once been a monk or abbot in one of the Roman basilical monasteries and that he used the style of liturgy familiar to him. A second is that he had been taught this liturgy by someone associated with the Roman basilicas and was prepared to combine it with rural monastic life. A third possibility might be that the liturgical sections of the rule are not original and could have been inserted or substituted at a later date.

The Diffusion of the *Rule*

Questions also surround the routes by which the Benedictine *Rule* was first disseminated. From the days of the great monastic historian Mabillon in the late seventeenth century up to the 1950s, it was generally believed that it was taken to Rome by monks of Monte Cassino fleeing the Lombard invasion in the 570s; that these monks took refuge in the Lateran monastery in Rome; and that they passed on their knowledge of both Benedict and his *Rule* to Pope Gregory I (590–604) who not only followed the rule himself but also composed a spiritual biography of Benedict in Book II of his *Dialogues*, written in 593–4. Towards the end of Book II, the *Dialogues* not only praise Benedict, but recommend his *Rule*:

> With all the renown he gained by his numerous miracles, the holy man was no less outstanding for the wisdom of his teaching. He wrote a rule for monks that is remarkable for its discretion and its clarity of language. Anyone who wishes to know more about his life and character can discover in his rule exactly what he was like as an abbot, for his life could not have differed from his teaching.[81]

This recommendation was regarded as marking the beginning of the diffusion of the Benedictine *Rule* beyond Italy and Rome, as the mission to convert the English, headed by a monk of Gregory's own monastery, would naturally have carried it with them when they set off in 596.

Belief in the existence of links between Benedict and his *Rule* and Rome, Gregory and ultimately the world beyond Italy went unquestioned by scholars for centuries. But in 1957, this opinion was challenged for the first time. Ferrari demonstrated that the Benedictine *Rule* was not used in Rome in the sixth or seventh centuries (although he believed that Gregory the Great knew it),[82] while Hallinger questioned the extent to which Gregory's monastic ideas reflected the prescriptions of the *Rule* itself, pointing out numerous highly significant differences between the two over, for example, novitiate, postulants, the prior and the election of the abbot.[83] While Porcel quickly replied to Hallinger's contentions,[84] the ideas that the Benedictine *Rule* was used in Rome and that Pope Gregory the Great had ever lived by the *Rule*, had been effectively undermined. From this point onwards, Gregory was regarded not as someone who followed the *Rule*, but rather as someone who knew of Benedict and recommended his *Rule*, a disciple in the broadest sense of the word. This revised picture of Gregory fitted rather more comfortably with the very limited appearances made by the Benedictine *Rule* in the Pope's writings. Although the *Dialogues* recommend the *Rule*, of all Gregory's works, only his *Commentary on I Kings* contains any direct quotation from it. However, the connection between Gregory and Benedict has been further questioned recently by the revelation that the *Commentary on I Kings*, long attributed to Gregory, is the work of a twelfth-century Benedictine abbot of La Cava in southern Italy.[85] This leaves the *Dialogues*, with their spiritual biography of Benedict and their recommendation of the *Rule*, as the only remaining link between Benedict and Gregory.

This link is itself less than secure as the *Dialogues* themselves are a highly controversial and problematic text. Like the *Commentary on I Kings*, their authenticity has been questioned by a variety of scholars over several centuries. The late 1980s saw the publication of a two-volume work by Francis Clark which maintained that they had been composed in Rome in the 670s, on the basis of fragments of genuine Gregorian writings, some of which still survive, along with others of recognizably Gregorian style which must have been available in the papal archives, but are now lost.[86] Despite his production of much evidence to support its main contention that the *Dialogues* are not, as a whole, authentic, Clark's work has not found favour with a number of scholars who accept the traditional attribution to Gregory – although others have agreed with some or all of his conclusions or at least kept an open mind.[87]

The *Life of Benedict* in Book Two of the *Dialogues*

While archaeological evidence indicates the existence of a monastery on the summit of Monte Cassino, where the *Dialogues* testify that Benedict eventually settled,[88] the author of the most famous of all monastic rules still remains an enigma as an historical figure. The *Dialogues* suggest that Benedict first entered the religious life as a hermit, without any cenobitic training and it is not at all clear how he might have acquired the extensive knowledge of monastic literature and cenobitic practice which inform his *Rule* as a whole. The problem of explaining Benedict's liturgical instructions is not resolved, either, by the *Dialogues* as they make no explicit connection between Benedict and the Roman basilical monasteries, alluding only to a secular career as a student, before he left Rome, disgusted by his fellow-students' excesses.

The *Rule* as a whole indicates that Benedict's ideal is that of a rural monastery cut off as far as possible from society, in which visitors are only allowed to speak with the abbot, who also carefully controls all contacts with the exterior with the help of the porter, or doorkeeper, a key figure in the monastery's regime. Yet, surprisingly, the Benedict of the *Dialogues* emerges as a monastic leader with many contacts with the outside world In addition to the assertion that he is head of a congregation of monasteries in the region of Subiaco and in charge of a community established by a pious Christian at Terracina,[89] the *Dialogues* portray Benedict as an evangelist who uses the Subiaco house as a base for preaching in the surrounding countryside and Monte Cassino itself as a centre of conversion. He destroys a pagan temple on the summit of the mountain to create churches and converts the pagan peasants of the neighbourhood to Christianity.[90] The dedication of one of these churches to John the Baptist even suggests that it was used as a baptismal church. Benedict's spiritual development and activities are explicitly assimilated to those of the clergy.[91]

The figure of the monk as an evangelist also figures large in Book One of the *Dialogues*. There, the narrative of the career of another monastic leader, Equitius, contains an account of the way in which he is miraculously empowered to preach and teach in the province of Valeria, though not in holy orders. He becomes the object of clerical wrath and is reported to the pope for his activities – but the pope, who is never identified by name is then warned by God in a dream to leave the holy man alone.[92]

The *Dialogues'* portrayal of the monastic leader as evangelist is at variance with the picture of Italian monasticism which can be constructed from other evidence of the period.[93] When monks and monasteries were involved with evangelization this was generally in areas on the fringes of Christendom, where dioceses were being established or extended and in association with the episcopate. Pockets of paganism still existed in sixth-century Italy, but it was the business of the Italian bishops and parochial clergy to deal with them[94] and pope Vigilius (537–555), when Benedict was writing his *Rule*, forbade two deacons to preach without episcopal permission.[95] Equitius' and Benedict's supposed evangelizing activities have left no trace in the historical record and the tales in which they are enshrined have been characterized in the recent and authoritative work on monastic Italy as 'exhortatory'.[96] All this might lead to the conclusion that the *Dialogues* are indeed inauthentic, neither an accurate portrait of the composer of the Benedictine *Rule* nor a genuine work of Gregory the Great. However, another explanation for the nature of the portraits of Benedict and Equitius may be that Gregory was not reporting accurately on their careers exactly as they had been narrated to him, but elaborating on them to fashion a blueprint for a new, more active form of monasticism.

Gregory the Great (590–604) and the Active and Contemplative Lives

Gregory was the first monk to become pope. He was born around 540 in to a wealthy, pious and aristocratic family, one of the most distinguished left in Rome after the wars of reconquest. His great-great-grandfather had been Pope Felix III and he was also related to Pope Agapetus. He had been prefect of the city of Rome for the year of 573, in charge of its aqueducts, grain supplies and its finance, invested with supreme civil power over the city and the surrounding area. In 574–5, a year or so year after occupying this high office, Gregory converted to the monastic life: he sold his patrimony in Sicily, founding no less than six monasteries there and turned his father's palatial house, on the Cælian Hill, into a monastery dedicated to St Andrew – next to the library which Cassiodorus had intended to be the centre of his Christian university in Rome. But he was not permitted to remain in his monastery for long. About five years after he retired from public life, the pope made him one of the deacons of Rome, a group of clergymen entrusted with practical responsibilities for the Christian community of the city and in *c.* 579 he was sent as *apocrisarius* to Constantinople, entrusted with a mission to the Emperor to ask for help in the face of a Lombard invasion of Italy and the inactivity of the imperial Exarch at Ravenna. In Constantinople Gregory – who never learned much Greek – lived in a monastic group with some of his monks from St Andrew's and made a number of clerical friends including the former patriarch Anastasius of Antioch, and the Spanish bishop Leander of Seville. Leander, along with Gregory's own monks, would later encourage him to set down his set of expositions on the Book of Job, the *Magna Moralia*, which he had originally delivered in Constantinople. In 585 or 586, he returned to Rome and spent the next few years in the quiet of his monastery occupied in study, meditation and prayer. However, in 590 Pope Pelagius II died in one of the outbreaks of plague which had devastated Italy since the 540s and the clergy, nobles and people turned to Gregory, whose combination of personal sanctity with the administrative experience which he had gained as city prefect and *apocrisarius* made him the natural choice for office. Unwilling once again to be wrenched from his monastery, he resisted appointment – but his letter to the emperor, asking him to refuse to accept the election, was intercepted by his own brother Palatinus and his elevation was confirmed.[97]

Although Gregory would frequently plead helplessness and bewail the manner in which he had been wrenched from contemplation, he brought – despite frequent illness – considerable energy to his role as pope. When Rome was struck by famine, he organized supplies of food for the starving population. He became, in effect, a civil as well as religious leader, in 593 holding off by bribery the Lombard threat to the city. Should Gregory's protestations at his removal from monastic contemplation therefore be regarded less than seriously, on a par with the rhetoric of inarticulacy and helplessness which he frequently deployed to strengthen his own position? Did he, in fact, come to believe that monks, with their superior spiritual training, might even replace clerics in important positions at the head of the church as he himself had done?

In Gregory's career, the tensions between monastic life and involvement in society as a leader of the church are all too apparent. In discussing the conflict between the two, which he does on many occasions, he opposes the concept of the 'contemplative' life of the monastery to the 'active' life of pastoral involvement.

> Under the pretence of being made a bishop [i.e. pope], I am brought back into the world; for I am now more in bondage than ever I was as a layman. I have lost the deep joy of my quiet and while I seem outwardly to have risen, I am inwardly falling down. Wherefore I grieve that I am driven daily from the face of my maker... I loved the beauty of the contemplative life... but by some judgement, I know not what, I have been wedded to... the active life.[98]

Gregory's use of the terms 'active' and 'contemplative' shows how understanding of them has evolved since Evagrius and Cassian. In his *Fourteenth Conference*, Cassian had declared that the 'spiritual knowledge' attained through preparation (*praktike*) would bring 'a learning that is not barren and worthless, but one that is alive and fruitful'.[99] This implied that 'spiritual knowledge' would bring with it the ability – even the obligation – to teach. While this was an obligation to teach *within* the monastery, the association between teaching and contemplation now brought the contemplative ideal within the grasp of the clergy[100] and this in turn began to shift the meaning of the 'active' life in a clerical context to encompass pastoral activity rather than ascetical preparation alone.

Even before his elevation, Gregory, as a monk who had also become a cleric and papal envoy, devoted much thought to the relationship between the active and contemplative lives and the great burden of pastoral care. His own situation led him to reason that those charged with this heavy burden were, in fact, strengthened by periods of retreat into the contemplative life. In the *Moralia* he wrote of the 'preachers' within the church, those who took on the office of leading and teaching, as being raised up by the contemplative life. Elsewhere in the *Moralia* holy men

> are sent and go forth as lightnings, when they come forth from the retirement of contemplation to the public life of employment.[101]

Gregory's view of the relationship between the active and contemplative lives has been characterized as a 'mixed' form of life, though he himself would never use this terminology and the expression may itself imply a greater degree of elision between the two types of existence than he ever envisaged.[102] Rather, Gregory saw an alternation between the two forms. In his *Homilies on Ezechiel*, composed in 592–3, he compares the active and contemplative lives to the Biblical figures of Rachel and Leah: Rachel, the contemplative life, is more beautiful; but Leah, the active life, though less beautiful, is more fruitful. There are moments when:

> the soul often reverts profitably from the contemplative life to the active, so that the contemplative life having kindled the mind, the active life might be the more perfectly led.[103]

To what extent, then, did Gregory envisage a church led by those who, like himself, had brought a monastic background and training into active life and who were fitted by their contemplative training to become what he called 'preachers'? Peter, formerly a monk of his own monastery, was sent as papal rector to Sicily; Cyriacus, the 'father of many monasteries' was despatched to act as joint leader of the mission to the pagan Barbaricini in Sardinia and was also sent as envoy to the Franks.[104] Augustine, prior of Gregory's own monastery of St Andrew's in Rome, was made head of a mission to England. Was Gregory attempting to circumvent their power by making monks literally into 'preachers' and were Benedict and Equitius models for this grand design for a new monasticism?

The reality is both more subtle and more prosaic. Gregory's own construction of the 'preacher' did not involve just the physical act of preaching. Instead it denoted a person who was a leader in the church by virtue of spiritual power. The spiritual power of Peter, Cyriacus and Augustine, in Gregory's view, derived from their contemplative train-ing.[105] But these were special assignments and, whatever he felt about the shortcomings of the Roman clergy, Gregory did not attempt to alter the fundamental relationship between monks and clerics. When, in the 590s, he took the running of the Roman basilica of San Pancrazio in *via Aurelia* away from clerics and put it in the hands of the monks who sang the office there, Gregory wrote to its abbot Maurus that the cure of souls 'clearly belongs to the priestly offices' and instructed him to appoint a *peregrinus presbiter* to administer the eucharist.[106] For him the monastery was still the place of contemplation and liturgical intercession and had to be protected as such. In a letter of 594 to bishop John of Ravenna he insisted that no one

> can serve as a clerk and persist under order in the monastic rule, nor can he be bound by the restraint of the monastery who is forced to remain in the daily service of the church... The duties of each office separately are so weighty, that no-one can rightly discharge them. It is very improper that one man should be considered fit to discharge the duties of both.[107]

He expressed himself in similar vein on a number of occasions and while he entrusted a few trusted monks with special duties, he never broke with the conventional structures of the church to do so. Although overseen by Cyriacus, the mission to the Barbaricini was also headed by a bishop, while the defunct see of Fausiana was revived as a mission-base.[108] Augustine was consecrated bishop at an early stage in the mission and the forty monks who set out with him from Rome were accompanied by Frankish clerics who would be able to communicate more easily with the English; once the mission met with some success a cathedral and a basilical monastery were established at Canterbury.[109] Gregory himself envisaged the evangelization of a new English church proceeding not from a series of monastic centres, as in the *Dialogues'* account of Benedict's activities, but from twenty-six conventional dioceses established in Roman cities.[110] Even if he believed in the spiri-tual superiority of contemplatives like himself in an active context, it was not Gregory's intention, as older interpretations of his actions might suggest, to clericalize monastic life. If anything, he hoped to achieve the reverse by making some of his clergy live a monastic lifestyle which he hoped would imbue them with contemplative virtue.[111] This was not an original idea: in the early sixth century, the African Augustinian writer Julianus Pomerius[112] promoted the contemplative ideal for clergy and both Fulgentius of Ruspe and Cæsarius of Arles, bishops who had for-merly been monks, had imposed a monastic lifestyle on some of their clergy.

Italian Monasticism at the End of the Sixth Century

With the advantage of hindsight, the most important monastic development in sixth-century Italy is the composition of the comprehensive and
authoritarian Benedictine *Rule* which would eventually become the paramount monastic rule of the early medieval West. Unfortunately, we have
no way of knowing exactly how far its use had spread in the forty or so
years after Benedict's death. Monte Cassino is believed to have been
destroyed in the 570s or 80s by the Lombard invasions, but the traditional belief that the *Rule* was carried to Rome by fleeing monks is belied
by the fact that it was not used there in either the sixth or the seventh
century. Instead, another route of diffusion suggests itself: its adaptation
in the *Rule of the Master* and use by the Frankish monasteries of Columbanus' congregation in the seventh century, suggest that the Benedictine
Rule had become known in northern Italy by the 630s and was transmitted from Bobbio to north-eastern Francia. The first monastic pope,
Gregory I, was not a Benedictine even in the broadest sense of the term:
instead, his authentic writings reveal the influence of highly traditional
monastic writings on his thought. Not only did he absorb the Cassianic
classification of the 'eight principal faults' and reshape them into the
Seven Deadly Sins, but his concept of the spiritual power which springs
from contemplation is a development of Cassian's view of contemplation
expressed in *Conference Fourteen*. Gregory's writings are also permeated
by the Gospel theme of love of God and one's neighbour, Basil's guiding
monastic principle, which Gregory characteristically applied in a wider
ecclesiastical framework.[113] In practical terms, Gregory found himself
confronted in the last years of the sixth century and the opening ones of
the seventh with a lengthy list of everyday problems – those of under-
endowment of monasteries, of episcopal interference and of admission,
probation and the appointment of priors.[114] What might possibly have
caught his attention as unusual in Roman monasticism at this point was
not the Benedictine *Rule* but the first influx of Greek monks, who would
settle in the city in increasing numbers in the seventh century.[115] As for
the disputed *Dialogues*, it appears increasingly likely that the first reliable
witnesses to the existence of the text as a whole date from the later seventh
century,[116] while its postulation in Book IV of a systematized process of
intercession for the release of the souls of the dead derives its basis from
the evolution of a tarriffed penitential system which had begun to develop
in Britain and Ireland and was virtually unknown on most of the continent
at this stage. The *Dialogues*' picture of monks as evangelists and of
monasteries which served as pastoral centres appears out of place in
sixth-century Italy, but is much more appropriate to another area and a
slightly later stage of monastic history.

7

Britain and Ireland

The Evolution of Monasticism in Roman and Celtic Britain

Christianity had been introduced to Britain during the Roman and continued to exist there in the sub-Roman period, after the official withdrawal of Roman troops in 410. Contacts continued between western Britain and other parts of the Roman Empire and Mediterranean world. Archaeology reveals the existence of trade between many areas of western Britain – Cornwall and Devon, south-west and north-west Wales, Man, the Solway area and Galloway – with Gaul, Spain and even North Africa, creating opportunities not only for the arrival of continental and eastern artefacts but also for the appearance of new ideas. These may also have been promoted by the church hierarchy which arrived from abroad to deal with perceived problems in the British church. Bishop Victricius of Rouen, an admirer of Martin of Tours and supporter of the ascetic movement, had visited Britain in the 390s, possibly to deal with some heresy or theological controversy. The so-called 'British heresy', Pelagianism, appears only to have been developed by the Irish or British lawyer Pelagius after he left the British Isles for the continent in 410: but it quickly spread to Britain and was considered to be such a threat by the Church that Bishops Germanus of Auxerre and Lupus of Troyes were despatched to Britain in 429 to deal with it.[1] Germanus and Lupus belonged to the circle of French bishops associated with Lérins and could have brought with them some of the monastic and ascetic ideas associated with that monastery. However, we do not know which areas were visited by the episcopal missions and Christianity in the south and east of the island began to be overwhelmed by the Anglo-Saxon invasions from the fifth century onwards.

There is evidence for a number of different types of monastery in fifth and early sixth-century Britain, mostly in those areas which had escaped the Saxon invasions of the south and east. Some of this evidence comes from Roman villas, the kind of gentleman's monastery found in Roman Gaul and Italy, where members of the upper classes turned their own houses into religious centres. Of these, Lullingstone in Kent (possibly as early as the late fourth century), Llandough and Llancarfen in Southern Wales are probably the best-known examples.[2] The later fifth and sixth centuries saw the growth of more organized asceticism – the closest continental parallels here may be the Jura monasteries. One such example is that of Llantwit Major in Glamorgan, the site of the monastery of St Illtud, a major monastic figure in fifth or sixth century Wales, which was itself built by the site of a Roman villa. Illtud himself might have been either the son of a sub-Roman landowner who retreated to lead an ascetic life on the margins of the family estate, just as Romanus and Lupicinus did in fifth-century Gaul, or a later Briton who built his monastery near the villa ruins. Both Illtud's foundation and Lann Docco, the monastery of Docco in northern Cornwall (probably an offshoot of a Welsh community) were clearly cenobitic monasteries. The former was of some importance – a *monasterium*, later described as *magnificum*, was combined with a *schola* where the future St Samson was sent to be educated probably about 490–500.[3] Samson himself was the son of an aristocrat from Demetia in Wales, a kingdom ruled by Christians of Irish origin: he later founded a cenobium somewhere in southern Cornwall on a site apparently granted to him by influential locals.[4] That smaller and possibly more austere monasteries, possibly organized along eremitical lines, were also created in south-west Britain is also illustrated by the *Life of Samson*: before leaving Wales for Cornwall and ultimately Celtic Brittany he had spent some time in a smaller monastery 'recently established' as an offshoot of Llantwit under a *presbyter* named Piro. This was Ynys Byr – the island of Piro, now identified as Caldey Island. Another island monastery was created on Lundy in the sixth century by Brychan, a Christian king of Demetia who retired there with a number of his followers.[5] The idea of retreat to a smaller contemplative centre – eremitic or not – had also appealed to Samson and his father before they ever left Wales when they found a small Roman fort near the Severn shore and lived within it for a period.

Even from the very little we know about these monasteries, it is possible to deduce that concepts of organized religious life inspired ultimately by eastern models had reached western Britain. Sub-roman Britain retained its version of Latin culture and Latin schools and works such as the *Life of Antony* and the writings of Cassian and Basil in translation could have been read and understood. The appearance of names with monastic association such as Macarius and possibly Amon (the name of Samson's father – Ammoun?) may even suggest a knowledge of other monastic literature such as the *History of the Monks in Egypt*. There seems not only to have been a differentiation between larger cenobitic monasteries and smaller ones located on islands – the far West's equivalent of the Egyptian desert as presented in the monastic literature – but also a consciousness of higher and lower standards, reflecting ascetic attempts, or lapses in them. Samson himself is credited with a more rigorous regime than some of his own monks; and when he visits the monastery of Docco, he is not admitted. The 'wisest' of the brethren, Uiniavus, is sent to turn him away, admitting that if Samson and his group are admitted their presence may cause discord because of the monastery's less strict standards.

Monachi peregrini

If there is much that recalls Egyptian or Roman monasticism to be found in the *Life of Samson*, it also contains the distinctively Celtic feature of the religious as *peregrinus*, literally 'pilgrim' but in reality occupying a status somewhere between that of hermit and pilgrim. In the tribal societies of Ireland and Wales, pilgrimage, with its withdrawal and detachment of the individual from the family group, came to represent one of the highest forms of penance and self-mortification.[6] Samson, who had become head of Illtud's community, was offered the opportunity to become a bishop – but, inspired by a divine vision, he, his father, now a cleric or monk, and a band of other clerics and retainers left Wales for Cornwall *c.* 530; ultimately Samson himself reached Brittany. As *peregrinus*, Samson ministered to apostates in Cornwall, recalling them to Christianity and confirming their baptisms. Such provision of pastoral care was entirely incidental to Samson's main purpose which was self-mortification and the desire to draw closer to God: but as a Christian religious he could not, in all conscience, ignore those who had lapsed from Christianity. There was no established episcopal hierarchy in Cornwall to minister to this group in the interior of the peninsula or to pagans and it is therefore not surprising that Samson became involved with pastoral matters. However, the *Life* suggests that pastoral activity was not his main goal and he refused the request of the reclaimed apostates to become their bishop. In his search for spiritual perfection, he moved on to found his monastery in southern Cornwall before his spiritual odyssey took him further afield to Brittany. There, he founded monasteries at Dol and, according to the *Life*, Pentale in Normandy and acted as bishop to the Bretons, using his monastery at Dol as his base. Although the evidence of the *Life* is not clear on this point, it appears that once again, Samson's pastoral activity was an offshoot of his status as *peregrinus* – although on this last occasion he appears finally to have become a bishop.

Samson's career shows the possible evolution of a monastic career and of monasteries on the fringes of organized Christianity. His monastic career began conventionally within a sub-Roman diocese, that of Bishop Dubricius, St Dyfrig, whose clergy would have been responsible for all pastoral care. Samson's status as a *peregrinus* led him into territory which had been evangelized but where there were no permanent ecclesiastical structures or hierarchy – it is not inconceivable that the original conversions had been carried out by earlier monastic *peregrini*, including Docco; and though Samson felt he had to do his duty by the lapsed Christians whom he found there, he did not stay to minister to them permanently, even though we are told that he had been ordained priest earlier in his career. It is just possible that he later used his monastery in southern Cornwall as a centre for conversion and baptism – but on the whole, given his continued wanderings, it seems more likely that he still regarded himself as a *peregrinus* until he arrived in Brittany and finally decided to assume pastoral responsibility as bishop. There, in an area technically part of the diocese of Rouen but in linguistic and religious terms outside the control of its bishops, he found that a monastery was a convenient centre from which to effect conversions. Similar features may be found in the late life of Paul Aurelian, another British monk who fetched up in Brittany and whose monastery became the centre of another northern Breton diocese, St Pol de Léon.[7]

While wandering *peregrini* might find themselves accepting the role of bishop and their monasteries serving as centres of conversion and baptism, officially-appointed bishops and missions to non-urbanized areas might use monasteries as bases for the same purpose. The evidence of inscribed stones in Galloway suggests the existence in the fifth century of an ecclesiastical organization, headed by Gallic priests or bishops. Where the original centre of this diocese (or dioceses) was is uncertain though its bishops and a sub-deacon are commemorated on stones at Kirkmadrine and Curghie in the Rhinns. It then seems to have shifted eastwards around the beginning of the sixth century to Whithorn and a church and monastery which Bede called *ad Candidam Casam* – 'at the White House'. Both this – a Latin version of the meaning of the original Celtic name for Ligugé, the monastery established by Hilary of Poiters and Martin of Tours – and, more plausibly, the dedication of the monastery to St Martin of Tours, once again suggest Gallic links. This may well be another case of a monastery set up on the edge of Christianized territory as a convenient centre for preaching and conversion. According to Bede, its founder Ninian conducted a mission to the 'southern Picts'; and while Ninian has usually been identified as a fifth-century figure, one recent suggestion is that Ninian may in fact be a misreading of the British name UUinniau. UUinniau was also a major figure in Irish monastic life in the sixth century, where he can be identified as either Finnian of Moville in

Bangor (near the north-eastern coast of Ulster and not far by sea from Whithorn) or Finnian of Clonard – or both.[8]

Christianity and Monasticism in Ireland

In the early seventh century the Irish monk Columbanus would describe himself in a letter to Pope Boniface as coming from 'the world's edge'.[9] Ireland, at the beginning of the fifth century, had never been part of the Roman Empire. Christianity and monasticism arrived in a non-urbanized and entirely rural society, divided into about one hundred and fifty petty kingdoms (*tuatha*, sing. *tuath*), each ruled by a king, who possessed much less land than any of the 'barbarian' kings on the continent. 'Overkings' might control three or four of the lesser kings (*rí tuaithe*) while the basic unit of social organization was the *derbfine* or four generation kin-group and land was owned by the kin-group rather than the individual. None of these rulers was Christian and Latin had never been the language of law or administration.[10]

Though non-Romanized, Ireland was not entirely isolated from Britain and the Continent or from Christian and monastic ideas. Contacts between Ireland and Britain and the continent made possible the gradual spread of both and the eventual transformation of Irish society from the fifth century onwards. It is true that trading links were originally not extensive and that the Irish mercenaries who served rulers in Britain would probably have returned home with only a limited store of new ideas and beliefs. More powerful vehicles for change are likely to have been provided by a series of migrations of Irish peoples into Britain – to Cornwall, north Wales and south-west Wales – which have left distinct traces in the archaeological record. The close cultural relations between Cornwall, and south-west Wales and southern Ireland are indicated by the ogham stones found in all these areas.[11] South-eastern Ireland, then, was potentially open to sub-Roman and perhaps even Christian influences from Britain.

The first bishop in Ireland of whom we know was Palladius, an aristocratic deacon of Auxerre, despatched by Pope Celestine to the 'Irish believing in Christ' (some of whom may have been Britons) in 431 AD.[12] Two years earlier, Celestine had sent Germanus, bishop of Auxerre on a mission to counter the growth of Pelagianism in Britain and appears to have been sufficiently concerned about its possible spread amongst Christians in Ireland to send out this second mission. Palladius' sphere of activity seems to have the south and east of the country, as place-names associated with the other churchmen sent with him and the existence of *domnach* place names (from the Latin *dominicum*, indicating a the presence of an early church), also confirm legendary accounts which state that he landed and worked in the south east of the islands.

Did Palladius – connected with Arles – introduce monasticism to Ireland? If he did, as guardian of anti-Pelagian orthodoxy he might not have brought the works of Cassian with him. The major problem in tracing the Palladian mission and its possible monastic offshoot is that evidence for Palladius has been overshadowed by and conflated with the activities of Patrick, the 'apostle of Ireland'.[13] Exactly when and where in the fifth century Patrick was active are still controversial questions. From his own writings we can gather that he was a Christian Briton. Captured in his youth by raiders and carried off to northern Ireland as a slave, he escaped after several years, later returning as a clerical missionary to spread the Christian faith. Although a saying attributed to Patrick refers to journeys in Gaul, Italy and the islands of the Tyrrhenian sea and though a much later life by Muirchu says that he visited Auxerre, such later accounts may be unreliable and may even have originated in descriptions of Palladius' career. His story as a whole is a very unusual one: in undertaking missionary activity amongst pagans, he was going beyond what most fifth-century churchmen would have considered to be their remit – especially as his story suggests the existence of a mission to Ireland independent of any Christianisation produced by settlement and kinship links.

Although Patrick is thought of as 'the apostle of Ireland' his main sphere of activity was in the north, in Ulster and Connacht, areas untouched by earlier Christian activities. Patrick's own *Testament* describes the very great difficulties which he faced and the ancient churches associated with his name are situated mainly in the north. It is also now recognized that the conversion of Ireland to Christianity was a gradual process and one about which we actually know very little. His *Testament*, however, suggests that he recruited both women and men of high status to the monastic life:

> and sons and daughters of Irish underkings are seen to be monks (*monachi*) and virgins of Christ.[14]

It is not clear whether the *monachi* were monks or clergy organized as formal communities or even ascetically-living converts to Christianity. Beyond the existence of a number of *domnach* (*dominicum*) place names, the Patrician mission seems to have left few surviving traces behind it. There is no clear evidence to suggest the development of monasteries endowed with land by Christian converts and their families and it may only have been after Patrick's lifetime that we see their emergence. On the other hand, while some scholars think that there are no monastic elements to be detected in his writings, others have found echoes of Augustine's *Confessions* and even of Basil's *Rule* in his words.

But even if Patrick did inspire some conversions to asceticism and monasticism, there may, in the fifth century, have been little further support for the monastic movement in the barely-Christianized area of Ulster and Connacht or even Palladian Leinster.

The patterns of monastic development in a country which was in the process of gradually accepting Christianity in the fifth and sixth centuries are not easy to trace. The southern third of Ireland contains a large number of monastic sites whose name is prefixed by words suggesting an eremitic origin such as *dísert*. Here, the original Christianizing influences may have come from links to western Britain, but while it is tempting to assume that these sites are of early origin it is usually impossible to tell how old such names are. The major cenobitic monasteries which had emerged by the seventh and eighth centuries are, by contrast, largely situated in the northern two-thirds of the island, including the areas originally covered by the Palladian and Patrician missions. While many details of monastic foundations from this period come from late and highly embroidered saints' lives, it nevertheless seems that the most important period for the establishment of such houses begins in the first half of the sixth century and that by about the 550s, a number of important monasteries had been created. Clonard was established by Finnian; Cluain moccu Noise (Clonmacnoise) by Ciarán (whose death from plague is recorded in 549); Clonfert and Birr by Brendan, the super-*peregrinus*, later credited with the remarkable voyage or *Navigatio* which took him as far as America. Ciarán and Brendan are both traditionally depicted as disciples of Finnian of Clonard; other famous Irish monastic leaders were Comgall of Bennchor (Bangor) and Coemgen (Kevin) of Glenn dá Locha (Glendalough). At Bangor, Comgall trained Columbanus, who as a *peregrinus* would take Irish-style monasticism to the continent of Europe in the 590s. Other houses and founders, including Achad Boe (Aghaboe) and Cork, are traditionally associated with a slightly later period. Iona, outside Ireland itself but within the orbit of the Northern Irish Dál Riata, was created at some point after the arrival of Colum Cille in 563.[15]

Contacts with Britain, an obvious source of ideas and literature, also played a part in the development of Irish monasticism. In a letter to Pope Gregory the Great written at the end of the sixth century, the monk Columbanus, who was educated at the monastery of Bangor not far from Moville, writes that he has read works by the British churchman Gildas and that he is familiar with a correspondence about wandering monks between Gildas and '*Uennianus auctor*' – UUinniau or Finnian of Clonard/Moville.[16] Fragments of the correspondence between Gildas and UUinniau survive and in the remains of Gildas' instructions on what to do with monks who leave their monastery to seek a stricter observance there are echoes of Augustine and possibly Basil.[17] The works of both Cassian and Basil as well as writings by Jerome were known in Ireland and could have reached the island *via* Britain or from the Rhône valley.[18] Exactly when knowledge of these works arrived in Ireland is not clear, although they were known and appreciated by the late sixth century. The *Amra*, a praise-poem composed on the death of Colum Cille, records that:

> He applied the judgements of Basil,
> who forbids acts of boasting by great hosts.
> He ran the course which runs past hatred to right action.
> The teacher wove the word.
> by his wisdom, he made the glosses clear.
> he fixed the psalms,
> he made known the books of Law,
> those books Cassian loved.
> He won battles with gluttony.

The *Amra*'s panegyric not only describes Colum Cille in terms which evokes the spiritual language of both Cassian and Basil:

> He was holy, he was chaste
> he was charitable, a famous stone in victory

but also alludes to the practice of confession to a spiritual adviser

> he was obedient. . .
> . . . he was a physician in every sage's heart. . . [19]

The Irish seem to have particularly cherished Cassian: his terms *praktike* and *theoretike* were given their equivalents in Irish. In the seventh century, accusations of Pelagianism were levelled against them,[20] perhaps because of Cassian's popularity. Irish monasticism, including communal monasticism, would retain a strongly contemplative element. The great monastic leaders would frequently retreat from full cenobitic life to recharge their spiritual forces in solitary contemplation: Colum Cille to a solitary hut (*tegoriolum*) near the shore on Iona where he sometimes received visitors but usually wrote, meditated or copied the gospels.[21] On one occasion he shut himself up in a house on Hinba for three days to commune with the Holy Spirit.[22] Kevin of Glendalough is reputed to have built a hermitage, the remains of which are still pointed out to the visitor. A great success on the continent, Columbanus retired to the forests which lay between his three monastic foundations of Luxeuil, Annegray and Fontaines to pray and meditate. Cuthbert, who represented the Irish tradition in seventh-century Northumbria, used to retreat to the edge of Lindisfarne, itself an island monastery off the coast – and even when he was made a bishop he spent the last part of

his life in contemplative retreat on the Farne Islands.[23] Hermits or
anchorites might live in and around monastic communities or independent of any monastic community. Thus the *Life of Columbanus* records
that when he was an adolescent, his first spiritual adviser was a holy
woman who lived alone not far from his parents' house.[24] Closely related
to the practise of reclusion was the concept of monk as *peregrinus*. The
Irish distinguished between 'red' or physical martyrdom, 'green martyrdom' which took the form of penance, and the 'white martyrdom' of
exile.[25] Brendan, as *peregrinus*, is believed to have founded monasteries in
Scotland on Tiree and in Perthshire. Colum Cille, an aristocrat of the Uí
Néill clan, made his first monastic foundation at Derry in 546: but in 563
he was exiled from Ireland. His hagiographer and distant kinsman Adamnan (abbot of Iona, d. 704) always presents him as a *peregrinus*, though
most historians now believe that he was exiled in punishment for his
involvement in war. Adamnan says only that he was unfairly censured at a
synod held at Tailtiu in 562. Colum Cille's body is said to have borne a
livid scar to which Adamnan attributes a supernatural origin, but which
may indicate that he personally took part in the battle of Cúl Dremne, the
year before Tailtiu. Even if Colum Cille's exile was forced, his actions
were very much those of a monastic *peregrinus*. He arrived in Scotland
where his first monastery may have been at Hinba (perhaps on Jura),
while another was on Tiree (Mag Luinge, where he sent penitents). But
his most famous foundation and his eventual burial-place was on Iona, on
the edge of territory of the Cenel Loairne, within Dál Riata control.
Colum Cille's period of exile must have eventually come to an end: he
visited Ireland several times after settling on Iona and he founded another
monastery at Dairmag (Durrow) in the 580s.[26]

Monasticism and the Secular Church

Until the Vikings disrupted the sea-routes between Scotland and Ireland,
Colum Cille's monastery of Iona was the spiritual head of a family of
monasteries which stretched from the west coast of Scotland to central
Ireland. It has been argued that by the seventh century, other major
monasteries such as Clonmacnois built up their own networks of dependent monasteries scattered across the country. Belief in the existence of
such *familiae* combined with a number of other features has suggested to
some historians that Irish monasticism evolved in a peculiar way. This
traditional view of the development of the church in Ireland was partly
influenced by the late and unhistorical *Catalogus Sanctorum Hiberniae*,
which posited an age of bishop saints followed by an age of abbot saints –
thus leading to the view that the paramount position of bishops in the
early church was overtaken by that of abbots. The idea arose that Ireland

evolved its own anomalous and anarchic church structure in which some abbots – by the seventh century heads of great federations of monasteries – were the predominant influence in the church. The bishops' powers, it was reasoned, were originally limited by being confined by the territorial extent of a *tuath*: later they either disappeared into monasteries or, in a few cases, began to attempt to build up power beyond that of the *tuath* in imitation of that of the heads of monastic confederations. An earlier generation of historians believed that the major monasteries acted as pastoral centres for much of the population.

Since the 1960s, first Hughes and later Sharpe have begun to move away from the traditional notion that the original episcopal hierarchy of Ireland, established from the fifth century on, had been supplanted in the sixth by an 'order of abbots' and that monasteries were responsible for the pastoral care of the surrounding localities, with the monastic church acting as parish church.[27] Sharpe in particular argued vigorously that the pastoral needs of the Irish were mainly served by conventional means – through bishops and dioceses, 'mother-churches' of comparatively early foundation (*domnach, andóit* and 'old' churches) and smaller, perhaps newer, churches served by a single priest. Legal texts testify to the importance of bishops and dioceses. The so-called *Synod of Patrick, Auxilius and Iserninus*, the core of which dates from the fifth century and was possibly the work of Palladius and his associates, reveals the presence of bishops, priests (who may be married) and deacons and the whole hierarchy of clerical offices from sexton upwards. The powers of the bishop are upheld: priests from one diocese may not work in another without episcopal permission and British clergy are not admitted without a licence – possibly from fear of the taint of Pelagian heresy. In the 560s, the decision to exile Colum Cille was taken by a synod of bishops, while in the seventh century synods decided a number of important matters affecting the Irish church. Legal texts from the seventh and eighth century envisage pastoral care being carried out by bishops and priests and in non-monastic churches: the *Riágail Phátraic* of the eighth century envisages a single priest serving three or four churches. While the later canon law creates a system of tithes rather too closely modelled on Old Testament ideas to be entirely practical, a substantial number of early churches and their sites have been identified and it is assumed that the majority of these were centres of pastoral care for the population at large.

The attractions of the newer model of pastoral care along more conventional lines lie partly in the way it undermines outdated notions of the existence of a distinctive and anomalous 'Celtic Christianity' – a notion which would have offended the Irish who thought of themselves as completely orthodox Christians. Yet there still remains, in the minds of some, the suspicion that Irish monks arrived elsewhere in Europe with the advantage as 'missionaries' of a highly-developed concept of the pastoral monastery. Columbanus' letters could be read to imply that he may have taken a bishop, Aed, with him to the continent[28] – suggesting a degree of domination of the episcopal by the monastic church. In the eighth century, the English monk-historian Bede described the Irish-influenced community of Lindisfarne, off the coast of Northumbria, where in the seventh century a bishop had lived in a monastic community and – according to Bede at least – was subject to the abbot's authority. Such cases may be misleading. It is not entirely clear that Aed ever accompanied Columbanus to the continent and even if he did, he was, like Columbanus, a *peregrinus*, who had left his homeland in search of spiritual perfection. Lindisfarne was not just a monastery but also an episcopal centre from which Cuthbert attempted to minister to the vast Northumbrian diocese and Bede stresses that in combining monastic and clerical life, Cuthbert, like Augustine at Canterbury, was simply following the way of life of the primitive church.[29] It is likely that in non-urbanized Ireland, bishops lived in monasteries with communities of clergy and monks, but this does not mean that in terms of ecclesiastical organization they were always subordinate to abbots.

In this discussion, the concept of 'pastoral care' needs to be defined carefully and put into the context of the diffusion of Christianity in Ireland. The latter is still controversial as there is no clear picture of the territorial advance of the new religion and establishment of dioceses. One of the few clues which we possess – apart from the putative foundation-dates of some of the principal monasteries – about the progress of Christianization is that the last high king to rule from the pagan sanctuary of Tara, Diarmait mac Cerbaill, died as late as the 560s. In these circumstances, when Christianity was still in the process of spreading, it seems logical to assume that monks occasionally played some part in the initial process of *conversion* – just as the monks of Lann Docco or Samson did in Cornwall. The Basilian monastic injunction to love of God and neighbour combined with the simple need to ensure Christianity's survival, when Ireland was still largely pagan, may have led to the use of the monastery as a base for preaching (accompanied by the promotion of tariffed penance) and the baptism of pagans. *Monachi peregrini* may also have taught and baptized. But this has to be distinguished from regular and continued pastoral care – baptism of children, eucharist, burial – which does not seem to have been regarded as a legitimate facet of monastic activity. Chapter 50 of the *Penitential of Uuinniau* indicates that in the sixth century, monks had carried out baptisms, but it forbids such practices, indicating that they created disputes over income with the regular clergy, within whose province the performance of baptism properly lay. If baptism by monks following on conversion was impermissible, then day-to-day pastoral care – burial, the administration of the eucharist – must have been at least as unacceptable.

Did monks on occasion preach, when they had a message of vital importance? The *Life of Fursey*, composed in Francia in the 650s, claims that the monk Fursey, after experiencing a stupendous vision of the afterlife, became a *peregrinus* and toured Ireland recounting his vision and urging the populace to penance. By contrast, Adamnan's *Life of Colum Cille*, composed in the 690s, about a century after the saint's death, conveys a complex message on the subject of pastoral care, indicating that by this time it was separating into a number of strands. None of them, however, involved the use of a major monastery as a 'parish church'. Colum Cille is never portrayed employing his monastery of Iona as a baptismal or eucharistic centre for the laity – on the contrary, he is depicted as recognizing and deferring to a bishop who visits Iona disguised as a simple priest, an incident which suggests that Adamnan was carefully taking up a position in relation to monastic–clerical disputes nearer his own time.[30] But the *Life* also refers to his travels north and east of Iona in an attempt to evangelize the Picts and to his baptism of a Pictish leader on Skye.[31] Here, Adamnan may be attempting to claim credit for Colum Cille for laying some ground for later evangelizers' success. Significantly, Adamnan also reveals that one of Iona's monks, Diún, presided over a *cella*, possibly a priory on the shores of Loch Awe. This site would be identified, perhaps as early as the seventh century, as an andoit, later 'annat' – a term based on the Old Irish *andóit*, indicating an 'old' church with pastoral responsibilities.[32] On the continent this type of *cella* was a feature of the period when well-established monasteries with Irish connections such as Corbie and Bobbio acquired large estates in areas where Christian belief was poorly implanted and created smaller dependent houses which served as agricultural, monastic and baptismal centres (see pp. 184–6 below). It is impossible to tell from Adamnan whether or not the *cella Diuni* had evolved in this fashion in his day, but it has been suggested that Diún was a deacon as well as a monk. In Ireland or Scotland the preface *Kil*, derived from *cella*, is often simply translated as 'church' and no systematic comparison has yet been carried out between Insular monastic *cellae* and monastic *cellae* of the continental type which developed in the seventh century; but it is, perhaps, possible that in Ireland and Scotland smaller monastic outposts developed some pastoral responsibilities. If this is the case, it would be interesting to know whether the model came from the continent (Adamnan may be projecting development of his own era back into Colum Cille's time) or whether it was suggested by the practice of sending penitents to outlying monasteries or by the growth of monastic estates. However, the original success of many Irish-trained monks in evangelizing parts of the continent in the seventh and eighth centuries seems not to have sprung from any developed and exclusively 'Irish' concept of a monastery ready to provide regular pastoral care. Instead, it was usually due to the presence of Irish and British *peregrini* on the peripheries of Christendom who believed that they were doing their Christian duty by preaching the word of God to pagans, apostates or the very recently converted.

Tariffed Penance

Associated with the preaching of the Christian faith was a system of private confession and tarriffied penance for the laity. The continental church mainly upheld the very strict penitential traditions which had been developed in previous centuries for a smaller church of committed believers and also used to reconcile schismatics. The class of penitents in the Christian church was a public one – major sins were publicly confessed. The penitent wore sackcloth, could not perform military service and was condemned to a life of celibacy. Penitents had to leave the church as a group when the eucharist was administered during mass. This conspicuously humiliating status lasted for the rest of the penitent's life. The inevitable result of such stringent procedures was that most who confessed to sins did so on their deathbeds – despite the fact that clerical leaders such as Pope Leo I and Bishop Cæsarius of Arles sought to moderate the rigours of traditional penance in some respects. Cæsarius developed the classification of sins into capital and venial offences, listed twelve means of remission for the latter and allowed younger people to perform penance twice, thus effectively limiting its duration. But although Cæsarius was an exceptional churchman whose pastoral concerns are evident in the way in which he addressed himself to the question of the non-Christian beliefs of the pagani or country-dwellers of his diocese, he never went as far as the Irish did in modifying the penitential system.

In Ireland, the church made penance limited, repeatable and non-public and allowed laypeople to confess in private. The idea of set penances for major offences derived from the native Irish legal system with its longs lists of penalties and compensations graded according to the nature and severity of the offence and the rank of those involved in any dispute. The major influences upon the earliest Irish penitential, or extensive set of tariffed provisions, attributed to UUinniau (d. 549) were the Synod attributed to Patrick and the works of Cæsarius of Arles and Cassian. From Cassian, UUinniau took the ideas of the 'eight principal faults' and of 'curing contraries by contraries', though he seems to apply these monastic, psychological techniques primarily to clerics rather than to the laity. It may also be Cassian who inspired UUinniau to list a particularly stringent form of fast on a measured allowance of bread and water (most ordinary penances were based on bread and water but did not restrict quantity). The interaction between the Welsh and Irish churches in the sixth century is indicated in the way in which Welsh synods began to issue similar penitential legislation and provisions, although in Wales, these (and even the *Penitential* compiled by Gildas) seem to have been applied initially more to monks and clergy than to the laity.[33]

Once converts had been gathered in by episcopal or even, occasionally, monastic preaching, the control of the church could be cemented and apostasy or backsliding punished through the system of tariffed penance. The so-called *Synod of Patrick, Auxilius and Iserninus* assigns penances of one year for laypeople who have confessed to killing or fornication, and six months for thieves. The crime of consulting diviners or soothsayers – in other words reverting to some familiar pagan practices – is punished by one year's penance.[34] The status of an exiled penitent could become assimilated to that of the *peregrinus*: both on and outside Iona, Colum Cille heard the confessions of both clerics and laypeople and assigned penances to individuals including Libran 'of the reed plot' who 'put on clerical dress', became a *peregrinus* to expiate his sins, and journeyed from Connacht to Iona where he was sent to Tiree for seven years.[35] On the continent, Columbanus would establish a similar penitential outpost for his foundation of Luxeuil at Fontaines, several miles away, where penitents could expiate their sins before returning to the world. The growth in the number of monasteries appears to have been fuelled by a strict application of penitential codes by charismatic monastic leaders.

The Irish Monastery

Established monastic communities were essentially places of prayer, contemplation and work and as such had to evolve strategies for interaction with the laity. Satellite monasteries, such as that on Tiree, might house penitents. The boundaries of Colum Cille's community on Iona were the shores of the island itself: one sinner who had committed fratricide and incest was only permitted to kneel on the shore to hear what his penance was to be. Comparatively few Irish monastic sites have been excavated but the surviving physical remains together with the surviving literature reveal a life led within a *vallum*, usually curvilinear in form, sometimes an actual wall (which could be based on the remains of an older cashel or fort), elsewhere created by a ditch. Monks often slept one or two to individually constructed cells (though there is also evidence of dormitories in the literature), while the abbot had his own house. The monks sometimes slept in and generally ate and wrote or copied manuscripts in the major building of the monastery: the *tech mor* – great house – otherwise known as the *praindtech* (literally house of the *prandium* or dinner) or simply the *monasterium*. However, the most striking feature of the evolution of Irish monasteries was the way in which their internal space became divided into more sacred and less sacred zones. The focus of communal monasteries was, naturally, the church which might contain the relics of a saint. The church was surrounded by the most sacred space or sanctuary, the *termonn* (from the Latin terminus). The remains of the monastery of Nendrum, the oldest of which date as far back as the eighth or ninth century, indicate that the *termonn* itself was surrounded by a wall. Nendrum was divided into three concentric spheres of activity – the holiest near the church, then the next holiest, corresponding to the *platea* mentioned in many texts, and a third or outer region where smiths and other artisans set up their workshops and where pilgrims and visitors might be accommodated.[36] Columbanus' so-called *Communal Rule*, though composed on the continent, still provides valuable insights into Irish monasticism. It reveals the importance, to the Irish, of the boundaries between sacred and less sacred space – monks were to cross themselves when entering and leaving the *domus*, here perhaps meaning the main building rather than the monastery itself.[37] The practice of propitiatory crossings and blessings seems to have extended itself from accompanying the crossing of the monastic limits to the ritual sanctification of everyday objects: in the 620s, the abbot of Luxeuil, one of the continental monasteries founded by Columbanus, declared that:

> It does not seem to me to be entirely contrary to religion to trace the sign of the cross on the spoon which a Christian licks or on whatever vessel or drinking cup, because the sign of the Lord chases by its coming the deadly adversary who opposes us.[38]

The proliferation of gesture in Irish monasticism and the Irish church in general is yet another reflection of their origins in a country where Latin culture was only introduced with Christianity. Both the monastic office and the mass were conducted in a language incomprehensible even to the elite, making it necessary to accompany them with ritual. Irish monks invested gesture and ceremonial with a significance unknown elsewhere in Europe before their arrival: as late as the ninth century, the Carolingian author Wahlafrid Strabo tells us that the Irish were known for their practice of genuflection. At the same time, to read sacred texts and sing the liturgy, monks and clergy in Ireland themselves had to learn Latin, a language of which they had no previous experience. Irish monasticism produced Christian equivalents of older centres of learning, and outstanding writers such as Columbanus and Colum Cille (author of the *Adiutor laborantium* and at least part of the hymn *Noli Pater*) emerged from monasteries such as Clonard and Bangor; but the restricted nature of Irish horizons in comparison with those of Cassiodorus in Italy is illustrated by the *Ars Asporii*, an adaptation of the Latin grammarian

Donatus' *Ars Minor*, dating from the first part of the seventh century. Whereas Cassiodorus could attempt to conscript the Seven Liberal Arts into the service of religion, the *Ars Asporii*, composed for those with no previous knowledge of Latin, turns a secular grammar into one based on religious vocabulary. Later in the seventh century the study of grammar and exegesis would be extended as grammarians other than Donatus were discovered and Ireland acquired classical learning from the works of Isidore of Seville, probably transmitted through Galicia.[39] Their learning and methods of teaching Latin from scratch were now eagerly sought by Anglo-Saxon students of the seventh century, who did not know Latin either. Bede, writing in the eighth century, records that in the 660s, many English nobles travelled to Ireland to pursue religious studies or lead a life of stricter discipline. There, some became monks while others preferred to travel, studying under various teachers in turn. Bede claims that the Scots (i.e. the Irish) welcomed them all kindly, and without asking for any payment provided them with daily food, books and instruction.

The seventh-century text, the *Hisperica Famina*, illustrates the teaching methods of the time, in an elaborate parody of the question-and-answer technique. The language of the *Hisperica* is tortuous and elaborate: when pupils make a simple request for food from the local populace they couch their request in grandiloquent terms:

> Who will ask these possessors to grant us their honied abundance; for an Ausonian chain (i.e. the obligation to speak in Latin) binds me; hence I do not utter the mellifluous Irish tongue (*Scotigenum eulogium*).[40]

While the Irish monastic schools seem to have valued classical learning, the classicizing poems formerly attributed to Columbanus are now recognized as the product of a later hand, while the role of the Irish monasteries on the continent in the preservation of secular classical culture was small: at both Bobbio and Luxeuil, monks created palimpsests out of magnificent manuscripts which had formerly contained treatises on law, philosophy, or other secular subjects. The exception to the general destruction was Virgil, whose work was valued because it was thought to prophesy the coming of Christ: a surviving commentary on him has been attributed at least in part to Adamnan of Iona.[41]

Irish monastic schools placed great value on the skill of computus, the compiling of ecclesiastical calendars. The *Amra* records of Colum Cille that:

> Seasons and calendars he set in motion.
> He separated the elements according to figures among the books of the Law.
> He read mysteries and distributed the Scriptures among the schools,
> and he put together the harmony concerning the course of the moon,
> the course which it ran with the rayed sun,

and the course of the sea.
He could number the stars of heaven...[42]

The Irish method of calculating the date of Easter – the most important function of computus – is probably based on an Irish forgery of the
sixth century and reflected old methods out of step with the variety of
calculations used throughout the rest of Europe.[43] Yet when he arrived
on the continent, Columbanus felt confident enough to defend it against
both French bishops and the pope, believing it to be the correct and
oldest form of the Easter calculation. Columbanus had been taught,
according to his biographer Jonas, by 'Sinlanus'. Sinlanus was Mo-Sinu
maccu Min, later fourth abbot of Bennchor (Bangor) and the pioneer of
computistical studies in Ireland:

> Mo-Sinu maccu Min, scholar and abbot of Bennchor was the first of the
> Irish who learned the computus by heart from a certain learned Greek.
> Afterwards, Mo-Chuaroc maccu Neth Semon, whom the Romans styled
> doctor of the whole world and a pupil of the aforesaid scholar... com-
> mitted this knowledge to writing lest it should fade from memory.[44]

The southern Irish would, by the 630s, bring themselves into line with
western Europe; but it took until the 660s for Irish-influenced Northumbria and even longer for the northern Irish and Iona to conform.[45]
However much Irish monks and clergy were prepared to meet the needs
of a society converting from paganism, they also displayed a passionate
attachment to what they felt to be the common Christian tradition, an
older and to them superior way of reckoning the date of Easter.

The *Monastic Rule* of Columbanus, composed after his arrival on the
continent, reveals that the Irish followed the traditional *psalterium currens* and still celebrated only six offices in every twenty-four hour period.
But at the same time Columbanus also describes an elaborate system of
night psalmody designed to cope with the long winter and short summer
nights of Ireland. The night office reached its maximum of thirty-six
psalms during the long winter nights from the first of November to the
first of February. On Saturdays and Sundays double time was spent in the
church and the monks of Luxeuil therefore sang almost the whole psalter,
in these two nights. Conversely, the Saturday and Sunday office was at its
shortest at the summer solstice, gradually increasing until the beginning
of winter.[46] Columbanus also reveals that not all the Irish were willing to
innovate and he is careful to acknowledge other, older, systems. He
remarks that there are still

> some Catholics who have the same canonical number twelve of psalms
> whether on short night or on long ones, but they render this canon in four
> portions during the night; that is at nightfall and at midnight and at cock-

crow and at morning. And as this office seems small to some in winter, in summer it is found burdensome and heavy enough, while with its frequent risings in the night's short length it causes not so much weariness as exhaustion.[47]

Another Irish rule composed on the continent in the seventh century, the *Rule of a Certain Father for Monks*, also reveals the continued existence of this traditional type of office, based on eastern practice, in Ireland.[48]

Some monasteries cemented the relationship between themselves and society by liturgical intercession in return for 'alms' or donations. Columbanus' *Monastic Rule* specifies that a series of intercessory versicles be said at each of the daytime offices:

> first for our own sins, then for all Christian people, then for priests and the other orders of the holy flock that are consecrate to God, finally for those that do alms, next for the concord of kings, lastly for our enemies, that God reckon it not to them for sin that they persecute and slander us, since they know not what we do.[49]

These instructions may have their origins in the practice of Bangor, where Columbanus trained, as the last phrase suggests that they evolved in a country where Christianity was still being established.

By the eighth century, there were dozens of larger monasteries as well as many smaller houses and eremitic foundations scattered across Ireland, the larger houses being mainly found in the eastern, central and northern areas of the island. One circumstance which may have initially inhibited the growth of monasteries but later, once the idea caught on, actually encouraged it, was property-law. In founding new monasteries, donors had to work within the rules governing ownership of property and in doing so turned many Irish monasteries into family concerns.[50] Although it is possible to see a gradual transition – under the influence of Christianity – to a greater emphasis on the individual in early medieval Irish society, the power of the kin group was still very strong as late as the seventh century and the kin as opposed to the individual retained control of family lands. Thus an individual could not give family property away, but only property which he had acquired independently of the kin group. It was however, possible to found a monastery or give land for its foundation where the kin group retained a controlling interest in the monastery by appointing the abbot from among its own number: and the Irish monastery became an extension of the interests of the kin group. This phenomenon is apparent by the end of the sixth century at Iona where Colum Cille's successor was his cousin Baithene while the third abbot was the son of another cousin. The succession passed to a different branch of the family before returning to

Laisren's nephew Segene. Until the death of Adamnan in 704 all the abbots except one were descendants of Colum Cille's kin, the Cenel Conaill branch of the Uí Néill, even although some were only distantly related to their immediate predecessor.[51] The duration of such arrangements is reflected as late as the eighth century in the *coibse* (public declaration) and testament of the monastic founder Feth Fio in a legal compilation regulating the succession to the abbacy of Drumlease, County Leitrim:

> that there is no family right of inheritance to Drumlease save for the race of Feth Fio, if there be any of the family who is noble, devout and conscientious or able. If there is not, it should be seen whether such a person can be found from among the community of Drumlease or its monastic clients. If that is not possible an outsider belonging to Patrick's community (i.e. Armagh or one of its network of churches and monasteries) should be installed.[52]

This text and its marginal gloss show the way in which succession to the abbacy is designed to remain in the family of its *érlam* or founding 'saint' whose family had given the land for the foundation. So strong was the identification between families and monasteries that the word *monasterium* – Irish *muintir* – became the accepted word for family grouping. The abbot himself was the *comarba* or 'heir' of the founder, a term usually associated with his control over the temporalia or landed properties of the house. By the eighth century, at houses such as Slane and Lusk, a non-celibate abbot might pass on control of a monastery to his son who ruled not only over real monks but also over *manaig* – lay tenants or clients designated as monks in the secular lawcodes.

Women in Irish Monasticism

Though male monasticism managed to adapt very successfully to Ireland's social and circumstances, female houses fared less well in these conditions.[53] Since the days of Patrick, women had played a part in ascetic and monastic life in Ireland, and several religious communities for women were established in the course of the sixth century. St Brigit, a legendary figure who appears to be a Christian reincarnation of an earlier, pagan, deity ranks along with Patrick as one of the two major Irish saints and her shrine at Kildare became one of the most prominent monasteries of Ireland.[54] It housed a congregation of nuns as well as clergy; the other major female communities were those of Monnena at Killevy and Ite at Killeedy. But it is noticeable in the later *Lives* of Irish saints, accounts of men far outnumber those of women: while at least one hundred and nineteen female saints or groups of religious are mentioned in the *Martyrology of Tallaght*, only four *Lives* of female saints survive. In these *Lives* women are credited with less spectacular and more domesticated forms of asceticism than men. While they fast, pray, heal and prophesy, they do not enter into single-handed conflict with the devil. In the works of the hagiographers, the first indication of their virtue is their chastity – as Patrick is alleged to have preached to Monnena herself. The monastic enclosure is often portrayed as protecting the chastity of women, though lecherous nuns are also stereotypes of these accounts. How far such later works reflect the reality of female – as opposed to male – sanctity and monastic life is difficult to estimate. While saints such as Molua and Coemgen (Kevin) are later credited with a particular desire to avoid females, the *Life of Columbanus*, composed less than thirty years after his death, claims that the first person he consulted about leading the religious life was a female hermit. The seventh-century *Life of Brigit* claims that she preached, and a ninth-century *Life* even claims that she was consecrated a bishop: but later versions of the story suggest that this was an error committed by Bishop Mel, intoxicated by the grace of God! This suggests that women may have been regarded as less worthy of respect as time went on and monasteries became more associated with family or tribal groups. But even in the earliest legal texts women were regarded as being under the permanent control of their family, natural or marital. In a society where many women became wives, concubines and servants of high-status males or were controlled by their fathers, they could encounter much hostility should they decide to enter the religious life. Women were regarded by the aristocracy as a resource, their existence tied to the production of heirs or the cementing of political alliances through marriage, and the *Lives* contain many motifs which reflect parental or societal opposition to women's becoming nuns: according to the earliest *Life* by Cogitosus, Brigit ran away to avoid marriage. Female houses were usually subordinated to those of men. Although they acted as centres of hospitality and offered some women the chance of education, only one female religious house, Tamnach, appears not to have been established on family land. Many houses may have existed for the founder's lifetime only, being dissolved when she died and the land returned to her family. Even more than male monasticism, female religiosity in Ireland appears, with the passage of time, to have become increasingly subordinated to the needs of family and tribe.

8

Irish *peregrini* and European Monasticism

Up to the end of the sixth century, Gaul had seen the foundation of two hundred and twenty monasteries, with their numbers spread more or less equally between southern and northern France.[1] By the end of the seventh, an additional three hundred and twenty communities had been established and the focus of monastic activity had now switched from the Mediterranean to the north. From being a largely urban and suburban phenomenon, mostly controlled by bishops, with some estate monasteries and a number of hermits such as the 'recluses' described by Gregory of Tours,[2] Frankish monasticism in the seventh century swept into the countryside, where monasteries directed by family groups became centres of aristocratic power as well as religious cult. This revitalization and extension of monastic life in the north-east, particularly in the region between the Seine and the Meuse, was result of the coincidence of the arrival of *peregrini* from Ireland in the northern parts of the Frankish kingdoms with the ambitions and interests of the Frankish aristocracy.

The Impact of Columbanus in Francia

Columbanus and his companions, Irish 'exiles for the sake of God', probably made their first landing on the continent in Brittany. They travelled into Francia which, in the 590s, was ruled by the same family but divided into three rival kingdoms. Welcomed by the ruler of Frankish Austrasia, the small band of *peregrini* moved on into the solitudes of the densely-forested region of the Upper Saône on the borders of Austrasia and Burgundy. There, with royal support, they began to build a monastery on the remains of an old Roman fort at Annegray, reconstructing the walls to form a monastic enclosure and reconsecrating the temple of Diana as a church dedicated to St Peter. As Columbanus attracted more followers, he established a second monastery on a more suitable site at the ruins of the Roman thermal springs at Luxeuil, some eight miles away from Annegray. According to Jonas of Bobbio, the author of the *Life of Columbanus*,

> people were rushing from all directions to the remedy of penance and ... the walls of one monastery could with difficulty hold such a great throng of converts.[3]

He therefore founded a third community at Fontaines, three miles north of Luxeuil, following the same pattern of detached penitential administration as Colum Cille, who sent penitents to satellite houses at Hinba and Tiree.

Jonas presents the activities of Columbanus and his companions as a calculated drive to spread the word of God among people who were only nominally Christian:

> They wanted zealously and shrewdly to inquire into the disposition of the inhabitants in order to remain longer if they found they could sow the seeds of salvation ...[4]

This looks like justification after the event: Columbanus' activities were those of a conscientious monastic *peregrinus* who had removed himself from his homeland and centres of Christian cult, only to feel obliged to preach to those whom he encountered on his way. The problem was that he was not quite far enough from local centres of ecclesiastical power. Annegray and Luxeuil may have lain on the borders of the Austrasian and Burgundian kingdoms, but they were still within the jurisdiction of the bishop of Besançon and friction quickly developed between Columbanus and the episcopate.[5] Jonas would justify Columbanus' actions by claiming that Christianity had nearly vanished from north-eastern Francia largely on account of episcopal negligence, commenting that the 'saving grace of penance'[6] was to be found only among a few. In reality, though private penance was mistrusted, less drastic procedures than the normal system of penance had been operated by a few outstanding churchmen such as Cæsarius of Arles, and Columbanus' *Penitential* (see below) suggests that some of the principles of penance which he was administering were already known.[7]

From the bishops' point of view, Columbanus was a rival focus of authority. Technically, he had encroached on their privileges by preaching and administering his version of the discipline of penance, while he had broken ecclesiastical law by creating his three foundations without

permission from a diocesan – the altar-stone of Luxeuil had been consecrated by an Irish bishop. But as long as Columbanus enjoyed the
backing of the ruling family, there was no possibility of attacking him
outright. Even so they must have begun agitating against him, because in
600 Columbanus took the step of writing to Pope Gregory I, defending
the Irish method of calculating the date of Easter.[8] This was based on an
obsolete system of reckoning and meant that he had several times
celebrated Easter at a different date from the Frankish church, thus giving
the local bishops an excellent opportunity to accuse him of being a
schismatic or even a heretic.

In his letter to Gregory, Columbanus put up a robust defence of Irish
practice, demanding that the Frankish cycle be suppressed and for good
measure, accusing the Frankish bishops of simony and immorality. The
bishops may have miscalculated in thinking that criticism of the Irish
calculation of Easter was a trump card, as Rome followed a third and
different system; and Pope Gregory would naturally have been concerned
about Columbanus' accusations of simony. While he did not reply directly
to Columbanus, the pope took no action against him and appears to have
commended him to the protection of the abbot of Lérins.[9] But the
bishops did not forget their grievances and Columbanus was summoned
to a synod to be held in 603 at Chalon. He refused to attend, sending a
public letter stating his case to the bishops and also writing to Rome once
more. At this stage, Columbanus still enjoyed royal favour: but his strict
principles eventually got him into trouble with the royal house of Burgundy, when he criticized King Theuderich for keeping concubines and
refused to bless his illegitimate children. Theuderich attempted to send
him back to Ireland and had him escorted across Francia to Nantes. The
boat was unable to leave harbour and Columbanus disembarked. Finding
that no one wished to stop him, he began a journey back to his monasteries. But he was eventually forced out of Luxeuil altogether by Theuderich and with a few monks he left Francia with the intention of making
a new settlement at Bregenz with the support of King Theudebert,
Theuderich's rival. Although Columbanus never returned to Francia,
his enemies Theuderich and Brunechildis were dead by 613 and Burgundy and Neustria were finally united. Chlothar II's rule was established
over all three Frankish kingdoms by 613 – an event, according to Jonas,
prophesied by Columbanus.[10]

The Ambitions of the Aristocracy

Despite the difficulties of his relationship with the royal family and
episcopate, Columbanus' spiritual teachings appealed to the aristocracy.
Previously, monasticism had principally been identified with the basilicas

established by royalty or with the senatorial aristocracy and its values and had offered little to the Frankish nobility of the north-east. But Columbanus' preaching and charisma soon attracted members of the local aristocracy to his communities. We do not know exactly what he preached in Francia, but some of the sermons composed at a later stage of his career for his monks focus on the terrors of Judgement and the need for repentance.[11] Luxeuil lay on the borders of Austrasia and Burgundy and his recruits Eustasius and Waldebert, who became the second and third abbots of Luxeuil, were members of the family of Duke Waldelenus of Burgundy. This family's connections stretched into Provence and would prove highly influential in seventh-century Frankish politics. Waldelenus and his wife Flavia themselves asked Columbanus to pray that their marriage might be blessed with children. Columbanus astutely cemented connections between Luxeuil and the ducal family by agreeing, provided that they dedicate their firstborn to a life of religion. They sent their first son, Donatus, to Luxeuil as a child: subsequently he became bishop of Besançon. Columbanus was even able to turn the failure of Theuderich's attempts to exile him to his own advantage. He was able to gain the favour of Theuderich's rival, Chlothar, and visited the estates of Chagneric's family near Meaux where, according to Jonas, he 'consecrated to the Lord' Burgundofara, Chagneric's young daughter. In the same region, he also paid a similar visit to the family of Autharius and blessed their sons – Ado, Dado and (according to a later source Rado). Dado and Ado went on to found the monasteries of Rebais-en-Brie and Jouarre, and Dado later became bishop of Rouen. A number of Austrasian supporters of Chlothar, the Neustrian king, became monks at Luxeuil including Romaric (later the founder of Remiremont) and Chagnoald, son of Chagneric. Bertulf, who was kinsman to Arnulf of Metz, one of the most prominent of the Austrasian aristocracy and a supporter of Chlothar II, followed Columbanus when he left Francia.

Eustasius and Waldebert, Columbanus' successors at Luxeuil, were able to consolidate and extend his work. Eustasius' rule as abbot of Luxeuil (612–629) coincided with the reign of Chlothar over Francia and the first nine years of his successor Waldebert's abbacy with the reign of Dagobert I – altogether the 'most peaceful, prosperous and significant period in Frankish history since the time of Clovis'.[12] Eustasius' background as a member of the Burgundo-Frankish aristocracy helped save Luxeuil from potential isolation after Columbanus' departure and he also managed to fend off a threat from within the monastic community itself. In the 620s Eustasius continued the evangelical tradition of the *peregrini* by directing preaching campaigns to the Warasci, some of whom were pagans and others 'Bonosiac' heretics: the fact that the *Penitential* ascribed to Columbanus mention this group indicates that at least part of it dates from after his death. With Agilus, the future abbot of Rebais-en-Brie, he then undertook a mission to the Bavarians. It is unlikely that the mission was a spontaneous extension of monastic activity: instead, it appears to have been politically inspired, undertaken at the request of the ruling Frankish dynasty which was attempting to extend its authority further east.

Agrestius, one of the monks sent on the Bavarian mission, returned to Francia via Aquileia, where he came to support the 'Three Chapters' schismatics – much of the northern Italian church which had been in schism since the 550s over a Christological dispute. According to Jonas, he came to present a very real threat to Luxeuil's existence as he also criticized many of the practices of Luxeuil – the multiplicity of blessings with which the monks of Luxeuil surrounded many everyday actions and also the multiplicity of prayers and collects in their liturgy, and persuaded his relation, the bishop of Geneva, to summon Eustasius to a church council. Jonas claims that Eustasius made a successful defence of Columbanian practice at the Council of Macon in 626. This episode suggests that the Columbanian rules were still being fully used in Luxeuil and that they had not yet been replaced by a mixture of the Columbanian rules with that of Benedict (see below) though Jonas may not be informing us fully about the background to all these events. Eustasius' work was consolidated under Waldebert, when, with the accession of Dagobert and the final Christianization of the foremost Franks, a strong alliance developed between the new style of monasticism and the Frankish court.[13]

Aristocratic Monasteries in Francia

In his *Life of Columbanus* Jonas claims that:

> The children of the nobles from all directions strove to come thither; despising the spurned trappings of the world and the pomp of present wealth, they sought eternal rewards.[14]

There were also many earthly rewards to be gained by the aristocracy as monasteries became the centre of estates which combined an ecclesiastical function with domination of territory, ensuring the extension of aristocratic power by ecclesiastical means. Families might set up monasteries on their own lands, but there was also the highly advantageous alternative of establishing a religious house on land newly acquired from the king. In the 630s, *Fontanella* (St Wandrille) was founded by Wandregisil who had been a monk first at Columbanus' Italian foundation of Bobbio (see below) and subsequently at Romainmoutier, on land which had previously been part of the royal fisc. In the same area, Filibert created Jumièges on royal land; in Aquitaine, Solignac was founded in the same way. The monasteries of Millebeccus and Longoretus were founded on land given by Dagobert to the nobleman Sigeramnus in 632. Clovis II granted land for Montier-la-celle and there are numerous other examples of royal generosity towards monasticism.[15] By appointing relations to rule over monasteries created on former royal land, aristocratic clans thus managed to extend their own interests – incidentally at the expense of the king, who nevertheless expected to benefit from the prayers of the monks in these new foundations which he had helped create.

During the peaceful end of Chlothar II's reign (from 613 to 629) and under Dagobert II (629–639), control of monasteries was established as one of the building-blocks of aristocratic power in Francia. The growth of Pipinnid power in Francia was partly achieved through control of the monasteries of St Wandrille, Fleury-en-Vexin and Jumièges, while the foundation of the abbey of Weissenburg was connected to Pippinid ambitions east of the Rhine in the early eighth century. In Brabant, Gertrudis and Begga also extended Pippinid influence with the foundation of Nivelles and Andenne. Arnulf, Bishop of Metz, the ancestor of the Carolingian dynasty, had trained at Remiremont.[16] Creating monasteries could be a good way of ensuring good relations with the church as well as control of land: although his brother Donatus was bishop of Besançon, Chrammelenus, who held the trans-Juranian dukedom, assured his association with the metropolitan of Doubs by his monastic foundations or reformations.

The new style of aristocratic monasticism was rural and estate-based: many monasteries were founded on land which had to be cleared and brought under cultivation. Columbanus' own houses undertook clearance and cultivation on a more ambitious and organized scale than earlier Gallic rural monasteries. Gregory of Tours claims that Lupicinus, head of the Jura monasteries of Condat and Lausinne in the later fifth century, had appealed to King Chilperic for support, but turned down a generous offer of fields and vines. Although the Jura monasteries prided themselves on the fact that they their monks worked with their hands, they were unwilling to extend this labour too far and were granted produce and money for clothing instead.[17] The *Rule of Tarn*, composed in southern Gaul in the sixth century, revealed that some monks were involved in cultivation. However, Jonas describes not only how Columbanus was frequently involved in the monasteries' agricultural enterprises, but the spectacle of no less than sixty monks hoeing the fields and preparing to sow the crops at Fontaines.[18] By inspiring the foundation of rural monasteries in which agriculture was carried out on a relatively large scale, Columbanus and his successors had helped evolve a style of monasticism perfectly in tune with the background as well as the aspirations of the Frankish nobility. Estate-monasteries of a kind had provided the setting for aristocratic monasteries since the late fourth century: now they were not just the centres of a life of ascetic retreat but of aristocratic exploitation and domination of the countryside.

The Rise of the Frankish 'Double House'

The emergence of the institution of the double house headed by an abbess is another testament to the way in which monasticism and aristocratic politics fused in seventh-century Francia. From the fourth century onwards a tradition of strict monastic segregation had sprung up, in response to the increasing disapproval of influential figures such as Athanasius and Jerome. Female communities associated with those of men, such as those of Basil or Pachomius, were ruled over by the male superior or in some way subordinated to the male part of the congregation.[19] Now many double houses emerged ruled over by an abbess who was a member of a noble family; these included *Evoriacum* (Faremoutiers), Chelles, les Andelys, Jouarre, Marchiennes, Nivelles, Hasnon, Laon, Maubeuge, Troyes, Fécamp, and Pavilly.[20] The initial decision to create a monastery ruled over by an aristocratic daughter or widow often appears to be a response to the political as well as a religious situation. The lives of a number of prominent abbess-founders in seventh-century Francia record attempts to marry them off against their will as a prelude to taking the veil. Women now had some rights of inheritance – early seventh-century legislation records that daughters took precedence over more distant male relations if a nobleman died intestate – and kings might aim to reward followers without depleting their own resources, by providing them with rich or noble brides.[21] The *Lives* of several prominent abbesses contain dramatic narratives of struggles to avoid arranged marriages. Jonas of Bobbio claims that Burgundofara, founder of *Evoriacum*, twice refused to marry, braving her father's wrath and even an attempt on her life: according to Jonas, she was remaining true to her 'consecration to the Lord' by Columbanus himself, who had blessed her when she was only ten years old. The tale may be a convenient fabrication, designed to excuse both Burgundofara and her family for their refusal of a husband chosen by the king: in Jonas' account her father, on Eustasius' advice, abandons his threats to kill his disobedient daughter and she builds a nunnery on her patrimonial soil.[22] The *Life* of Sadalberga, thought to be the daughter of the dux Gundoin who founded Grandval (Grannfelden) in the Sorgau, claims that as a young woman she was inspired by Eustasius' teaching and was attracted to the religious life. Nevertheless, she was married off by her family, and when widowed compelled to make another marriage with one of the supporters of King Dagobert. After bearing five children, she and her husband were at last converted to the monastic life by Waldebert, Eustasius' successor.[23] The *Life* of Rictrude, who became abbess of Marchiennes, recounts how, as a widow, she escaped a marriage about to be forced on her by the king by publicly veiling herself at a banquet.[24] The accounts given of resistance to unwelcome suitors, to parental opposition or to forced marriage do not resort to the stereotypes of the Roman virgin martyrs, as some *Lives* of Anglo-Saxon female saints do.

To whatever extent the foundation of monasteries headed by females was a response to the new religious climate ushered in by Columbanus, it also represented an opportunity for families to retain control of wealth which might otherwise pass to another family through marriage. When Pippin of Landen's widow Ida founded Nivelles on the lands of a villa which her daughter Gertrudis inherited on his death, she kept her portion of the family lands out of royal hands. The community was still under the control of the family – in the shape of her niece, Wulftrudis – when the Pippinids began to assume real power in Francia.[25] At the most basic level the creation of one of these new-style nunneries represented the endowment of an estate which, if the family continued to provide abbesses for it, could remain in their control forever. Thus the father of Burgundofara – after the intervention of Abbot Eustasius – allowed her to create her nunnery on 'patrimonial land between the Grand Morin and Albetin rivers'. The dynastic and family nature of the initial foundation is shown by the way in which Burgundofara's brother – one of the monks of Luxeuil – was entrusted with her training in the monastic rule by Eustasius, while Jouarre, initially a monastery, soon became a double house with the founder's cousin Theodochildis, who had first entered the religious life at *Evoriacum*, ruling as abbess. Sadalberga's entire family joined the religious life and Sadalberga founded her own house, initially at Langres, which she endowed with her own revenues from the lands of her hereditary paternal succession. Her daughter Anstrudis succeeded her as abbess of the house which Sadalberga had meanwhile moved to Laon. The succession of daughters or nieces to the control of these new-style nunneries was a common feature of seventh-century monastic life in Francia. The only problem which might follow a foundation on patrimonial land was the reluctance of some of the family to see a portion of their inheritance disappear: thus the *Life of Sadalberga* complains that 'her brother Bodo had, by illicit usurpation, retained the farms which she had bestowed on the convent'.[26] But a solution was soon reached through the mutual confirmation of charters. Similarly, Burgundofara's will shows that she was compelled to bribe her siblings with bequests to prevent them contesting the extensive provision she had made for *Evoriacum*, to which she wished to leave all her land.[27] However two of its later abbesses, Æthelburh and Sæthryd, came from the royal family of Kent in England, achieving this status, according to Bede the Venerable, because of their holiness. The political dimension underlying these elevations can only be guessed at.[28]

The reasons behind the emergence of nunneries with male communities attached have been much discussed and it has been suggested that that the male community was there to act as chaplains to the nuns.[29] But it did not take a whole monastery of men to provide the eucharist even for several hundred nuns. (Some of the double houses may have been very large: Sadalberga's hagiographer claims that her convent at Laon housed three hundred nuns, while at the other end of the scale Pavilly had less than twenty-five nuns; the author of the *Life of Austreberta* remarks on the smallness of this foundation.[30]) The popularity of double houses in Francia and also in Frankish-influenced England reflects the importance of aristocratic – or in England, aristocratic and royal – family interests. In Francia, the monks appear in the *Lives* in a subordinate capacity, working as gardeners or on the monastery's estates.[31] The social and political realities of the situation in seventh-century Francia (and also in England) were such that it was acceptable, for the moment, for women to exercise authority over men of lower rank in a monastic context.

The Royal Court

If the Hiberno-Frankish monastic movement could be used by the aristocracy to extend its own power, the Frankish court would also find it a useful aid to the extension of their control over outlying and marginal areas. One of the key figures linking these two phenomena is the royal *referendarius* Dado, who would play an important role in establishing a second generation of Columbanian-influenced houses in northern Francia and lent his support to both the monastery of Jumièges and the nunnery of Pavilly. In 641 Dado was appointed to the see of Rouen. At the same time Eligius, a Gallo-Roman goldsmith from Limoges, whose talents had taken him to the court under Chlothar, and who had founded Solignac, became bishop of Noyon. Columbanus' biographer Jonas lists a number of future bishops – all members of the Frankish aristocracy – who were educated in the monastic life at Luxeuil: Chagnoald, brother of Burgundofara, who became bishop of Laon; Acharius, bishop of Vermandois, Noyon and Tournai; Rachnachar of Basle; and Audomar of Boulogne and Thérouanne. This last diocese was re-established by Dagobert I who aimed at the extension of his power in the north by establishing ecclesiastical structures which would begin to introduce royal control to the area.[32] Amand, a native of Aquitaine who had been deeply influenced by Luxeuil and founded Bairisis-au-Bois and Elnone, had been sent by Dagobert to evangelize the area around Tournai, Ghent and Antwerp. The monastic movement which, under Columbanus, had struggled for its life against the machinations of the Frankish bishops, now provided a monastically-trained episcopate on the fringes of Frankish control. Columbanian monasticism made less impact in southern Burgundy, where the influence of the older Roman monasteries was still strong, but King Sigebert III (along with his palace mayor and the bishop of Cologne) established the famous double house of Stablo-Malmédy in the Ardennes in 648.[33]

Political as well as religious motivations are clearly seen in the foundation of the male house of Corbie in Picardy and the nunnery of Chelles-sur-Cher near Paris. Both were the creations of Queen Baldechildis, an Anglo-Saxon who became the wife of Clovis II, king of Neustria and Burgundy (639–657). Baldechildis, as a woman and a former slave, relied on her ecclesiastical and monastic patronage to secure her own position and that of her minor sons on the death of her husband in 657. She established Corbie between 657 and 661, summoning monks from Luxeuil to form the nucleus of a community. Her favourite house, however, was Chelles, built at a slightly later date on the site of a Roman villa and to which she was forced to retire in or after 664.[34]

The Monasteries of Fursey

Neustrian court patronage of Irish-influenced monasticism continued after 640, now partly directed toward another charismatic Irish *peregrinus* who had arrived on the continent. To the east of Paris on the River Marne, Erchinoald, mayor of the palace to Clovis II before 650, established Lagny.[35] Its first abbot was Fursey, another successful preacher of the doctrine of penance. According to the anonymous author of his *Life*, he had preached his vision of the afterlife, in which angels and demons fought for control of his soul, so powerfully in his native Ireland that huge crowds came to hear him. After ten years, unable to cope with his own popularity and – according to his hagiographer – the jealousy of others, he left the country for England. There, he established a monastery at *Cnobheresburg* in East Anglia, once more gained a large popular audience and so moved on to Lagny in Francia, where he was followed by his brothers Ultán and Foílleán.[36] The activity of all three brothers had profound effects on the religious life of this northerly area of Francia and beyond. The Pippinid nunnery of Nivelles had links with Ultán and after Fursey's death, Erchinoald built another monastery around his tomb at Péronne. This famous monastery was known as *Peronna Scottorum*, Péronne of the Irish, and would for a long time retain strong connections with Ireland, perhaps acting as channel through which continental monastic ideas were funnelled back to its patron's native country. When Erchinoald expelled him from Péronne, Foílleán founded Fosses with Gertrudis' help.[37]

The Self-Sanctification of the Aristocracy

The new model of aristocratic monasticism offered even more advantages than those of guaranteed personal salvation combined with the ability to retain control of estates and build up a political ascendancy: it also provided the Frankish aristocracy with a spiritual means of underpinning its hegemony. Aristocratic families now scrambled to associate themselves with the prestige of sanctity.[38] This growth in the cults of monastic founders or abbots and abbesses was partly aided by the change in burial practices which had begun to take place from the middle of the sixth century onwards and which eventually allowed monasteries to function partly as places of cult centred round their tombs. The Frankish royal family had begun to have themselves interred in churches from the time of Clovis onwards and this practice was gradually copied by the aristocracy. At Amay (now in the province of Liége, Belgium), the noblewoman Chrodoara was buried in one of the churches which she had founded in the first half of the seventh century.[39] Monasteries now began to house the graves of their founders or abbots and abbesses and perhaps even family and associates. Communities were acutely aware of the prestige which came with the possession of relics and shrines. When the holy abbot Fursey inconveniently died outside Lagny and in the home of another aristocrat, his mentor Erchinoald promptly arrived to demand the return of his body – 'Give me back my monk otherwise tomorrow God will judge between you and me!' – and then built the monastery of Peronne around Fursey's grave.[40] At Nivelles, after Gertrudis' death, she became the object of a saintly cult (effectively becoming the first saint of the Carolingnian dynasty). Her bed, a miracle-working relic, was first moved into an existing church and then into one specially constructed to enable pilgrims to visit it.[41] The most famous monastic burials are those of the crypts of Jouarre, which contain the tombs of Theodochildis, Jouarre's first abbess and her brother Acgilberht, bishop of Wessex and later bishop of Paris; of Audo, who had founded the house; and of three other female relations. The original tombs were modelled for the burial of Acgilberht and Theodochildis' own tomb may date from the eighth century, suggesting the continuing or increasing importance of the burial site as a locus of sanctity and of monastic and aristocratic prestige and influence.[42]

The *Lives* and *Miracles* of this new group of saints was set down in writing by members of their communities. The penetration of Frankish monastic life by aristocratic values and interests is nowhere made more apparent than in the *Lives* of aristocratic founders and abbots. These were deliberate works of propaganda which sought to strengthen or publicize the combination of the material and spiritual interests already inherent in the monastery-estate. The system of values which they propagated was robustly aristocratic. Monastic sanctity was not now a matter, as it had been in the fifth century, of a personal rejection of materialism: in its new Frankish version, sanctity was reflected back on the family of the saint. The *Life of Germanus*, abbot of Moutier-Grandval, emphasizes his high rank and notes the important position of his brother at the royal court. As Germanus, attended by servants and accompanied by another of his brothers, enters the monastery, he is welcomed with great jubilation and thanks are given to God that a man of such high standing had been called by God to his service. The nature of life in rural monasteries allowed the writers of the *Lives* of abbots and abbesses frequent scope for emphasizing their humility. When Germanus is later described cutting wood and carrying it to the monastery, the rhetoric is not, as in earlier *Lives*, directed towards emphasizing a strict asceticism and bodily mortification: instead, the accent is laid on the fact that that a man of such illustrious birth was humiliating himself by carrying out work normally associated with the peasantry.[43] An identical emphasis is present in the *Life* of Sadalberga: an archdeacon of the city of Laon is miraculously informed that the Abbess is cooking for her sisters and that it is a sight which he should see for himself![44]

Columbanus' Teaching: *Penitentials and Rules*

The existence of a *Penitential* ascribed to Columbanus confirms the statement of Jonas and the evidence of at least one of his later sermons that the preaching of repentance and penance formed an important part of his monastic activity. The surviving *Penitential* may not be entirely his own work but an adaptation dating from later in the seventh century: even so it gives an idea of the way in which British and Irish penitential thinking was introduced to the continent and then adapted. It declares that it relies partly on the 'traditions of the elders' and is also written 'in part according to our own understanding' and assigns penances to monks, clerics and laity.[45] Columbanus knew and elaborated on the *Penitential of Finnian* (UUinniau – see pp. 150–1 above) and was also aware of the work of Gildas and of the British synods of the sixth century.[46] The second part of the *Penitential* ascribed to him is prefaced by a declaration of a medicinal approach to penance and the need to apply appropriate remedies in different cases, deriving partly from Basil's idea of the spiritual physician:

> The diversity of offences makes a diversity of penances. For doctors of the body also compound their medicines in diverse kinds: thus they heal wounds in one manner, sicknesses in another, boils in another, bruises in

another, festering sores in another, eye diseases in another, fractures in another, burns in another. So also should spiritual doctors treat with diverse kinds of cures the wounds of souls . . .[47]

Another penitential, ascribed to a later period by some historians, but viewed by others as the genuine, primitive nucleus of Columbanus' work, also stresses the need for a curative approach, offering a number of 'medicaments' to cure corresponding evils.[48] The idea of cures was particularly important to Columbanus as he was active amongst laity and went much further than UUinniau in dealing with them. It was no longer enough simply to abstain from murder and fornication: Columbanus extended the discipline of penance over offences punishable by secular law, thus narrowing the gap between clergy and laity.[49]

The earliest surviving monastic rules of Irish origin are attributed to Columbanus and, according to Jonas, were composed when both Luxeuil and Fontaines had been built and when he divided his time between the two.[50] The *Monastic Rule* is Columbanus' *summa* of what he considers to be essential monastic teaching. By continental standards, it is old-fashioned in its approach, setting down no formal administrative structures. Instead it is concerned with the basics of monastic life and conduct, enjoining in ten brief chapters that a monk should be obedient, silent, eat and drink little, have no possessions, overcome greed, vanity and lust and observe discretion. It opens with the Gospel injunction which forms the basis of Basil's monastic thought:

> to love God with all our heart and all our soul and our neighbour as ourselves.[51]

The doctrine which he goes on to expound is adapted from the works of Basil, Cassian, Jerome, and Faustus of Riez. The influence of Cassian is apparent in the passage in which he lists the 'perfections' of the monk:

> nakedness and disdain of riches are the first perfection of monks, but the second is the purging of vices . . .[52]

Finally in a passage closely based on Jerome's Letter 125, Columbanus enjoins a monastic 'perfection' based upon complete mortification and self-abnegation:

> Let the monk live in a community under the discipline of one father and in company with many, so that from one he may learn lowliness, from another patience. For one may teach him silence another meekness. Let him not do as he wishes; let him eat what he is bidden, keep as much as he has received, complete the tale of his work, be subject to whom he does not like. Let him come weary to his bed and sleep walking, and let him be forced to rise

when his sleep is not yet finished. Let him keep silence when he has suffered wrong, let him fear the superior of his community as a lord, love him as a father, believe that whatever he commands is healthful for himself, and let him not pass opinion on the judgement of an elder...[53]

Columbanus' doctrine of monastic obedience – set out not just in his *Monastic Rule* but also in the monastic section of his *Penitential* and also in the *Communal Rule* attributed to him – is in some ways closer to that of Benedict than that of Cassian or even Basil, from whom it derives in part.[54] For him, as for Benedict, the focus is not just on obedience, but on total obedience to the superior:

He who does something by himself without asking, or who contradicts and says, I am not doing it, or who murmurs, if it is a serious matter, let him do penance with three impositions, if a slight one, with one....[55]

Any monk who rejects the judgement of a superior is to do forty days' penance on bread and water.[56] This severity of approach went beyond other Irish monastic regulations such as that of Cummean's *Penitential*,[57] suggesting that Columbanus' rigour in these matters was not just a product of his Irish inheritance.

A charismatic abbot himself, Columbanus nevertheless felt it necessary to set out the duty of obedience owed by monks, perhaps anticipating that his subordinates and successors would need more support than he himself required. It has even been suggested that he may have been influenced by reading Benedict's *Rule*. The grouping together of chapters on obedience and silence recalls part of the schema of Benedict's opening chapters, and in places the opening chapter of the *Monastic Rule* appears to echo not only Basil but also Benedict's fifth chapter.[58] However, this could result from a convergence of thought and principle over the importance of obedience. It is hard to see Benedictine influence elsewhere: in terms of scale and approach the contrast between the two authors could not be greater. While Benedict takes a highly detailed, organizatory approach, in Columbanus' short *Monastic Rule* only two chapters are devoted to practical matters. Columbanus leaves even more than Benedict to the discretion of the abbot and does not privilege the rule to the extent that Benedict does. On the other hand, while Benedict contents himself with outlining disciplinary procedures, the *Communal Rule* ascribed to Columbanus, in the spirit of the Irish penitential tradition, allocates detailed and severe penalties to regulate discipline within the monastery and to enforce seemly behaviour during liturgy and eucharist. Even more vividly than the Pachomian legislation, the *Communal Rule* highlights problems which might arise in a community: the sins punished range from stubbornness and disobedience to drunkenness and vomiting up the host. Penalties might range from 'impositions' of extra psalms to severe physical punishment:

> If any spits and touches the altar, twenty-four psalms; if he touches a wall, six. If he forgets chanting or reading, three psalms.

> If any comes too slowly to the prayers, fifty [lashes] or noisily, fifty, or if he is too slow in doing what he is told, fifty… If he has replied stubbornly, fifty. If he eats without prayer, fifty. If he has come into the house with his head covered, fifty lashes. If he does not ask a prayer when he enters the house, fifty. If he eats without prayer, fifty.[59]

Community Life

From the *Communal Rule*, together with Jonas' *Life of Columbanus*, it becomes possible to gain some insight into life in the triple community of Luxeuil-Fontaines-Annegray. The monks lived within an enclosure and the successive versions of the *Communal Rule* indicate the existence of sacred zones; Columbanus – apparently unlike Frankish abbots – refused to allow laypeople into the interior of the monastery, saying that a 'special place' was reserved for visitors or pilgrims. The Irish practice of gestures of benediction is also mentioned: before eating, work, or when entering or leaving the house, each monk had to 'bless' himself, that is, make the sign of the cross.[60] Thus each task, each meal and the limits of the monastic enclosure, were all sanctified by gesture. The *Communal Rule* emphasizes the need to treat the Eucharist with decorum and reverence and implies that it was celebrated on Sundays and feast-days.

The main practical matters dealt with by Columbanus' *Monastic Rule* were diet and liturgy. Columbanus did not share Benedict's relatively relaxed view of the monastic diet, describing a traditionally severe régime which allowed only one meal a day consisting of grains and vegetables.[61] However, according to both the *Communal Rule* and Jonas, the monks of Luxeuil were allowed to drink beer[62] – and beer-brewing is mentioned in a rule for a Columbanian double house. His liturgical directions contained both traditional and innovative elements. By establishing a pattern of intercession for named groups, Columbanus made a further move in the direction of the intercessory superstructure which had already begun and would come to surround the monastic office in subsequent centuries. Though specific groups are mentioned, the overall schema adds up to prayer for all of society – including 'our enemies'. Columbanus himself maintained an impartial stance, reflecting his certainty of God's ultimate justice. When asked to pray for his supporter King Theudebert against his enemy King Theuderich he answered:

Your advice is foolish and irreligious, for God, who commanded us to pray for our enemies has not so willed. The just Judge has already determined what He wills concerning them.[63]

The *Antiphonary of Bangor* produced at Columbanus' Italian foundation of Bobbio in the later seventh century contains a similar, if more developed series of intercessions, this time for fifteen different groups.[64]

Jonas of Bobbio's account of Agrestius' attacks on the practices of Luxeuil reveals that the Columbanian practices of blessings and intercessory versicles were still in existence in the mid-620s. By this stage, or very soon after, the *Rule* of Benedict of Nursia became known to the Columbanian congregation in Francia, where some of its prescriptions began to be combined with those of Columbanus in what became known as 'mixed rules'. It is not certain how knowledge of the *Rule* had reached northern Francia. According to one source, a monastic founder named Venerandus wished the *Rule* to be used in his monastery and sent a copy to the Bishop of Albi in the south around 620. But the lateness of the manuscript (it dates from the fifteenth century), the inaccurate description of Benedict as *abbas Romensis* – more characteristic of the eighth century – together with the fact that the Benedictine *Rule* made no impact on the south for several decades, suggests that this is an unreliable and possibly interpolated text. Older styles of monasticism predominated in the Rhône valley and on the southern coast and there is no other evidence of knowledge of Benedict in the area for decades. A mixed Benedictine–Columbanian rule only arrived at Lérins in the period 660–667, brought from northern Francia by monks of Fleury under Aigulf whose attempts to impose it led to a revolt. By the end of the seventh century, the mixed Benedictine–Columbanian rule – along with sections of the *Rule of Macarius* – was in use only at one other southern monastery, that of St Victor-Graselle at Vaison.[65] It is possible that the *Rule* may have arrived in northern Francia directly from Bobbio, the Italian monastery founded by Columbanus in the seventh century (see below). With its detailed provisions for running a rural monastery and its strong support for the figure of the abbot, it must have been eagerly seized on by aristocratic monastic leaders looking for practical as well as spiritual guidance.

Mixed *Rules* for Women

No examples of the combined Columbanian–Benedictine rule for men survive from Francia, but two rules for female houses show the Benedictine *Rule* being used along with the work of Columbanus. Although it is anonymous, the *Rule of a Certain Father to the Virgins* has been tentatively identified with the rule which Waldebert (629–670), third abbot of Luxeuil, composed for Burgundofara and Evoriacum, using Columbanus and Benedict as his basis.[66] Waldebert's contemporary Donatus, ex-monk of Luxeuil and bishop of Besançon, compiled a rule for his mother's foundation of Jussanum and its abbess Gauthstrudis, to whom the rule is addressed. In the preface to his work, Donatus reveals that Abbess Gausthrudis persuaded him to read and use Cæsarius' *Rule*, written specially for women:

> you have often urged me to explore the rule of the holy Cæsarius which was specially devoted to Christ's virgins along with those of the most blessed Benedict and the Abbot Columbanus, and select for you the choicest blooms . . .

How Gausthrudis came to know of Cæsarius' rule is not clear but she was apparently successful in her attempts to get Donatus to consider its value for a female community. He used substantial sections of it – for instance on admission, conduct and possessions, while taking other aspects from Benedict (for example, the steps of humility, the abbess and her officials) and from Columbanus, from whom he derives his ideas on confession, punishments and the liturgy. In fact, Donatus' abbess appears as a less autocratic figure than the abbess of the *Rule of a Certain Father*: this is, in part, a result of his reliance on Cæsarius and might suggest that Jussanum was an urban house, or one over which he hoped to exert control, rather than the more independent rural nunnery of the *Rule of a Certain Father*. Jussanum seems, like Cæsarius' nunnery in Arles to have had a *provisor*, who supplied the house with its material needs. There is no reference to any male community. On the other hand, the existence of a male section of the house is also hard to discern in the *Rule of a Certain Father*, even though it is suggested that it was composed for Faremoutiers, the first double house.

The importance of the abbess is made plain in Waldebert's *Rule* which makes her authority paramount. Waldebert does not follow Benedict in making provision for electing a successor to the abbess – so she can pass the abbacy on to a member of her own family. Nor does his abbess have to take advice from anyone – in both respects she is even more powerful than the Benedictine abbot.[67] Donatus' perspective is slightly different to that of Waldebert, because he was not writing for an abbess-founder: his mother Flavia, was (like Radegund, rather than most seventh-century female founders) a member of the community and not its head. His opening chapter on the abbess, while by its position acknowledging her importance, makes no reference to her rank. The abbess does not have the right to choose her own successor – she is to be elected 'unanimously' by the whole congregation for her wisdom and talents, not because of her birth or because she is loved: but in fact, after Gauthstrudis' death, Flavia seems to have appointed her own daughter Siruda to succeed her.[68]

Donatus' view of the abbess' authority is based partly on Benedict's second chapter, but to a large extent also on his sixty-fourth, which stresses the pastoral rather than the autocratic features of the governance of the abbot. But her control is strengthened to some extent, insofar as Donatus, in addition, employs Benedict's devices for severing ties between individuals and the outside world and adapts Benedict's text to prevent the growth of family-based cliques: order of seniority is based on the date of entry to the convent and nuns are forbidden to defend their relations.[69] Waldebert, by contrast, did not consider it necessary to use the first measure, but includes the second.[70] Donatus attempts to keep order by formally restating some of Benedict's more authoritarian prescriptions as well as through a system of penances and punishments. Waldebert too is aware of the possibility of unrest in the community: nuns are urged to show mutual respect and affection and on occasion he, too, resorts to Columbanian-style punishments.[71] But he relies to a considerable degree on the authority of the abbess who is, effectively, superior to the *Rule*, and backs this up with a clear statement of the duties and qualities of her main subordinates, the prioress, cellarer and doorkeeper. The chapters dealing with these officers are not mere copies of Benedict, but adaptations clearly inspired by the idea of a powerful head of community with a strong hierarchy of officials.[72]

One question which arises from both *Rules* is their attitude to enclosure. Donatus does not think strict enclosure practical for the nuns of Jussanum:

> though holy Cæsarius may himself have dedicated his rule to virgins of Christ, their stability of place is not in the least suitable to your circumstances...[73]

He also quotes from Columbanus' regulations for crossing oneself when leaving the monastery.[74] But Donatus also omits the chapters in which Benedict describes monks going outside the monastery and repeats Cæsarius' injunctions against letting men into the house, so it is not at all certain to whom or how far any relaxation of enclosure actually applied. *The Rule of a Certain Father* prescribes manual work for the nuns between the morning office of *Secunda* and the later one of Nones – milling, baking and brewing. Such work was undertaken by teams of four, supervised by a senior. It is not clear whether this took place in the nuns' enclosure or an outer enclosure of the double monastery where a mill, bake-houses and brewery (*braxatorium*) might have been situated.[75] Whether, in practice, nuns actually left their enclosure for other reasons is doubtful. According to Jonas, Faremoutiers had three gates but also a substantial wall or palisade designed to keep the religious in as well as undesirables out: a group of misguided nuns who attempted to escape needed a ladder to climb them.[76] The *Lives* of the most famous abbesses of the time do not suggest that they ever travelled about on business, conventual or family, or on pilgrimage: but at the same time while it is specifically affirmed that Rictrude never ventured beyond her convent walls, she is also shown accompanying a holy visitor a little way on his journey as he left the house.[77] Waldebert is recorded as visiting Sadalberga at Laon as is an archdeacon who came to see her cooking for her nuns and while the *Rule of a Certain Father* forbids visitors, male or female, to eat within the boundaries of the nunnery, restricting them to an external guest house, it appears to allow pilgrims into the monastic enclosure. If this the case, it is an important regulation which would facilitate the opening up of nunneries as cult centres as laypeople came to visit the tombs of their founders.

One of the most striking aspects of the *Rule of a Certain Father* is its insistence that the nuns are to make confession to the abbess or a senior nun. This takes place no less than three times every day – after the morning office of *Secunda*, after Nones, and at Compline.[78] While the Columbanian *Communal Rule* prescribes confession at certain times ('before meat or entering our beds or whenever it is opportune'), Columbanus never went as far as actually imposing three sessions of confession a day. This, of course, could in part be continuation of the *Rule*'s disciplinary measures, designed to bolster the authority of the abbess and her officials. But it could also reflect a belief that females are more prone to sins of thought and deed than men. Confession at *Secunda* was intended to purge the sisters of any unchaste thoughts or dreams they may have had during the night. Elsewhere in the *Rule* it is laid down that nuns are to sleep two by two, but not facing each other in case talk should excite desire.[79] Donatus is only slightly less enthusiastic in his advocacy of frequent confession, again to the abbess.[80] There is also suggestion of a particular consciousness of the need to prevent women forming close personal or sexual links – Donatus forbids nuns to hold each other by the hand and call each other 'little sister'.[81] A fragment of a third women's rule from an unidentified nunnery somewhere in the Columbanian sphere of influence demonstrates a traditional concern with ritual purity: menstruating nuns were forbidden to take communion and made instead to stand with the community's penitents in church.[82]

Although the abbess of the *Rule of a Certain Father* appears all-controlling and all-powerful, her gender places limitations on the way in which she can be described. The language which is used to outline the abbess' role and authority is often strikingly different from that applied by Benedict to the abbot. Benedict describes the abbot as vice-gerent of

Christ in the monastery. Waldebert is unable to apply such language to a woman. Instead, he instructs that the abbess should be wise and holy, the flower of continence and chastity, adorned by the benevolence of charity, a carer for pilgrims and the ill, a corrector of the erring and the lazy.[83] Despite her great authority over her community, the role of abbess is constructed at this point as one of feminine nurturer rather than a masculine leader and shepherd. Donatus similarly omits the idea of the abbess as Christ's representative.[84] Both writers, however (Waldebert more explicitly), suggest that she can fulfil one traditional abbatial role – that of teaching her congregation. Several of the more important double houses became famed transmitters of learning and specifically Christian culture in a world where cultural possibilities had rapidly diminished with the end of Roman civilization and the rise of a predominantly rural society. From Nivelles, Gertrudis sent to Rome for books as well as relics.[85] Chelles would become the home of a famous scriptorium in which the nuns copied manuscripts which were sent to many other houses.[86] The epitaph of the abbess Theodochildis inscribed on her splendid tomb at Jouarre records that she 'burned for sacred doctrine'.[87] Yet while nunneries and double houses of the seventh century were centres of aristocratic power, Christian civilisation and learning in a pagan countryside, it still remains to be seen how far they were governed by male clerical assumptions.

The Monastic Environment

Both the written sources and archaeological evidence reveal that many of the Columbanian and Frankish houses were constructed on the site of older buildings.[88] These were attractive to monastic founders for a variety of reasons. On the most basic level, they provided defence and the beginnings of the monastic buildings. The *Life* of Columbanus mentions a fort at Annegray and baths at Luxeuil. While the written sources give the impression that Amatus built Habendum-Remiremont on the site of a deserted fort, archaeological studies suggest that it might still have been inhabited or used up to the period of his arrival.[89] Most importantly, as at Luxeuil, near a Roman temple, or at Nivelles (*Niuwale*, the site of the sacrifice), the implanation of a monastery might deliberately signal the triumph of Christianity over paganism.

The new rural monasteries were surrounded by a *vallum*, consisting of a wall, hedge or ditch. Some monasteries may have used substantial older walls as their boundaries. Fursey, 'founder' of Péronne, lived within the Roman fortification of Burgh Castle[90] before coming to the continent and it has been suggested that Filibert founded Jumièges within a similar

Gaulish Saxon Shore fort.[91] The sources also suggest that considerable variety of buildings existed in some monasteries. There are numerous references to a dormitory – though the word *dormitorium* itself is only found in connection with Evoriac (Faremoutiers). For Donatus, the dormitory is the *domus*; for Waldebert, who devotes a chapter to the dormitory, it is (as in Caesarius and Aurelian of Arles) the *schola* or, once again, *domus*.[92] The same rule envisages the provision of separate cells for the sick. There appears to have been no standard practice in this, however, as Donatus – like Benedict – prefers the idea of one building for the sick.[93] Written sources also make reference to the existence of a refectory. Ten years after Gertrudis' death, a fire broke out at Nivelles and a monk reported a vision, during the conflagration, of Gertrudis standing on the roof of the refectory, 'in her old form and habit', fanning the flames back from the house.[94] The *Rule of a Certain Father to the Virgins* refers to the existence of baths,[95] while Luxeuil itself was built on the site of Roman baths.

A single oratory or church was often insufficient to fulfil all the community's roles. Many double houses contained separate churches for the male and female parts of the community.[96] Monasteries and nunneries might incorporate funerary churches in which abbots or abbesses were interred, as at Jouarre. While Chelles is unusual in that only one church has been found there, Andenne on the Maas, founded in the 690s by Gertrudis' sister Begga, after the assassination of her husband, possessed an abbatial church dedicated to the Virgin; a burial church dedicated to St Peter, where Begga and her husband were interred; a church dedicated to St John, perhaps used by the monks of the double community; and two others. The *Lives* of Sadalberga and Anstrudis name two churches in Sadalberga's large double house at Laon – the abbatial church (St John) where the abbess' chair as head of the congregation was placed and the funerary church dedicated to the Virgin. Seventh- and eighth-century texts mention four churches at Nivelles. Excavations have revealed three of the four churches, all with signs of red-painted floors and white plaster walls. The largest, fourteen metres wide and perhaps twice as long, with, unusually, two side aisles, can be identified with St Mary's. This was originally where the office was celebrated and abbess's chair – from which she presided solemnly over her community – was placed. According to Gertrudis' hagiographer, this church possessed a portico dedicated to St Agatha, where she died. The smallest was St Paul's: about nine-and-a-half metres by seven internally, with a small rectangular apse. Later and not necessarily reliable tradition makes this the monks' church. St Peter's, later known as St Gertrudis', is presented in the *Life* as the funerary church – Ida (d. 652), Gertrudis (d. 659) and Wulftrudis, the second abbess (d. 662) were all buried there. When a cult swiftly began to develop around Gertrudis after her death, the bed which she had used was transferred to St Paul's and at the end of the seventh century, her body was transferred to a place of honour in a small rectangular chevet, not much larger than her tomb, at the end of the funerary church. The fourth abbess, Agnes, built a completely new church dedicated to Gertrudis herself, thus conferring the status of a saint on her only a quarter of a century after her death. The nuns immediately began celebrating the office there and her chair was transferred from St Paul's. The series of posthumous miracles attached to the *Life of Gertrudis* reveals the way in which even nunneries could be opened to lay worshippers on feastdays.

Columbanus in Switzerland and Italy

Although he had laid the foundations of aristocratic monasticism amongst the Franks, Columbanus himself was not able to see it develop: he left Francia for what is now Switzerland before the defeat of his enemy Theuderich and the uniting of the Frankish kingdoms. Theuderich's rival, King Theudebert, persuaded him to move into the territory of Alamannia south of the Rhine over which he had been trying to extend his authority since 610. This area had been partly Christianized under the Romans and one diocese existed, centred on Constance. There were also many pagans and Columbanus, though not entirely happy with his situation, remained true to the evangelizing traditions of Irish *peregrini*. Even before his expulsion from Austrasia by Theuderich he had considered the conversion of the Wends – though he himself admitted that he had been deterred by accounts of their 'coolness' in the face of such initiatives. In one controversial passage from the *Life*, Jonas recounts that he decided to spread Christianity amongst the Alamanni.[97]

The later *Lives* of his disciple Gall claims that though seriously ill with fever, Gall asked to be allowed to remain in the area to the south of Lake Constance to continue his work of conversion and that Columbanus attempted to prevent him. The historicity of this passage has been debated and the evidence does not appear to support the idea of missionary activity in this area at this time.[98] Columbanus' enemy Theuderich conquered Austrasia and Columbanus was once more forced to move on. Jonas claims that while he had thought of converting the pagan Wends to Christianity, he was dissuaded by a vision and decided, instead, to make his way south, crossing the Alps and entering the Lombard kingdom of Northern Italy in 612. There, he appears to have been welcomed because its ruler, Agilulf, was an enemy of Theuderich.

The religious environment in which Columbanus now found himself was an extraordinarily complex one. The Catholic Church in northern Italy had itself been split for over fifty years by the so-called 'Three Chapters' (Tricapitoline) Schism, while the Lombards under their king Agilulf were Arians. Agilulf's wife, Queen Theudelinda, was a supporter of the

Catholics in schism with Rome. Columbanus evidently felt an obligation to help bring the schism to an end especially as he appears to have been told that Pope Boniface IV himself followed Pope Vigilius in favouring Nestorianism. He wrote peremptorily to the pope:

> I summon you, my fathers and my own patrons, to dispel confusion from before the face of your sons and disciples ... and ... to remove the cloud of suspicion from St Peter's chair. So call a conference, that you may clear the charges laid against you ...[99]

At times, Columbanus appears to be confused, but is only, in coded terms making references which would have been understood at the time, attempting to reconcile Roman, Aquileian and even Byzantine concerns.[100] The Irish, Columbanus proudly asserted, may have been 'inhabitants of the world's edge' but they were also

> disciples of Saints Peter and Paul and of all the disciples who wrote the sacred canon by the Holy Ghost and we accept nothing outside the evangelical and apostolic teaching; none has been an heretic, none a Judaizer, none a schismatic; but the Catholic faith as it was delivered by you first, who are the successors of the holy apostles, is maintained unbroken.[101]

He demanded that the pope put an end to the schism and he himself took action by preaching against both Arianism and the schism within the Catholic church. His sermon 'Concerning the Faith' opens with a statement of his intention to teach true doctrine:

> Since I bear the responsibility for very needful teaching, first of all I may briefly speak of the first thing for all to know. I desire that what is the basis of all men's salvation should be the foundation of our talk and that our doctrine should commence from that point where all that is arises and what has not been begins ...[102]

It also encapsulates a credal formula which stressed the linear and inclusive nature of the Trinity, in effect a counter to both Arians and schismatics:

> Let each man then who wishes to be saved believe first in God the first and last, one and three, one in substance, three in character; one in power, three in person; one in nature three in name; one in Godhead Who is Father and Son and Holy Spirit, one God, wholly invisible, inconceivable, unspeakable ...[103]

This statement resembles very closely the *Quicunque vult*, a creed associated with the Columbanian monastery of Bobbio in the Apennines, which he founded in 614.

Bobbio and the First Monastic Exemption

Columbanus died at his newly-created monastery in November 615. His career had been one of a *peregrinus* who found himself, whether because of his administration of private penance or because of the religious situation in northern Italy, at the centre of religious events and controversy. Whether we should regard his monasticism as having an overtly missionary dimension is doubtful: one of his letters reveals that he had considered preaching to pagans but had been easily discouraged.[104] However, his penitential does reveal a degree of concern for the Christian laity. And after his death, Bobbio would develop a network of smaller dependent houses which assumed some pastoral functions.

Columbanus was succeeded as abbot by Attala, one of the monks of Luxeuil who had accompanied him to Italy. Attala's period in office was marked, according to Jonas, by a rebellion of a number of monks who found Columbanian discipline too strict and left the house to live in 'hermitages'. In 628, under Attala's successor Bertulf, Pope Honorius I granted Bobbio the first-ever monastic exemption from episcopal authority, when Bertulf complained that Probus, bishop of Tortona, was attempting to extend episcopal power over the monastery and its territories. The reaction against Columbanian discipline, the establishment of 'hermitages' and the issuing of the first complete immunity from episcopal authority would combine to change the character of Bobbio in a number of ways.

In the early 640s, the Lombard king Rothari conquered Liguria. In the wake of this conquest, in a bull which was later altered, but in which the framework of the original can still be discerned, Pope Theodore I confirmed Bobbio's freedom from episcopal interference. The bull reveals that by the early 640s, Bobbio possessed tithes and baptismal churches and that the bishop was obliged to provide these churches with chrism for baptism and could only intervene in Bobbio's affairs if the abbot did not observe the precepts of the rule.[105] The churches to which the bull refers were a number of small dependent houses or *cellae* some of them perhaps originating in the hermitages to which monks had escaped in Attala's time. The rural areas surrounding Bobbio contained Arians as well as Catholics and were still home to pagans and pagan cults. By the 640s, as a centre of Catholic as opposed to Arian Christianity, Bobbio was now a monastery with dependent cells which served as baptismal centres for the rural population of a wide area extending, after Rothari's invasion, into eastern Liguria.

Bobbio and the *Rule of the Master*

According to the bull of 643, bishops could only intervene in the affairs of Bobbio if its abbot refused to follow the rule, which, according to the same bull, was the rule 'of Benedict of holy memory and of the aforesaid reverend Columbanus, its founder'. There is a great deal of evidence to suggest that the rule combining Benedictine and Columbanian features referred to in the bull of 643 can be identified as the *Rule of the Master*. Characterized by many historians as a rule composed in the early sixth century and as the major source for Benedict of Nursia, the *Rule of the Master* instead fits the description of the rule referred to by Pope Theodore.[106] Its version of Benedict's chapter 'The Instruments of Good Works' opens by quoting part of the *Quicunque vult*, the creed particularly associated with Columbanus' anti-Arian and anti-Tricapitoline crusade in northern Italy. It follows Columbanus' own *Monastic Rule* in arranging an increasing and decreasing system of liturgy for the night office. Although the system is slightly different from that of the *Monastic Rule*, partly in order to take into account Bobbio's more southerly location where the difference between the length of nights and days in winter and summer is not so great as in Ireland (or even Luxeuil), it is organized around the same equinoctial dates as those used by Columbanus. These equinoctial dates are distinctive as they had been abandoned in Europe in the 520s, but were still adhered to by the Irish: the southern Irish discontinued their use in the 630s, but the northern Irish adhered to them for much longer. Columbanus' adherence to a spring equinox dated to March 25 formed part of his anomalous system of calculating the date of Easter. The Celtic origins of the rule are also evident in the degree of ritual, including the blessing of food, with which it surrounds many actions and its use of Latin term *secundarius* to mean a successor-designate, in this case to the office of abbot. Such usage is confined in the early middle ages to Insular Latin, where it translated terms such as *tanaise rig* and *ætheling*, words used to denote successors to a king. The Columbanian, northern Italian background to the *Rule of the Master* is also revealed by its use of the terms *rogus* and *saltuarius*, both of which appear in the laws of the Lombards.[107]

Although the *Rule of the Master* contains many pointers to a Columbanian background, much of its structure and some of its wording derives from the *Rule of Benedict*. It is not difficult to understand why such a lengthy rule should have emerged. Columbanus' disciplinary provisions were often harsh and his *Monastic Rule* was so brief and unspecific that parts of the Benedictine *Rule* were welcomed throughout the Columbanian congregation as a supplement to it. The *Rule of the Master* uses Benedict's disciplinary procedures rather than Columbanus' penitential code suggesting that the revolt of the monks under Abbot Attala – if not immediately successful in alleviating the harshness of Columbanian discipline – may have eventually borne fruit under Bertulf. The compiler of the *Rule of the Master* seems to have embraced the idea of written directions with enormous enthusiasm – to the extent that what emerged from his pen was around four times as long as Benedict's *Rule*. The *Rule of the Master* goes to the opposite extreme from Columbanus, often trying to set out every eventuality in as much detail as it can muster. Its instructions for abbatial succession are enormously detailed. In one of a number of instances where he either enters into dialogue with the Benedictine *Rule* or appears to be responding to it, the writer takes Benedict's worries about the appointment of a prior so seriously that he does not appoint one. He also counsels the abbot against appointing a *secundarius* or designated successor

> The abbot should beware that no-one adjudges himself *secundarius* or installs anyone in third place. Why? So that no-one should be puffed up by the honour; and by promising the honour of succeeding him to him who behaves in a holy fashion let him make them all contend in good actions or in humility...[108]

The chapter advises the current abbot to keep the monks constantly guessing who is to become the *secundarius*. The writer is anxious that the abbot might designate an unworthy successor, only to have a more suitable candidate then enter the monastery. The following chapter gives instructions for succession to the abbacy: ideally, the abbot, when he feels he is dying, should designate his own successor, have him consecrated by the bishop, and immediately hand over the government of the monastery to him. It reveals that the only circumstance in which a *secundarius* can overtly emerge is when the abbot falls ill, designates a successor (who is then consecrated) but subsequently recovers from his apparently mortal illness, having inadvertently created a situation whereby there are now two abbots. Then the new appointee may be given special honours and treated as a *secundarius*, by virtue both of his choice and his consecration. From that day on, he is, in the words of the *Rule*, a *Cæsar designatus*.[109]

All this makes for a description of abbatial succession of complexity and detail unparalleled in any other monastic rule and is typical of the verbal and conceptual lengths to which the author is willing to go. Amongst the other concepts which he feels need to be spelled out are those of the rewards which await the disciple who has mastered the '*Ars Sancta*' or climbed the twelve steps of the ladder of humility. Whereas Benedict echoes Cassian in having the monk who has reached the top of the ladder achieve the perfect love which casts out fear, the *Rule of the Master* follows with a lengthy and highly sensual description of the joys of eternal life, borrowed from the *Passio Sebastiani*, a popular martyrdom-tale. The *Rule of the Master* is generally characterized by a higher use of excerpts from popular lives and deaths of saints than Benedict – who himself quotes from them from time to time. Part of the *Rule*'s prologue consists of a commentary on the Lord's Prayer, largely modelled on Ambrose's *De Sacramentis* and analogous to the type of explication of this prayer given by the bishop to those about to be baptized.

The priorities of the monastery according to the *Rule of the Master* were liturgical: manual work, which seems to have been largely agricultural under Attala and Bertulf, is now confined to garden and kitchen and the domains of the monastery are now run by a lay *conductor*. While in Benedict the property of the monastery appears to be held by the abbot, in this case it is now corporate, belonging 'to everyone and to no one'. The writer attempts to keep the local bishop at arm's length – he is only allowed to consecrate the abbot once elected, a situation achieved by the exemptions of 628 and 643.

The *Rule* Attributed to Eugippius and the *cellae* of Bobbio and Corbie

Of the two earliest manuscripts of the *Rule of the Master*, one contains the full text, but the other only a few selected chapters, which themselves form part of another rule made up also from extracts from Cassian, Basil, a text known as the *Sentences of Novatus*, Jerome, Pachomius and the *Rule of the Four Fathers*. The whole collection is prefaced by the *Ordo Monasterii*, ascribed to Augustine and his *Regula Tertia*. For some time now, the whole collection has been identified with the rule which, according to Isidore of Seville, Eugippius composed for his monastery of Lucullanum at Naples (see pp. 112–3 above). Not only is this identification based partly on the idea that the *Rule of the Master* dates from the first part of the sixth rather than the seventh century, but it also takes no account of the unsuitability of the rule for an organization such as Lucullanum, a monastery founded by an aristocrat and containing a famous scriptorium. The emphasis in this collection of texts on the monastery's tools and utensils and the importance placed on manual work suggests very strongly that this may have been a rule put together for use in Bobbio's cells, which were centres of agricultural production as well as of evangelization, and where the manual labour of the monks may have initially (as at Bobbio itself) included agricultural work.[110] The *Lives* of Abbots Attala and Bertulf of Bobbio certainly reveal a level of agricultural aptitude on the part of Bobbio's monks and those who lived in its *cellae* brought a degree of technical expertise to the regions in which they were settled –

for example in the manufacture and use of the plough.[111] The rule also cites a chapter of Basil which refers to the entry of 'pilgrims' into an area of the monastery where crafts are practised. The comparatively restricted liturgy set out in the *Ordo Monasterii* may have been thought suitable for a small church to which the public was admitted. Two chapters on penitents (taken from Basil) suggests that the house may have in part fulfilled the function of a penitentiary, while other sections outline the responsibilities of the abbot – presumably the abbot of Bobbio, the central cenobium – and the *praepositus* – the head of the *cella*? The whole collection concludes with extracts adapted from Basil and from Jerome's Letter 125 (the text which Columbanus' *Monastic Rule* itself concludes) forbidding monks to leave the community to become hermits. This prohibition recalls forcibly a series of incidents described in Jonas' *Life* of Abbot Attala, where a number of monks attempt to escape the disciplinary rigour of Bobbio, still at this early stage following the Columbanian rule, by leaving for hermitages.[112] Some of the cells may even have been created as a result of the revolt and it looks as if the memory of threats to abbatial authority and the discipline of the cenobium was still present when this short rule was created.

The script of the two earliest surviving manuscripts containing the *Rule of the Master* – its full version and the extracts forming part of a second rule – is similar to that of a sixth-century copy of Prudentius which had found its way into Bobbio's library and we may presume that they were copied there. By around 700, both had crossed the Alps and entered the library of one of the most prominent 'Columbanian' houses in Francia, Corbie in Picardy. Between 657 and 661, its founder, Queen Baldechildis, had endowed the monastery with no less than twelve estates. These became the sites of small monastic centres which acted as centres of Christianity in the area, and in 664 the monks of Corbie obtained a charter of exemption from the bishop of Amiens, which restricted his powers over them to a level of disciplinary control. It is not surprising that copies of the two rules were sent to Corbie which was part of the same monastic movement and which, with its satellites, had come to occupy a position very similar to that of Bobbio. Further north, Sithiu (St Bertin) also developed in a similar fashion, as did Jumièges (*Fontanella*), both founded in a diocese presided over by Dado, bishop of Rouen. The *Life of Filibert*, who trained at Rebais, describes him as a bee who drew nectar from the flowers of earlier monastic writers, especially Basil, Macarius, Benedict and Columbanus. This suggests that he may have created a rule similar to that produced for Bobbio's and Corbie's *cellae*.[113]

In rural Liguria and on the northern margins of Francia, with its populations of Gallo-Romans, Franks and Saxons, rural monastic cells probably acted initially as a centre for preaching and baptism and evolved over the subsequent century or two centuries into viable pastoral centres.[114] The existence of monastic cells – agricultural centres, retreats and baptismal centres combined – foreshadowed the possession of dependent churches by monasteries throughout other areas of Europe. Over the next few centuries, the performance of the *cura animarum* by monks became more usual as monastic estates grew and monasteries took over rural churches.

Spiritual Life and Monastic Theology

The first generation of Irish monastic leaders, Columbanus and Fursey, were themselves living exemplars of the Irish tradition in which monastic leaders alternated communal life and preaching with periods of retreat and solitary contemplation, and they brought with them the Irish veneration for Cassian and Basil, texts long popular in continental monasticism. There may have been a copy of Pelagius at Corbie in its early days, while the Bobbio manuscript containing the *Rule of the Master* also includes works by Augustine and was read and annotated carefully by a monk keenly interested in ideas of grace and predestination. Corbie was rich not only in patristic tests but also in Greek and Eastern works.[115] On the other hand, although the scriptorium of Luxeuil copied manuscripts for other monasteries, not all houses would have possessed the same texts – one had a useful 'start-up' collection of material necessary to a new monastery, including Isidore and Biblical commentaries, while another possessed material with an anti-Arian slant which appears to have originated in northern Italy. The activities of Irish *peregrini* had led to the foundation of monasteries from the Apennines to the Scheldt and it would be misleading to think of this as a coherent movement producing a single spiritual or theological identity. The former could fragment along gender lines – the visions of Aldegund of Maubeuge have long been differentiated from those of early medieval males. Aldegund is a classic 'type two' visionary: while the experiences of men were unique and involved an overwhelming experience in which the visionary was given a tour of a compartmentalized afterlife, Aldegund experienced a number of visions from her childhood onwards, in which she saw heaven as a mansion with seven columns and was visited by Christ, St Peter, the Holy Spirit, by angels, by a young girl dressed in gold and even once by the devil.[116]

A Monastic and Penitential Theology: the emergence of purgatory

The popularisation of the concept of repeatable, tariffed penance was connected with the evolution of the concept of purgatory. The ecclesiastical view of post-mortem purgation began slowly to change in the seventh century as the use of tariffed penance began to spread. Once this practice began to gain currency, the vista of the afterlife began slowly to change. What, for example, would happen if an individual died with their penance incomplete?

In the early seventh century Columbanus' sermons still – although he himself operated a severe penitential system – present a traditional and terrifying prospect.

> as the Apostle says, Fire shall try each man's work, of what sort it is. You see the scheme of the misery of human life, from earth, on earth to earth, from earth to fire from fire to judgement, from judgement to Hell or else to life; for from earth you were made, earth you tread and to earth you shall return, from earth you shall arise, in fire you shall be tried, you shall await judgement and thereafter you shall obtain either an eternal punishment or an eternal reign . . . [117]

Columbanus is speaking here of the human body, but his sermon conforms to a view of the afterlife suggested centuries earlier by Augustine and turned into certainty by his followers such as Julianus Pomerius and Cæsarius of Arles. In this schema, the souls of the very good and very bad pass straight to Hell or a state of bliss in an individual judgement which anticipates the great eschatological ordering at the end of time in which bodies will be united with souls for eternity in either Heaven or Hell. Meanwhile, the souls of the not very bad await the Last Judgement in 'dwelling-places' or the bosom of Abraham. Before the Last Judgement, they are purged or purified of their minor sins through fire, a belief based on the text of Paul's *Epistle to the Corinthians*. Augustine had also thought that suffering or tribulation in this life might purge minor sins, while Julianus Pomerius would affirm as certainty Augustine's speculations that prayers for the departed or the offering of the Eucharist might ease the passage of souls through purifying fire.[118] While Columbanus makes no reference here to the practice of suffrages for the departed, he makes no alterations to the traditional view of the afterlife.

A slightly different perspective is revealed in the work of Columbanus' hagiographer, Jonas of Susa, who narrates the deaths of a number of the nuns of Faremoutiers, describing the passage of their souls into the afterlife according to their conduct on earth. Much of this is traditional: the souls of the saintly are seen to ascend to heaven, while those of two nuns who attempt to escape from the convent are punished by hellish torment. Physical suffering and illness are presented as trials which purify the soul in preparation for death. Jonas also narrates visions in which the souls of nuns are carried up to heaven only to be returned temporarily to complete their preparations for death: they are allowed a certain amount of time, thirty or forty days, in which to amend their conduct or be purified through suffering.[119] Such returns to the living may have precedents, but the quantified periods perhaps suggests the influence of the penitentials, with their set tariffs and terms of penance. However, the traditional schema of the progress of the soul after death remains unaltered and the soul of one nun appears before Christ the Judge before being returned to earth.

A dramatically new development can be found in the *Life of Fursey*, the first major account of the journey of a soul in the other world to be composed in the early medieval period.[120] Fursey made this vision the focus of a preaching tour of Ireland which lasted ten years and he must also have publicized it in the time he spent in England and on the continent. The written version, set down in northern Francia *c*.656–7, several years after Fursey's death, is a work of great intensity and detail. In it, Fursey, gravely ill and unconscious, is swept up into another world by angels so that he may gaze down on the earth below. Seeing a gloomy valley with four fires burning in it, he is told that these fires will burn and consume the wicked. The four fires merge and grow nearer, alarming Fursey greatly; but his angel explains to him that he will not be harmed. According to the angel, this fire tests everyone according to their deserts and will burn them to the extent that illicit desires are still present. Just as the body is set on fire by unlawful desires, so the soul will burn according to the penalty owed.

With these words, the connection between an immediate post-mortem purgation and the Celtic system of tariffed penance begins to be made explicit. Several devils pursue Fursey and attempt to capture him from his angelic guides, claiming him as a sinner who has not purged his sins. One devil poses the question: has God not promised that what was not purged on earth would be punished by heaven? Here, he declares, there is no place of penance. But Fursey's accompanying angels not only defend him but reject this claim affirming that God's hidden justice still operates: here in the afterlife, they insist, penance may also exist.[121] The point has been made clear for Fursey's audience: those who have not completed penance in this life may continue to do so in the next. On to the late antique notions of post-mortem purgation or purification and intercession developed by Augustine and his followers has now been grafted the concept of post-mortem penance.

The structure and contents of the text reveal not only that that its author was familiar with the Irish *De duodecim abusivis saeculi* (composed very shortly before) but also that he probably knew the work of Columbanus and used the *Penitential* of UUinniau and perhaps even that of Cummean.[122] The picture of the afterlife would be conditioned by the structures of Irish tariffed penance outlined in the latter works. Tarriffed penance possessed similar characteristics to Irish law, sharing its private rather than public nature and its automatic penalties for specified offences. Here, applied to the afterlife, were the rudiments of what would soon begin to take shape as the early medieval structures of purgatory and intercession, from which the figure of God the Judge was now noticeably absent. Certain lesser sins would gradually begin to be thought of as automatically earning finite periods in purgatory.[123] The natural conco-mitant of this idea would, in turn, be the development of the concept of quantified periods of intercession which would automatically obtain the release of the soul from its purgatorial state.

There is evidence that the view of the afterlife as locus of penance expounded in the *Life of Fursey* was not accepted without a struggle even within monastic circles. The *Vision of Barontus*, another vision-text composed barely twenty years later, and in a related monastic envir-onment, the Frankish monasteries of Longoretus and Millebeccus, maintains the traditional belief that the souls of those who have com-mitted minor sins will await judgement in locations which are neither heaven, hell nor purgatory.[124] Although one of the purposes of the text is the promotion of private penance, it places a great weight on the poss-ibility of earning forgiveness of minor sins through the giving of alms. The emphasis on forgiveness though almsgiving centres on the fact that Barontus himself has secreted money in defiance of the monastic rule and is told by angels that he may earn pardon by giving it away as charity.

This episode appears to be a direct response to the concepts of post-mortem penance and quantified intercession, as they appear laid down in the *Dialogues*. Although attributed to Pope Gregory the Great,[125] the authenticity of this work has been disputed and it appears to have been compiled at a later date in an area where such ideas had begun to develop as a result of the spread of the practice of tarriffed penance. In Book IV, the story is told of Justus, a monk of Gregory's own monastery who similarly secretes gold coins. His misdeeds are discovered when he is fatally ill and Gregory orders that he be sent to coventry and buried in a dungheap. But after a time, Gregory repents of his harshness and orders that mass be said daily for period of thirty days: when this period is up, Justus appears in a dream to another monk to announce his liberation from fiery torments.[126] The *Vision of Barontus* is one of the earliest authentic witnesses to the existence of the *Dialogues* as a whole[127] and clearly takes issue with the idea that a sin such as that of Justus may be purged in the afterlife through the offering of the eucharist for a set period of time. Instead, it proffers the more traditional remedy of remis-sion of sin in this life, through the giving of alms.

However, the notion of post-mortem purgation and quantified inter-cession was once again promoted in a monastic environment in the eighth century, when the English monk and author, Bede the Venerable, not only recounted Fursey's vision in his *Ecclesiastical History* but also added a similar vision, attributed to a Northumbrian named Dryhthelm, which makes a clear link between post-mortem penance and intercessory prayer or the offering of the Eucharist.[128] Belief in purgatory and set forms of intercession, particularly Eucharistic intercession, began to change the shape of monastic life from the eighth century on. While other elements – such as the desire to replicate the solemn stational liturgies of Rome – would also lead to the multiplication of masses in monasteries, the idea of purgatory became one of the foundations of the medieval superstructure of monastic intercession, with its elaborate systems of liturgy and multi-plication of 'private' masses, offered for intercessory purposes.[129] In the seventh century it is thought that comparatively few monks were priests, but from the eighth onwards, such numbers increased as monasteries accepted payment for priest-monks to say votive masses and masses for the dead. A new chapter in monastic history was gradually beginning to unfold.

9

England in the Seventh Century

The Diffusion of the Benedictine *Rule*

After its introduction to Francia by the Columbanian monasteries, the combined Benedictine–Columbanian rule made great headway in northern and eastern and also to some extent central Francia. Queen Baldechildis, who retired to her own foundation of Chelles in 664, was not only involved in the foundation of Corbie, St Wandrille and Jumièges but had a 'regular' way of life – based on the combined rules – introduced at some of the oldest and most prominent Frankish basilical monasteries – St Denis at Paris, St Germanus in Auxerre, St Médard, Soissons, St Aignan, Orleans and even that of St Martin at Tours.[1] The *Rule* of Benedict, used at first in conjunction with Columbanian *Rules*, began gradually to rise to a position of dominance where it was used on its own: a charter issued by Bishop Drauscius of Soissons in 667 for the convent dedicated to the Virgin in his city stipulates that the nuns are to follow the *Rules* of Benedict and Columbanus but also prescribes the use of Benedict's – rather than Columbanus' – liturgy.[2] One of the nuns of this convent was the mother of Bishop Leodegar of Autun (663–679), who attempted to impose the use of the Benedictine *Rule* on all the monasteries of his diocese. The spread of the cult of Benedict as a saint in northern Francia, inspired in the first place by knowledge of the *Rule*, itself in turn helped to promote the *Rule*'s popularity. A ninth-century text claims that the monks of Fleury-sur-Loire, a foundation generously endowed by both Chlothar II and Theuderich III,[3] mounted an expedition in 653 to recover the relics of St Benedict from Monte Cassino which had been destroyed by the invading Lombards and now lay in ruins. The truth of this claim has been much disputed[4] and it seems likely that if the expedition ever took place it was not at this early stage, but only after the *Dialogues*, with their second book devoted to Benedict's life and miracles, had begun to circulate in Francia. The first secure evidence for this dates from the 670s, when the *Dialogues* are referred to or quoted in the *Vision of Barontus* and the *Passio Praejecti*.[5]

The mixed Columbanian and Benedictine *Rule*, however, made slower progress in the south where older styles of monasticism predominated in the Rhone valley and on the southern coast: the first evidence of its use – apart from the abortive attempt to introduce it to Lérins where it was identified with intrusive northerners – is at the monastery of St Victor in the diocese of Vaison in the late seventh century.[6] Neither rule seems to have found its way into the Iberian peninsula, where monasticism was based on traditional texts: the Pachomian *Rules*, Augustine, Basil and Cassian. In the sixth century Bishop Martin of Braga, founder of the monastery of Dumio, had composed moral treatises which borrow heavily from the *Institutes* and *Conferences* and when Isidore of Seville composed his own monastic *Rule* in the early seventh century, he was highly dependent on the thought of earlier monastic writers. Whether any traces of knowledge of Benedict can be found in his *Rule* is doubtful as the resemblances between the two authors are slight and may be a matter of parallelism rather than dependence.[7] Isidore's younger brother Leander of Seville based his work, *On the Training of Nuns*, on Cassian, Cyprian, Jerome and Augustine.[8]

Leander of Seville was a friend and correspondent of Pope Gregory the Great. When it was believed that Gregory followed the Benedictine *Rule* himself, it was naturally also held that he would have promoted its use elsewhere and that the head of his English mission, his prior Augustine, would have brought the Benedictine *Rule* to England with him. But the notion of Gregory's own Benedictinism is now under attack and there are no quotations from the *Rule* in Gregory's undisputedly authentic writings.[9] The observance brought by Augustine to England would have been based on that of Gregory's own monasticism – resonant with the thought of Basil and Cassian. Augustine also set up a basilical monastery in Canterbury on the model of the Roman basilicas. Elsewhere in seventh-century England, the dominant monastic influences were Irish and Frankish. While Irish traditions were based on the more diffuse Basilian rules and the writings of Cassian, the close contacts between England and Francia led to knowledge of the mixed Benedictine and Columbanian *Rules*. It is even possible that the *Rule of a Certain Father to the Virgins* was known in England: this may have been composed for Faremoutiers and could also have been used at Les Andelys and Chelles. The later *Life* of Abbess Bertilla tells us not only that Chelles served as a training-ground for English nuns but that even from over the seas the faithful Kings of the Saxons, through trusted messengers, asked her to send some of her disciples for the learning and holy instruction they heard were wonderful in her, that they might build convents of men and nuns in their land.[10]

A version of the Benedictine–Columbanian rule used by the male monasteries of double houses and the Luxovian group may also have arrived in the country around the 650s or 60s. Even before this, it is likely that Birinus (who, according to Bede, came to Britain at the direction of Pope Honorius I in 635 and was consecrated by Asterius, Bishop of Genoa) brought knowledge of both Benedictine and Columbanian *Rules* from Bobbio when he arrived in England in the 630s as Bishop of the West Saxons. English travellers to the continent were also responsible for bringing the Benedictine *Rule* to England. Benedict Biscop, founder and abbot of Monkwearmouth-Jarrow in Northumbria, laid down a way of life for his monks based on the customs of no less than seventeen different monasteries which he had visited in the late 650s and 660s. Biscop's reverence for Benedict of Nursia is shown in the way in which he took Benedict's name, although at what stage in his career he adopted it is unknown. Bede's *Lives of the Abbots of Monkwearmouth-Jarrow* records Biscop's attempt, in 690, to prevent his brother from succeeding to the abbacy by invoking the Benedictine *Rule*.[11] The hagiographer of Bishop Wilfrid of Northumbria (one of whose patrons was Acgilberht, bishop of Wessex and brother of Theodochildis of Jouarre) claimed that he 'brought about a great improvement' by introducing the Benedictine rule to Northumbria in the late 660s. Like Benedict Biscop, Wilfrid, too may have come across it in his travels in Francia and recognized its usefulness.[12]

The Liturgy of Monkwearmouth-Jarrow and the Benedictine *Rule*

The anonymous *Life* of Abbot Ceolfrid of Jarrow tells us that when many of the community at Jarrow died of plague, Ceolfrid ordered that the antiphonal singing of psalms should cease except at vespers and matins.[13] This practical instruction parallels one given in Chapter 17 of the Benedictine *Rule* which directs that antiphons should cease if numbers are small and has been read as evidence of the use of the *Rule* of Benedict at Monkwearmouth-Jarrow.[14] But are the liturgical instructions of the Benedictine *Rule* as transmitted to us in manuscripts from the eighth century onwards part of the original *Rule* itself? As they stand, they resemble the public liturgy of the Roman basilicas rather than the traditional, contemplative monastic office, based around the *psalterium currens*.[15] The

possibility that the *Rule* originally contained different liturgical instructions, for which a Roman-based liturgy was later substituted should be
considered.[16] The first surviving manuscripts of the *Rule* of St Benedict
date from as late as the eighth century: the earliest of all comes from
England – probably south-western England – but has possible Northumbrian connections[17] and contains the liturgy that we know today. The
Roman basilical liturgy had arrived in Kent with Augustine and reached
Northumbria with Paulinus; now under Benedict Biscop, Monkwearmouth-Jarrow enjoyed very strong connections with Rome and the
papacy. Biscop made several journeys to Rome and Bede records of his
fifth expedition that he returned with a variety of treasures: books 'of
every sort', relics, and a papal privilege of exemption granted by Pope
Agatho. Amongst the books was a pandect of the Bible which originated
in Cassiodorus' monastery of Viviarium. Working from and adapting this
original with the help of other version of the Bible, the monks of
Monkwearmouth-Jarrow later produced three massive Bibles – one for
each of their two monasteries and a third to be presented to the pope,
which still survives as the famous Codex Amiatinus, now in Florence.
Biscop also introduced to his monastery

> the order of chanting and singing the psalms and conducting the liturgy
> according to the practice in force at Rome. To this end Pope Agatho, at
> Benedict's request, offered him the services of the chief cantor of St Peter's
> and abbot of the monastery of St Martin, a man called John. Benedict
> brought him back to Britain to be choirmaster in the monastery. John
> taught the monks at first hand how things were done in the churches in
> Rome and also committed a good part of his instruction to writing. This is
> still preserved in memory of him in the monastery library.[18]

This statement, with its precise reference to an order of chanting and
singing the palms suggests that more than just Roman *cantilena* was
being taught. Bede thought John's work important enough to record it
in his *Ecclesiastical History* as well. Could John the cantor's instructions
on the Roman *cursus* have provided the ultimate inspiration for the
liturgical instructions which now appear in the Benedictine *Rule*?

Monasteries and Pastoral Care in England

Although a British church survived in the west of England, much of the
country was under Anglo-Saxon control and only converted to Christianity in the course of the seventh century. At first, the mission sent by
Pope Gregory I to Kent, headed by Augustine, appeared to enjoy considerable success. Its path was smoothed by Aethelbehrt's Frankish Queen

Bertha, like Chrodechildis a daughter of King Charibert, who had been practising the Christian religion in her own household for thirty-five years. Gregory wrote to Bishop Eulogius of Alexandria in July 598 announcing the baptism of more than ten thousand *Angli*, on Christmas Day 597 and Bede recounts the baptism of the Kentish king, Aethelbehrt, and also the establishment of dioceses at London and Rochester. However, this achievement proved to be short-lived and a pagan reaction set in after Aethelbehrt's death. His own son, Eadbald and three sons of his nephew, Saberht of the East Saxons, who had converted along with his uncle, reverted to paganism on their fathers' deaths. Redwald, King of the East Angles, who had converted to Christianity when Aethelberht was in power, now refused to abandon altogether his old religion, keeping a Christian altar along with pagan ones in the same temple.

Further north, the mission appeared poised to enjoy greater success, when King Edwin of Northumbria married the Christian princess Ethelberga of Kent, who took north with her Paulinus, one of the Roman monks of Gregory's mission. Even so, while Paulinus' arrival in Northumbria took place perhaps as early as 619, political conditions were not right for the Northumbrian king, Edwin, to convert to Christianity until 627. Along with him was baptized his young great-niece Hild who would later become the abbess of Streonaeshalch/Whitby. However, the Canterbury mission in the north then collapsed with Edwin's death in 633. Paulinus fled his diocese leaving behind only a deacon named James who remained in York until his death preaching, baptizing and teaching the faithful to sing in church 'after the uses of Rome and Canterbury'. In Kent, the Augustinian mission recovered ground, though Augustine's four successors to the see of Canterbury were all members of the original Roman mission and it was not until 644 that an Englishman, Ithamar, was appointed to one of the Kentish dioceses, that of Rochester.[19]

The first monasteries were in the south and played an important part in the Gregorian mission to Kent: set up first in Canterbury and then in Rochester and London, they helped provide liturgical service at the cathedrals, in the same way that the basilical monasteries assisted with the daily liturgy at the major Roman basilicas. Outside Kent, however, conditions were different and England in the period of the conversion presented a very different picture of ecclesiastical organization to that found in Francia or Italy. Instead of operating from continental-style dioceses centred on former Roman cities, seventh-century English bishops were appointed to individual kingdoms and peoples, thus creating large dioceses which followed tribal divisions. They might be semi-peripatetic and on occasion operate out of monasteries as a more convenient way of preaching, baptising and also of remaining in contact with the king. Other purposes too might be served by a monastic base: after the failure of the Canterbury mission to Northumbria, King

Oswald, a Bernician who had lived in Ireland turned to Colm Cille's monastery of Iona to provide him with a bishop. The first candidate sent proved unsuitable, but was quickly replaced by Aidan, who established a monastic centre for his episcopal activities at Lindisfarne, off the Northumbrian coast. By choosing Lindisfarne as the centre of his diocese and using a monastery as his base, Bishop Aidan of Northumbria combined evangelizatory and pastoral activities with a contemplative, monastic life.

Writing in the eighth century Bede held Aidan up as an example to the clergy of his own day. He

> gave his clergy an inspiring example of self-discipline and continence and the highest recommendation of his teaching to all was that he and his followers lived as they taught. He never sought or cared for any wordly possessions and loved to give away to the poor who chanced to meet him whatever he received from kings or wealthy folk...His life is in marked contrast to the apathy of our own times, for all who walked with him, whether monks or laymen were required to meditate, that is, either to read the scriptures or to learn the psalms.[20]

Cuthbert, who became a bishop in Northumbria in the 680s, also combined an episcopal with a contemplative life.[21] But Bede also indicates that there had been a specifically pastoral dimension to the activity of the monastery of Melrose where Cuthbert himself had trained, claiming that while prior, he had followed the example of his superior Boisil and

> did not restrict his teaching and influence to the monastery but worked to rouse the ordinary folk far and near to exchange their foolish customs for a love of heavenly joys. For many profaned the faith that they professed by a wicked life and at a time of plague some had even abandoned the Christian sacrament and had recourse to the delusive remedies of idolatry...Following Boisil's example, in order to correct such errors, he often used to leave the monastery, sometimes on horseback but more frequently on foot and visit the neighbouring towns...Cuthbert was so skilful a speaker, and had such a light in his angelic face, and such a love for proclaiming his message, that none presumed to hide his innermost secrets...He mainly used to preach in the villages that lay far distant...it could sometimes be a week...and occasionally an entire month, before he returned home after staying in the mountains to guide the peasants heavenwards by his teachings and virtuous example.[22]

Though Bede's picture is an idealized one, it shows how, for him, preaching, teaching monks were a reality.[23] Melrose lay in the northern part of the vast diocese of Northumbria and where other ecclesiastical personnel and structures were thin on the ground, it must have seemed natural for a number of monasteries to exercise some sort of pastoral role at least where the initial stages of conversion were concerned. Bede's own monastery of Monkwearmouth-Jarrow (a dual community) also carried out pastoral work. There are two churches at Jarrow, of which the second and smaller may have served as a baptismal church. The wording of some of Bede's homilies, which have been preserved in Latin but which would have been delivered in the vernacular, suggests that on certain major feast days he may have preached to an audience not only of monks but of those recently-baptized or about to be baptized. At other times he may have addressed an audience which included an 'additional troop of brethren', probably the workers on the monastery's estates.[24] Bede pairs the activities of the clergy with those of abbots:

> By pastors are understood not only the bishops, priests and deacons, but also the heads of monasteries and all the faithful who have the care of even small households.[25]

Excavations at Monkwearmouth have revealed the existence of a lay cemetery, containing the bones of men, women and children.[26] A pastoral as well as an educational role has also been postulated for Hild's double monastery of Whitby/*Streonaeshalch*, where the first English poet Cædmon lived and worked.[27] Not only was she regarded as *magistra* and *doctrix* who fufilled the roles of teacher and counsellor, but she presided over what was in effect a family of dependent smaller monasteries at locations such as Hackness and *Osingadun*.[28]

In other areas, too, some monasteries undertook an active role in the early stages of conversion. Bede records that the small Irish community at Bosham in southern England attempted to get the local populace to listen to their preaching – even if they enjoyed no success.[29] The monks of the double houses of Minster-in-Sheppey and Minster-in-Thanet may have carried out pastoral services.[30] The monastery of Medeshamstede (Peterborough) had extensive dependencies which also seem to have operated as – or been associated with – pastoral centres. The monks of one of its dependencies, Breedon, were obliged to leave a priest behind to continue pastoral services when they left the site and the important pastoral role of Medeshamstede – even if it was not the original purpose of these monasteries – may account for the extensive exemptions later claimed for it in the *Anglo-Saxon Chronicle*.[31]

Bede, as a monk, naturally emphasizes monastic involvement in evangelization and pastoral care and gives a less than full picture of the other means by which both were provided in England. There also existed churches at *villae regales* as well as baptismal churches and the latest model of pastoral care in England suggests that much of it was provided by clergy working at or from 'minsters' – a term which derives from *monasterium* – with pastoral responsibilities for large areas, 'the institutions that lay behind the mother-churches' referred to in the Domesday Book.[32] Current thinking stresses the fluidity of the Latin word *monasterium*, which was used interchangeably to describe both types of community. But in Northumbria in the early days of conversion, it is possible that not only Monkwearmouth-Jarrow, but also the monasteries controlled by Bishop Wilfrid at Hexham and Ripon, played important pastoral or baptismal roles.

However any involvement by monasteries – as opposed to clerical 'minsters' – in pastoral care must have begun rapidly to diminish in importance, when Theodore of Tarsus arrived in England as Archbishop of Canterbury in 669. This period sees the initiation of a period in which more conventional diocesan hierarchies and structures gradually replaced the arrangements which had evolved in many areas.[33] The huge diocese of Northumbria was a case in point. Theodore proposed a reorganization of the English dioceses, but was stalled at the Council of Hertford in 672. When Wilfrid was exiled by his king in 678, Theodore was able to divide his diocese into three. In 681, a new bishopric was created at Hexham, as part of the further ecclesiastical reorganization of Northumbria carried out by Theodore, who now split the diocese into five. This created more manageable units (although one of them, Ripon, would disappear by the eighth century and there were no dioceses west of the Pennines). Two different conceptions of episcopal office and activity had confronted each other: the English one where the diocese was co-terminous with the kingdom or people and Theodore's which, although it took account of tribal divisions, was more like that of Gregory the Great, where a diocese was a smallish administrative unit.[34] In the former model, aspects of pastoral care had sometimes been provided through monasteries. In the latter, Theodore's vision of church organization was a more conventional clerical one. Theodore was also astute enough to see that control of monasteries such as Hexham and Ripon had brought Wilfrid control of immense wealth – a wealth perceived and resented by the Northumbrian royal family and which may have led to his expulsion from his diocese.[35] Both monasteries now became the centres of new dioceses, undoubtedly for financial as well as administrative reasons.

The debate at Hertford and the subsequent division of Northumbria and conversion of monasteries into diocesan centres must have been unsettling for the new foundations of Jarrow-Monkwearmouth. The creation of the diocese of Hexham may explain the fact that several years later Abbot Ceolfrid petitioned Pope Sergius (d. 701)

> to obtain an indult granting privileges for the protection of the monastery similar to those granted by Pope Agatho to Benedict [Biscop]. When it was brought back and produced before the synod, the assembled bishops and the noble King Aldfrid confirmed it with their signatures in the same way,

as is well known, the former privilege was publicly confirmed in synod by the king and bishops of the time.[36]

Theodore's work had begun to undermine any possible claims by monasteries to the right to perform pastoral work. While Bede, in his *Homilies*, was still able to count burial as a pastoral duty performed by monks, he does not mention either baptism or the administration of the Eucharist. Perhaps, by Bede's time, monasteries had ceased even occasionally to administer or control the administration of the latter, while still burying the dead. By 747, the provisions of the Council of *Clofesho* do not contain any clear indication that monasteries still undertook any forms of pastoral care.[37] For a brief period, some English monasteries had taken an active role in pastoral work, but once the initial period of conversion had been superseded by one of reorganization and consolidation that era drew to a close.

The *Dialogues* and Monks as Preachers and Teachers

Is Northumbria – at the point when Theodore first proposed the division of the disocese – an alternative context for the composition of the *Dialogues*? (see pp. 130–6 and 189 above). Their portrayal of monastic evangelizing and pastoral activity, anomalous in the context of sixth-century century Italy, becomes suddenly relevant in the Northumbria of the early 670s, when some of the major monasteries were threatened with having pastoral responsibilities (and with this, income) removed from them. The assertion that monastic leaders in the past, especially St Benedict, had been successful preachers may have been thought to strengthen their claim to a continuance of their activities. The caricatured hostility of the clergy to Benedict's and Equitius' activities – the denunciation of Equitius to the pope by a cleric, the priest Florentius' attempt to poison Benedict – all suggest the existence of considerable tensions between monks and clergy over the right to preach and teach when these passages were composed.

If, as is suggested here, the *Dialogues* might have been composed in seventh-century Northumbria, many other puzzling features of their contents would begin to fall into place. The dichotomy between the recommendation of the *Rule* and its portrayal of Benedict fits into a scene where the *Rule* was revered but not necessarily followed in its entirety. It would also explain the way in which the *Dialogues*' characterization of post-mortem purgation appears to develop from the Irish system of tarriffed penance, with which Gregory I cannot have been familiar in 593–4.[38] The *Dialogues* are a multi-faceted work and their thoughts on the soul and the afterlife as expressed in Book Four would prove a useful textbook for those engaged in the work of teaching and conversion.[39] Northumbrian monastic circles associated with Benedict Biscop and Wilfrid – both of whom made several journeys to Rome, where they could have acquired the 'unpublished' Gregorian material in the *Dialogues* – had both motive and opportunity to create a text enshrining their view that monastic leaders should preach and teach and also a theology of purgatory which was a development of the system of private confession and tariffed penance. Attributed to Gregory, such a theology – recently developed and not necessarily acceptable to all as the reaction of the *Visio Baronti* indicates – might carry real weight in England. Gregory's importance to the English rested not only on the fact that he had been pope but on his attempts to bring the Christian faith to England and while his cult only developed in a limited way among his friends and admirers in Rome, it took off in a major way there in the later seventh century.[40] In the late seventh century and early eighth, Northumbria – in marked contrast to southern England – produced a large number of saints' *Lives*, such as those of Wilfrid, Ceolfrid and the abbots of Monkwearmouth-Jarrow as well as the Whitby *Life* of Pope Gregory the Great.[41] As they have come down to us, the *Dialogues* might possibly constitute yet another product of this highly political and polemical period of Northumbrian literary activity.

Royal and Aristocratic Monasteries

Just as kings and aristocrats in Ireland and Francia had swiftly taken over monasticism, so one of the most noticeable features of the Christianization of England was the extent and rapidity of royal involvement in monastic foundations. Missionary bishops and monks had targeted rulers and their families, who then accepted Christianity before their peoples and promptly founded monasteries which naturally reflected their dynastic and political as well as religious aims and aspirations. From the point of view of the church, the rapid foundation of monasteries by newly-converted kings and their families was welcome as it both stood as witness to the commitment to Christianity of royal families as well as providing training-colleges for priests. As in seventh-century Francia, monasteries represented the merging of religious and elite secular interests: they were centres of the cult of royal saints, of liturgical intervention for the souls of the dead and at the same time royal or aristocratic estates and centres of family power. Gilling, in Deira, was founded by King Oswiu, on the recommendation of Queen Eanfled, to atone for his sin of killing Oswine, the Deiran king.[42] There, the monks were to pray continuously for the souls of both murdered and murderer. Whitby was the burial-place of King Edwin of Deira, the southern Northumbrian Kingdom, and the focus of his cult.[43]

Royal involvement may be seen in the foundation of Monkwearmouth-Jarrow (the two houses were established in 674 and 682 respectively by the nobles who became its first abbots, Benedict Biscop and Ceolfrid). It was also richly endowed by King Ecgfrith – who gave fifty or seventy hides in the case of Monkwearmouth, rather less in the case of Jarrow. Biscop spent a great deal of time at the royal court advising the king and according to the *Life* of Ceolfrid, abbot of Jarrow, this foundation was established for the salvation of the king's soul. Significantly, Bede's homily on Benedict Biscop specifies that the monastery's endowment came from the king's own estates. This would seem to differentiate Monkwearmouth-Jarrow from other aristocratic houses and suggests that that it had much closer connections with the king. Other factors tend to confirm this view. By 716 the combined communities are said to have had six hundred monks – though this number may have included estate workers – and to have owned one hundred and fifty hides of land.

If English royalty was quick to use monasteries as centres of royal power, their aristocracies did not lag far behind them. Warrior nobles were eager to acquire land by charter – 'bookland' – from the king. This, unlike land which was part of the kin inheritance and could therefore not be alienated without consent, could be disposed of at will. Kings may have given such grants in return for warrior-service by nobles in the belief that they could recover the land, only to find that nobles chose to create family monasteries instead and the land thus technically became unrecoverable church land. The major rush to do so in Northumbria came, according to Bede, after the death of King Aldfrid in 705.[44] Though this was essentially the same process that led, on the continent, to the foundation of some of the greatest Frankish monasteries, Bede is highly uncomplimentary about some examples of Northumbrian aristocratic monasticism:

> [Nobles] give money to the kings and under pretence of building mon-asteries they acquire possessions, wherein they more freely indulge their licentiousness; and procuring these by a royal edict to be assigned to them in inheritance, they get the deed by which these privileges are con-firmed . . . And thus having gained possession of farms and villages, they free themselves from every bond . . . and in the character of superiors over monks, though they are but laymen, they do nothing but gratify their desires therein . . . Moreover, they display the same folly in acquiring land for their wives, as they claim, to erect convents, and these, equally foolish, though also laypeople, permit themselves to become the superiors over Christ's handmaidens.[45]

Historians have rightly emphasized the positive aspects of this fusion of warrior culture and Christianity: Bede himself, a product of the great and distinguished Northumbrian community of Monkwearmouth-Jarrow, was probably over-exacting in his expectations. Some family monasteries were, like royal monasteries and double houses, vibrant centres of Christian culture and even of pastoral or missionary activity directed towards those who lived on their estates. But while not all 'family' monasteries in either Northumbria, the rest of England or Francia were as bogus as those castigated by Bede, the vehemence of his complaints reveals the way in which the institution of monasticism could potentially be abused to the point where it lost all but the most superficial religious character. On his deathbed in 690, Benedict Biscop, the first abbot and founder of Monkwearmouth-Jarrow, attempted to prevent his brother succeeding to his office as was often the norm, undoubtedly fearing the dilution of his religious ideals.

Women's Monasteries in England

Just as in Francia, women's monasticism in England was a highly significant social and religious force. The earliest nunnery established in England was at Folkestone, founded around 630: but at least a dozen double houses appeared in the following decades in Kent, Essex, Northumbria, East and Middle Anglia, Mercia, Sussex and Wessex. Amongst the most prestigious and best known in the seventh and eighth centuries were Whitby, Hartlepool, Coldingham, Wenlock, Minster-in-Thanet, Minster-in Sheppey, Barking, Repton and Wimborne. Many double houses – Whitby, Coldingham, Ely, Wimborne, Much Wenlock, Minster-in-Thanet, and Bardney in Mercia – were founded for or by, or endowed by, royal women.[46] Both royalty and aristocracy in England seem to have endowed houses for women following the same principle that the Frankish aristocracy had adopted: that a nunnery or double house headed by a daughter or widow was a good means of keeping both land and influence within the family, thus securing the position and power of royal or aristocratic dynasties. As in Francia, the position of abbess usually passed to daughters, sisters or nieces.

The double house ruled by a royal princess, widow or even divorcée, was one of the most important political, religious and cultural institutions of seventh-century England. Handing over some ecclesiastical functions to the female side of the line kept more males free to act as warriors. First-generation royal converts embraced a version of the monastic ideal which combined religious with secular functions, as royal women who became abbesses maintained the important female role of counsellor, adviser and mediator (a role normally played by royal brides, married off to strengthen their family's position). Hartlepool was founded by Heiu, the first woman in Northumbria to be consecrated a nun. After Heiu's departure, the royal Hild was first put in charge of Hartlepool and then founded Streaneshalch. Her successor as abbess was Ælfflæd, granddaughter of King Edwin who ruled jointly with her mother Eanfled. Eanfled had been baptized as an infant by Paulinus and, according to Bede, was the first native Northumbrian to become a Christian. Bede records that, as abbess, Hild functioned as counsellor to both commoners and royalty and presided over the Synod of Whitby in 664, where the differences between 'Celtic' and 'Roman' customs were discussed.[47] This mediatory role reflects the continuation of the role which Hild might previously have played as a woman of high secular status, while the *Life* of Wilfrid describes her successor, Abbess Ælfflæd, as the 'best counsellor and a constant source of strength to the whole province'.[48]

Frankish influence was from the beginning apparent in the fashion for female religious houses. Bede records that Earcongota daughter of the Kentish King Earconbert

> was a nun of outstanding virtue who served God in a convent in Frankish territory founded by the noble Abbess Fara at a place called Brie [*Evoriacum*/Faremoutiers], for as yet there were few monasteries built in English territory and many who entered conventual life went from Britain to the Frankish realm of Gaul for that purpose. Girls of noble family were also sent there for their education or to be betrothed to their heavenly Bridegroom, especially to the houses of Brie, Chelles and Andelys.[49]

Æthelburh, daughter of King Anna of Kent, and his stepdaughter Sæthryd, both became abbesses of Faremoutiers. One of the Anglo-Saxon royal women who travelled to Chelles was Hereswith, the sister of Hild of Whitby (614–680). Hild was thirty-three years old when she decided to take up the religious life – it is possible that she had previously been married and widowed, though Bede merely remarks that she spent her time 'most nobly in secular occupations'. When she decided to abandon secular life

> and serve God alone, she went to the province of the East Angles, whose king was her kinsman; for having renounced her home and all that she possessed, she wished if possible to travel on from there into Gaul and to live an exile for Our Lord's sake in the monastery of Chelles . . . For her sister Hereswith, mother of Aldwulf, king of the East Angles, was already living there as a professed nun and awaiting her eternal crown. Inspired by her example, Hild remained in the province a full year, intending to join her overseas.[50]

But Hild never reached Chelles. Instead she was recalled by Bishop Aidan and given a single hide of land on which she and a handful of companions observed the monastic rule for a year. This appears to have been probationary period imposed by Aidan to test her resolve and capacities. It was after this that she became abbess of Hartlepool and finally founded *Streonaeshalch*, identified as Whitby.

Along with Monkwearmouth-Jarrow and the monasteries of Ripon and Hexham, Whitby was one of the premier religious houses in Northumbria. The functions of this great double house, though it was headed by a woman, were analogous to those of male monasteries. Bede credits Whitby with the education of no less than six men who were consecrated as bishops (five of whom actually ruled as such). How far Hild herself was personally responsible for their instruction is not clear. It has been argued that Bede was sufficiently imbued with male clerical prejudice to understate her role, although others have taken his account of her career at face value and characterized her primarily as a wise administrator and counsellor.[51] Two of her clerical trainees who became bishops were sent on to Canterbury to study further with Theodore of Tarsus: the curriculum followed by one, Oftfor, was primarily reading and scriptural study which seems, according to Bede, to have been the Whitby curriculum. The extent of learning demonstrated by the monk or possibly nun of Whitby who composed the anonymous *Life of Gregory the Great* between 704 and 714 is mainly Biblical, although there are references to Augustine and Jerome.[52] However these may have come from anthologies and a solitary quotation from Horace almost certainly originates in a grammar. But while knowledge of Gregory's own works might have been based on books borrowed from other centres, it is possible that John and Oftfor transmitted back to Whitby information acquired at Canterbury, such as the eastern text, the *Spiritual Meadow* of John Moschos, brought to England by Theodore of Tarsus. A considerable level of learning may have been possible at some houses: abbess Cuthswith of Inkberrow in Worcestershire – a 'family' monastery – owned an Italian manuscript of one of Jerome's commentaries.[53] The nuns of Barking in Essex must have possessed an impressive library as they were exhorted to study not merely grammar and scripture but also patristics, the *Conferences* of Cassian and the *Moralia* of Gregory the Great, as well as exegesis, history and chronology.[54]

Earlier excavations have revealed styli (as well as loom-weights, evidence that the nuns practised traditional 'feminine' monastic crafts) in what may now prove to be the women's part of the Whitby community as well as toiletry items which show that secular values had not been abandoned altogether by members of this high-status community.[55] The latest excavations at Whitby will reveal more about the extent of separation between the male and female sections of the house. If Hild did indeed teach six future bishops herself, it suggests that even if there were two separate residential enclosures, boundaries between them were to some extent permeable. Examples of these contacts could be multiplied: at Barking, for example, while there were separate enclosures or quarters for the monks and nuns, they appear to have used the church simultaneously and a dying boy scholar called for one of the nuns, Æsica, by name. In England as in Francia, strict active enclosure seems to have been considered 'less suitable' as Bishop Donatus of Besançon had written, for seventh-century double houses headed by noblewomen or royalty. Royal abbesses could both receive male clerical guests in the nunnery – to take only one example Cuthbert visited Coldingham – and travel outside to give advice and counsel, as Ælfflæd did, when she attended the synod on the Nidd to speak in support of Wilfrid. In the early eighth century, nuns travelled to hear St Boniface teach at his monastery of Nursling.[56] The one text which suggests strict segregation and enclosure, the *Life* of the eighth-century Abbess Lioba, was composed in the ninth century and cannot be considered reliable as strict enclosure had been back on the agenda since the eighth century as episcopal and clerical control of the church became more institutionalized.[57]

The importance of women and double houses in English monastic and ecclesiastical life in the seventh century is reflected in the *De virginitate* (*On virginity*) of Bishop Aldlhem, produced for Abbess Hildelith and the nuns of Barking in the late seventh or more probably the early eighth century. The plan of *De virginitate* itself reflects its composition for a double house: its martyrology includes both women and men. Aldhelm recognizes the important role played by the nuns in both monastic life and the church when he addresses them in the same terms as men – as *milites Christi* or soldiers of Christ, fighting the good fight, participants, through their learning, which brings them nearer to God in the struggle to covert and Christianize the English kingdoms. Aldhelm is also conscious of a high proportion of widows or even of women who had divorced their husbands among the nuns of Barking: Abbess Hildelith had probably once been a married woman herself. In English double houses in general, evidence for unmarried women flocking to join the religious life in great numbers is scarce. Aldhelm even went as far as reformulating Jerome's classic evaluation of the relative rewards which virginity and marriage would reap in heaven – thirty, sixty and one hundred fold – by introducing the idea that chastity as opposed to simple physical virginity also has a value. By postulating a moral conception of purity rather than a strictly physical one, Aldhelm was responding not only to the status of Hildelith but also to that of others such as Cuthburg, sister of the kings of Wessex, who left her husband Aldfrith of Northumbria and eventually founded Wimborne.[58]

Although Aldhelm is prepared to tamper with the conventions established by an authority such as Jerome in response to the peculiarities of the English situation, other aspects of his thinking are more conventional. Even while he is bending inherited views of virginity to suit the social conventions of his time, he is also maintaining that suicide in the defence of virginity is not only permissible but laudable. In his view, the nuns of Barking are not only soldiers of Christ, but, more conventionally, Brides of Christ who must resist the temptation to deck themselves out in finery, curl their hair or file their nails. A little later in the eighth century Bede, in his *Ecclesiastical History*, launches a thinly disguised polemic against the double house when he writes of Coldingham that both nuns and monks were either 'sunk in unprofitable sleep or awake only to sin', and that the nuns dressed themselves up to attract the attention of outsiders of the opposite sex.[59] Bede stands accused of elsewhere underplaying or undermining the achievements of the royal abbesses Hild and Ælfflæd: he does not record Hild as ever speaking at the Council of Whitby, though she presided over it. His rewriting of the anonymous *Life of Cuthbert* transforms its construction of the relationship between Ælfflæd and Cuthbert from one of 'soul-friendship' to one where Ælfflæd is portrayed as an importunate woman who, excluded from sharing Cuthbert's insights, interrupts him when he is saying mass and detains him at a feast, which symbolizes profane activity.[60] By the time Aldhelm composed *De Virginitate*, the English church had begun to move towards the segregation of sexes and a separation of pastoral and monastic functions which would render the double house redundant. The *Penitential* attributed to Theodore of Tarsus, the Greek Archbishop of Canterbury who arrived in the country in 669, notes disapprovingly that:

> it is not permitted for men religious to have women [among them], nor for women, men: nonetheless we shall not overthrow that which is the custom of this province.[61]

But the custom of the province would eventually vanish under the weight of ecclesiastical disapproval and the disappearance of the double houses' social role and function in the process of conversion. The English monk Boniface's use of nunneries as well as monasteries in his efforts to convert the Germans in the 730s, however, perpetuated the institution of the powerful abbess.

The decline of the famed Anglo-Saxon double houses, like their Frankish counterparts, indicates not only the extent of ecclesiastical disapproval of these anomalous institutions, but also that they were no longer considered to fulfil a useful dynastic function. Irish nunneries declined in importance as their land was re-absorbed by the kin-group. Evidence not just from England and Francia but from all over Christian Europe in the seventh century indicates the extent to which monasticism was affected, one way or the other by the interests of the landowning groups. In Italy, it was not until the Lombard King Liutprand II in the early eighth century legalized donations to the church that aristocratic patronage of monasteries really took off.[62] By contrast, in north-western Spain, although the alienation of land to the church was difficult if not impossible, the founding of a monastery became so attractive to a middle class of landowners that a new type of monastic rule evolved to meet their needs. Late seventh-century Galician monasticism, very different from that of the rest of the Iberian peninsula, fragmented into unusual patterns. On the one hand, there was the group of monasteries headed by St Fructuosus of Braga, monk-bishop of Dumio from 653–4 who aimed to promote a monasticized episcopate in opposition to secular bishops. This group of abbots and abbesses was governed by the *Sancta Communis Regula* and a *pactum* was made between each abbot and his monk which limited the powers of the abbot. On the other, there was the radically egalitarian *Consensoria monachorum* which emerged from the family monasteries which sprang up in the wake of Fructuosus' preaching. Although small landed proprietors and their families were inspired to take up the religious life, they could not alienate family land even to the church. The result was that the monasteries which they founded were unmistakably private and proprietorial affairs, and the *Consensoria* embodies a strong sense of ownership inconsistent with traditional concepts of monastic poverty.[63]

Out of the Desert – the seventh century in the history of monasticism

By the seventh century, monasticism, which had originally arisen from the desire for self-mastery, self-transcendence and union with God, embracing the ideal of the voluntary removal of the individual from society, had become closely identified with land-owning and the interests of royalty and aristocracy. From being a movement in which all levels of Egyptian society were represented, the diffusion of its ideal through literature in the west meant that it became associated with the upper classes at an early date. Although endowed with a charitable dimension by an eastern bishop, Basil of Cæsarea, its original spiritual objectives soon became regarded as theologically dangerous and in the early fifth century it was reshaped by Cassian whose identification of contemplation with scriptural study increased its appeal to late Roman elites. The *Rule* of Benedict – which was composed in late Roman Italy and was representative of a more austere strand of monastic tradition – was transmitted to the 'barbarian' kingdoms of the North in the seventh century. There, its insights would help sustain the rural estate-monasteries and shrines created by Frankish and Anglo-Saxon aristocracies, a process culminating in its promotion as a whole by the Carolingian dynasty in the eighth and ninth centuries. The driving forces behind many developments in seventh-century monasticism came from northern Europe, where the popularity of private and tarriffed penance in societies with compensatory law-codes would lead to the first development of the concept of purgatory, reshaping older ideas of commemoration of the dead. In monastic terms, this would, over the centuries, lead to the growth of confraternities and also to much greater liturgical elaboration, as the intercessory aspect of monasticism increased exponentially and more and more monks became priests in order to extend the service of eucharistic intercession to society in return for donations – a development which had the incidental effect of downgrading the religious contribution of nuns who could not offer this themselves. In the seventh century, some monasteries had gained exemption from episcopal authority and answered only to the pope,[64] thus contravening the principles for control of monasteries laid down in the fifth century.

The trends which emerged in monasticism by the seventh century would develop and coalesce in the early tenth with the foundation and development of Cluny, in Burgundy, soon the most powerful monastery in European history. Established by an aristocrat as a penance for a murder, it was exempt from episcopal authority and answerable only to the pope. Local landholders vied with each other in donating land which might then be 'reclaimed' by relations who would abandon such claims in return for burial in this holiest of holies. To be buried at Cluny, which had grafted a magnificently elaborate rhythm of liturgy and intercession on to the bare bones of the Benedictine regulations, or to be commemorated in the prayers of its monks in return for donations was to be guaranteed entrance to heaven. In the eleventh century, its rebuilt church, which surpassed St Peter's in Rome in size, was the largest building in Europe, financed by generous donations of gold from kings in faraway Spain. Monks following the Benedictine *Rule* could be found throughout rural Europe, their lifestyles less magnificent and their liturgy less elaborate than those of Cluny, but, like the Cluniacs, offering intercession and the eucharist in return for donations of land. Yet in numerous monasteries throughout western Europe between the seventh and eleventh centuries, the memory of the more contemplative origins of monasticism was still to some extent kept alive – whether in the Egyptian style 'hermitage' perched on the tip of the tiny island monastery of Skellig Michael off the west coast of Ireland or in the scriptoria of great continental houses such Bobbio and Corbie which preserved some of the writings of Basil and Cassian or even of Evagrius and Origen. Just as Cluny reached the zenith of its prestige and its power in the early eleventh century, the first signs of a different type of monasticism began to appear. More modest, contemplative and eremitic in their orientation, the monks of monasteries such as Camaldoli, Vallombrosa and Fonte Avellana were the pioneers of a new monastic consciousness in western Europe. In response to the growth of an urbanised society and a monetary economy, they were able to turn once again – as guides and as symbols of their intention to return to a different set of spiritual values – to the literature of the Egyptian desert and the early monastic life.

Notes

1   The Emergence of Christian Eremitism

1   E. A. Judge, 'The earliest use of Monachos for "monk" (P. Coll. Youtie 77) and the origins of monasticism', *Jahrbuch für Antike und Christentum* 20 (1977) pp. 77–89.

2   For monasticism as a protest against 'institutional' Christianity, see H. B. Workman, *The Evolution of the Monastic Ideal* (London, 1913); also C. W. Griggs, *Early Egyptian Christianity from its Origins to 451* CE (Leiden, 1990) esp. pp. 102, 146–8, 152. For an older resumé of the different opinions on the origins of monasticism see K. Heussi, *Der Ursprung des Mönchtums* (Tübingen, 1936) pp. 280–304.

3   E. E. Malone, *The Monk and the Martyr* (Washington, D.C., 1950).

4   E. R. Dodds, *Pagan and Christian in an Age of Anxiety: Some Aspects of Religious Experience from Marcus Aurelius to Constantine* (Cambridge, 1965).

5   See J. C. O'Neill, 'The origins of monasticism', in *The Making of Orthodoxy. Essays in Honour of Henry Chadwick*, ed. Rowan Williams (Cambridge, 1989) pp. 270–87, which advances this theory while also indicating many possible counter-arguments.

6   For instance, W. H. C. Frend, 'The monks and the survival of the East Roman Empire in the fifth century', *Past and Present* 54 (1972) pp. 3–24, esp. pp. 10–11; W. H. C. Frend, 'Town and countryside in early Christianity', *The Church in Town and Countryside*, ed. D. Baker, Studies in Church History 16 (Oxford, 1979) pp. 27–8.

7   Athanasius, *The Life of Antony and the Letter to Marcellinus*, trans. Robert C. Gregg (Classics of Western Spirituality, New York, 1989). See D. Brakke, *Athanasius and the Politics of Asceticism* (Oxford, 1995) for background and also B. R. Brennan, 'Dating Athanasius' *Vita Antonii*, *VC* 30 (1976) pp. 52–4.

8   *Life*, ch. 2.

9   *Life*, ch. 14.
10 *Life*, ch. 3.
11 *Life*, ch. 14.
12 S. Rubenson, *The Letters of St. Antony. Monasticism and the Making of a Saint* (Minneapolis, 1995), p. 211. (This was originally published without translations of the letters themselves as *The Letters of St. Antony: Origenist Theology, Monastic Tradition and the Making of a Saint* [Lund, 1990].)
13 Ibid., pp. 197–202.
14 Ibid., pp. 187–9.
15 H. Crouzel, *Origen*, trans. A. S. Worrall (Edinburgh, 1989); H. Crouzel, 'Origène, précurseur du monachisme', in *Théologie de la Vie Monastique, Études sur la Tradition Patristique*, Théologie 49 (Paris, 1961) pp. 15–38.
16 Letter 2, Rubenson, *Letters*, p. 203.
17 Letter 1, Rubenson, *Letters*, p. 198.
18 Letter 2, Rubenson, *Letters*, pp. 203–5.
19 C. H. Roberts, *Manuscript, Society and Belief in Early Christian Egypt* (1979) pp. 65–6.
20 Rubenson's arguments in favour of a clear relationship between Origenist theology and Platonist philosophy rather than a diluted or popular version of both have been criticized by G. Gould, 'Recent work on monastic origins: a consideration of the questions raised by Samuel Rubenson's *The Letters of St Antony*', *Studia Patristica* XXV, ed. E. A. Livingstone (Leuven, 1993) pp. 405–16. Gould also questions the association of all monastics with Origenism – see his 'The image of God and the anthropomorphite controversy in fourth century monasticism', *Origeniana Quinta*, ed. R. J. Daley (Leuven, 1992), pp. 549–57. Rubenson has defended his views in 'Christian asceticism and the emergence of monastic tradition' in *Asceticism*, ed. Wimbush and Valantasis, pp. 49–57. See also Roberts, *Manuscript, Society and Belief* pp. 59–63.
21 Dodds, *Pagan and Christian*, p. 29, but see also M. A. Williams, *Rethinking 'Gnosticism'. An Argument for Dismantling a Dubious Category* (Princeton, 1997), p. 118 and R. Valantasis, 'Is the gospel of Thomas ascetical? revisiting an old problem with a new theory', *JECS 7* (1999) pp. 55–81. See also H. Chadwick, 'The domestication of Gnosis', pp. 3–36 of B. Layton, ed., *The Rediscovery of Gnosticism: Proceedings of the International Conference on Gnosticism at Yale, New Haven, Connecticut, March 28–31, 1978*, 2 vols, Studies in the History of Religions (Supplements to *Numen* 41, Leiden, 1980–1).
22 R. Valantasis, 'Adam's body: Uncovering esoteric traditions in the *Apocryphon of John* and Origen's *Dialogue With Heraclides*', in *The Second Century* 7, (1989) pp. 150–62; R. Valantasis, 'Daemons and the perfecting of the monk's body: monastic anthropology, daemonology and asceticism', *Semeia* 58 (1992), pp. 47–79; R. Valantasis, 'Is the Gospel of Thomas Ascetical?'
23 G. G. Harpham, *The Ascetic Imperative in Culture and Criticism* (Chicago and London, 1987); K. Ware, 'The way of the ascetics: Negative or affirmative' in *Asceticism*, ed. V. L. Wimbush and R. Valantasis (Oxford–New York, 1995) pp. 3–15; R. Valantasis, 'Is the Gospel of Thomas ascetical?'; R.

Valantasis, 'Constructions of power in asceticism', *Journal of the American Academy of Religion* 63 (1995) pp. 775–821. See also V. L. Wimbush, *Ascetic Behavior in Greco-Roman Antiquity: A Sourcebook* (Minneapolis, 1990) p. 1.

24 D. Brakke, *Athanasius*, pp. 44–51.

25 For Syrian Christianity and encratism, see S. H. Griffith, 'Asceticism in the church of Syria: the hermeneutics of early Syrian monasticism', in *Asceticism*, pp. 220–45.

26 A. H. Vööbus, *History of Asceticism in the Syrian Orient*, vol. I (Louvain, 1958) pp. 66–78.

27 *The Gospel of Thomas in The Nag Hammadi Library in English*, gen. ed. J. M. Robinson (2nd edn, 1984), Saying 22, p. 129.

28 Ibid., Saying 75, p. 134.

29 Letter 1, Rubenson, *Letters of St. Antony*, p. 198.

30 Ibid.

31 See Griffiths, 'Asceticism in the church of Syria' for a discussion of similarities but also very real differences between the terms *iḥidaya* and *monachos*.

32 *Life of Antony*, ch. 3.

33 J. E. Goehring, 'Through a glass darkly: Diverse images of the Apotaktikoi(ai) of early Egyptian monasticism', *Semeia* 58 (1993) pp. 25–46.

34 *Life of Antony*, ch. 14: Antony's body is neither wasted nor fat but totally unchanged after twenty years.

35 *Life of Antony*, ch. 7.

36 *Life of Antony*, ch. 20.

37 For theological developments, see R. P. C. Hanson, *The Search for the Christian Doctrine of God: the Arian Controversy 318–381* (Edinburgh, 1988) and H. Chadwick, *The Early Church* (revised edition, Harmondsworth, 1993).

38 Rubenson, *Letters*, p. 211.

39 *Life of Antony*, ch. 13.

40 Brakke, *Athanasius*, pp. 249–65.

41 *Life of Antony*, ch. 91; D. Brakke, ' "Outside the places, within the truth": Athanasius of Alexandria and the localization of the holy', in *Pilgrimage and Holy Space in Late Antique Egypt*, ed. D. Frankfurter (Leiden, 1998) pp. 445–82.

42 Brakke, *Athanasius*, chs 1 and 2.

43 Ibid., pp. 236–8.

44 Ibid., pp. 3–6; J. E. Goehring, 'Melitian monastic organization: A challenge to Pachomian originality', *Studia Patristica XXV*, ed. E. A. Livingstone (Leuven, 1993) pp. 388–95.

45 H.-C. Puech, *Sur le manichéisme et autres essais* (Paris, 1979); P. Brown, 'The diffusion of manichaeism in the Roman Empire', *JRS* 59 (1969) pp. 92–103; G. Stroumsa, 'The Manichaean challenge to Egyptian Christianity', in *The Roots of Egyptian Christianity*, ed. B. A. Pearson and J. E. Goehring (Philadelphia, 1986) pp. 307–19.

46 G. Stroumsa, 'Monachisme et marranisme chez les manichéens d' Égypte', *Numen XXIX*, (1982), pp. 184–201.

47   W. H. C. Frend, ' "And I have other sheep" – John 10:16' in *The Making of Orthodoxy*, ed. R. Williams, pp. 24–39 at p. 33.

48   The literature on 'gnosticism' is enormous, but a recent survey of the field which changes the terms of reference of the debates about its existence and meaning is M. A. Williams, *Rethinking 'Gnosticism'*. Williams proposes that we should regard 'gnostic' groups as Biblical-demiurgic.

49   See H. M. Jackson, 'Plato, Republic 588A–589B', p. 318 of *The Nag Hammadi Library*.

50   On Mani as an ascetic, see Frend, ' "And I have other sheep" ', p. 33.

51   *Life of Antony*, ch. 68, states that Antony did not profess friendship to the Manichaeans.

52   Originally it seems to have indicated a more complete severing of ties with society than that of the apotactics: see Goehring, 'Through a glass darkly', esp. pp. 35–6.

53   Suggested by N. Kelsey, 'The body and the desert in the *Life of St. Antony*', *Semeia* 57 (1992) pp. 132–51.

54   J. E. Goehring, 'The encroaching desert: literary production and ascetic space in Early Christian Egypt', *JECS* 1 (1993) pp. 281–96; see also n. 89 below.

55   Jerome, ep. 122, in *The Letters of St. Jerome*, trans. C. C. Mierow and intro. by T. C. Lawler, vol. 1 (1963) p. 170.

56   Brakke, *Athanasius*, pp. 111–29.

57   *Life*, ch. 14.

58   H. G. Evelyn White, *The Monasteries of the Wadi 'n Natrun, The History of the Monasteries of Nitria and of Scetis Part II* (New York 1932) pp. 45–9.

59   *Life of Antony*, ch. 15.

60   W. K. L. Clarke, trans., *The Lausiac History of Palladius* (London, 1918), ch. 57.

61   *Historia Monachorum In Ægypto*, in the translation by B. Ward and N. Russell under the title *Lives of the Desert Fathers* (London and Oxford, 1981), Prologue, 10.

62   *Lausiac History*, ch. 8.

63   *Lausiac History*, ch. 17.

64   A. Guillaumont, 'Histoire des moines aux Kellia', *Orientalia Lovanensia Periodica* 8 (1977) pp. 187–203; J. Jacquet, 'L'adoption par les ermites d'un milieu naturel et ses consequences sur leur vie quotidienne', *Le site monastique copte des Kellia. Sources historiques et explorations archéologiques. Actes du Colloque de Genève, 13 au 15 août 1984* (Geneva, 1986) pp. 21–9.

65   *Apophthegmata* Lucius I, in *The Sayings of the Desert Fathers, The Alphabetical Collection*, trans. by Benedicta Ward SLG (London, 1975). This is a translation of the Greek Alphabetical Series.

66   *Lausiac History*, ch. 7.

67   *Lausiac History*, ch. 10.

68   Guillaumont, 'Histoire des moines aux Kellia'.

69   *History of the Monks in Egypt*, XVIII.

70   *Life of Antony*, ch. 6.

71   *Lausiac History*, ch. 23.

72 A. Rouselle, *Porneia: On Desire and the Body in Antiquity*, trans. F. Pheasant (Oxford, 1988) pp. 172–8; T. M. Shaw, 'Creation, virginity and diet in fourth-century Christianity: Basil of Ancyra's *On the True Purity of Virginity*', *Gender and History* 9 (1997) pp. 579–96. See also now T. M. Shaw, *The Burden of the Flesh. Fasting and Sexuality in Early Christianity* (Minneapolis, 1998).

73 Antony, Letter I, Rubenson, pp. 199–200; D. Brakke, 'The problematization of nocturnal emissions in Early Christian Syria, Egypt and Gaul', *JECS* 3 (1995) pp. 419–60, which indicates the way in which emissions, originally seen as making the individual vulnerable to attack by demons in the third century, came to be considered as a register of the moral condition of the individual in the fourth and the fifth.

74 John Cassian, *De Institutis Coenobiorum et De Octo Principalium Vitiorum remediis Libri XII*, trans. by J. Bertram as *The Monastic Institutes, consisting of On the Training of a Monk and The Eight Deadly Sins* (London, 1999) Book IV, 11 and 21–22; John Cassian, *Conlationes*, trans. and ed. by B. Ramsey, *John Cassian: the Conferences* (New York – Mahwah 1997), Conferences XII 5 and XXII 2 and 3.

75 *History of the Monks in Egypt*, XX, 17.

76 *Apophthegmata Patrum* Antony 19.

77 *History of the Monks in Egypt*, V, Oxyrhynchus, for the classification of charisms.

78 Rubenson, *Letters of St. Antony*, pp. 145–62 argues for the carefully constructed nature of this work, assembled after the Origenist controversy of 399 and therefore, he suggests, not entirely accurate in its picture of Antony's teaching. G. Gould regards the *Apophthegmata* as more reliable (see his 'Recent work on monastic origins') and uses the text as a whole in his book, *The Desert Fathers on Monastic Community* (Oxford, 1993). For the transition from the spoken to the written word and the teachings of the *Apophthegmata* in general, see also D. Burton-Christie, *The Word in the Desert. Scripture and the Quest for Holiness in Early Christian Monasticism* (Oxford, 1993).

79 *Apophthegmata* Poemen 54.

80 *Apophthegmata* Poemen 108.

81 *Apophthegmata* Or 7.

82 *Apophthegmata* John the Dwarf 1; John Cassian, *Institutes*, iv, 24.

83 *Apophthegmata* Pistus.

84 *Apophthegmata* Joseph of Panephysis, 7.

85 See E. Wyschogrod, *Saints and Postmodernism: Revisioning Moral Philosophy* (Chicago, 1990).

86 *Life*, ch. 48.

87 *Apophthegmata* Arsenius 28.

88 G. Frank, 'Miracles, monks and monuments: the *Historia Monachorum in Ægypto* as pilgrims' tales', in *Pilgrimage and Holy Space in Late Antique Egypt*, ed. D. Frankfurter (Leiden, 1998) pp. 483–505.

89 Though see Wipszycka, 'Le monachisme égyptien et les villes', in *Travaux et Mémoires* 12 (1994) pp. 1–44, esp. pp. 10–12 for the problems concerning the question of the establishment of monks on this site

90　*Life of Antony*, chs 21–43; Brakke, *Athanasius*, pp. 217–26; see also N. Baynes, 'St. Antony and the Demons', *Journal of Egyptian Archaeology* 40 (1954) pp. 7–10.

91　*History of the Monks in Egypt*, VI.

92　P. Brown, 'The rise and function of the holy man in Late Antiquity' *JRS* 61 (1971) pp. 80–101; but also see P. Brown, 'The Saint as exemplar in Late Antiquity', *Representations* 1 (1983) pp. 1–25 and 'Rise and function of holy man in Late Antiquity 1971–1997', *JECS* 6 (1998) pp. 353–77.

93　See J. E. Goehring 'The world engaged: the social and economic world of Early Egyptian monasticism', in *Gnosticism and the Early Christian World: in Honour of James M. Robinson*, ed. J. E. Goehring, C. H. Hedrick, J. T. Sanders, with H. D. Betz (Sonoma, 1990) pp. 134–44 and G. Gould, 'Lay Christians, Bishops and Clergy in the *Apophthegmata Patrum*', *Studia Patristica* XXV, ed. E. A. Livingstone (Leuven, 1993) pp. 296–304.

94　*Lausiac History*, XI: for another version of the story see Socrates, IV, 23.

95　Stroumsa, 'Monachisme et marranisme'.

96　For Evagrius, see A. Guillaumont, 'Histoire des moines aux Kellia'; A. Guillaumont, *Les 'Kephalaia Gnostica' d'Évagre le Pontique et l'Histoire de l'Origénisme chez les Grecs et chez les Syriens* (Patristica Sorbonensia, 5, Paris, 1962); A. Guillaumont, 'Un philosophe au désert: Évagre le Pontique', *RHR* 181 (1972) pp. 29–56; A. Guillaumont, 'Le texte véritable des 'Gnostica' d'Évagre le Pontique', *RHR* 142 (1952) pp. 156–205; J. Driscoll, 'Gentleness in the *Ad Monachos* of Evagrius Ponticus', *SM* 32 (1990) pp. 295–321; J. Driscoll, *The 'Ad Monachos' of Evagrius Ponticus. Its Structure and a Select Commentary*, Studia Anselmiana 104 (Rome, 1991). Of great importance is the work of G. Bunge: 'Évagre le Pontique et les deux Macaire', *Irénikon* 56 (1983) pp. 215–27, 323–60; *Das Geistgebet. Studien zum Traktat, "De Oratione" des Evagrios Pontikos*. Koinonia XXV (Köln, 1987); 'Origenizmus-Gnostizismus: zum geistgeschichtlichen Standort des Evagrios Pontikos', *VC* 40 (1986) pp. 24–54; 'Palladiana I: Introduction aux fragments coptes de l'Histoire Lausiac', *SM* 32 (1990) pp. 79–129 and *Briefe aus dem Wüste*, Sophia, vol. 24 (Trier, 1986). See also E. A. Clark, *The Origenist Controversy. The Cultural Construction of an Early Christian Debate* (Princeton, 1992).

97　G. Gould, 'The image of God and the anthropomorphite controversy' questions the existence of the simple 'anthropomorphite' monk, suggesting that this term may caricature monks who did not believe in the incorporeality of God.

98　Bunge 'Origenismus-Gnostizismus'.

99　See XX 15 and p. 120 of the version by Ward and Russell, *Lives of the Desert Fathers*.

100　The *Sentences to Monks* are to be found in the seventh-century western manuscript BN. Lat. 12634, which probably originated in the monastery of Bobbio.

2 The Development of Communal Life

1 Stroumsa, 'Monachisme et marranisme'.

2 Goehring, 'Melitian monastic organization'.

3 See T. Orlandi, 'Coptic literature', in B. A. Pearson and J. E. Goehring, eds, *Roots of Egyptian Christianity*, pp. 51–81; Goehring, 'New frontiers'.

4 See P. Rousseau, *Pachomius. The Making of a Community in Fourth-Century Egypt* (Berkeley–Los Angeles–London (1985), chapter II; A. Veillleux, *La liturgie dans le cénobitisme pachômien au quatrième siècle*, Studia Anselmiana 57 (Rome, 1968); A. De Vogüé 'Les pièces latins du dossier pachomien. Remarques sur quelques publications recents', *RHE* 67 (1972) pp. 27–67; A. De Vogüé, 'La Vie arabe de saint Pachôme et ses deux sources présumées', *AB* 91 (1973) and Veilleux, *Pachomian Koininia*, vol. I.

5 For the Pachomian sources in translation, see A. Veilleux, *Pachomian Koinonia, The Lives, Rules and Other Writings of Saint Pachomius and His Disciples*, with a foreword by A. de Vogüé. Vol. I, *The Life of Saint Pachomius and His Disciples*, Cistercian Studies 45 (Kalamazoo, 1980); vol. II, *Pachomian Chronicles and Rules*, Cistercian Studies 46 (Kalamazoo, 1981), and vol. III, *Instructions, Letters and Other Writings of Saint Pachomius and His Disciples*, Cistercian Studies 47 (Kalamazoo, 1982).

6 For Pachomius, his career and foundations, see principally Rousseau, *Pachomius* together with J. E. Goehring, 'New frontiers in Pachomian studies', in *The Roots of Egyptian Christianity*, ed. B. A. Pearson and J. E Goehring (Philadelphia, 1986) pp. 237–57; J. E. Goehring, 'Withdrawing from the desert; Pachomius and the development of village monasticism in Upper Egypt', *Harvard Theological Review* 89 (1996) pp. 267–85; J. E. Goehring, *The Letter of Ammon and Pachomian Monasticism*, Patristische Texte und Studien 27 (Berlin, 1988); and T. G. Kardong, 'The monastic practices of Pachomius and the Pachomians', *SM* 32 (1990) pp. 58–78.

7 Stroumsa, 'Monachisme et marranisme', p. 187, notes the probability that the Thebaid rapidly became a home to Manichaean communities.

8 *Bohairic Life*, 105, *Pachomian Koinonia* I, p. 149.

9 *First Sahidic Life*, Fragment III, 6 and 7, *Pachomian Koinonia* I, p. 428.

10 Ibid. 11, pp. 430–1.

11 Rousseau, *Pachomius*, pp. 137–42.

12 See Goehring, 'New frontiers' and the other literature listed in note 6 above and their references.

13 *First Sahidic Life*, Fragment II, 4, *Pachomian Koinonia* I, p. 427.

14 Ibid. Introduction, pp. 1–26; F. Wisse, 'The Nag Hammadi Library and the Heresiologists' *VC* 25 (1971) pp. 205–23; Williams, pp. 46–9; Valantasis, 'Is the Gospel of Thomas ascetical?'

15 F. Wisse, 'Gnosticism and early monasticism in Egypt;' in *Gnosis, Festschrift für Hans Jonas*, ed. B. Aland (Gottingen, 1978); F. Wisse, 'The Nag Hammadi Library and the Heresiologists', *VC* 25 (1971) pp. 205–23; F. Wisse, 'Language mysticism in the Nag Hammadi texts and in early Coptic monasticism I: Cryptography', *Enchoria* 9 (1979) pp. 101–20; Valantasis, 'Is the Gospel of Thomas ascetical?'.

16 The cartonnage of the manuscripts is packed with other papyri, including a letter from Papnoute to Pachom. Whether the recipient is Pachomius himself and the sender was Paphnoute the steward of Phbow has not definitively been proved: see A. Veilleux, 'Monasticism and Gnosis in Egypt', in Pearson and Goehring, *Roots of Egyptian Christianity*, pp. 271–306 and J. Shelton, Introduction to *Nag Hammadi Codices: Greek and Coptic Papyri from the Cartonnage of the Covers*, ed. J. W. B. Barns, G. M. Browne and J. C. Shelton (Leiden, 1981).

17 Rousseau, p. 77 is highly critical of A. H. M. Jones, *The Later Roman Empire*, vol. 2 (Oxford, 1964) p. 929 and E. Amand de Mendieta 'Le système cénobitique basilien comparé au système cénobitique pachômien', *RHR* 152 (1957) pp. 31–80.

18 *Lausiac History*, ch. 32. This may in any case be interpolated in places.

19 Ibid.

20 See *Pachomian Koinonia* II, pp. 141–223.

21 See B. Büchler, *Die Armut der Armen: Über den ursprünglischen Sinn der mönchischen Armut* (Munich, 1980) pp. 9–36.

22 Precepts 49, *Pachomian Koinonia II*, pp. 152–3.

23 Rousseau, *Pachomius*, ch. 5.

24 *Bohairic Life*, ch. 72.

25 See Büchler, *passim*.

26 *Bohairic Life*, ch. 144.

27 For the difficulties surrounding these texts and the problems of attributing part, or indeed any, of them to Pachomius himself, see the properly cautious judgements of Rousseau, *Pachomius*, chapter 2, esp. pp. 48–53.

28 Rousseau, *Pachomius*, p. 80; J. Dyer, 'Monastic Psalmody of the Middle Ages', *RB* 100 (1990) pp. 41–84.

29 See *Bohairic Life*, ch. 28.

30 *Bohairic Life*, ch. 48.

31 *Pachomian Koinonia* II, pp. 175–9.

32 *Greek Life*, ch. 69, *Pachomian Koinonia* I, p. 344.

33 *Precepts* 95, *Pachomian Koinonia* II, p. 161.

34 *Precepts* 2, *Pachomian Koinonia* II, p. 145.

35 *Precepts* 92, *Pachomian Koinonia* II, p. 161.

36 *Precepts and Judgements 7, Pachomian Koinonia* II, p. 177.

37 *Precepts* 143, *Pachomian Koinonia* II, pp. 166–7.

38 J. E. Goehring, 'Withdrawing from the desert'; E. Wipszycka, 'Les terres de la congrégation pachômienne dans une list de payements pour les apora', in J. Bingen et al., eds, *Le monde grec. Pensée, litterature, histoire, documents: Hommages à Claire Preaux* (Brussels, 1975) pp. 623–36; E. Wipszycka, 'Le monachisme égyptien et les villes', *Travaux et mémoires* 12 (1994) pp. 1–44.

39 Wipszycka, 'Le monachisme égyptien et les villes'.

40 Suggested by S. Elm *'Virgins of God'. The Making of Asceticism in Late Antiquity* (Oxford, 1994) pp. 296–7, but not by Goehring, 'New frontiers'.

41 See Goehring, 'Withdrawing from the desert'.

42 For Shenoute, see principally J. Leipoldt, *Schenute von Atripe* (Leipzig, 1903); J. Timbie, 'The state of research on the career of Shenoute of

Atripe', in *The Roots of Egyptian Christianity*, ed. B. A. Pearson and J. E. Goehring (Philadelphia, 1986) pp. 258–70; D. N. Bell, trans., *The Life of Shenoute by Besa*, Cistercian Studies 73 (Kalamazoo, 1983).

43 C. C. Walters, *Monastic Archaeology in Egypt* (Warminster, 1974) pp. 36–7. Cf. W. Liebeschuetz, 'Problems arising from the conversion of Syria', *The Church in Town and Countryside*, Studies in Church History 16 (Oxford, 1979) pp. 17–24: p. 21 on the way in which Syrian Monophysite monasteries seem more open to the public than their Chalcedonian equivalents.

44 Though he eventually seems to have reconsidered its effectiveness – Timbie, 'State of research', p. 264.

45 Gregory of Nazianzus, *Orationes* 43, 62: ed. and trans. C. G. Browne and J. E. Swallow, Nicene and Post-Nicene Fathers 7 (Ann Arbor, 1955) pp. 415 ff. For what follows, see principally, P. Rousseau, *Basil of Cæsarea* (Berkeley, 1994); P. J. Fedwick, ed., *Basil of Cæsarea: Christian, Humanist, Ascetic*, 2 vols (Toronto, 1991), especially the contributions by Spidlik and Karayannopoulos; J. Gribomont, 'Le monachisme au IVe siècle en Asie Mineur du Gangres au Messalianisme', *Studia Patristica* 3, ed. K. Aland and F. L. Cross (Berlin, 1957) pp. 400–15.

46 Bunge, *Briefe aus dem Wüste*, p. 58 on the place of Gregory of Nazianzus in this tradition.

47 Ep. 2, see Rousseau, *Basil* pp. 79–80

48 Ibid.

49 The Longer (F) and Shorter (B) Rules have been rendered into English by W. K. L. Clarke, *The Ascetic Works of St Basil* (London 1925) whose translation is cited here. See F2 for these and other 'Origenist' themes.

50 Ep. 223.

51 See J. Gribomont, *Histoire du texte des ascétiques de saint Basile*, Bibliothèque du Muséon 32, (Louvain, 1953).

52 Rousseau, pp. 191–2.

53 F 1.

54 F 9.

55 B 85. For Basil's attitude to property and wealth I follow G. Gould, 'Basil of Cæsarea and the problem of the wealth of monasteries', in W. Sheils and D. Wood, *The Church and Wealth*, Studies in Church History 24 (Oxford, 1987) pp. 15–24.

56 Ibid.

57 B 187.

58 Ibid. In Ep. 284 (*PG* 32, 1020 B–C) Basil asks that monks be exempt for taxation as they devoted their wealth entirely to charity.

59 B 304 and 305.

60 F 37.

61 B 207.

62 F 37.

63 F 7.

64 F 27.

65 F 47.

66 F 43.

67   F 28.
68   F 26 title.
69   F 51.
70   See *Precepts and Judgements 7, Pachomian Koinonia* II, p. 177.
71   F 15: see this chapter for his regulations for children in general.
72   A. Meredith, 'Asceticism – Christian and Greek', in *JTS* (n.s.) 27 (1976) pp. 313–32, p. 325.

3   Women in Early Monasticism

1   Galatians 3: 28.
2   Timothy 2: 11.
3   C. Trevett, *Montanism: Gender, Authority and the New Prophecy* (Cambridge, 1996).
4   J. C. Davies, 'Deacons, deaconesses and the minor orders in the patristic period', *JEH* 14 (1963) pp. 1–15.
5   See Brakke, 'Nocturnal emissions', pp. 424–5. On pollution in general, see Mary Douglas, *Pollution and Danger: an Analysis of Concepts of Pollution and Taboo* (London, 1966).
6   See E. A. Clark, 'Devil's gateway and bride of Christ', in her *Ascetic Piety and Women's Faith: Essays on Late Ancient Christianity*, Studies in Women and Religion 20 (Lewiston, 1986) pp. 23–60, p. 26.
7   Origen, *Commentary on Genesis* 4,5; 5.2.6, *PG* 12, cols. 186, 190.
8   Brown, *Body and Society*, pp. 168–77.
9   V. E. F. Harrison, 'Male and female in Cappadocian theology', *JTS* n.s., 41 (1990), pp. 441–71. See also Elm, '*Virgins of God*', pp. 198–9.
10   *St Gregory of Nyssa: The Life of St Macrina*, trans. W. K. L. Clarke (London, 1916) p. 18.
11   G. Gould 'Women in the writings of the fathers: Language, belief and reality', in *Women in the Church*, Studies in Church History 27, ed. W. J. Sheils and D. Wood (Oxford, 1990); A. Cameron, 'Virginity as metaphor: women and the rhetoric of early Christianity', in A. Cameron, ed. *History as Text: the Writing of Ancient History* (London, 1989) pp. 181–205.
12   *De vera virginitatis integritate*, *PG* 30, cols. 669–809, where it is appended to the works of Basil of Cæsarea. See Elm, '*Virgins of God*', pp. 113–25. For an alternative view of Basil, see T. M. Shaw, 'Creation, virginity and diet in fourth-century Christianity: Basil of Ancyra's "On the true purity of virginity"', *Gender and History* 9 (1997) pp. 579–96.
13   See M. Douglas, *Natural Symbols: Explorations in Cosmology* (Harmondsworth, 1979) and M. Douglas, *Risk and Blame: Essays in Cultural Theory* (London, 1992). I have not been able to see K. Aspegren, *The Male Woman: a Feminine Ideal in the Early Church* (Stockholm, 1990).
14   *Nag Hammadi Library in English*, p. 138. See also the *Gospel of Mary* in the same volume, pp. 523–7. In this text, Mary Magdalene confronts Peter who cannot believe that Christ gave revelation to a woman.
15   G. P. Corrington, ' "The Divine Woman"? Propaganda and the power of chastity in the New Testament Apocrypha', *Helios* 13 (1986), pp. 151–62;

J. Anson, 'The female transvestite in early monasticism: the origin and development of a motif', *Viator* 5 (1974) pp. 1–32; E. Patlagéan, 'L'histoire de la femme déguisée en moine et l' évolution de la sainteté féminine à Byzance', *Studi Medievali*, 3rd ser., XVII (1976) pp. 597–623.

16 Brown, *Body and Society*, pp. 81–2.

17 D. F. Stramara Jr., 'Double monasticism in the Greek East, fourth through eighth centuries', *JECS* 6 (1998) pp. 269–312.

18 *Lausiac History*, ch. 49.

19 Elm, '*Virgins of God*', pp. 263 ff.

20 For a later account of Syncletica's teaching, see Pseudo-Athanasius, 'The life and activity of the holy and blessed teacher Syncletica', in *Ascetic Behavior*, ed., Wimbush, pp. 265–311.

21 *Apophthegmata* Sarah I.

22 Elm, '*Virgins of God*', pp. 287–97.

23 For the introduction of monasticism to Rome and the role of women there see, R. Lorenz, 'Die Anfänge des abendländischen Mönchtum im 4. Jahrhundert', *ZKG* 77 (1986) pp. 1–61; J. N. D. Kelly, *Jerome. His Life, Writings and Controversies* (London, 1975), chs 9–11; G. D. Gordini, 'Origine e sviluppo del monachesimo a Roma', *Gregorianum 37* (1956), pp. 220–60; G. Jenal, *Italia Ascetica atque Monastica. Das Asketen- und Mönchtum in Italien von den Anfängen bis zur Zeit den Langobarden (ca. 150/250–604)*, Monographien zur Geschichte des Mittelalters, 39, 2 vols (Stuttgart, 1995), vol. 1, pp. 28–93; G. Clark, *Women in the Church: Pagan and Christian Lifestyles* (Oxford, 1993); G. Cloke, *This Female Man of God. Women and Spiritual Power in the Patristic Age, AD 350–450* (London, 1995); E. A. Clark, *Ascetic Piety*, especially Part II; E. A. Clark, *Jerome, Chrysostom and Friends. Essays and Translations*, Studies in Women and Religion 2 (Lewiston, 1979).

24 A. Yarborough, 'Christianisation in the fourth century: the example of Roman women', *Church History* 45 (1976) pp. 149–65. P. Veyne, 'The Roman Empire', pp. 5–234 of P. Ariès and G. Duby, *A History of Private Life*, vol. I (Cambridge, MA, 1987); ibid., P. Brown, pp. 235–312, 'Late Antiquity'; P. Brown, *The Body and Society. Men, Women and Sexual Renunciation in Early Christianity* (London, 1989), *passim*; B. Shaw, 'The age of Roman girls at marriage: a reconsideration', *JRS* 77 (1987) pp. 30–46; A. Cameron and A. Kuhrt, eds, *Images of Women in Antiquity* (London, 1983).

25 In the East, the most prominent example of a women of high rank who adopted a life of religion was Olympias. See Palladius, *Lausiac History*, ch. 56; *Vita Sanctae Olympiadis Diaconissae, AB* 15 (1896), pp. 409–23; Cloke, *Female Man* pp. 94–9; Clark, *Jerome, Chrystostom and Friends*.

26 For a comprehensive account of Jerome's life and writings, see Kelly, *Jerome*.

27 Kelly, *Jerome*, pp. 76, 85, 98, 164, 169, 178, 196 and *passim*.

28 Kelly, *Jerome*, ch. 6.

29 *Jerome*, Ep. 125

30 Kelly, *Jerome*, p. 109

31 *Jerome*, Ep. 108.

32 *Lausiac History*, ch. 55.

33 *Jerome*, Ep. 108.
34 Ibid.
35 *Lausiac History*, ch. 10.
36 Kelly, *Jerome*, p. 121.
37 *Lausiac History*, ch. 46.
38 *Lausiac History*, ch. 61; Gerontius, *The Life of Melania the Younger*, ed. E. A. Clark (Lampeter, 1984).
39 *Lausiac History*, ch. 41.
40 ibid., ch. 55.
41 *Sententiae ad Virginem* 54, *PG* 40, cols. 1282–6.
42 Palladius, *Lausiac History*, ch. 41.
43 Ibid.
44 Brakke, *Athanasius and the Politics of Asceticism*, ch. 1.
45 Elm, '*Virgins of God*', Part I.
46 See Harrison, 'Male and female', pp. 452–3: 'Thus Basil's literal and rigorist interpretation of biblical precepts combines with his strong sense of the closeness of eschatological realities to prevent his drawing of many social realities from his ontology of gender.'
47 Elm, '*Virgins of God*', pp. 197–8.
48 Elm, '*Virgins of God*', pp. 292 ff.
49 *Bohairic Life*, ch. 27, *Pachomian Koinonia* I, p. 50 and *First Greek Life*, ch. 32 ibid., p. 319, the latter adding that visitors were to forget their 'kinship of the flesh', which rather invalidates their reasons for visiting in the first place!
50 *Second Greek Life*, ch. 29.
51 *Lausiac History*, ch. 33.
52 See A. de Vogüé, *Césaire d'Arles, Oeuvres Monastiques* I (Paris, 1988) pp. 71–3.
53 Elm, '*Virgins of God*', pp. 303 ff.
54 S. Brock and S. Ashbrook Harvey, *Holy Women of the Syrian Orient* (Berkeley, 1987); ibid., 'Women in Early Syrian Christianity', in Cameron and Kuhrt, *Images* pp. 288–98; B. Ward, ed., *Harlots of the Desert* (Oxford, 1987).
55 Brown, *Body and Society*, p. 195.
56 D. S. Wiesen, *St Jerome as a Satirist*, Cornell Studies in Classical Philology 34 (Ithaca, 1964).
57 *Vita Hilarionis*, ch. 7, *PL* 23, 32; P. C. Miller, 'Jerome's Centaur: A hyper-icon of the desert', *JECS* 4 (1996) pp. 209–33 for a more nuanced treatment of this symbol.
58 His later eulogy of Marcella would claim that she had rarely appeared in public, and at home spent long hours in study and meditation – although in reality she had run her household, received some visitors and prayed at the basilicas and burial-places of the martyrs. See Ep. 127.
59 P. C. Miller, 'The blazing body: Ascetic desire in Jerome's letter to Eustochium', *JECS* 1 (1993) pp. 21–45.
60 Ibid, p. 21. See also on this theme M. Allen, 'The martyrdom of Jerome', *JECS* 3 (1995) pp. 211–13.

61 For Ambrose and his writings, see N. B. McLynn, *Ambrose of Milan: Church and Court in a Christian Capital*, The Transformation of the Classical Heritage, vol. XXII (Berkeley, 1994) pp. 60–8; V. Burrus, 'Reading Agnes; the rhetoric of gender in Ambrose and Prudentius', *JECS* 3 (1995) pp. 25–46; Cameron, 'Virginity as metaphor'.

62 Ambrose *On Virginity*, trans. D. Callam (Toronto, 1980) VII 41, p. 24.

63 Brown, *Body and Society*, Part Three.

64 Clark, *Jerome, Chrysostom and Friends*, pp. 55–6 for Jerome's allusions to women as male.

65 Jerome, Ep. 108.

66 *Lausiac History*, ch. 61.

67 *Life of Melania the Younger*, chs 40, 41, 49. See J. T. Lienhard, *Paulinus of Nola and Early Western Monasticism* (Köln–Bonn, 1977) p. 72 for the formal separation of men and women in the community of Nola in Southern Italy.

68 G. Lawless, *Augustine of Hippo and His Monastic Rule* (Oxford, 1987), Parts Two and Three. See pp. 118–20 on the rule.

69 K. Power, *Veiled Desire. Augustine's Writing on Women* (London, 1995) esp. Parts III and IV.

70 Power, p. 120; Gould 'Women in the writings of the Fathers', p. 7.

71 Ep. 94, *PL* 33, pp. 471–2. See also Power, pp. 117–20.

72 *PG* 40, cols. 1282–6.

73 Although Origen had seen virgins as particularly capable of achieving union with God and as fulfilling the union of Christ with the Church, he did not write of the virgin as Bride of Christ. See E. A. Clark, 'The uses of the song of songs: Origen and the later Latin Fathers', pp. 386–427 of her *Ascetic Piety and Women's Faith*, and D. C. Hunter, 'Helvidius, Jovinian and the virginity of Mary in late fourth-century Rome', *JECS* 1 (1993) pp. 47–71.

4 The Meaning of Asceticism

1 For all these, see M. A. Williams, *Rethinking 'Gnosticism'*, pp. 18–23; R. Lorenz, 'Die Anfänge des abendländischen Mönchtum'; G. D. Gordini, 'Origine e sviluppo del monachesimo a Roma', *Gregorianum* 37 (1956) pp. 220–60; G. Jenal, *Italia Ascetica atque Monastica*, vol. 1, pp. 12–93.

2 McLynn, *Ambrose*, pp. 60–8.

3 For Jerome, see principally J. N. D. Kelly, *Jerome. His Life, Writings and Controversies* (London, 1975) and P. Rousseau, *Ascetics, Authority and the Church in the Age of Jerome and Cassian* (Oxford, 1987).

4 J. Fontaine, 'Hilaire et Martin', pp. 59–86 of *Hilaire de Poitiers. Évêque et docteur* (Paris, 1969), esp. pp. 68–75.

5 Kelly, *Jerome*, pp. 27–33.

6 Augustine, *Confessions*, 8, 6. The translation is that of R. S. Pine-Coffin (London, 1961) pp. 167–8.

7 Kelly, *Jerome*, p. 33, pp. 46–56.

8 Some of the accusations levelled against the monastic movement can be found in a text dating from the early fifth century, the *Consultationum*

Zacchei Christiani et Apollonii Philosophi Libri Tres, PL 20, cols. 1071–166.

9   Brown, *Body and Society,* p. 377; Hunter, 'Resistance to the virginal ideal'; Hunter, 'Helvidius, Jovinian and the virginity of Mary', *JECS* 1 (1993) pp. 47–71.

10 Palladius, *Lausiac History,* ch. 54.

11 Jerome, Ep. 66; Jenal, *Italia Ascetica atque Monastica* pp. 364–6.

12 For Sulpicius see C. Stancliffe, *St Martin of Tours and his Hagiographer. History and Miracle in Sulpicius Severus* (Oxford, 1983), ch. 2; for Paulinus, J. T. Lienhard, *Paulinus of Nola and Early Western Monasticism* (Köln–Bonn, 1977) pp. 128–41.

13 For Martin, I follow Stancliffe, *St Martin of Tours;* Fontaine, 'Hilaire et Martin'; Rousseau, *Ascetics, Authority and the Church in the Age of Jerome and Cassian* (Oxford, 1978) Part Four; *Saint Martin et Son Temps,* Studia Anselmiana 46 (Rome, 1961). The *Vita Martini* is edited by J. Fontaine, *Vie de Saint Martin* I (*SC* 133, Paris, 1967) and there is also an older English translation of the *Life,* and the *Dialogues* of Sulpicius Severus, *Library of the Nicene and Post-Nicene Fathers* XI (Oxford and New York, 1894), pp. 2–54.

14 Jerome, *Contra Vigilantium,* PL 23, cols. 353–68; Kelly, *Jerome,* p. 289; Stancliffe, *St Martin,* ch. 21; D. G. Hunter, 'Vigilantius of Calagurris and Victricius of Rouen: ascetics, relics and clerics in late Roman Gaul', *JECS* 7 (1999) pp. 401–30.

15 Stancliffe, *St Martin,* ch. 3; the quotation is in her translation, p. 35.

16 Ibid.

17 E.g. *Life,* ch. 14.

18 The literature on Augustine is vast, but for a biographical approach see P. R. L. Brown, *Augustine of Hippo* (Berkeley, 1969) and for his views on asceticism, grace, and sin the same author's *Body and Society,* Part Three. On Augustine as monastic thinker see especially T. J. van Bavel, ' "Ante omnia" ' et "in Deum" dans la "Regula Sancti Augustini" ', *VC* 12 (1958) pp. 157–65; and the many works of L. Verheijen on the subject, including *Saint Augustine's Monasticism in the Light of Acts 4: 32–35* (Villanova, 1979) and *Nouvelle Approche de la Règle de saint Augustin* (Abbaye de Bellefontaine, 1980). An extensive bibliography is given in G. Lawless, *Augustine of Hippo and His Monastic Rule* (Oxford, 1987), which contains Augustine's rules and English translations as well as essential background and analysis. The translations given here are those of Lawless, who comes down in favour of Augustine's *Regula Tertia* as a rule given to monks rather than to clerics.

19 See Lawless, *Augustine of Hippo and His Monastic Rule,* Part Three 'Disputed questions'.

20 *Life of Antony,* ch. 2.

21 *Rule,* ch. 8, Lawless, pp. 102–3.

22 Lawless, Appendix II, '*Ordo monasterii*: Current state of research', pp. 170–1, notes Italian symptoms in the *Ordo,* to which it might be added that the noticeable variants in the length of the Night Office (see pp. 74–5)

between winter, spring and autumn and summer, would suggest that these instructions originated in a northern, rather than, as he suggests, a southern Italian background. See M. Dunn, 'The Master and St Benedict: a rejoinder', *EHR* 107 (1992), pp. 104–11.

23 For details of his stay there, see Kelly, *Jerome*, pp. 46–56.

24 *Life of Paul the First Hermit, PL* 23, Cols. 17–360; trans. P. B. Harvey in Wimbush and Valantasis, eds, *Ascetic Behavior*, pp. 357–69. Jerome's *Letter to Heliodorus* (Letter 14) an invitation to Heliodorus to join him in the desert is a highly rhetorical construction, which he himself later condemned (Kelly, p. 52).

25 See Kelly, *Jerome*, pp. 170–4 for the way in which Jerome's later *Lives* of Malchus and Hilarion, hagiographies based on real figures, reflect his own ideas and obsessions.

26 See, for instance, Kelly, *Jerome*, pp. 144, 146–7.

27 Ibid., p. 98.

28 For what follows, see principally Clark, *The Origenist Controversy* and Kelly, *Jerome*, but also Bunge, *Briefe*, Introduction; J. Dechow, *Dogma and Mysticism in Early Christianity: Epiphanius of Cyprus and the Legacy of Origen*, North American Patristic Society Patristic Monograph Series 13 (Macon, 1988).

29 For the accusations levelled against Origen by Epiphanius, Jerome and others, see Crouzel, *Origen*, pp. 169–79 and Clark, *The Origenist Crisis*, especially chapters three and four.

30 Ep. 84, *To Pammachius*; and see Brown, *Body and Society*, p. 382.

31 A. Veilleux, ed., *Pachomian Koinonia* vol. II, pp. 141–223. Jerome's preface, pp. 141–2.

32 See Rufinus' translation in *Basilii Regula a Rufino latine versa*, ed. K. Zelzer, *CSEL* 86 (Vienna, 1986); Jenal, *Italia Ascetica atque Monastica*, vol. I, pp. 96–8; Rousseau, *Basil of Cæsarea*, pp. 354–9; K. Zelzer, 'Der Rufinus-übersetzung der Basiliusregel im Spiegel ihrer ältesten Handschriften', *Latintät und Alte Kirche. Festschrift für Rudolf Hanslik zum 70 Geburtstag*, ed. H. Bannert and J. Divjak (Wien–Köln–Graz, 1977) pp. 341–50; J. Gribomont, *Histoire du texte des Ascétiques de S. Basile*, Bibliothèque du Muséon, 32 (1953).

33 *Historia Monachorum in Aegypto*, ed. A.-J Festugière (Brussels, 1961, 1971); an English translation has been made under the title *The Lives of the Desert Fathers* by B. Ward and N. Russell (London and Oxford, 1981). While the recent English editors regard the account of the journey as basically reliable clues to its artificial nature may be gleaned from both the careful construction of the opening chapter on John of Lycopolis and from the assertion in the Epilogue that the group had seen many more Desert Fathers and that the author had 'selected a few to represent the many'. But see also G. Frank, 'Miracles, monks and monuments'.

34 *Lives of the Desert Fathers*, p. 146.

35 Clark, *Origenist Controversy*, ch. 5 and pp. 144–7. See also R. Evans, *Pelagius: Inquiries and Reappraisals* (New York, 1957).

36 Jerome, *Dialogue Against the Pelagians, PL* 23, col. 562.

37 Augustine, *Confessions*, Book X; Chadwick, *The Early Church*, p. 227: 'the use of these words seems to Pelagius to undermine moral responsibility and to preach cheap grace'. See also P. R. L. Brown, 'Pelagius and his supporters; Aims and environment', *JTS* n.s. 19 (1968) pp. 93–114; P. R. L. Brown, *Religion and Society in the Age of St Augustine* (London, 1977); and 'Sexuality and society in the fifth century' in E. Gabba, ed., *Tria Cordia. Scritti in Onore de Arnaldo Momigliano* (Como, 1983) pp. 49–70.

38 *Rule*, ch. 8; Lawless, p. 103.

39 For analysis of Augustine's position, see, as well as the works cited earlier, C. Kirwan, *Augustine* (London, 1989), chapters 5 and 6.

40 Bunge, *Briefe*, p. 73.

41 *De Institutis Coenobiorum et De Octo Principalium Vitiorum remediis Libri XII*, trans. J. Bertram as *The Monastic Institutes, consisting of On the Training of a Monk and The Eight Deadly Sins* (London, 1999); *Conlationes*, trans. and ed. B. Ramsey, *John Cassian: the Conferences* (New York – Mahwah, 1997).

42 For a summary of conjectures on Cassian's background, see Stewart, *Cassian*, pp. 4–6.

43 *Conference Ten* 1–5.

44 For Cassian, see principally O. Chadwick, *John Cassian* (2nd edition, Cambridge 1968); R. Markus, *The End of Ancient Christianity* (Cambridge, 1990), chs 11–14; Rousseau, *Ascetics, Authority and the Church*, Part Five; Rousseau, 'Cassian, contemplation and the cenobitic life', *JEH* 26 (1975) pp. 113–26; K. S. Frank, 'John Cassian on John Cassian', *Studia Patristica* 30 (Leuven, 1996) pp. 418–33; and now, C. Stewart, *Cassian the Monk* (Oxford, 1998).

45 V. Burrus, 'Ascesis, authority and text: *The Acts of the Council of Saragossa*', *Semeia* 58 (1992) pp. 95–108 argues in favour of broadening our understanding of officially-unpopular 'eremitism' to include 'alternative' forms of asceticism which the episcopate was attempting to control.

46 See Chadwick, *John Cassian*, pp. 70–8 on the difficulties of Cassian's instructions, as they stand, on the liturgical hours and also R. Taft, *The Liturgy of the Hours in East and West* (Collegeville, 1986) pp. 191–209.

47 See Chadwick, pp. 58–9 and A. Veilleux, *La liturgie dans le cénobitisme pachômien* for Cassian and the discrepancies between his and Palladius' version of how the set quantities of communal psalmody were handed down (to the primitive Christian community, according to Cassian, and to the Pachomians according to Palladius) by an angel. See also Stewart, *Cassian*, p. 140, 'Secondhand tales'.

48 See chapter 5 below, pp. 84–90.

49 Chadwick, pp. 14–15.

50 See most recently Stewart, *Cassian*, pp. 11–12; but Frank, 'John Cassian', pp. 427–8 thinks Cassian may never have actually visited Kellia.

51 See Chadwick, pp. 18–22 for a discussion of the authenticity of the *Conferences* and also Stewart, *Cassian*, pp. 8–12, 28, 36 and 'Appendix: Cassian on Monastic Egypt'.

52 For the texts he used, see Stewart, *Cassian*, pp. 36–7.

53 *Conference Thirteen* III, 5.
54 Ibid., 8, 3, and 18, 2.
55 *Conference Four* 12, 13.
56 *Conference Twenty-three* 7.
57 For Cassian's more general approach to aims and ends in the monastic life, see Stewart, *Cassian*, pp. 38–9.
58 See in particular the comments of Stewart, pp. 42–7, on this terminology.
59 *Institutes*, Books 5, 14, 4; 9, 10; 9, 13; 12, 12; and 12, 15, 2. *Conference One*, 8, 3; *Conference Ten* 6, 4 and 7, 3; *Conference Twenty-three* 5. 1; 8, 1; 11, 2; 15, 5; 15, 6.
60 *Conference Ten* 1–5.
61 See *Conference Three* 3–4 and Rubenson, *Letters*, pp. 85, n. 5; *Kephalaia Gnostica* I, 78–80 cf. *Conference Three* 6.
62 See M. Foucault, 'The Battle for Chastity', pp. 14–25 of *Western Sexuality*, ed. P. Ariès and A. Béjin (Oxford, 1985): Foucault does not deal with the theological context.
63 See also *Institutes* VI 8 and 20 and *Conference Twenty-two* 'Nocturnal Illusions': see D. Brakke, 'The Problematization of Nocturnal Emissions', esp. pp. 446–60.
64 *Conferences Twelve* and *Twenty-two; Institutes*, Book 6. See Brakke, 'Nocturnal Emissions', pp. 446–58.
65 Sulpicius, *Dialogue* I, ch. 5.
66 *Institutes*, Book 4, 21.
67 Here I follow Rouselle, *Porneia*, pp. 176–7 as much as Stewart, *Cassian*, p. 73.
68 *Institutes*, Book I, 10.
69 *Conference* 24, 1–2.
70 *Lausiac History*, ch. 33.
71 *Institutes*, Book II, 5.
72 *Institutes*, Book II, 4.
73 *Conference Eighteen*, 'On the kinds of monks'.

5 The Evolution of Monasticism in the West

1 See M.-D. Valentin, *Vie de Saint Honorat*, SC 245 (Paris, 1977), introduction; S. Pricoco, *L'Isola dei Santi* (Rome, 1978) pp. 70 ff. This criticizes aspects of F. Prinz's theory of Lérins as *Flüchtlingskloster* – see *Frühes Mönchtum im Frankenreich. Kultur und Gesellschaft in Gallien, den Rheinlanden und Bayern am Beispiel der monastischen Entwicklung* (München–Wien, 1965) pp. 47–87; C. Kasper, *Theologie and Askese. Die Spiritualität des Inselmönchtum Lérins im 5. Jahrhundert* (Münster, 1991) pp. 149–50.
2 Prinz, *Frühes Mönchtum*, p. 60.
3 *Vita Honorati*, 22.
4 P. Courcelle, 'Nouveaux aspects de la culture lérinienne', *Revue des Études Latines* 46 (1968) pp. 379–409; P. Riché, *Education et culture dans l'occident barbare 6e–8e siècle* (Paris, 1962) pp. 141–5; Kasper, pp. 181–5.
5 *VH* 18, 1 and Basil F 30 and 31.

6   *VH* 18, 1 and Basil F 25 (see also F 24–7 in general for confession).

7   *VH* 17, 8 and Basil F 43.

8   *VH* 37, 3 and Basil B 138.

9   *VH* 18, 5, cf. Basil F 1.

10 *VH* 21.

11 See M.-D. Valentin's edition of Hilarius, *Vie de Saint Honorat*, pp. 119 and 124; M. Carrias, 'Vie monastique et règle à Lérins au temps d'Honorat', *Revue d'histoire de l'Église de France* 74 (1988) pp. 191–211. A. de Vogüé, 'Aux Origines de Lérins: la Règle de Saint Basile?', *SM* 31 (1989) pp. 259–66 has attempted to deny the presence of the Basilian rule there and claims that the *Rule of the Four Fathers* was composed at Lérins. Kasper (note 4 above) criticizes Zelzer's claims in *CSEL* 86 that the sub-archetype of the MSS of Rufinus' version of Basil goes back to the sixth and not the fifth century. But Zelzer's suggestions may find confirmation in the work of Valentin and Carrias; and Rufinus' translation was not the only one to circulate in the west. Kasper argues that initially there were only parallels between Basil and Lérins – see esp. pp. 111–13.

12 Chadwick, *John Cassian*, p. 64.

13 *Vie des Pères de Jura*, ed., F Martine, *SC* 142 (Paris, 1968) ch. 20.

14 *Vie des Pères de Jura*, ch. 170.

15 I. Wood, 'A Prelude to Columbanus: the monastic achievement in the Burgundian territories', *Columbanus and Merovingian Monasticism*, pp. 4–8.

16 Translations cited are from *Early Monastic Rules. The Rules of the Fathers and the Regula Orientalis*, trans. C. V. Franklin, I. Havener, and J. Francis (Collegeville, 1981). Full edition by A. de Vogüé, *Les Règles des Saints Pères*, 2 vols, *SC* 297 and 298 (Paris, 1982).

17 *Rule of the Holy Fathers Serapion, Macarius, Paphnutius and another Macarius*, ch. 2, *Early Monastic Rules*, pp. 16–31.

18 *Rule of the Four Fathers*, ch. 5.

19 *Rule of the Four Fathers*, chs. 6–14.

20 *Second Rule of the Fathers*, in *Early Monastic Rules*, pp. 32–9, Preface.

21 *Rule of Macarius*, in *Early Monastic Rules*, pp. 40–51.

22 *Third Rule of the Fathers*, in *Early Monastic Rules*, pp. 52–9.

23 *Early Monastic Rules*, pp. 60–85.

24 *Oriental Rule*, ch. 1.

25 *Rule of the Four Fathers*, ch. 13.

26 *Rule of Macarius*, ch. 24.

27 *Second Rule of the Fathers*, ch. 6.

28 *Rule of the Four Fathers*, ch. 10; *Second Rule of the Fathers*, ch. 5.

29 Ch. 24.

30 *Rule of Macarius*, ch. 11; *Third Rule*, ch. 5.

31 *Rule of Macarius*, ch. 2.

32 *Third Rule*, ch. 14; ch. 13; ch. 4; ch. 2.

33 In favour of the production of the rules at Lérins, A. de Vogüé, *Les Règles des Saints Pères*; A. de Vogüé, *Les Règles Monastiques Anciennes (400–700)*, Typologie des Sources du Moyen Âge Occidental 46 (Turnhout, 1985);

A. de Vogüé, 'La Vie des Pères de Jura et la datation de la *Regula Orientalis*', *RAM* 47 (1971) pp. 121–7; A. Mundó, 'Les anciens synodes abbatiaux et les *Regula SS. Patrum*', *Studia Anselmiana* 44 (1959) pp. 107–25.

34 Pricoco, pp. 88–97.

35 *Life* composed by Jonas of Bobbio in *MGH SS Rer Mer*, vol. III, pp. 502–17.

36 De Vogüé, *Règles des Saints Pères*, p. 32 suggests that John had probably found the Rule of Macarius at Lérins. The rule is also mentioned in two charters which date from the second half of the seventh century: see Prinz, *Frühes Mönchtum*, p. 73.

37 A. Wilmart, 'Les *Monita* de l' abbé Porcaire', *RB* 26 (1909) pp. 475–80. The resemblance betwen the *Monita's* '*Orationi nihil praeponas tota die*' and *Macarius* 14 (= 2 RP 31) '*nihil orationi praeponendum est*' may merely reflect what was becoming a general monastic principle. Similarities between *Monita* lines 64–5 and RIVP 2, 32–3 appear to be based on a common knowledge of Cassian, *Institutes* 4, 34.

38 A. de Vogüé, ed., *Césaire d' Arles Oeuvres Monastiques*, vol. 1, *Oeuvres pour les Moniales*, SC vol. 345 (Paris, 1988) pp. 45–7, 180–91. The verbal resemblances noted between the *Rules of the Fathers* and Cæsarius at p. 181 n. 2, p. 191 n. 12, p. 190 n. 13, 2 are slight. Elsewhere, similarities may arise because similar issues are being treated.

39 Theories of Italian origin have been advanced by J. Neufville 'Règle des Pères et Second Règle des Péres. Texte critique', *RB* 75 (1965) pp. 307–12. See also J. Neufville, 'Les Éditeurs des *Regulae Patrum*: Saint Benoît d'Aniane et Lukas Holste', *RB* 76 (1966) pp. 327–43; J. Neufville, 'Sur le texte de la Règle des IV Pères', *RB* 75 (1965) pp. 47–95.

40 J. Percival, 'Villas and Monasteries in Later Roman Gaul', *JEH* 48 (1997) pp. 1–21. The sequence of events where villa or house monasteries did gradually become centres of communities is not clear from archaeological evidence – especially in cases where later sequences of mosaics in public parts of the building suggest a level of luxury incompatible with monastic vocation.

41 N. Gussone, 'Adventus-Zeremoniell und Translatio von Reliquien: Victricius von Rouen *De Laude Sanctorum*', *Frühmittelalterliche Studien* 10 (1976) pp. 125–33; P. Andrieu-Guitancourt, 'La vie ascétique à Rouen au temps de saint Victrice', *Recherches de science réligieuse* 40 (1952) pp. 90–106.

42 J. T. Lienhard, *Paulinus of Nola and Early Western Monasticism* (Köln-Bonn, 1977).

43 *Lives of the Fathers of Jura*, ch. 155.

44 F. Benoît, 'Le martyrium de l'abbaye Saint-Victor', Actes du Congrès sur l'Histoire de l'Abbaye Saint Victoire de Marseille, *Provence Historique* XVI (1966) pp. 259–96; G. Demians d'Archimbaud, 'Fouilles récentes de Saint-Victor de Marseille', *Comptes rendus de L'Académie des Inscriptions et des Belles-Lettres* (1974) pp. 313–46; M. Vieillard-Troiekouroff, *Les Monuments Religieux de la Gaule d'après les Oeuvres de Grégoire de Tours* (Paris, 1976) pp. 161–5 questions the identification of St. Victor with Cassian's monastery church; Stewart, *Cassian*, p. 16.

45 Vieillard-Troiekouroff, pp. 252–3; Prinz, pp. 42, 105–7, 137, 159, 167 ff., 193 ff., 260 ff., 274 ff.

46 F. Masai, 'La "Vita Patrum iurensium" et les débuts du monachisme a Saint-Maurice d'Agaune', in *Festschrift Bernard Bischoff, zu seinem 65 Geburtstag* (Stuttgart, 1971) pp. 43–69.

47 S. Burnell, *Merovingian to Early Carolingian Churches and their Founder-Graves in Southern Germany and Switzerland: the Impact of Christianity on the Alamans and the Bavarians*. D.Phil. Thesis (Oxford, 1988) pp. 265–7.

48 G. Ferrari, *Early Roman Monasteries. Notes for the History of the Monasteries and Convents at Rome from the V through the X Century*, Studi di antichità cristiana 23 (Città del Vaticano, 1957) ch. 10, Basilical Monasteries.

49 Ferrari, p. 365, points out that 'in a certain sense all Roman monasteries were basilical, in so far that their principal occupation was the recitation of the divine office in their own chapel or church or in a nearby basilica'.

50 *Lives of the Fathers of Jura*, chs 12–13, 18.

51 Palladius, *Lausiac History*, ch. 7.

52 *Apophthegmata* Lucius I.

53 J. Dyer, 'Monastic Psalmody of the Middle Ages', *RB* 99 (1989) pp. 241–74.

54 See Basil, F 37 and Taft, *The Liturgy of the Hours*, pp. 191–209.

55 L. Duchesne, *Christian Worship: Its Origins and Evolution* (4th English edn, London, 1912) pp. 492–4.

56 Lawless, *Augustine of Hippo and His Monastic Rule*, pp. 167–71.

57 *Corpus Consuetudinum Monasticarum* I (Siegburg, 1963) pp. 77–91.

58 F. Villegas, La 'Regula cuiusdam Patris ad Monachos' *Revue de l'Histoire de la Spiritualité* 49 (1973); *Sancti Columbani Opera*, ed., G. S. M. Walker (Dublin, 1957) pp. 128–33.

59 *Rule for Nuns* of Cæsarius of Arles, ch. 66 in *Césaire d'Arles, Oeuvres Monastiques*, vol. I, ed., A. de Vogüé, SC 345 (Paris, 1988) pp. 252–3.

60 O. Heiming, 'Zum Monastischen Offizium von Kassianus bis Kolumbanus', *Archiv fur Liturgiewissenschaft* 7 (1961–2), pp. 89–156.

61 T. P. McLaughlin, *Les Très Ancien Droit Monastique de l'Occident*, Archives de la France Monastique, vol. XXXVIII (Ligugé–Paris, 1935) pp. 129–52. For the reception of the decrees of Chalcedon in Italy, see Jenal, *Italia Ascetica Atque Monastica*, vol. II, pp. 714 ff. and Ch. 6 in this volume.

62 Ibid.; E. Lesne, *Histoire de la propriété ecclésiastique en France*, Mémoires et Travaux des Facultés Catholiques de Lille VI, vol. I (Paris–Lille, 1910) pp. 126–7; McLaughlin, pp. 111–28.

63 Gregory of Tours, *Glory of the Martyrs*, trans. and intro. by R. van Dam (Liverpool, 1988) ch. 61 translates the 'clerics' and 'monks' of the original as 'monks' throughout.

64 *TADMO*, p. 113.

65 J. Laporte, 'Les origines du monachisme dans la province de Rouen', *RM* 31 (1941) pp. 1–13.

66 Eugippius, *Vita sancti Severini* IV, 6, ed. P. Knoell (Vienna, 1886).

67 J. Orlandis, *Estudios sobre las institutiones monasticas medievales* (Pamplona, 1971) ch. 6, esp. pp. 106 ff. and C. J. Bishko, *Spanish and Portuguese Monastic History 600–1300* (London, 1984) pp. 18–20.

68 Leo I, Ep. 118, 2; 119, 6; 120, 6.

69 *TADMO*, p. 121.

70 *Lives of the Fathers of Jura*, ch. 26. Ch. 60 states that Romanus died at Baume – probably a sign that he regarded himself as head of the female community, rather than of any relaxation of active enclosure. For definitions of 'strict passive' and 'strict active' enclosure, see J. T. Schulenburg, 'Strict active enclosure and its effects on female monastic experience (ca. 500–1100)', in *Distant Echoes*. Vol. I of *Medieval Religious Women*, ed. J. A. Nichols and L. T. Shank (Kalamazoo, 1984) pp. 51–86

71 For Cæsarius' episcopate in general, see. W. Klingshirn, *Caesarius of Arles. The Making of a Christian Community in Late Antique Gaul* (Cambridge, 1994) and the bibliography given there.

72 The precise location of the re-founded nunnery and its basilica is disputed. See A. de Vogüé and J. Courreau, *Césaire d'Arles, Oeuvres monastiques* vol. I. *Ouevres pour les moniales*, Sources chrétiennes 345 (Paris, 1988) pp. 98–112, 500 and P.-A. Février, 'Arles', in *Topographie chrétienne des cités de la Gaule*, ed., N. Gauthier et J.-Ch. Picard, vol. III, *Provinces ecclésiastiques de Vienne et d'Arles* (Paris, 1986) pp. 73–84.

73 Klingshirn, *Caesarius* pp. 117–24, 250–6.

74 Full edition with French trans. A. de Vogüé and J. Courreau, *Césaire d'Arles, Oeuvres monastiques* vol I. *Ouevres pour les moniales*, pp. 35–273. For an English translation of the entire rule see M. C. McCarthy, *The Rule for Virgins of Saint Cæsarius of Arles: A Translation With a Critical Introduction* (Washington, 1960).

75 *Rule*, ch. 2.

76 First section = chapters 1–16; section 2 = 17–35; section 3 = 37–47; *Recapitulation* 48–66; liturgy, fasts and conclusion 67–73. For structure and dating of the rule, see de Vogüé and Courreau, pp. 45–68 and for the influence of Augustine, see L. de Seilhac, *L'utilisation par S. Césaire d'Arles de la Règle de S. Augustin. Étude de terminologie et de doctrine monastiques*, Studia Anselmiana 62 (Rome, 1974).

77 *Rule for Virgins*, ch. 1.

78 *Rule for Monks*, ch. 11 in A. de Vogüé and J. Courreau, *Césaire d'Arles, Oeuvres monastiques* vol II, *Oeuvres pour les moines*, SC 398 (Paris, 1994).

79 *Rule for Virgins*, ch. 36.

80 *Rule for Virgins*, ch. 25. See also ch. 54.

81 Ibid., ch. 38.

82 Ibid., chs 46, 27, 28

83 See D. Hochstetler, 'The meaning of monastic cloister for women according to Cæsarius of Arles', in *Religion, Culture and Society in the Early Middle Ages*, ed. T. F. X. Noble and J. J. Contreni (Kalamazoo, 1987) pp. 27–40. Hochstetler thinks that the abbess might sometimes dine outside the nunnery, but this seems unlikely. See *Rule*, ch. 41.

84 Letter *Vereor*, ch. 5, *Oeuvres pour les moniales*, p. 314.

85 *Rule for Virgins*, chs 7, 19–20.

86 Augustine, *Rule for Nuns*, ch. 20.

87 Ibid., ch. 18.

88 For officials, see ch. 30.

89 *Rule for Virgins*, ch. 7.

90 Basil F 15 = Rufinus, ch. 7.

91 M. de Jong, *In Samuel's Image: Child Oblation in the Early Medieval West* (Leiden, 1986) pp. 19–22; J. Boswell, *The Kindness of Strangers. The Abandonment of Children in Western Europe from Late Antiquity to the Renaissance* (Harmondworth, 1988) p. 257 on Salvian's complaint in the fifth century.

92 Ibid., chs 7, 44–5. See also the *Recapitulation*.

93 *Rule for Virgins*, ch. 30.

94 Ibid., ch. 26.

95 *Vereor*, ch. 8.

96 *Rule for Virgins*, ch. 6.

97 For legislation, see S. F. Wemple, *Women in Frankish Society. Marriage and the Cloister 500–900* (Philadelphia, 1981) pp. 157–8.

98 Ibid., ch. 56.

99 Ibid., ch. 69.

100 See Taft, *The Liturgy of the Hours*, pp. 191–209; M. Dunn, 'Mastering Benedict', pp. 576–80 and 'The Master and St Benedict: A Rejoinder', *EHR* 107 (1992) p. 110.

101 See *Rule*, chs 67–73 and for liturgy and many other aspects of female monastic life, see G. Muschiol, *Famula Dei. Zur Liturgie in merowingischen Frauenklöstern*, Beiträge zur Geschichte des Alten Mönchtums und des Benediktinertums 41 (Münster, 1994).

102 P. Jay, 'Le purgatoire dans la prédication de saint Césaire d'Arles', *Revue de Théologie Ancienne et Médievale* 24 (1957), 5–14; Cæsarius, Sermons 5, 14, 18, 31 and 137 in *Sermones, Corpus Christianorum*, vols 103–4, (Turnhout, 1953).

103 P.-A. Février, 'Arles', in *Topographie chretienne des cités de la Gaule*.

104 Klingshirn, *Caesarius*, pp. 260–6.

105 For Aurelian's *Rules*, see *PL* 68, cols. 385–404.

106 See Wemple, p. 156.

107 Gregory of Tours, *Glory of the Confessors*, trans. and ed. R. van Dam (Liverpool, 1988) p. 18.

108 There is now a large and growing bibliography on Radegund which cannot all be cited here. For what follows see principally Wemple, *Women in Frankish Society* 38–9, 132, 140–2, 155, 158, 165, 176, 181, 183–5, 220–1; B. Brennan, 'St Radegund and the early development of her cult at Poitiers', *JRH* 13 (1984–5) pp. 311–23; *La Riche Personnalité de Sainte Radegonde, Conférences et homélies prononcées à Poitiers à l'occasion du XIVe centenaire de sa mort (587–1987)* (Poitiers, 1908); *Sainted Women of the Dark Ages*, ed. and trans. J. A. Macnamara and J. E. Halborg with E. G. Whatley (Durham and London, 1992) pp. 60–106 including a transla-

tion of the *Life*; and the items listed below. See also Prinz, *Frühes Mönchtum*, pp. 57 ff.

109 I. Moreira, '*Provisatrix optima*: St. Radegund of Poitiers' relic petitions to the East', *JMH* 19 (1993) pp. 285–305.

110 *History of the Franks* 9, 40. This testimony is, however, rejected by de Vogüé and Courreau vol I, pp. 443–60, who believe that the *Rule* was sent to Radegund and Richildis – whom they identify with Agnes – by Cæsaria the Younger, Cæsarius' niece and the second abbess of St Jean.

111 *Glory of the Confessors*, ch. 104.

112 J. George, *Venantius Fortunatus: A Latin Poet in Merovingian Gaul* (Oxford, 1992); *Sainted Women of the Dark Ages*; S. Gabe, 'Radegundis: sancta, regina, ancilla: Zum Heiligkeitsideal der Radegundisviten von Fortunat und Baudonivia', *Francia* 16 (1989) pp. 1–30; J. Leclercq, 'La Sainte Radegonde de Venance Fortunat et celle de Baudovinie. Essai d'hagiographie comparée,' *Fructus centesimus. Mélanges offerts à Gérard J. M. Bartelink à l'occasion de son soixante-cinquième anniversaire, Instrumenta patristica* 19 (Steenbrugge, 1989) pp. 207–16; S. F. Wemple. 'Female spirituality and mysticism in Frankish Monasteries: Radegund, Balthild and Aldegund', in *Peace Weavers. Medieval Religious Women*, vol. II, ed. J. A Nichols and L. T. Shank (Kalamazoo, 1987) pp. 39–53 and the bibliographies given in all. Macnamara and Halborg, p. 65, state that both biographies were composed after the revolt of the nuns of Holy Cross while J. T. Schulenburg, *Forgetful of their Sex. Female Sanctity and Society ca. 500–1100* (Chicago and London, 1998) p. 42 dates Venantius' *Life* to the period before 590.

113 For the revolt of the nuns of Poitiers, see Gregory of Tours, *History of the Franks* trans. and ed. L. Thorpe (Penguin Classics, 1974) Books IX 38–43; X 14–17, 20.

6 The *Rule* of St Benedict and its Italian Setting

1 The most comprehensive account of Italian monasticism in this period is to be found in Jenal, *Italia Ascetica*, vol. I, pp. 145–311, who notes pp. 192–203 the anomalous picture given in the *Dialogues* attributed to Pope Gregory the Great.

2 *TADMO*, p. 121.

3 Jenal, *Italia Ascetica*, pp. 709–24.

4 Ibid., p. 178.

5 For Fulgentius, including a translation into French of Ferrandus' *Vita Fulgentii* the standard work is still G. Lapeyre, *Saint Fulgence de Ruspe. Un évêque catholique africain sous la domination vandale* (Paris, 1929). See also J. J. Gavigan, *De vita monastica in Aftrica septentrionali inde a temporibus S. Augustini usque ad invasiones Arabum* (Rome–Turin, 1962) pp. 145 ff; Jenal, pp. 180–90, 223–4.

6 Jenal, *Italia Ascetica*, pp. 157–62.

7 *De viris illustribus*, 26, 34.

8 *Eugippii Regula*, ed. F. Villegas and A. de Vogüé, *CSEL*, vol. LXXXVII (Vienna, 1976).

9 The principal exponent of this theory is A. de Vogüé; see his 'La Règle d' Eugippe retrouvée?', *RAM* 47 (1971) pp. 233–65 and the other items in his collection *Le Maître, Eugippe et saint Benoît* (Hildesheim, 1984), principally section II, *La Règle d'Eugippe*. For an earlier but useful treatment of the contents of the manuscript in which the rules are found as a whole, see A. Genestout, 'Le plus ancien témoin manuscrit de la Règle du Maître: le *Parisinus* Latin 12634', *Scriptorium* 1 (1946–7) pp. 129–42. For arguments against de Vogüé and the varying views on the dating of BN Lat. 12634, see M. Dunn, 'Mastering Benedict: monastic rules and their authors in the early medieval West', *EHR* 105 (1990) pp. 567–94. I agree with Genestout that the manuscript is written in hands dating from the seventh century.

10 J. J. O'Donnell, *Cassiodorus* (Berkeley, 1979); P. Courcelle, 'Le site du monastère de Cassiodore', *Mélanges d'archéologie et d'histoire* 55, (1938) pp. 259–307; P. Courcelle, 'Nouvelles Recherches sur le monastère de Cassiodore', *Actes du Ve Congrès International d'archéologie chrétienne, Aix-en-Provence*, Studi di antichità cristiana XXIII (Vatican–Paris, 1957), pp. 511–28.

11 Jenal, *Italia Ascetica*, vol. II, pp. 635 ff.

12 Ibid., vol. I, pp. 145–214, 226–8.

13 *La Règle de Saint Benoît*, Sources Chrétiennes 181–6 (Paris, 1971–2), vol. 2, pp. 887–903 for a complete list of Benedict's citations. See also the interpretation of the areas treated below and of the rule in general in this and in A. de Vogüé, *La communauté et l'abbé dans la Règle de Saint Benoît*, Textes et Études Théologiques (Paris, 1961). The following treatment differs from these in many fundamental respects: see Dunn, 'Mastering Benedict'; A. de Vogüé, 'The Master and St Benedict: a reply to Marilyn Dunn', *EHR* 107 (1992) 95–103; and Dunn, 'The Master and St Benedict: a Rejoinder', ibid., pp. 104–11. De Vogüé's contribution to the literature on Benedict and the Master is enormous and only some of it can be cited here: but see in particular the studies collected in his *Le Maître, Eugippe et saint Benoît*.

14 *RB*, ch. 48; for writing-instruments, see *RB*, ch. 33.

15 *RB*, ch. 1 cf. Cassian, *Conference Eighteen*.

16 *RB*, Prologue, 1. The English translation used here is by J. McCann, *The Rule of St Benedict* (London, 1970), while the numbering of individual lines in each chapter is that of de Vogüé's edition.

17 RB, chs 1, 6–9. This description ultimately goes back to Jerome's Letter 22 to Eustochium and his complaints about the *remnuoth*; Cassian is nearer to him than Benedict is to Cassian.

18 C. Vagaggini, 'La posizione di San Benedetto nella questione semiepelagiana', *Studia Anselmiana* 17–18 (1947) pp. 17–83 discusses both 'semi-Pelagian' and 'Augustinian' statements in Benedict.

19 Based on Basil B 201: cf. Rufinus 108 and Cassian, *Conference* 23 vi.

20 *RB* ch. 4, 50.

21   *RB*, Prologue, 46.
22   *RB*, ch. 73, 8.
23   *RB* ch. 73, 1.
24   *RB* ch. 73, 5.
25   E.g. RB c. 1, 3; c. 1, 12; c. 58, 17.
26   *RB*, ch. 5.
27   *RB*, ch. 68.
28   *RB*, ch. 6.
29   *RB*, ch. 3, 7–11.
30   *RB*, ch. 3, 11.
31   *RB*, ch. 2, 2–3.
32   *RB*, ch. 2, 11–12, 16.
33   *Regula Orientalis* ch. 1 'The abbot...shall freely make decisions on all matters within the monastery'.
34   *RB*, c. 3, 3–6. *RB*, ch. 61 notes that pilgrim monks, who are treated as guests when they arrive in the monastery and therefore dine with the abbot are allowed 'modestly' to censure or charitably remark on any defects which they may perceive in the running of the community: but the fact that they are treated as guests means that it is the abbot who hears their comments.
35   *Oriental Rule*, ch. 17 in *Rules of the Fathers and the Regula Orientalis.*
36   *RB*, ch. 65, 1–4.
37   *RB*, ch. 21.
38   *RB*, ch. 60.
39   *RB*, ch. 71, 4.
40   *RB*, ch. 72, 8.
41   *RB*, ch. 31.
42   *RB*, ch. 32.
43   *RB*, ch. 66.
44   *RB*, ch. 63.
45   *RB*, ch. 62.
46   E.g. *RB*, chs 36, 37, 57.
47   *RB*, ch. 57, 1.
48   *RB*, ch. 63. 10.
49   *RB*, ch. 63, 9.
50   *RB*, ch. 58.
51   *RB*, ch. 69.
52   De Jong, *In Samuel's Image*, pp. 23–7.
53   *RB*, chs. 23–30.
54   Basil F 28
55   *RB*, ch. 28; F 28. Rufinus 76 (cf. Basil B 4) also uses the simile of amputation, but does not go through the procedures or the extended similes and metaphors of F 28 which are close to Benedict.
56   E. M. Vilanova. *Regula Pauli et Stephani*, Edicia critica i comentari (Montserrat, 1959), ch. 39.
57   *RB*, ch. 53.
58   Ibid.
59   *RB*, ch. 62.

60 *RB*, ch. 64. The legislation of 546 replaced earlier a law of the 530s which had been interpreted to mean that the prior could succeed. See K. Hallinger, 'Das Wahlrecht der Benediktusregula', *ZKG 76* (1965) pp. 233–45; K. Hallinger, 'Regula Benedicti 64 und die Wahlgewohnheiten des 6–12 Jahrhunderts,' *Latintät und alte Kirche. Festschrift für Rudolf Hanslik zum 70 Geburtstag*, ed. H. Bannert and J. Divjak (Vienna–Cologne–Graz, 1977); Jenal, *Italia Ascetia* vol. I, pp. 237–8; K. Hallinger, 'Papst Gregor der Grosse und der heiliger Benedikt', *Commentationes in Regula Sancti Benedicti*, ed. B. Steidle, Studia Anselmiana 42 (Rome, 1957) pp. 231–319, esp. pp. 309–17.

61 *RB*, ch. 64, 5.

62 *RB*, ch. 48.

63 *Regula Pauli et Stephani*, chs 10, 11, *Regula Tarnatensis*, ch. 9, *PL* 66, col. 981.

64 *RB*, ch. 32.

65 *RB*, ch. 35.

66 *RB*, ch. 39.

67 *RB*, ch. 40, 5–7

68 *RB*, chs 36 and 37.

69 *RB*, chs 48 and 42.

70 De Vogüé, *Règle*, vol. 1, p. 170.

71 The most detailed account is still that of T. Hodgkin *Italy and Her Invaders* vol. IV, pp. 535–53 (Oxford, 1885) and vol. V, pp. 3–47.

72 Hallinger, 'Papst Gregor der Grosse', p. 316; Jenal, *Italia ascetica*, pp. 811–16.

73 *Regula Tarnatensis*, *PL* 66, cols. 977–86; and F. Villegas, 'La "Regula monasterii Tarnantensis". Texte, sources et datation', *RB 84* (1974) pp. 7–65; G. Holzherr, *Regula Ferioli. Ein Beitrag zur Entwicklungsgeschichte und zur Sinndeutung der Benediktinerregel* (Einsiedeln, 1961); E. M. Vilanova. *Regula Pauli et Stephani*.

74 This view was first advanced by A. Genestout in the 1930s and published in 'La Règle du Maître et la Règle de S. Benoît', *RAM* 21 (1940) pp. 51–112. For the subsequent lengthy controversy and its bibliography, see B. Jaspert, *Die Regula Benedicti-Regula Magistri Kontroverse* (2nd edn, Hildesheim, 1977). The view of the *Rule of the Master*'s priority was reworked by A. de Vogüé and enshrined in his editions of the two rules, *La Règle du Maître*, SC 105–7 (Paris, 1964) and *La Règle de Saint Benoît*, SC 181–6 (Paris, 1971–2), with extensive commentary in both, particularly the latter. I have taken issue with this view in the articles cited at note 13 above, as has M. Tosi, 'La presenza della *Regula Benedicti* nel monastero di S. Colombano in Bobbio', *Archivum Bobiense* 3 (1981) pp. 7–58.

75 *Regula Magistri* = *RM* Prologue; *RM*, ch. 1, 1–26; 'Thema'.

76 *RB*, ch. 66, 8 and also on the related question of the 'pure' and 'interpolated' manuscript version of *RB*, see P. Meyvaert, 'Towards a history of the textual transmission of the Regula S. Benedicti', *Scriptorium* 17 (1963) pp. 83–111.

77 See pp. 129–33 below for Benedict's monasteries; for clothing according to climate, see *RB*, ch. 55, 1.

78 Oxford, Bodley Hatton 38.

79 See Dunn, 'Mastering Benedict', pp. 576–82 and the references given there, especially O. Heiming, 'Zum monastischen Offizium von Cassianus bis Kolumbanus,' *Archiv fur Liturgiewissenschaft* vii (1961–2) pp. 89–156 and P. Nowack, 'Die Strukturelemente des Stundengebets der Regula Benedicti', *Archiv für Liturgiewissenschaft* XXVI (1984) pp. 253–304.

80 *RB*, ch. 18, 25.

81 Gregory the Great, *Dialogues*, Book IV, ch. 36. The most detailed modern edition with French translation by P. Antin and extensive commentary by A. de Vogüé is *Grégoire le Grand, Dialogues, SC* 251, 260, 265 (Paris, 1978, 1979, 1980). Quotations given here are based on the English translation by O. J. Zimmermann in the *Fathers of the Church* series (Washington D. C., 1959).

82 Ferrari, *Early Roman Monasteries*, ch. 10, 'Roman Monastic Observance'.

83 K. Hallinger, 'Papst Gregor der Grosse' und der heiliger Benedikt' esp. pp. 309–17.

84 O. Porcel, 'San Gregorio Magno y el Monachato. Cuestiones controvertidas', *Monastica* I (Montserrat, 1960) pp. 1–95.

85 See A. de Vogüé, 'L'Auteur du Commentaire des Rois attribué à S. Grégoire: un moine de Cava?' *RB* 106 (1996) pp. 319–31.

86 F. Clark, *The Pseudo-Gregorian Dialogues*, Studies in the History of Christian Thought XXXVII and XXXVIII (Leiden, 1987).

87 Among defenders of the traditional view of the *Dialogues* are R. Godding, 'Les *Dialogues*... de Grégoire le Grand. À propos d'un livre récent', *AB* 106 (1988) pp. 201–29; P. Meyvaert, 'The enigma of Gregory the Great's *Dialogues*: a response to Francis Clark', *JEH* 39 (1988) pp. 335–81; P.-P. Verbraken, 'Les Dialogues de saint Grégoire le Grand: sont-ils apocryphes? À propos d'un ouvrage récent', *RB* 98 (1988) pp. 272–7; A. de Vogüé, 'Grégoire le Grand et ses "Dialogues" d' après deux ouvrages récents', *RHE* 83 (1988) pp. 281–348; de Vogüé, 'Les Dialogues, oeuvre authentique et publiée par Grégoire lui-même', in *Gregorio Magno e il suo tempo* (Rome, 1991) vol. 2 pp. 27–40; de Vogüé ' "Martyrium in occulto" Le martyre du temps de paix chez S. Grégoire le Grand, Isidore de Séville, et Valerius de Bierzo', *Fructus centesimus. Mélanges offerts à Gérard J. M. Bartelink à l'occasion de son soixante-cinquième anniversaire* (*Instrumenta patristica* 19, Steenbrugge, 1989) pp. 125–40. Clark has replied to his critics in several places, most notably in 'St Gregory and the Enigma of the *Dialogues*: a response to Paul Meyvaert', *Journal of Ecclesiastical History* 40 (1989) pp. 323–43, but also in 'The authorship of the *Dialogues*: an old controversy renewed', *Heythrop Journal* 30 (1989) pp. 257–72; 'The renewed debate on the authenticity of the Gregorian *Dialogues*', *Augustinianum* 30 (1990) pp. 75–105; and 'The renewed controversy about the authorship of the *Dialogues*', *Gregorio Magno e il suo tempo* (Rome, 1991) vol. II, pp. 5–25 and his work has been favourably reviewed by R. Gillet, *Dictionnaire d'Histoire et de Géographie Ecclésiastiques* XXI (1409–11) and

H. Wansbrough in *Heythrop Journal* 30, (1989) pp. 356–7. G. Cremascoli, 'Se i *Dialogi* siano opera di Gregorio Magno', *Benedictina* 36 (1989) pp. 179–92 considers the question still open.

88 *Dialogues* II, 8; A. Pantoni, *L'Acropoli di Montecassino e il Primitivo Monastero di San Benedetto* (1980) pp. 55–6, 81. This work, like others before it, uses the narrative of the *Dialogues* to interpret the archaeological remains found on Monte Cassino. The temple found there seems to have been dedicated to Jove rather than to Apollo as the *Dialogues* maintain.

89 *Dialogues* II, 1–8. See also Jenal, *Italia Ascetica* I, pp. 196–203 and the references given there.

90 *Dialogues* II, 8.

91 Ibid.

92 *Dialogues* I, 4. This last incident contains incidents which resemble those in the story told of the bishop of 'Romilla' in the *Spiritual Meadow* of the eastern writer John Moschos, composed in the early seventh century: see *The Spiritual Meadow of John Moschos*, trans. and ed. J. Wortley, *Cistercian Studies* 139 (Kalamazoo, 1992) ch. 150, pp 122–4. J. M. Petersen, *The Dialogues of Gregory the Great in their Late Antique Cultural Background* (1984), maintains the authenticity of the attribution of the *Dialogues* to Gregory, but her discussion of Equitius-narrative of the *Dialogues* pp. 79–80 reveals its resemblance to one of the Italian *Gesta Martyrum*. A. de Vogüé, 'Le pape qui persecuta Saint Equitius. Essai d' identification', *AB* 100 (1984) pp. 319–25 treats the story as authentic.

93 Jenal, *Italia Ascetica*, vol. I, pp. 193–214, 224–6.

94 For the pastoral organization of Italy in late antiquity and the early middle ages see C. E. Boyd, *Tithes and Parishes in Medieval Italy* (Ithaca, 1952) pp. 47–58.

95 Vigilius, *Ep. ad Rusticum et Sebastianum, PL* 69, 48b.

96 Jenal, *Italia Ascetica* II, p. 219.

97 For biographies of Gregory, see F. Homes Dudden, *Gregory the Great: his Place in History and Thought*, 2 vols (London, 1905); J. Richards, *Consul of God* (London, 1980); R. Markus, *Gregory the Great and His World* (Cambridge, 1997). The last gives some idea of the vast bibliography that has grown up on the subject of Gregory and his writings. See in particular, C. Dagens, *Saint Grégoire le Grand. Culture et expérience chrétiennes* (Paris, 1977) esp. pp. 149–63 for what follows below; C. Straw, *Gregory the Great. Perfection in Imperfection* (Berkeley and Los Angeles, 1988); J. Fontaine, R. Gillet and S Pellistrandi, eds, *Grégoire le Grand*, Colloques internationaux du CNRS (Paris, 1986) and *Gregorio Magno e il suo tempo*, Studia Ephemeridis 'Augustinianum' 34 (Rome, 1991); J. C. Cavadini, ed., *Gregory the Great: A Symposium* (Notre Dame and London, 1995).

98 *Moralia in Iob Libri XXIII–XXXV*, ed. M. Adriaen (*Corpus Christianorum*, vol. CXLIII B, Turnhout, 1985), Book XXXI, xxv, 49.

99 Cassian, *Conference Fourteen*, 16, 9.

100 Markus, *End of Ancient Christianity*, pp. 187 ff.

101 *Moralia* XXX ii, 8.

102 R. Rudmann, *Mönchtum und kirchlicher Dienst in den Schriften Gregors des Grossen* (St Ottilien, 1956) ch. 3, 2, suggests that Gregory held 'conflicting' views on whether monks should embrace the active or the contemplative life, but singles out exceptional cases when Gregory entrusted special tasks to monks whom he knew. See also R. Gillet, 'Spiritualité et place du moine dans l'eglise selon saint Grégoire le Grand', *Théologie de la vie monastique*, coll. Théologie 49 (Paris, 1961) pp. 323–51.

103 *Homiliae in Hiezechielem* II, pp. 10–11: C. Morel, 'Grégoire le Grand', *Homélies sur Ézéchiel, SC* 327, 360 (1986, 1990) vol. II, pp. 110–13.

104 Richards, *Consul of God*, ch. 5.

105 C. Leyser, ' "Let me speak, let me speak": vulnerability and authority' in *Gregorio Magno*, vol. II, pp. 169–82.

106 *Epistolae* IV, 18.

107 *Epistolae* V, 1. See also iv, 11; vi, 28; vii, 40 for similar statements.

108 Gregory, *Epistolae* iii 59; iv, 29; iv, 23, 25–29.

109 *Epistolae* vi, 51; vi, 53; vi, 55; vi, 60. The view that Gregory purchased English slave boys (mentioned in Ep. vi, 10) to train as monks and send on the mission needs to be treated with caution. They were pagans when purchased in 595 and Gregory arranged for Franks to act both as priests and interpreters to the mission. See also N. Brooks, *The Early History of the Church of Canterbury* (Leicester, 1984), chs 1 and 5.

110 E. John, 'The social and political problems of the early English church', *Journal of Agricultural History* 18 (1970) Supplement in Honour of G. Finsberg, ed. J. Thirsk, pp. 54–6.

111 Jenal, *Italia Ascetica*, vol. II, pp. 826–31.

112 Julianus Pomerius, *The Contemplative Life = De Vita Contemplativa, PL* 59.

113 The relative frequency of the use of the Gospel injunction may prove to be a test of the authenticity of Gregory's works.

114 Endowment: *Epistolae* I, 54; VIII, 5; IX, 233; XIII, 16; IV, 14; for the episcopate and monasteries, especially Ravenna, see Markus, *Gregory*, pp. 71–2 and 152 ff. For priors, probation etc., see Hallinger, 'Papst Gregor der Grosse' who indicates the many contrasts between Benedict and Gregory.

115 See J.-M. Sansterre, *Les Moines grees et Orientaux à Rome aux époques byzantine et Carolingienne (milieu du vie siècle-fin du lxe siècle)* 2 vols. (Brussels, 1983).

116 Godding, 'Les *Dialogues*... de Grégoire le Grand', p. 205 shows that the earliest MSS of the *Liber testimoniorum*, an anthology of Gregorian material composed by the notary Paterius date from the eighth century, so that the *lemmata* identifying excerpts as coming from the *Dialogues* could have been added long after the compilation was made and once the *Dialogues* as we know then came into circulation. See the debate indicated at note 87 above.

7 Britain and Ireland

1 C. Thomas, *Christianity in Roman Britain* (London, 1981) pp. 53–60, 295–302, 333

2 Ibid., pp. 90–2; C. Thomas, *And Shall These Mute Stones Speak? Post-Roman Inscriptions in Western Britain* (Cardiff, 1994) ch. 14; L. Olson, *Early Monasteries in Cornwall* (Woodbridge, 1989) ch. 2.

3 *Life of St Samson*, ed. T. Taylor (Llanerch, 1991). For some of the many problems associated with this text see Thomas, *And Shall*, ch. 14. The late date proposed for the *Life* by J. C. Poulin, 'Hagiographie et Politique: la première Vie de St Samson de Dol', *Francia* V (1978) pp 1–26 has not, apparently, hindered its use as an indicator of relations between monks and episcopate.

4 Identified by Olson, pp. 12 ff., as Golant and Thomas, *And Shall*, pp. 232–3 as Fowey.

5 Thomas, *And Shall*, ch. 10.

6 See T. Charles-Edwards, 'The social background to Irish peregrinatio', *Celtica* II (1975) pp. 43–59; K. Hughes, 'The changing theory and practice of Irish pilgrimage', *Journal of Ecclesiastical History* 11 (1960) pp. 143–51; A. Angenendt, *Monachi Peregrini* (Munich, 1972) pp. 124–51.

7 G. H. Doble, *The Saints of Cornwall* (Llanerch, 1997–8) pp. 10–60.

8 For literature and archaeological information on Whithorn – except the identification of UUinniau–Finnian with Ninian, which has been proposed by T. O. Clancy – see J. Macqueen, *Saint Nynia* (Edinburgh, 1990) and P. Hill, *Whithorn and Saint Ninian. The Excavation of a Monastic Town* (Stroud, 1997).

9 G. S. M. Walker, ed., *Sancti Columbani Opera*, Scriptores Latini Hiberniae col. II (Dublin, 1957), Letter V, 8.

10 For Irish background, see most recently D. Ó. Cróinín, *Early Medieval Ireland 400–1200* (London, 1995).

11 Ó Cróinín, pp. 14–20.

12 Ó Cróinín, pp. 20–23; T. Charles-Edwards, 'Palladius, Prosper and Leo the Great; mission and primatial authority', in D. Dumville, ed., *Saint Patrick* AD 493–1993 (Woodbridge, 1993) pp. 1–12.

13 A. B. E. Hood, trans. and ed., *St Patrick, His Writings and Muirchu's Life* (London, 1978); Ó Cróinín, pp. 23–9; Dumville, ed., *Saint Patrick*.

14 *Confessio* 41.

15 For Irish monasteries and monasticism in general, there is still that old standby, J. Ryan, *Irish Monasticism. Origins and Early Development* (Dublin and Cork, 1931, 2nd edn, 1972) but it is now outdated in many respects. See also J. R. Walsh and T. Bradley, *A History of the Irish Church 400–700* AD (Blackrock, 1991) chs 5 and 6.

16 *Sancti Columbani Opera*, Letter I, 6.

17 See M. Lapidge, 'Gildas' education and the Latin culture of sub-Roman Britain', in M. Lapidge and D. Dumville, *Gildas: New Approaches* (Woodbridge, 1986) pp. 27–50.

18 C. Stancliffe, 'Venantius Fortunatus, Ireland, Jerome: The Evidence of Precamur Patrem' *Peritia* 10 (1996) pp. 91–7, demonstrates that we should not over-estimate the importance of trade-links with Aquitaine in this context.

19 *Amra Choluimb Chille* in *Iona. The Earliest Poetry of a Celtic Monastery* (Edinburgh, 1995) ed. and trans. T. O. Clancy and G. Márkus, pp. 97–128.

20 Clancy and Márkus, pp. 77–80.

21 *Adomnan's Life of Columba*, ed. and trans. A. O. Anderson and M. O. Anderson (London, 1961), 29a.

22 Ibid., 119a.

23 Bede, *Ecclesiastical History* IV, 28–9.

24 Jonas, *Life of Columbanus, PL* 87, cols. 1014–46, ch. 8.

25 See note 6 above.

26 For Colum Cille, see A. Smyth, *Warlords and Holy Men. Scotland* AD *80–1000* (Edinburgh, 1984), ch. 3; Clancy and Márkus, pp. 1–128. For the monastic *familia* of Iona, see M. Herbert, *Iona, Kells and Derry: The History and Hagiography of the Monastic 'Familia' of Columba* (Oxford, 1988).

27 K. Hughes, *The Church in Early Irish Society* (London, 1966); R. Sharpe, 'Some problems concerning the organisation of the early Irish church', *Peritia* 3 (1984) pp. 230–70; R. Sharpe, 'Churches and communities in early medieval Ireland: towards a pastoral model', *Pastoral Care before the Parish* (Leicester, 1992), ed. J. Blair and R. Sharpe, pp. 81–109. See also ibid., pp. 63–80; T. Charles-Edwards, *The pastoral role of the churches in the early Irish laws*; D. Ó Corráin, 'The early Irish churches: some aspects of organization' in D. Ó Corráin, ed., *Irish Antiquity: Essays and Studies Presented to Professor M. J. O' Kelly* (Cork, 1981) pp. 327–41; C. Etchingham, 'The early Irish church: some observations on pastoral care and dues', *Eriu* 42 (1991) pp. 99–118; Ó Cróinin, *Early Medieval Ireland*, ch. 6; W. Davies, 'The myth of the Celtic Church', in N. Edwards and A. Lane, eds, *The Early Church in Wales and the West* (Oxford, 1992) pp. 12–21.

28 Columbanus, *Opera* Letter IV, 4.

29 Bede, *Ecclesiastical History*, IV, 27.

30 Adamnan, ed. Anderson and Anderson, 45b.

31 Ibid., 82b for Colum Cille's journey to the King of the Picts; baptism of Artbranna 34b–35a.

32 T. O. Clancy, 'Annat in Scotland and the origins of the parish', *Innes Review* 42 (1995) pp. 91–115.

33 On penitentials and the development of penance, see L. Bieler, *The Irish Penitentials* with an appendix by D. A. Binchy (Dublin, 1963); A. Frantzen, *The Literature of Penance in Anglo-Saxon England* (New Brunswick, NJ, 1963); J. Laporte, *Le Penitentiel de saint Colomban* (Tournai–Paris–Rome–New York, 1958). References here are to the translations in J. T. McNeil and H. M. Gamer, *Medieval Handbooks of Penance: A Translation of the Principal Libri Poenitentiales* (New York, 1938, 1990). Ó Cróinin, ch. 8. See also T. Charles-Edwards, 'The Penitential of Theodore and the *Iudicia Theodori*' in *Archbishop Theodore* ed. M. Lapidge (Cambridge, 1995) pp. 96–129.

34 McNeill and Gamer, pp. 76–80.

35 Adamnan, *Life of Columba*, 87b–92b.

36 On the organization of monasteries in general, see A. D. S. MacDonald, 'Aspects of the monastery and monastic life in Adomnan's life of Columba', *Peritia* 3 (1984) pp. 271–302. L. Bitel, *Isle of the Saints. Monastic settlement and Christian Community in Early Ireland* (Ithaca and London, 1990); M. Herity, 'Early Irish hermitages in the light of the *Lives* of Cuthbert', in *St. Cuthbert, his Cult and his Community to AD 1200*, ed. G. Bonner, D. Rollason, and C. Stancliffe (Woodbridge, 1989) and the references given there.

37 *Columbani Opera*, p. 146.

38 Jonas, *Life of Columbanus* II, 9.

39 See Ó Cróinin, ch. 8; Clancy and Márkus, *Iona* pp. 27–35, 'Iona as a literary centre'.

40 Quotation by Ó Cróinin, p. 179.

41 Ó Cróinin, *Early Medieval Ireland*, ch. 8; Clancy and Márkus, pp. 27–35.

42 Clancy and Márkus, p. 109.

43 See *Columbani Opera*, introduction, pp. xvi–xvii.

44 Quoted Ó Cróinin, p. 177

45 Ó Cróinin, *Early Medieval Ireland*, pp. 152–3.

46 *Monastic Rule*, ch. 7, Walker, pp. 128–31.

47 Ibid.

48 F. Villegas, 'La *Regula cuiusdam patris ad monachos*', *Revue d'histoire de la spiritualité* 49 (1973) pp. 3–39.

49 *Monastic Rule*, ch. 7, Walker, pp. 128–31.

50 See Hughes, *Church in Early Irish Society*, pp. 160–2; Ó Cróinin, *Early Medieval Ireland* pp. 162–3.

51 Clancy and Márkus, pp. 9–13.

52 Quoted by Ó Cróinin, p. 163.

53 For what follows, see L. Bitel, 'Women's monastic enclosures in early Ireland: a study of female spirituality and male monastic mentalities', *Journal of Medieval History* 12 (1996) pp. 15–37; D. Ó Corráin, 'Women in early Irish society', in M. MacCurtain and D. Ó Corráin, eds, *Women in Irish Society* (Westport, 1980), pp. 1–13.

54 For Brigit and the absorption of pagan material into Christian literature, see K. McCone, 'Brigit in the seventh century; a saint with three lives?', *Peritia* 1 (1982) pp. 107–45; ibid., *Pagan past and Christian present in early Irish literature*, Maynooth Monographs iii (Maynooth, 1990).

8 Irish *peregrini* and European Monasticism

1 H. Atsma, 'Les monastères urbains du Nord de la Gaule, *Revue d' Histoire de l'Église de France*, vol. 62 (1976) pp. 163–87; H. Atsma, 'Die christlichen Inschriften Galliens als Quelle für Kloster und Klosterbewohner bis zum Ende des 6 Jahrhunderts', *Francia* 4 (1976) pp. 1–57.

2 Gregory of Tours, *Life of the Fathers*, trans. and ed. E. James (Liverpool, 1985) X, XI, XX.

3 Jonas, *Life of Columbanus, Vita Columbani abbatis discipulorumque eius, Monumenta Germaniae Historica, Scriptorum rerum merovingicarum* vol. 4 pp. 1–60, c. 10; English translation, ch. 16. For a comprehensive critical account of Columbanus' career and the reliability of Jonas' *Life*, see D. A. Bullough, 'The career of Columbanus', in M. Lapidge, ed., *Columbanus; Studies on the Latin Writings* (Woodbridge, 1997) pp. 1–28.

4 *Life of Columbanus*, ch. 5, English translation, ch. 10.

5 For a discussion of these issues, see Bullough, pp. 9–11.

6 *Life of Columbanus* ch. 5, English translation ch. 11.

7 J. Laporte, *Le Penitentiel de saint Colomban* (Tournai–Paris–Rome–New York, 1958) pp. 47–8; Charles-Edwards, 'Penitential of Theodore'.

8 *Columbani Opera*, Letter I.

9 Gregory I, *Epistolae* X, 9.

10 Jonas, *Life*, ch. 48. For the political situation in Francia, see I. N. Wood, *The Merovingian Kingdoms 470–751* (London, 1994) chs 6 and 9, and for monasticism, ch. 11; P. Geary, *Before France and Germany* (Oxford, 1988) ch. 5 for the Merovingians and monasticism. See also Prinz, *Frühes Mönchtum* Parts II and III. There are valuable studies by Wood, James, Riché, Prinz, Ganz, McKitterick and others in H. B. Clarke and M. Brennan, eds, *Columbanus and Merovingian Monasticism* (Oxford, 1981). See also *Jonas de Bobbio, Vie de saint Colomban et de ses disciples*, ed. and trans. A de Vogüé in collaboration with P. Sangiani, *Aux sources du monachisme colombanien* I (Bellefontaine, 1988). Two important collections on the impact of Irish monks and monasteries in Europe in general are H. Löwe, ed., *Die Iren und Europa im Frühen Mittelalter*, 2 vols, (Stuttgart, 1982) and P. Ní Catháin and M. Richter, eds, *Ireland and Europe: the Early Church* (Stuttgart, 1984).

11 *Columbani Opera*, Sermons, IX and X, pp. 96–107. For the authenticity of these works, see C. Stancliffe, 'The thirteen sermons attributed to Columbanus and the question of their authorship', in *Columbanus*, ed. Lapidge, pp. 93–202.

12 Geary, p. 151.

13 See Wood, *Merovingian Kingdoms* p. 192.

14 *Life of Columbanus* ch. 10, English translation ch. 17.

15 Wood, *Merovingian Kingdoms* pp. 193–4.

16 See Prinz, *Frühes Mönchtum* II, v.

17 E. James, ed., *Gregory of Tours: Life of the Fathers* (Liverpool, 1985) pp. 33–4.

18 Jonas, *Life of Columbanus* ch. 13.

19 See Stramara, 'Double monasteries' and also chapter 5, note 91 above.

20 For what follows, see principally S. F. Wemple, *Women in Frankish Society. Marriage and the Cloister 500–900* (Pennsylvania, 1981), Part Two, chs 6 and 7; J. A. McNamara, J. E. Halborg and E. G. Whatley, *Sainted Women of the Dark Ages* (Durham and London, 1992) (which contains translations of several important saints' *Lives*); J. A. McNamara, 'Living sermons: consecrated women and the conversion of Gaul', pp. 19–37 in L. T. Shank and J. A. Nichols, eds, *Medieval Religious Women*, vol. II, *Peace Weavers*

(Kalamazoo, 1987); J. T. Schulenburg, 'Strict active enclosure and its effects on the female monastic experience', in L. T. Shank and J. A. Nichols, eds, *Medieval Religious Women*, vol. I, *Distant Echoes* (Kalamazoo, 1984) pp. 51–86; F. Lifshitz, 'Les femmes missionaires: l'exemple de la Gaule franque', *RHE* 83 (1988) pp. 5–33; S. F. Wemple, 'Female spirituality and mysticism in Frankish monasteries: Radegund, Balthild and Aldegund', *Peace Weavers*, pp. 39–65.

21 Wemple, *Women in Frankish Society*, pp. 44–9.
22 *Sainted Women*, ch. 9, 'Burgundofara, Abbess of Faremoutiers (603–45)'.
23 Ibid., ch. 10, 'Sadalberga, Abbess of Laon (ca. 605–70)'.
24 Ibid., ch. 11, 'Rictrude, Abbess of Marchiennes (ca. 614–688)'.
25 Prinz, *Frühes Mönchtum*, pp. 186–8; *Sainted Women*, ch. 12.
26 Ibid., p. 194.
27 J. Guerout, 'Le testament de Ste. Fare', *RHE* 60 (1965) pp. 762–821; Wood, *Merovingian Kingdoms*, pp. 206–7.
28 Bede, *Ecclesiastical History* III, 8
29 M. Bateson, 'Origins and early history of double monasteries', *TRHS* n.s. 13 (1899) pp. 137–98; S. Hilpisch, *Die Doppelklöster: Entstehung und Organisation* (Münster in Westphalia, 1928); J. Godfrey, 'Double monasteries in early English history', *Ampleforth Journal* 79 (1974) pp. 19–32; J. Godfrey, 'The place of the double monastery in the Anglo-Saxon minister system', in *Famulus Christi*, ed. G. Bonner (1976) pp. 344–50.
30 For Laon and Pavilly, see *Sainted Women*, pp. 188, 191 and 341.
31 E.g. *Miracles of Sadalberga*, ch. 22, *Sainted Women*, pp. 190–1.
32 Geary, p. 177.
33 *Frühes Mönchtum*, pp. 169–70.
34 For Baldechildis in general, see J. Nelson, 'Queens as Jezebels: Brunhild and Balthild in Merovingian history', in *Medieval Women*, ed. D. Baker (Oxford, 1978) pp. 31–78; for Baldechildis and Chelles, see Wemple, 'Female spirituality' and *Sainted Women*, ch. 14.
35 Prinz, *Frühes Mönchtum*, pp. 128–9.
36 *Vita et Miracula Fursei*, ed. W. W. Heist, in *Vitae Sanctorum Hiberniae* (Brussels, 1965) pp. 37–55.
37 Prinz, *Frühes Mönchtum*, pp. 128f.
38 Prinz, *Frühes Mönchtum*, pp. 492–3; T. Parsons, introduction to M. Weber *Sociology of Religion*, trans. E. Bischoff (Boston, 1963) pp. 84–5; B. K. Young, 'Exemple aristocratique et mode funeraire dans la Gaule Merovingienne', *Annales ESC* 41 (1986) pp. 370–407.
39 S. Burnell, *Merovingian to Early Carolingian Churches and their Founder-Graves in Southern Germany and Switzerland: The Impact of Christianity on the Alamans and the Bavarians*, D.Phil. Thesis (Oxford, 1988) pp. 204–5.
40 *Miracula Fursei* 1, ed. Heist, p. 50.
41 See E. James, 'Archaeology and the Merovingian monastery', in *Columbanus and Merovingian Monasticism*, pp. 33–58, esp. pp. 43–4.
42 M. de Maillé, *Les Cryptes de Jouarre* (Paris, 1971).
43 H. Keller, 'Mönchtum und Adel in den *Vitae patrum Jurensium* und in der *Vita Germani Abbatis Grandivalensis*', in K. Elm et al., eds, *Landesgeschichte*

und Geistesgeschiche: Festschrift für Otto Herdin zum 65 Geburtstag (Stuttgart, 1977) pp. 1–23; F. Graus, *Volk, Herrscher und Heiliger im Reich der Merowinger* (Prague, 1965) in general and pp. 295–6, 409 on menial work as a sign of humility.

44 *Sainted Women*, p. 91.
45 The text of the *Penitential* is given in *Columbani Opera*, pp. 168–81. See also *Saint Colomban, Règles et pénitentiels monastiques*, trans. and ed. A. de Vogüé in collaboration with P. Sangiani and J.-B. Juglar, *Aux sources du monachisme colombanien* II, (Bellefontaine, 1989); and particularly T. M. Charles-Edwards, 'The penitential of Columbanus', in *Columbanus*, ed. Lapidge, pp. 217–39 and the bibliography given there.
46 A translation of UUinniau's (Finnian's) *Penitential* is given by McNeill and Gamer, pp. 86–97. For the links between Columbanus, UUinniau, Gildas and the Welsh synods, see Laporte, pp. 29 ff, but more recently Charles-Edwards.
47 *Columbani Opera*, pp. 172–3.
48 M. Tosi, 'Arianesimo Tricapitolino norditaliano e penitenza privata Iroscozzese: due piste importanti per riprendere la questione critica delle opere di Colombano', *Archivum Bobiense: Rivista degli Archivi Storici Bobiense* X–XI (1988/9) pp. 9–118 and 12–13, pp. 5–144.
49 Charles-Edwards, 'Penitential', p. 238.
50 Jonas, *Life of Columbanus*, ch. 17.
51 *Columbani Opera*, pp. 122–3.
52 Ibid., pp. 126–7, cf. *Institutes* iv, 43, *Conference* xiv, 1
53 Ibid., pp. 140–3.
54 Cf. *Monastic Rule*, ch. 1, 3–7.
55 *Penitential 9, Columbani Opera*, pp. 170–1.
56 *Communal Rule, 8 Columbani Opera*, pp. 152–3.
57 McNeill and Gamer, p. 109; for a discussion of date and attribution see McNeill and Gamer, pp. 98–9.
58 Suggestion made by de Vogüé, *Règle de saint Benoît*, vol. 1, pp. 163–9, and de Vogüé, Sangiani and Juglar, pp. 47–8, 54–5. I would suggest that if, as is generally accepted, Columbanus composed his rule in Francia, he did not know of *RB* at this stage and that he is more likely to have acquired knowledge of it at Bobbio. See below.
59 *Communal Rule 13–14, Columbani Opera*, pp. 162–3.
60 *Communal Rule chs 2–4, Columbani Opera*, pp. 144–9.
61 *Monastic Rule ch. 3, Columbani Opera*, pp. 124–7.
62 Jonas, *Life of Columbanus*, ch. 25; *Communal Rule 3, Columbani Opera*, pp. 146–7.
63 Ibid., ch. 57.
64 M. Curran, *The Antiphonary of Bangor and the Early Irish Monastic Liturgy* (Dublin, 1984) pp. 106–9.
65 Prinz, *Frühes Mönchtum*, pp. 267 ff., 272, 277, 284.
66 *Rule of a Certain Father to the Virgins*, PL 88, 1053–70 and *Rule of Donatus*, PL 87, 273–98. Translations of both in *The Ordeal of Community* by J. A. McNamara (Toronto, 1993) are not always reliable.

67 Waldebert, ch. 1.
68 Donatus, chs 1–2, 77.
69 Donatus, chs 66, 74.
70 Waldebert, ch. 23.
71 E.g. ch. 12.
72 Chs 2–4.
73 Donatus, Prologue.
74 Ch. 27.
75 Waldebert, ch. 12.
76 *Life of Burgundofara*, ch. 19, *Sainted Women*, pp. 171–2.
77 *Life of Rictrudis*, ch. 32, *Sainted Women*, p. 218.
78 Waldebert, ch. 6.
79 Ibid., ch. 14.
80 Donatus, ch. 23.
81 Ch. 32.
82 O. Seebass, 'Fragment einer Nonnenregel des 7 Jahrhunderts', *Zeitschrift für Kirchengeschichte* 16 (1896), pp. 465–70.
83 Waldebert, ch. 1.
84 Donatus, ch. 1.
85 *Life*, ch. 2, *Sainted Women*, pp. 224–5
86 B. Bischoff, 'Die Kölner Nonnenhandschriften und das Skriptorium von Chelles', *Mittelalterliche Studien. Ausgewählte Aufsätze zur Schriftkunde und Literaturgeshichte* I (Stuttgart, 1966) pp. 16–33; R. McKitterick, 'Nuns' scriptoria in England and France in the Eighth Century', *Francia* 19 (1992) pp. 1–35.
87 See note 41 above.
88 See E. James, 'Archaeology and the Merovingian monastery', in *Columbanus and Merovingian Monasticism*, pp. 33–56; S. Bonde and C. Maines, 'The archaeology of monasticism: a survey of recent work in France, 1970–1987', *Speculum* 63 (1988) pp. 794–825. See also A. Erlande-Brandenbourg, 'Le monastère de Luxeuil au IX siècle. Topographie et fragments de sculpture', *Cahiers Archéologiques* 14 (1964) pp. 239–43. The journal *Archéologie Médiévale* has useful accounts of more recent monastic excavations, particularly in its 'Chronique des fouilles médievales'. See, for example, 1986 (16), 1992 (22), 1993 (23), 1995 (25), 1997 (27), and 1998 (28) for excavations at Chelles.
89 C. Kraemer, 'Le Saint-Mont: Première implantation monastique de Lorraine', *Archéologie Médiévale* 19 (1989) pp. 59–79.
90 Hughes, *Church in Early Irish Society*, p. 82.
91 James, 'Archaeology', p. 39.
92 Donatus, *PL* 87, col. 279; *Regula Cuiusdam Patris*, *PL* 88, col. 1065.
93 Donatus, ch. 12.
94 *Miracles of Gertrude*, ch. 2, *Sainted Women*, p. 230.
95 Waldebert, ch. 15.
96 For the following, see James, 'Archaeology', pp. 41–3.
97 *Life of Columbanus*, ch. 27, but see Bullough, 'The career' p. 19.
98 Bullough, 'The career', pp. 19–20.

99   Columbanus, Letter V, 10, ed. Walker, *Columbani Opera*, pp. 46–7.
100 P. T. R. Gray and M. W. Herren, 'Columbanus and the three chapters controversy – a new approach', *Journal of Theological Studies* 45 (1994) pp. 160–70, p. 170.
101 Columbanus, Letter V, 3, ed. Walker, *Columbani Opera*, pp. 38–9.
102 Sermon I, 1, ed. Walker, *Columbani Opera*, pp. 60–1.
103 Ibid., 2.
104 Letter IV, 5, ed. Walker, *Columbani Opera*, pp. 30–1.
105 C. Cipolla, ed., *Codice Diplomatico del Monastero di S. Colombano di Bobbio* vol I (*Fonti per la storia d'Italia* 52 Rome, 1918) no. XIII, pp. 104–12 and M. Tosi, 'I monaci colombaniani del secolo VII portano un rinnovamente agricolo-religioso nella fascia littorale Ligure', *Archivum Bobiense* XIV (1992) pp. 5–106.
106 See Dunn, 'Mastering Benedict'; de Vogüé, 'The Master and St Benedict'; Dunn, 'The Master and St Benedict: a Rejoinder'.
107 See M. Dunn '*Tánaise ríg*: the earliest evidence?' to appear in *Peritia*.
108 *Regula Magistri* 92, 1–2. De Vogüé's edition translates *secundarius* into French simply as 'second'.
109 *Regula Magistri* 93, 62.
110 J. Villegas-A. de Vogüé, *Eugippii Regula* (*CSEL* 87, 1976), ch. 3.
111 M. Tosi, 'I monaci colombaniani', esp. pp. 28–36.
112 Jonas, *Life of Columbanus* II, ch. 1.
113 D. Ganz, 'The Merovingian library of Corbie,' in *Columbanus and Merovingian Monasticism*, pp. 153–72. P. 163 points out that the final recension of the *Collectio corbeiensis* contains excerpts from Benedict, Columbanus, Macarius and Basil as well as material from the *Collectio hibernensis*.
114 J.-F. Lemariginer, 'Quelques remarques sur l' organisation ecclésiasatique de la Gaule du VIIe à la fin di IXe siècle, principalement au nord de la Loire', *Settimane di Studio del Centro Italiano di Studi sull' Alto Medioevo* XIII (Spoleto, 1966) pp. 451–86.
115 Ibid., p. 161.
116 See Wemple, 'Female spirituality and mysticism'; P. Dinzelbacher, *Vision und Visionsliteratur im Mittelalter* (Stuttgart, 1981) Monographien zur Geschichte des Mittelalters Band 23, pp. 229 ff.
117 *Columbani Opera*, Sermon IX, pp. 98–9.
118 Augustine, *Enchiridion*, chs 67 and 68; *City of God*, Book XXI, ch. 26; *de Fide et Operibus* XVI, 29. See R. Atwell, 'Aspects in St. Augustine of Hippo's Thought and Spirituality Concerning the State of the Faithful Departed', pp. 354–430, in *The End of Strife*, ed. D. Loades (Edinburgh, 1984) 3–13, against J. Ntedika, *L' Evolution de la Doctrine du Purgatoire chez Saint Augustine* (Paris, 1966); J. Ntedika, *L' évocation de l' au-delà dans la prière pour les morts* (Louvain, 1971); G. R. Edwards, 'Purgatory: birth or evolution', *Journal of Ecclesiastical History* 36 (1985) pp. 634–46; Jay, 'Le purgatoire dans la prédication de saint Césaire d' Arles', *Revue de Théologie Ancienne et Médievale* 24 (1957) pp. 5–14.

119 *Life of Burgundofara*, chs 12, 14, 15, 18, 20 in *Sainted Women*, pp. 163–73. A. de Vogüé, 'La mort dans les monastères: Jonas de Bobbio et les Dialogues de Grégoire le Grand', *Mémorial Dom Jean Gribomont*, Studia Ephemeridis "Augustinianum" 27 (Rome, 1988) pp. 593–619 argues that Jonas was dependent on the *Dialogues* attributed to Gregory I, but the resemblances are verbal rather than conceptual and it is argued here that the compiler of the *Dialogues* was familiar with Jonas' work.

120 *Vita S. Fursei*, in *Vitae Sanctorum Hiberniae*, ed. W. W. Heist, (Brussels, 1965) pp. 37–50, C. Carozzi, *Le voyage de l' âme dans l' au-delà d'après la littérature latine (Ve-XIIIe siècle)*, Collection de l'École Française de Rome 189 (Rome, 1994) ch. 2 and pp. 677–92; P. R. L. Brown, 'Vers la naissance du purgatoire', *Annales ESC* 52, 2 (1997) pp. 1247–71.

121 *Vita Fursei* 11.

122 Carozzi, pp. 113–4.

123 J. Le Goff, *La Naissance du Purgatoire* (Paris, 1981) has argued that the term *purgatorium* as such only emerged in the central middle ages and should not be applied to earlier periods; but the idea had taken shape long before then and its seems unnecessarily pedantic not to use it.

124 See Y. Hen, 'The structure and aims of the *Visio Baronti*', *JTS* n.s. 47 (1996) pp. 477–97; an English translation of the text in *Monumenta Germaniae Historica Scriptores rerum merovingicarum* 5, pp. 386–94 is given in J. N. Hillgarth, *Christianity and Paganism 350–750* (Philadelphia, 1986) pp. 195–204.

125 See chapter 6 above and especially notes 87 and 116 for the debate over the authenticity of this work and the problems surrounding its attribution to Gregory.

126 *Dialogues* IV, 57.

127 See Clark, 'The renewed controversy', for the gradual disappearance of some supposedly earlier testimonies and also chapter 6 esp. note 116 above. Hillgarth indicates some direct quotations from the *Dialogues* in the *Vision of Barontus*.

128 Bede, *Ecclesiastical History*, trans. L. Sherley-Price as *A History of the English Church and People* (Harmondsworth, 1955) III, 19 and V, 12. Bede's *Homilies* also affirm the reality of immediate post-mortem purgation. See *PL* 94, col. 30.

129 O. Nussbaum, *Kloster, Priestermönch und Privatmesse: ihr Verhältnis im Westen von den Anfängen bis zum hohen Mittelalter*, Theophaneia 14 (Bonn, 1961); A. A. Häussling, *Mönchskonvent und Eucharistiefeier*, Liturgiewissenschaftliche Quellen und Forschungen 58 (Münster, 1972).

9   England in the Seventh Century

1 Prinz, *Frühes Mönchtum*, pp. 174–5, 274–6.

2 *PL* 83, cols. 1183–4.

3 Prinz, *Frühes Mönchtum*, p. 177.

4 Ibid., pp. 276–7; P. Meyvaert, 'Peter the Deacon and the tomb of St Benedict', *RB* 65 (1955).

5   See chapter 8, note 119 above and also chapter 6, notes 37 and 115. *Passio Praejecti*, ed. B Krusch, *MGH Scriptores rerum merovingicarum* V. The preface to this narrative mentions both the work of Jonas of Bobbio and the *Dialogues*.

6   Prinz, *Frühes Mönchtum*, p. 277. Prinz indicates the problems surrounding a reference to the presence of the *Rule* at Albi in Southern France and to Benedict as *abbas Romensis*. This is likely to post-date the seventh century though others place more weight on its testimony. See J. Wollasch, 'Benedictus Abbas Romensis. Das römische Element in der frühen benediktinischen Tradition', in N. Kamp and J. Wollasch, eds, *Tradition als historischer Kraft. Interdisziplinäre Forschungen zur Geschichte des frühen Mittelatters* (Berlin and New York, 1992) pp. 119–37; K. Zelzer, 'Von Benedikt zu Hildemar. Zur Textgestalt und Textgeschichte der Regula Benedicti auf ihrem Weg zur Alleingeltung', *Frühmittelalterliche Studien* 23 (1989) pp. 112–30.

7   The similarities found by A. Linage Conde, 'El Monacato Betico del Sevillano San Isidoro', *SM* 32 (1990) pp. 131–8 are slight.

8   See *Iberian Fathers, Martin of Braga, Paschasius of Dumium, Leander of Seville*, Fathers of the Church 62, trans. C. W. Barlow (Washington, D.C., 1969)

9   See chapter 6 above.

10 *Life of Bertilla*, ch. 6, *Sainted Women*, p. 286.

11 Bede, *Lives of the Abbots of Wearmouth and Jarrow*, ch. 11 in *The Age of Bede*, trans. W. J. Webb and D. H. Farmer (Harmondworth, 1965) p. 196. For Benedict Biscop and the *Rule*, see C. P. Wormald, 'Bede and Benedict Biscop', in *Famulus Christi*, ed. G. Bonner (London, 1976) pp. 141–69; K. Zelzer, 'Zur Frage des Observanz des Benedict Biscop', *Studia Patristica* 20 (1989) pp. 323–9.

12 Eddius Stephanus, *Life of Cuthbert* in *The Age of Bede*, pp. 105–82.

13 *Historia Abbatum auctore Anonymo*, ch. 14, ed. C. Plummer, *Baedae Opera Historica* (Oxford, 1896) p. 393.

14 Wormald, 'Bede and Benedict Biscop', pp. 143–4.

15 See chapter 6, pp. 129–30 above.

16 In the 660s, Bishop Drauscius of Soissons prescribed the use of *cursus* of the Benedictine *Rule* for one of the convents of his diocese, but gave no further details. See Dunn, 'Mastering Benedict', p. 587.

17 See P. Sims-Williams, 'Varieties of monasticism', in his *Religion and Literature in Medieval England 600–800* (Cambridge, 1990) pp. 117–18. Sims-Williams suggests that this MS, Oxford Bodley Hatton 48, may have been written in a monastery in the south-west connected with Wilfrid, such as Bath.

18 *Lives of the Abbots*, ch. 6; *Ecclesiastical History* IV 18, where Bede also mentions that John committed to writing the way of celebrating festal days throughout the year. See also É. Ó. Carragáin, *The City of Rome and the World of Bede* Jarrow Lecture 1994 (Jarrow, 1994) and S. Van Dijk, 'The Urban and Papal Rites in Seventh and Eighth-Century Rome', *Sacris Erudiri* 12 (1961) pp. 411–87.

19   See H. Mayr-Harting, *The Coming of Christianity to Anglo-Saxon England* (3rd edn, London, 1991).
20   Bede, *Ecclesiastical History* III, 5
21   C. Stancliffe, 'Cuthbert and the polarity between pastor and solitary', in *Cuthbert, His Community and his Cult*, ed. Bonner, Rollason and Stancliffe, pp. 22–42.
22   Bede, *Ecclesiastical History*, IV, 27.
23   Bede also claims that Cuthbert, like Columbanus, administered penance. See also n. 29, below.
24   A. Thacker, 'Monks, preaching and pastoral care in England', *Pastoral Care before the Parish* pp. 140–41.
25   Bede, *Opera Homiletica* i, 7, quoted by Cubitt, p. 202.
26   R. J. Cramp, 'Excavations at the Saxon monastic sites of Wearmouth and Jarrow', *Medieval Archaeology* 13 (1969) pp. 24–66; R. J. Cramp, 'Monastic sites', in *Archaeology of Anglo-Saxon England*, ed. D. Wilson (London, 1976) p. 231.
27   See Thacker, 'Monks, preaching and pastoral care', pp. 143–45.
28   Ibid.
29   Bede, *Ecclesiastical History* IV, 13.
30   Thacker, 'Monks, preaching', p. 143.
31   Ibid., p. 146; F. M. Stenton, 'Medeshamstede and its Colonies', in *Preparatory to Anglo Saxon England*, ed. D. M. Stenton (Oxford, 1970); Morris, *Churches in the Landscape*, p. 132 stresses the separation of the priest provided at Breedon and the monastic community there. This may be the case, but the fact that Medeshamstede later claimed considerable exemptions suggests a connection between the monastery and some form of pastoral work, even if its dependencies were not originally designed as pastoral centres. At any rate, the link between pastoral care and claims of exemption should be considered. *Anglo-Saxon Chronicle*, trans. G. N. Garmonsway (1954), the Laud Chronicle, pp. 35–7.
32   The literature on the 'minster debate' is very extensive and only some of the studies on the topic can be cited here. See principally *Pastoral Care Before the Parish*; J. Blair, *Minsters and Parish Churches*, ed. J. Blair (Oxford, 1988); E. Cambridge and D. Rollason, 'The pastoral organisation of the Anglo-Saxon Church: a review of the "Minster Hypothesis"', *Early Medieval Europe* 4(1) (1995) pp. 87–104; S. Foot, 'Parochial ministry in early Anglo-Saxon England: the role of monastic communities', *Studies in Church History* 26 (1989); D. M. Palliser, 'The "Minster Hypothesis": a case study', *Early Medieval Europe* 5 (2) (1996) pp. 207–14. Quotation from S. Foot, 'Anglo-Saxon minsters: a review of terminology', in *Pastoral Care Before the Parish*, p. 215. See also E. Cambridge, 'The early church in County Durham: a reassessment', *Journal of the British Archaeological Association* 137 (1984) pp. 65–86.
33   Mayr-Harting, *The Coming of Christianity*, pp. 131–9, M. Brett, 'Theodore and the Latin canon law', in *Archbishop Theodore* ed. Lapidge, pp. 120–40.
34   Mayr-Harting, *Coming of Christianity*, ch. 9.

35   See M. Roper, 'Saint Wilfrid's landholdings in Northumbria', in *Saint Wilfrid at Hexham*, ed. D. P. Kirby (Newcastle, 1971) pp. 61–80.

36   Bede, *Lives of the Abbots* ch. 15; for relations between Wilfrid and Monkwearmouth-Jarrow, See I. Wood, *The Most Holy Abbot Ceolfrid*, Jarrow Lecture 1995 (Jarrow, 1995).

37   C. Cubitt, 'The 747 Council of Clofesho', pp. 203–5.

38   See chapter 8, pp. 186–9.

39   The passages in Gregory's *Gospel Homilies* which are repeated in the *Dialogues* look like interpolations in the former, e.g. the story of Count Theophanius in *Homily 36* which is repeated more or less word for word in *Dialogues* IV, 27. Such stories often deal with ideas of judgement and the afterlife. See the translation by D. Hurst in *Gregory the Great. Forty Gospel Homilies*, Cistercian Studies 123 (Kalamazoo, 1990).

40   A. Thacker, 'Memorializing Gregory the Great: the origin and transmission of a papal cult in the seventh and early eighth centuries', *Early Medieval Europe 7* (1998) pp. 59–84.

41   See D. Rollason, 'Hagiography and politics in early Northumbria', in *Holy Men and Holy Women: Old English Prose Saints' Lives and Their Contexts*, ed. P. E. Szarmach (Albany, 1996) pp. 95–114.

42   Mayr-Harting, *Coming of Christianity* p. 106.

43   Rollason, 'Hagiography and Politics', pp. 96–7.

44   C. P. Wormald, 'Bede and the conversion of England: the charter evidence', Jarrow Lecture (Jarrow, 1984), esp. pp. 19 ff.

45   Bede, *Epistola ad Ecgbertum Episcopum* 12, in Plummer, *Baedae Opera Historica* vol. 1, p. 415.

46   See in general Godfrey, 'Double monasteries in early English history' and 'The place of the double monastery in the Anglo-Saxon minster system'.

47   Bede, *Ecclesiastical History* IV, 23 gives his account of Hild's life. See C. Fell, 'Hild, Abbess of Streonaeshalch', in H. Bekker-Nielsen, P. Foote, J. H. Jorgensen and T. Nyberg, eds, *Hagiography and Medieval Literature* (Odense, 1981) pp. 76–99.

48   Eddius, *Life of Wilfrid*, ch. 60.

49   *Ecclesiastical History* III, 8.

50   Ibid., IV, 23.

51   See S. Hollis, *Anglo-Saxon Women and the Church: Sharing a Common Fate* (Woodbridge, 1992), chs 5 and 6. See also P. H. Blair, 'Whitby as a centre of learning in the seventh century', in M. Lapidge, H. Gneuss, eds, *Learning and Literature in Anglo-Saxon England* (Cambridge, 1985) pp. 3–32 and C. P. Wormald, 'St Hilda, Saint and Scholar (614–80)', in *The St Hilda's College Centenary Symposium*, ed. J. Mellanby (Oxford, 1993).

52   Ed. and trans. B. Colgrave, *The Earliest Life of Gregory the Great* (Lawrence, 1968); S. E. Mosford, *Critical edition of the Vita Gregorii Magni by an anonymous member of the community of Whitby*, D. Phil. thesis, University of Oxford, 1989.

53   Sims-Williams, *Religion and Literature*, pp. 191–7.

54   See Hollis, *Anglo-Saxon Women and the Church*, pp. 78–9.

55 R. J. Cramp, 'Monastic sites', in D. M. Wilson, ed., *The Archaeology of Anglo-Saxon England* (London, 1976) pp. 201–52; R. J. Cramp, 'A reconsideration of the monastic site of Whitby', in R. M. Spearman and J. Higgitt, eds, *The Age of Migrating Ideas* (Edinburgh and Stroud, 1993) pp. 64–73.

56 Hollis, pp. 78–9.

57 For this material, a discussion of these issues and the double monasteries in general, see D. B. Schneider, *Anglo-Saxon Women in the Religious Life: A Study of the Status and Position of Women in an Early Medieval Society*, Ph.D thesis, Cambridge University, 1985.

58 For Aldhelm and the *De Virginitate*, see Hollis, ch. 3. For *De Virginitate*, see *Aldhelm. The Prose Works*, trans. M. Lapidge and M. Herren (Ipswich, 1979).

59 *Ecclesiastical History* IV, 25.

60 Hollis, *Anglo Saxon Women and the Church*, ch. 6.

61 *Penitential of Theodore* VI, 8, McNeill and Gamer, *Medieval Handbooks of Penance*, p. 204.

62 Wickham, *Early Medieval Italy*, p. 43.

63 See C. J. Bishko, 'The pactual tradition in Hispanic monasticism', *Spanish And Portuguese Monastic History 600–1300* (London, 1984) pp. 1–42 and *Iberian Fathers*, vol. II, *Braulio of Saragossa, Fructuosus of Braga*, trans. C. W. Barlow (Washington, D.C., 1969).

64 Lesne, *Histoire de la Propriété Ecclésiastique*, pp. 124 ff.

Select Bibliography

Primary Sources

Adomnan's Life of Columba, ed. and trans. A. O. Anderson and M. O. Anderson (London, 1961).

Aldhelm, *De virginitate* in Aldhelm, *The Prose Works*, trans. M. Lapidge and M. Herren (Ipswich, 1979).

Ambrose, *De virginitate liber unus*, ed. E. Cazzaniga (Turin, 1954); English translation by D. Callam, *Ambrose, On Virginity* (Toronto, 1980).

Anglo-Saxon Chronicle, trans. G. N. Garmonsway (London, 1954).

Antony, *Letters*, in S. Rubenson, *The Letters of St. Antony. Monasticism and the Making of a Saint* (Minneapolis, 1995).

Apophthegmata Patrum, Greek Alphabetical Series, translated as *The Sayings of the Desert Fathers, The Alphabetical Collection* by B. Ward, (London, 1975).

Ascetic Behavior in Greco-Roman Antiquity, ed. V. L. Wimbush (Minneapolis, 1990).

Athanasius, *The Life of Antony and the Letter to Marcellinus* trans. R. C. Gregg. Classics of Western Spirituality (New York, 1989).

Augustine, *Confessions*, trans. R. S. Pine-Coffin (London, 1961).

Augustine, *Regula Tertia* and *Ordo Monasterii*, texts and translations in G. Lawless, *Augustine of Hippo and His Monastic Rule* (Oxford, 1988) pp. 64–118.

Aurelian of Arles, *Regula ad monachos, Regula ad virgines, PL* 68, cols. 385–404.

Basil of Ancyra, *De vera virginitatis integritate, PG* 30, cols. 669–809.

Basil of Cæsarea, *Longer* and *Shorter Rules, Regulae fusius tractatae, PG* 31, cols. 889–1052 and *Regulae brevis tractatae, PG* 31 cols. 1080–1320; English translation in W. K. L. Clarke, *The Ascetic Works of St Basil* (London, 1925).

Baudonivia, *Life of St Radegund, Monumenta Germaniae Historica, Scriptores rerum merovingicarum* 2, pp. 377–95; translation in *Sainted Women of the Dark Ages*, ed., McNamara and Halborg, pp. 86–105.

Besa, *Life of Shenoute*, trans. D. N. Bell as *The Life of Shenoute by Besa*, Cistercian Studies 73 (Kalamazoo, 1983).

Bede, *Ecclesiastical History*, trans. L. Sherley-Price as *A History of the English Church and People* (Harmondsworth, 1955).

Bede, *Epistola ad Ecgbertum Episcopum*, in C. Plummer, ed. *Baedae Opera Historica*, vol. 1. (Oxford, 1896) pp. 405–23.

Bede, *Lives of the Abbots of Wearmouth and Jarrow* in *The Age of Bede*, trans. W. J. Webb and D. H. Farmer, (Harmondworth, 1965).

Bieler, L. *The Irish Penitentials* (Dublin, 1963).

Cæsarius of Arles, *Rule for Virgins* and letter *Vereor* in A. de Vogüé and J. Courreau, eds, *Césaire d'Arles, Oeuvres monastiques*, vol. I. *Ouevres pour les moniales*, Sources chrétiennes 345 (Paris, 1988). English translation of the *Rule* by M. C. McCarthy. *The Rule for Virgins of Saint Cæsarius of Arles: a Translation With a Critical Introduction* (Washington, 1960).

Cæsarius of Arles, *Rule for Monks* in A. de Vogüé and J. Courreau, *Césaire d'Arles, Oeuvres monastiques* vol. II. *Ouevres pour les moines, SC* 398 (Paris, 1994).

Cæsarius of Arles, *Sermones, Corpus Christianorum*, vols 103–4 (Turnhout, 1953).

Cassian, John, *Conlationes*, ed. M. Petschenig, *CSEL* 13 (Vienna, 1886); trans. and ed. B. Ramsey, as *John Cassian: the Conferences* (New York – Mahwah, 1997).

Cassian, John *De Instiutis Coenobiorum et De Octo Principalium Vitiorum remediis Libri XII* ed. K. Petschenig, *CSEL* 17 (Vienna, 1888); trans. J. Bertram as *The Monastic Institutes, consisting of On the Training of a Monk and The Eight Deadly Sins* (London, 1999).

Cassiodorus, *Institutiones divinarum litterarum, PL 70*, cols. 1105–50.

Codice Diplomatico del Monastero di S. Colombano di Bobbio, vol. I, ed. C. Cipolla, *Fonti per la storia d'Italia* 52 (Rome, 1918).

Columbanus, *Letters, Rules and Penitentials* in *Sancti Columbani Opera*, ed. G. S. M. Walker, Scriptores Latini Hiberniae vol. II (Dublin, 1957).

Concilia Galliae anno 511-anno 695 ed. C. de Clercq *CC* 148a (Turnhout, 1963).

Consultationum Zacchei Christiani et Apollonii Philosophi Libri Tres, PL 20, cols. 1071–166.

Eddius Stephanus, *Life of Cuthbert* in *The Age of Bede*, trans. W. J. Webb and D. H. Farmer (Harmondsworth, 1965) pp. 105–82.

Eugippius, *Vita sancti Severini*, ed. P. Knoell (Vienna, 1886).

Eugippius, *Rule*, ed. J. Villegas and A. de Vogüé, *Eugippii Regula, CSEL* 87 (Vienna, 1976).

A. Guillaumont, *Les 'Kephalaia Gnostica' d' Évagre le Pontique et l'Histoire de l' Origénisme chez les Grecs et chez les Syriens* (Patristica Sorbonensia, 5, Paris, 1962).

Evagrius Ponticus, *Gnostikos*, ed. and trans. A. Guillaumont and C. Guillaumont as *Évagre le Pontique: le Gnostique, SC* 356 (Paris, 1969).

Evagrius Ponticus, *Praktikos*, ed. and trans. A. Guillaumont and C. Guillaumont as *Évagre le Pontique: Traité practique ou le moine, SC* 170–1 (Paris, 1971).

Evagrius Ponticus, *Sentences to Monks, Sententiae ad Monachos, PG* 40, cols. 1273–82; also ed. H. Gressmann, 'Nonnenspiegel und Mönchspiegel des Evagrios Pontikos', in *Texte und Untersuchungen zur Geschichte der Altchris-*

tlichen Literatur, 3rd series vol. (Leipzig, 1913) pt. 4, pp. 143–65 and J. Driscoll, *The 'Ad Monachos' of Evagrius Ponticus. Its Structure and a Select Commentary*, Studia Anselmiana 104 (Rome, 1991).

Evagrius Ponticus, *Sentences to a Virgin, Sententiae ad Virginem*, *PG* 40 cols. 1282–86; ed. Gressmann. H. 'Nonnenspiegel und Mönchspiegel des Evagrios Pontikos' in *Texte und Untersuchungen zur Geschichte der Altchristlichen Literatur*, 3rd series vol. (Leipzig, 1913) pt. 4, pp. 143–65.

Finnian (UUinniau) *Penitential* in McNeill, J. T. and Gamer, H., *Medieval Handbooks of Penance* (New York, 1938, 1990) pp. 86–97.

Gerontius, *The Life of Melania the Younger*, ed. E. A. Clark (Lampeter, 1984).

The Gospel of Thomas in *The Nag Hammadi Library in English*, ed. J. Robinson, (Leiden, 1988).

Gregory I, *Dialogues*, ed. A. de Vogüé, as *Grégoire le Grand, Dialogues*, SC 251, 260, 265, (Paris, 1978, 1979, 198); English translation by O. J. Zimmermann, in the *Fathers of the Church* series (Washington D.C., 1959)

Gregory I, *Epistolae*, ed. D. Norbert, *CC* vols. CXL, CXLA (Turnhout, 1982).

Gregory I, *XL homiliarum in Evangelia libri duo*, *PL* 76, cols. 1035–1312 translated as *Gregory the Great Forty Gospel Homilies* by D. Hurst, (Kalamazoo, 1990) Cistercian Studies 123.

Gregory I, *Homilies on Ezechiel*, ed. C. Morel, as *Grégoire le Grand, Homélies sur Ézéchiel*, SC 327, 360 (Paris, 1986, 1990).

Gregory I, *Moralia in Iob*, ed. M. Adriaen, *CC* vol. CXLIII (Turnhout 1985).

Gregory of Nazianzus, *Orationes*, ed. and trans. C. G. Browne, and J. E. Swallow, Nicene and Post-Nicene Fathers 7 (Ann Arbor, 1955).

Gregory of Nyssa, *Life of St Macrina*, trans. and ed. W. K. L. Clarke, *St Gregory of Nyssa: The Life of St Macrina* (London, 1916).

Gregory of Nyssa, *De virginitate*, ed. and trans. M. Aubineau, *Traité de la virginité*, SC 119 (Paris, 1966).

Gregory of Tours. *History of the Franks*, trans. L. Thorpe (Harmondsworth, 1974).

Gregory of Tours, *Life of the Fathers*, trans. and ed. E. James (Liverpool, 1985).

Gregory of Tours *Glory of the Confessors*, trans. and ed. R. van Dam, (Liverpool, 1988).

Gregory of Tours., *Glory of the Martyrs*, trans. and ed. R. van Dam, (Liverpool, 1988).

Hilarius of Arles, *Life of Honoratus*, trans. and ed. M.-D. Valentin, *Vie de Saint Honorat SC* 245 (Paris, 1977).

Historia Monachorum In Ægypto, History of the Monks in Egypt, ed. A.-J. Festugière, (Brussels, 1961, 1971). English trans. B. Ward and N. Russell as *Lives of the Desert Fathers* (London and Oxford, 1981).

History of the Abbots of Monkwearmouth-Jarrow, Historia Abbatum auctore Anonymo, ch. 14, C. Plummer, *Baedae Opera Historica* (Oxford, 1896).

Hucbald, *Life of Aldegund*, *PL* 132, cols. 857–876; translated in McNamara and Halborg, *Sainted Women of the Dark Ages*, pp. 235–63.

Hucbald, *Life of Rictrude, nun of Marchiennes*, prologue in *Monumenta Germaniae Historica, Scriptores rerum merovingicarum*, vol. 6, pp. 91–4 and *Vita* in

PL 132, pp. 829–48; translated in McNamara and Halborg, *Sainted Women of the Dark Ages*, pp. 195–219.

Iberian Fathers, Martin of Braga, Paschasius of Dumium, Leander of Seville, Fathers of the Church 62, trans. C. W. Barlow, (Washington, D.C., 1969).

Iberian Fathers, vol. II Braulio of Saragossa, Fructuosus of Braga, Fathers of the Church 63, trans. C. W. Barlow (Washington, D.C., 1969).

Iona, The Earliest Poetry of a Celtic Monastery, ed. and trans. T. O. Clancy, and G. Márkus (Edinburgh, 1995).

Jerome, *Dialogue Against the Pelagians, PL* 23, cols. 495–50.

Jerome, *Against Vigilantius, PL* 23, cols. 353–68

Jerome, *Letters*, ed. I. Hilberg, *CSEL* 54 (1910), 55 (1912) and 56 (1918).

Jerome, *Letter 122*, in *The Letters of St. Jerome*, trans. C. C. Mierow and intro. by T. C. Lawler, vol. 1 (1963).

Jerome, *Life of Paul the First Hermit, PL* 23, cols. 39–55; trans. P. B. Harvey in Wimbush and Valantasis, eds, *Ascetic Behavior*, pp. 357–69.

Jerome, *Life of Hilarion, Vita Hilarionis, PL* 23, cols. 55–65.

Jerome, *Life of Malchus, Vita Malchi, PL* 23, cols. 65–81.

John Moschos, *Pratum Spirituale, PG 87*, cols. 2851–3116 and *PL*, cols. 74 119–240 trans. Wortley, J. *The Spiritual Meadow of John Moschos*, Cistercian Studies 139 (Kalamazoo, 1992).

Jonas of Bobbio, *Life of Columbanus, Vita Columbani, Monumenta Germaniae Historica, Scriptores rerum merovingicarum* vol. 4 pp. 1–60. See also *Jonas de Bobbio, Vie de saint Colomban et de ses disciples*, ed. and trans. A. de Vogüé in collaboration with P. Sangiani. Aux sources du monachisme colombanien I (Bellefontaine, 1988). English translation of Part One of the *Life* in *Life of St Columban by the monk Jonas* (Llanerch, 1993).

Jonas of Bobbio, *Life of John of Réomé, Vita Johannis Reomaensis* in *Monumenta Germaniae Historica, Scriptores rerum merovingicarum* vol. 3 pp. 502–17.

Julianus Pomerius, *The Contemplative Life, De vita contemplativa, PL* 59, cols. 415–520.

Leo I, *Epistolae, PL* 54, cols. 593–1218.

Life of Balthild (Baldechildis), Latin text in *Monumenta Germaniae Historica, Scriptores rerum merovingicarum*, vol. 2, pp. 477–508; translated in McNamara and Halborg, *Sainted Women of the Dark Ages*, pp. 264–78.

Life of Bertilla Abbess of Chelles, Latin text in *Monumenta Germaniae Historica, Scriptores rerum merovingicarum*, vol. 6, pp. 95–109; translated in McNamara and Halborg, *Sainted Women of the Dark Ages*, pp. 279–88.

Life of Burgundofara, Latin text in *Monumenta Germaniae Historica, Scriptores rerum merovingicarum*, vol. 4, pp. 130–43; translated in McNamara and Halborg, *Sainted Women of the Dark Ages*, pp. 155–75.

Life of Gregory the Great, trans. B. Colgrave, as *The Earliest Life of Gregory the Great* (Lawrence, 1968). See also S. E. Mosford, *Critical Edition of the Vita Gregorii Magni by an Anonymous Member of the Community of Whitby*, D.Phil thesis, University of Oxford, 1989.

Life of Gertrude of Nivelles, Latin text in *Monumenta Germaniae Historica, Scriptores rerum merovingicarum*, vol. 2, pp. 453–64; translated in McNamara and Halborg, *Sainted Women of the Dark Ages*, pp. 220–34.

Life of Olympias, Vita Sanctae Olympiadis Diaconissae, AB 15 (1896), pp. 409–23.

Life and Miracles of Fursey, Latin text in W. W. Heist, ed., *Vitae Sanctorum Hiberniae* (Brussels, 1965) pp. 37–55.

Life of Sadalberga abbess of Laon, Latin text in *Monumenta Germaniae Historica, Scriptores rerum merovingicarum,* vol. 5, pp. 40–66; translated in McNamara and Halborg, *Sainted Women of the Dark Ages,* pp. 176–94.

Life of St Samson, ed. T. Taylor (Llanerch, 1991). Latin text in *AB* VI (1887) pp. 79–150.

Lives of the Fathers of Jura, Vie des Pères de Jura, ed. F. Martine, *SC* 142 (Paris, 1968).

Lives of St Mary of Egypt, Pelagia, Thais and Maria in B. Ward, trans., *Harlots of the Desert* (London, 1987).

The Nag Hammadi Library in English, revised edition, gen. ed. J. Robinson, (Leiden, 1988).

Pachomian Koinonia, ed. A. Veilleux, *The Lives, Rules and Other Writings of Saint Pachomius and His Disciples* with a foreword by A. de Vogüé, vol. I, *The Life of Saint Pachomius and His Disciples,* Cistercian Studies 45 (Kalamazoo, 1980); vol. II, *Pachomian Chronicles and Rules,* Cistercian Studies 46 (Kalamazoo, 1981) and vol. III, *Instructions, Letters and Other Writings of Saint Pachomius and His Disciples,* Cistercian Studies 47 (Kalamazoo, 1982).

Palladius, *Lausiac History* trans. W. K. L. Clarke as *The Lausiac History of Palladius* (London, 1918).

Passio Praejecti, ed. B. Krusch, *MGH Scriptores rerum merovingicarum* 5, pp. 212–48.

Patrick *Confessio* and *Letter* trans. and ed. A. B. E. Hood, *St Patrick, His Writings and Muirchu's Life* (London, 1978).

Pseudo-Athanasius, 'The life and activity of the holy and blessed teacher Syncletica', in *Ascetic Behavior,* ed. Wimbush, pp. 265–311.

Ratio de cursus qui fuerunt eius auctores, in Corpus Consuetudinum Monasticarum I (Siegburg, 1963) pp. 77–91.

Rufinus, Latin translation and adaptation of Basil's *Rules* in *Basilii Regula a Rufino latine versa,* ed. K. Zelzer, *CSEL* 86 (Vienna, 1986).

Rule of a Certain Father for Monks, F. Villegas, La 'Regula cuiusdam Patris ad Monachos', *Revue de l'Histoire de la Spiritualité* 49 (1973) pp. 3–39.

Rule of a Certain Father to the Virgins, PL 88, cols. 1053–70 and *Rule of Donatus, PL* 87, cols. 273–98. Translations of both in *The Ordeal of Community* by J. A. McNamara (Toronto, 1993).

The Rule of the Four Fathers, Second Rule of the Fathers, Third Rule of the Fathers, Rule of Macarius and Oriental Rule in *Early Monastic Rules. The Rules of the Fathers and the Regula Orientalis* trans. C. V. Franklin, I. Havener, and J. Francis (Collegeville, 1981). Full edition by A. de Vogüé, *Les Règles des Saints Pères,* 2 vols, *SC* 297 and 298 (Paris 1982).

Rule of the Master, ed. A. de Vogüé, *La Règle du Maître, SC* 105–7 (Paris, 1964).

Rule of Paul and Stephen, ed. E. M. Vilanova *Regula Pauli et Stephani,* Edicia critica i comentari (Montserrat, 1959)

Rule of St Benedict, ed. A. de Vogüé, *La Règle de Saint Benoît, SC* 181–6 (Paris, 1971–2); English translation of the text by J. McCann, *The Rule of St Benedict in Latin and English* (London, 1952).

Rule of Tarn, Regula Tarnatensis, PL 66, cols. 977–86; see also F. Villegas, 'La "Regula Monasterii Tarnantensis"'. Texte, sources et datation,' *RB* 84 (1974) pp. 7–65.

Sulpicius Severus, *Life of Martin of Tours, Dialogues*, Library of the Nicene and Post-Nicene Fathers XI (Oxford and New York, 1894), pp. 2–54; ed. J. Fontaine, *Vie de Saint Martin SC* 133, (Paris, 1967)

Venantius Fortunatus, *Life of the Holy Radegund, Monumenta Germaniae Historica Scriptores rerum merovingicarum* 2, pp. 364–77; translation in *Sainted Women of the Dark Ages*, ed. McNamara and Halborg, pp. 70–86.

Vigilius, *Epistola ad Rusticum et Sebastianum, PL* 69, 48b.

The *Vision of Barontus*, Latin text in *MGH Scriptores rerum merovingicarum* 5 (Hanover, 1910) pp. 386–94; English translation by J. N. Hillgarth *Christianity and Paganism 350–750* (Philadelphia, 1986) pp. 195–204.

Secondary Works

Allen, M., 'The martyrdom of Jerome', *JECS* 3 (1995) pp. 211–13.

Amand de Mendieta, E., 'Le système cénobitique basilien comparé au système cénobitique pachômien', *RHR* 152 (1957) pp. 31–80.

Andrieu-Guitancourt, P., 'La vie ascétique à Rouen au temps de saint Victrice', *Recherches de science réligieuse* 40 (1952) pp. 90–106.

Angenendt, A. *Monachi Peregrini* (Munich, 1972).

Anson, J., 'The female transvestite in early monasticism: The origin and development of a motif', *Viator* 5 (1974) pp. 1–32.

Asceticism eds. Wimbush, V. L. and Valantasis, R. (Oxford–New York, 1995)

Aspegren, K., *The Male Woman: a Feminine Ideal in the Early Church* (Stockholm, 1990).

Atsma, H., 'Les monastères urbains du Nord de la Gaule', *Revue d' Histoire de l'Église de France* 62 (1976) pp. 163–87.

Atsma, H., 'Die christlichen Inschriften Galliens als Quelle für Kloster und Klosterbewohner bis zum Ende des 6 Jahrhunderts', *Francia* 4 (1976) pp. 1–57.

Atwell, R., 'Aspects of St. Augustine of Hippo's Thought and Spirituality Concerning the State of the Faithful Departed', pp. 354–430 in *The End of Strife*, ed. D. Loades (Edinburgh, 1984).

Barnish, S. J. B., 'The work of Cassiodorus after his conversion', *Latomus* 48 (1989) pp. 157–87.

Bateson, M., 'Origins and Early History of Double Monasteries', *TRHS* n.s. 13 (1899) pp. 137–98.

Baynes, N, 'St. Antony and the demons', *Journal of Egyptian Archaeology* 40 (1954) pp. 7–10.

Benoît, F., 'Le martyrium de l'abbaye Saint-Victor', Actes de Congrès sur l'Histoire de l' Abbaye Saint Victoire de Marseille, *Provence Historique* XVI (1966) pp. 259–96.

Bischoff, B., 'Die Kölner Nonnenhandschriften und das Skriptorium von Chelles', *Mittelalterliche Studien. Ausgewählte Aufsätze zur Schriftkunde und Literaturgechichte* I (Stuttgart, 1966) pp. 16–33.

Bishko, C. J., 'The pactual tradition in Hispanic monasticism', in his *Spanish and Portuguese Monastic History 600–1300* (London, 1984) pp. 1–42.

Bitel, L., *Isle of the Saints. Monastic settlement and Christian Community in Early Ireland* (Ithaca and London, 1990).

Bitel, L., 'Women's monastic enclosures in early Ireland: a study of female spirituality and male monastic mentalities', *Journal of Medieval History* 12 (1996) pp. 15–37.

Blair, J., ed., *Minsters and Parish Churches* (Oxford, 1988).

Blair, J. and Sharpe, R. eds, *Pastoral Care Before the Parish* (Leicester, 1992).

Blair, P. H., 'Whitby as a centre of learning in the seventh century', in M. Lapidge and H. Gneuss, eds, *Learning and Literature in Anglo-Saxon England* (Cambridge, 1985) pp. 3–32.

Bonde, S. and Maines, C., 'The archaeology of monasticism: A survey of recent work in France, 1970–1987', *Speculum* 63 (1988) pp. 794–825.

Bonner, G., Rollason, D. and Stancliffe C., *St. Cuthbert, His Cult and His Community to AD 1200* (Woodbridge, 1989).

Boswell, J., *The Kindness of Strangers. The Abandonment of Children in Western Europe from Late Antiquity to the Renaissance* (Harmondworth, 1988).

Boyd, C. E., *Tithes and Parishes in Medieval Italy* (Ithaca, 1952).

Brakke, D., *Athanasius and the Politics of Asceticism* (Oxford, 1995).

Brakke, D., 'The problematization of nocturnal emissions in early Christian Syria, Egypt and Gaul', *JECS* 3 (1995) pp. 419–60.

Brakke, D., '"Outside the places, within the truth": Athanasius of Alexandria and the localization of the holy', in *Pilgrimage and Holy Space in Late Antique Egypt*, ed. Frankfurter, D. (Leiden, 1998) pp. 445–482.

Brennan, B. R., 'Dating Athanasius' *Vita Antonii*', *VC* 30 (1976) pp. 52–4.

Brennan, B., 'St Radegund and the early development of her cult at Poitiers', *JRH* 13 (1984–5) pp. 311–23.

Brett, M., 'Theodore and the Latin canon law', in *Archbishop Theodore* ed. M. Lapidge, pp. 120–40.

Brock, S. and Ashbrook Harvey, S., *Holy Women of the Syrian Orient* (Berkeley, 1987).

Brock, S. and Ashbrook Harvey S., 'Women in early Syrian Christianity', in Cameron and Kuhrt, *Images*, pp. 288–98.

Brooks, N., *The Early History of the Church of Camterbury* (Leicester, 1984).

Brown, P. R. L., 'Pelagius and his supporters; aims and environment', *JTS* n.s. 19 (1968) pp. 93–114.

Brown, P. R. L., *Augustine of Hippo* (Berkeley, 1969).

Brown, P. R. L., 'The diffusion of Manichaeism in the Roman Empire', *JRS* 59 (1969) pp. 92–103.

Brown, P. R. L., 'The rise and function of the Holy Man in Late Antiquity', *JRS* 61 (1971) pp. 80–101.

Brown, P. R. L., *Religion and Society in the Age of St Augustine* (London, 1977).

Brown, P. R. L., 'Sexuality and society in the fifth century', in E. Gabba, ed., *Tria Cordia. Scritti in Onore de Arnaldo Momigliano* (Como, 1983), pp. 49–70.

Brown, P. R. L., 'The saint as exemplar in late antiquity' *Representations* 1 (1983) pp. 1–25.

Brown, P. R. L., *The Body and Society. Men, Women and Sexual Renunciation in Early Christianity* (London, 1989).

Brown, P. R. L., 'Vers la naissance du purgatoire', *Annales ESC* 52 (2) (1997) pp. 1247–71.

Brown, P. R. L. 'Rise and function of Holy Man in Late Antiquity 1971–1997', *JECS* 6 (1998) pp. 353–77.

Büchler, B., *Die Armut der Armen: Über den ursprünglischen Sinn der mönchischen Armut* (Munich, 1980).

Bullough, D. A., 'The career of Columbanus' in M. Lapidge, ed., *Columbanus; Studies on the Latin Writings* (Woodbridge, 1997) pp. 1–28.

Bunge, J. G., 'Évagre le Pontique et les deux Macaire', *Irénikon* 56 (1983) pp. 215–27.

Bunge, J. G., 'Origenizmus-Gnostizismus: zum geistgeschichtlichen Standort des Evagrios Pontikos', *VC* 40 (1986) pp. 24–54.

Bunge, J. G., *Briefe aus dem Wüste*, Sophia, vol. 24 (Trier, 1986).

Bunge, J. G., *Das Geistgebet. Studien zum Traktat, "De Oratione" des Evagrios Pontikos.* Koinonia xxv (Köln, 1987).

Bunge, J. G., 'Palladiana I: Introduction aux fragments coptes de l'Histoire Lausiac', *SM* 32 (1990) pp. 79–129.

Burnell, S., *Merovingian to Early Carolingian Churches and their Founder-Graves in Southern Germany and Switzerland: the Impact of Christianity on the Alamans and the Bavarians.* D.Phil. Thesis (Oxford, 1988).

Burrus, V., 'Ascesis, authority and text: *The Acts of the Council of Saragossa*', *Semeia* 58 (1992) pp. 95–108.

Burrus, V., 'Reading Agnes; The rhetoric of gender in Ambrose and Prudentius', *JECS* 3 (1995) pp. 25–46.

Burrus, V., *The Making of a Heretic. Gender, Authority and the Priscillianist Controversy* (Berkeley, 1995).

Burton-Christie, D., *The Word in the Desert. Scripture and the Quest for Holiness in Early Christian Monasticism* (Oxford, 1993).

Cambridge, E., 'The Early Church in County Durham: A reassessment', *Journal of the British Archaeological Association* 137 (1984) pp. 65–86.

Cambridge, E. and Rollason D., 'The pastoral organisation of the Anglo-Saxon Church: a review of the "Minster Hypothesis"', *Early Medieval Europe* 4(1) (1995) pp. 87–104.

Cameron, A. and Kuhrt A., eds, *Images of Women in Antiquity* (London, 1983).

Cameron, A., 'Virginity as metaphor: women and the rhetoric of early Christianity' in A. Cameron, ed., *History as Text: the Writing of Ancient History* (London, 1989) pp. 181–205.

Carozzi, C., *Le voyage de l'âme dans l'au-delà d'après la littérature latine* (Ve-XIIIe siècle), Collection de l'École Française de Rome 189 (Rome, 1994).

Carrias, M., 'Vie monastique et règle à Lérins au temps d'Honorat', *Revue d' histoire de l' Église de France* 74 (1988) pp. 191–211.

Catháin, N. and Richter M., eds, *Ireland and Europe: the Early Church* (Stuttgart, 1984).

Cavadini, J. C., ed., *Gregory the Great. A Symposium* (Note Dame and London, 1995).

Chadwick, H, 'The Domestication of Gnosis', pp. 3–36 of B. Layton, ed., *The Rediscovery of Gnosticism: Proceedings of the International Conference on Gnosticism at Yale, New Haven, Connecticut, March 28–31, 1978.* 2 vols, Studies in the History of Religions (Supplements to *Numen* 41, Leiden, 1980–1).

Chadwick, H., *The Early Church* (revised edition, Harmondsworth, 1993).

Chadwick, O., *John Cassian* (2nd edn, Cambridge 1968)

Charles-Edwards, T., 'The social background to Irish peregrinatio', *Celtica* II (1975) pp. 43–59.

Charles-Edwards, T. M., 'The penitential of Columbanus, in *Columbanus*, ed. Lapidge pp. 217–39.

Charles-Edwards, T., 'Palladius, Prosper and Leo the Great; mission and primatial authority', in D. Dumville, ed., *Saint Patrick AD 493–1993* (Woodbridge, 1993) pp. 1–12.

Charles-Edwards, T., 'The pastoral role of the churches in the early Irish laws', in Blair and Sharpe, eds, *Pastoral Care*, pp. 63–80.

Charles-Edwards, T., 'The Penitential of Theodore and the *Iudicia Theodori* in *Archbishop Theodore* ed. M. Lapidge (Cambridge, 1995) pp. 96–119.

Clancy, T. O., 'Annat in Scotland and the origins of the parish', *Innes Review* 42 (1995) pp. 91–115.

Clark, E. A., *Jerome, Chrysostom and Friends. Essays and Translations*, Studies in Women and Religion 2 (Lewiston, 1979).

Clark, E. A., 'Devil's Gateway and Bride of Christ' in *Ascetic Piety and Women's Faith: Essays on Late Ancient Christianity* Studies in Women and Religion 20 (Lewiston, 1986) pp. 23–60.

Clark, E. A., 'The uses of the Song of Songs: Origen and the later Latin Fathers', pp. 386–427 of her *Ascetic Piety and Women's Faith*.

Clark, E. A., *The Origenist Controversy. The Cultural Construction of an Early Christian Debate.* (Princeton, 1992).

Clark, F., *The Pseudo-Gregorian Dialogues*, 2 vols, Studies in the History of Christian Life and Thought XXXVII and XXXVIII (Leiden, 1987).

Clark, F., 'St. Gregory and the enigma of the *Dialogues*: a response to Paul Meyvaert', *JEM* 40 (1989) pp. 323–43.

Clark, F., 'The authorship of the *Dialogues*: an old controversy renewed', *Heythrop Journal* 30 (1989) pp. 257–72.

Clark, F., 'The renewed debate on the authenticity of the Gregorian *Dialogues*', *Augustinianum* 30 (1990) pp. 75–105.

Clark, F., 'The renewed controversy about the authorship of the *Dialogues*', *Gregorio Magno e il suo tempo* (Rome, 1991) vol. II pp. 5–25.

Clark, G., *Women in the Church: Pagan and Christian Lifestyles* (Oxford, 1993).

Clarke, H. B. and Brennan M., eds, *Columbanus and Merovingian Monasticism* (Oxford, 1981).

Cloke, G., *This Female Man of God. Women and Spiritual Power in the Patristic Age, AD 350–450* (London, 1995).

Corrington, G. P., 'The Divine Woman'? Propaganda and the power of chastity in the New Testament Apocrypha', *Helios* 13 (1986), pp. 151–62.

Courcelle, P., 'Le site du monastère de Cassiodore', *Mélanges d'archéologie et d'histoire* 55 (1938) pp. 259–63.

Courcelle, P., 'Nouvelles recherches sur le monastere de Cassiodore', *Actes du Ve Congrès International d'archéologie chrétienne, Aix en Provence*, Studi di antichità cristiana XXIII (Vatican–Paris, 1957), pp. 511–28.

Courcelle, P. 'Nouveaux aspects de la culture lérinienne', *Revue des Études Latines* 46 1968) pp. 379–409.

Cramp, R. J., 'Excavations at the Saxon monastic sites of Wearmouth and Jarrow', *Medieval Archaeology* 13 (1969) pp. 24–66.

Cramp, R. J., 'Monastic sites', in *Archaeology of Anglo-Saxon England*, ed. D. Wilson (London, 1976) pp. 201–52.

Cramp, R. J., 'A reconsideration of the Monastic Site of Whitby', in R. M. Spearman and J. Higgitt, eds, *The Age of Migrating Ideas* (Edinburgh and Stroud, 1993) pp. 64–73.

Cremascoli, G., 'Se i *Dialogi* siano opera di Gregorio Magno', *Benedictina* 36 (1989) pp. 179–92.

Crouzel, H., 'Origène, précurseur du monachisme', in *Théologie de la Vie Monastique, Études sur la Tradition Patristique*, Théologie 49 (Paris, 1961).

Crouzel, H. *Origen*, trans. A. S. Worrall (Edinburgh, 1989).

Cubitt, C., 'Pastoral care and conciliar canons: the provisions of the 147 Council of Clofesho', in Blair and Sharpe, eds, *Pastoral Care*, pp. 193–211.

Curran, M., *The Antiphonary of Bangor and the Early Irish Monastic Liturgy* (Dublin, 1984).

Dagens, C., *Saint Grégoire le Grand. Culture et expérience chrétiennes* (Paris, 1977).

Davies, J. C., 'Deacons, deaconesses and the minor orders in the patristic period', *JEH* 14 (1963) pp. 1–15.

Davies, W. 'The myth of the Celtic Church' in N. Edwards and A. Lane eds, *The Early Church in Wales and the West* (Oxford, 1992) pp. 12–21.

De Jong, M., *In Samuel's Image: child oblation in the early medieval West* (Leiden, 1986).

de Maillé, M., *Les Cryptes de Jouarre* (Paris, 1971).

de Seilhac, L., *L'utilisation par S. Césaire d'Arles de la Règle de S. Augustin. Étude de terminologie de la doctrine monastiques*, Studia Anselmiana 62 (Rome, 1974).

de Vogüé, A., *La communauté et l'abbé dans la Règle de Saint Benoît*, Textes et Études Théologiques (Paris, 1961).

de Vogüé, A., *La Règle du Maître*, Sources Chrétiennes, 105–7 (Paris, 1964).

de Vogüé, A., 'La Règle d'Eugippe retrouvée?', *RAM* 47 (1971) pp. 233–65.

de Vogüé, A., *La Règle de Saint Benoît*, SC 181–6 (Paris, 1971–2).

de Vogüé, A., 'La *Vie des Pères de Jura* et la datation de la *Regula Orientalis*', *RAM* 47 (1971) pp. 121–7.

de Vogüé, A. 'Les pièces latins du dossier pachomien. Remarques sur quelques publications recents', *RHE* 67 (1972) pp. 27–67.

de Vogüé, A. 'La Vie arabe de saint Pachôme et ses deux sources présumées', *AB* 91 (1973) pp. 379–90.

de Vogüé, A., *Le Maître, Eugippe et saint Benoît* (Hildesheim, 1984).

de Vogüé, A., 'Le pape qui persecuta Saint Equitius. Essai d'identification', *AB* 100 (1984) pp. 319–25.

de Vogüé, A., *Les Règles Monastiques Anciennes (400–700)* Typologie des Sources du Moyen Âge Occidental 46 (Turnhout, 1985).

de Vogüé, A., 'Grégoire le Grand et ses "Dialogues" d' après deux ouvrages récents', *RHE* 83 (1988) pp. 281–348.

de Vogüé, A., 'La mort dans les monastères: Jonas de Bobbio et les Dialogues de Grégoire le Grand', *Mémorial Dom Jean Gribomont*, Studia Ephemeridis 'Augustinianum' 27 (Rome, 1988) pp. 593–619.

de Vogüé, A., 'Aux Origines de Lérins: la Règle de Saint Basile?' *SM* 31 (1989) pp. 259–66.

de Vogüé, A., '"Martyrium in occulto" Le martyre du temps de paix chez S. Grégoire le Grand, Isidore de Séville, et Valerius de Bierzo', *Fructus centesimus. Mélanges offerts à Gérard J. M. Bartelink à l'occasion de son soixante-cinquième anniversaire (Instrumenta patristica* 19, Steenbrugge, 1989) pp. 125–40.

de Vogüé, A., 'Les Dialogues, oeuvre authentique et publiée par Grégoire lui-même', in *Gregorio Magno e il suo tempo* (Rome, 1991), vol. II pp. 27–40.

de Vogüé, A., 'The Master and St Benedict: a reply to Marilyn Dunn', *EHR* 107 (1992) pp. 95–103.

de Vogüé, A., 'L'Auteur du Commentaire des Rois Attribué à S. Grégoire: un Moine de Cava?' *RB* 106 (1996) pp. 319–31.

Dechow, J., *Dogma and Mysticism in Early Christianity: Epiphanius of Cyprus and the Legacy of Origen* North American Patristic Society Patristic Monograph Series 13 (Macon, 1988).

Demians d'Archimbaud, G., 'Fouilles récentes de Saint- Victor de Marseille', *Comptes rendus de l'Academie des Inscriptions et des Belles-Lettres* (1974) pp. 313–46.

Dinzelbacher, P., *Vision und Visionsliteratur im Mittelalter* (Stuttgart 1981) Monographien zur Geschichte des Mittelalters Bd 23.

Doble, G. H., *The Saints of Cornwall* (Llanerch, 1997–8).

Dodds, E. R., *Pagan and Christian in an Age of Anxiety: Some Aspects of Religious Experience from Marcus Aurelius to Constantine* (Cambridge, 1965).

Douglas, M., *Pollution and Danger: an Analysis of Concepts of Pollution and Taboo* (London, 1966).

Douglas, M., *Natural Symbols: Explorations in Cosmology* (Harmondsworth, 1979)

Douglas, M., *Risk and Blame: Essays in Cultural Theory* (London, 1992).

Driscoll, J., 'Gentleness in the *Ad Monachos* of Evagrius Ponticus', *SM* 32 (1990) pp. 295–321.

Duchesne, L., *Christian Worship: Its Origins and Evolution* (4th English edn., London, 1912).

Dumville, D., ed., *Saint Patrick 493–1993* (Woodbridge, 1993).

Dunn, M., 'Mastering Benedict: monastic rules and their authors in the early medieval West', *EHR* 105 (1990) pp. 567–94.

Dunn, M., 'The Master and St Benedict: a Rejoinder', *EHR* 107 (1992), pp. 104–11.

Dyer, J., 'Monastic Psalmody of the Middle Ages', *RB* 99 (1989) pp. 241–74.

Edwards, G. R., 'Purgatory: Birth or Evolution', *JEH* 36 (1985) pp. 634–46.

Elm, S., *'Virgins of God'. The Making of Asceticism in Late Antiquity* (Oxford, 1994).

Erlande-Brandenbourg, A., 'Le monastère de Luxeuil au IX siècle. Topographie et fragments de sculpture', *Cahiers Archéologiques* 14 (1964) pp. 239–43.

Etchingham, C., 'The early Irish church: some observations on pastoral care and dues', *Eriu* 42 (1991) pp. 99–118.

Evans, R., *Pelagius: Inquiries and Reappraisals* (New York, 1957).

Evelyn White, H. G. *The Monasteries of the Wadi'n Natrun, The History of the Monasteries of Nitria and of Scetis Part II* (New York, 1932).

Fedwick, P. J., ed., *Basil of Cæsarea: Christian, Humanist, Ascetic*, 2 vols (Toronto, 1991).

Fell, C., 'Hild abbess of Streonaeshalch', in H. Bekker-Nielsen, P. Foote J. H. Jorgensen and Nyberg T., eds, *Hagiography and Medieval Literature* (Odense, 1981) pp. 76–99.

Ferrari, G., *Early Roman Monasteries. Notes for the History of the Monasteries and Convents at Rome from the V through the X Century*, Studi di antichità cristiana 23 (Città del Vaticano, 1957).

Février, P. -A., 'Arles', in *Topographie chrétienne des cités de la Gaule*, ed. N. Gauthier et J. -Ch. Picard, vol. III, *Provinces ecclésiastiques de Vienne et d'Arles* (Paris, 1986) pp. 73–84.

Fontaine, J., 'Hilaire et Martin' pp. 59–86 of *Hilaire de Poitiers. Évêque et docteur. Cinq conférences données à Poitiers à l' occasion du XVI centenaire de sa mort* (Paris, 1969).

Fontaine, J., *Saint Martin et son temps*, Studia Anselmiana 46 (Rome, 1961).

Foot, S., 'Anglo-Saxon minsters: a review of terminology', in Blair and Sharpe, eds, *Pastoral Care Before the Parish* pp. 212–25.

Foot, S., 'Parochial ministry in early Anglo-Saxon England: the role of monastic communities', *Studies in Church History* 26 (1989) pp. 43–54.

Foucault, M., 'The battle for chastity', pp. 14–25 of *Western Sexuality*, ed. P. Ariès and A. Béjin (Oxford, 1985)

Frank, G, 'Miracles, monks and monuments: the *Historia Monachorum in Ægypto* as Pilgrims' Tales', in *Pilgrimage and Holy Space in Late Antique Egypt*, ed. D. Frankfurter (Leiden, 1998) pp. 483–505.

Frank, K. S., 'John Cassian on John Cassian', *Studia Patristica* 30 (Leuven, 1996) pp. 418–33.

Frantzen, A., *The Literature of Penance in Anglo-Saxon England* (New Brunswick, NJ, 1963).

Frend, W. H. C., 'The monks and the survival of the East Roman Empire in the fifth century', *Past and Present* 54 (1972) pp. 3–24.

Frend, W. H. C. 'Town and Countryside in Early Christianity', *The Church in Town and Countryside*, ed. D. Baker, *Studies in Church History* 16 (Oxford, 1979) pp. 25–42.

Frend, W. H. C., ' "And I have other sheep" – John 10:16', in *The Making of Orthodoxy: Essays in Honour of Henry Chadwick*, ed. R. Williams (Cambridge, 1989) pp. 24–39.

Gabe, S., 'Radegundis: sancta, regina, ancilla: Zum Heligkeitsideal der Ragegundisviten von Fortunat und Baudonivia', *Francia* 16 (1989) pp. 1–30.

Ganz, D., 'The Merovingian library of Corbie', in *Columbanus and Merovingian Monasticism*, pp. 153–72.

Gavigan, J. J. *De vita monastica in Africa septentrionali inde a temporibus S. Augustini usque ad invasiones Arabum* (Rome–Turin, 1962)

Geary, P., *Before France and Germany* (Oxford, 1988).

Genestout, A., 'Le plus ancien témoin manuscrit de la Règle du Maître: le *Parisinus* Latin 12634', *Scriptorium* 1 (1946-7) pp. 129–42.

Genestout, A., 'La Règle du Maître et la Règle de Saint Benoît', *RAM* 21 (1940) pp. 51–112.

George, J., *Venantius Fortunatus: A Latin Poet in Merovingian Gaul* (Oxford, 1992).

Gillet, R. 'Spiritualité et place du moine dans l'église selon saint Grégoire le Grand', *Théologie de la vie monastique*, coll. Théologie 49 (Paris, 1961) pp. 323–51.

Gillet, R., 'Grégoire le Grand', in *Dictionnaire d' Histoire et de Géographie écclesiastiques* XXI, cols. 1387–420.

Godfrey, J., 'Double monasteries in early English history', *Ampleforth Journal* 79 (1974) pp. 19–32.

Godfrey, J., 'The place of the double monastery in the Anglo- Saxon minster system', in *Famulus Christi*, ed. G. Bonner (1976) pp. 344–50.

Godding, R. 'Les *Dialogues*... de Grégoire le Grand. À propos d' un live recent', *AB* 106 (1988) pp. 201–9.

Goehring, J. E. and Pearson, B., *The Roots of Egyptian Christianity* (Philadelphia, 1986).

Goehring, J. E., 'New frontiers in Pachomian studies', in *The Roots of Egyptian Christianity*, pp. 236–57.

Goehring, J. E. *The Letter of Ammon and Pachomian Monasticism*, Patristische Texte und Studien 27 (Berlin, 1988).

Goehring, J. E., 'The world engaged: the social and economic world of Early Egyptian monasticism', in *Gnosticism and the Early Christian World: in Honour of James. M. Robinson*, ed. J. E. Goehring, C. H. Hedrick, J. T. Sanders, with H. D. Betz (Sonoma, 1990) pp. 134–44.

Goehring, J. E., 'The encroaching desert: Literary production and ascetic space in Early Christian Egypt', *JECS* 1 (1993) pp. 281–96.

Goehring, J. E., 'Melitian monastic organization: a challenge to Pachomian originality', *Studia Patristica* XXV, ed. E. A. Livingstone (Leuven, 1993) pp. 388–95.

Goehring, J. E., 'Through a glass darkly: diverse images of the Apotaktoi(ai) of early Egyptian monasticism', *Semeia* 58 (1993) pp. 25–46.

Goehring, J. E., 'Withdrawing from the desert; Pachomius and the development of village monasticism in Upper Egypt', *Harvard Theological Review* 89 (1996) pp. 267–85.

Gordini, G. D., 'Origine e sviluppo del monachesimo a Roma', *Gregorianum* 37 (1956) pp. 220–60.

Gould, G., 'Basil of Cæsarea and the problem of the wealth of monasteries,' in W. J. Sheils, and D. Wood, eds., *The Church and Wealth*, Studies in Church History 24 (Oxford, 1987) pp. 15–24.

Gould, G., 'Women in the writings of the Fathers: language, belief and reality', in *Women in the Church*, Studies in Church History 27, ed. W. J. Sheils and D. Wood (Oxford, 1990) pp. 1–13.

Gould, G., 'The image of God and the anthropomorphite controversy in fourth century monasticism', *Origeniana Quinta*, ed. R. J. Daley (Leuven), 1992 pp. 548–57.

Gould, G., 'Lay Christians, bishops and clergy in the *Apophthegmata Patrum*', *Studia Patristica* XXV, ed. E. A. Livingstone (Leuven, 1993) pp. 296–404.

Gould, G., 'Recent work on monastic origins: a consideration of the questions raised by Samuel Rubenson's *The Letters of St Antony*', *Studia Patristica* XXV, ed. E. A. Livingstone (Leuven, 1993) pp. 405–16.

Gould, G., *The Desert Fathers on Monastic Community* (Oxford, 1993).

Graus, F., *Volk, Herrscher und Heiliger im Reich der Merowinger* (Prague, 1965).

Gray, P. T. R. and Herren M. W., 'Columbanus and the Three Chapters controversy – a new approach', *JTS* 45 (1994) pp. 160–70.

Grégoire le Grand, Colloques internationaux du CNRS (Paris, 1986) ed. J. Fontaine, R. Gillet, and S. Pellistrandi.

Gregorio Magno e il suo Tempo Studia Ephemeridis 'Augustinianum' 34, 2 vols (Rome, 1991).

Gribomont, J., *Histoire du texte des ascétiques de saint Basile*, Bibliothèque du Muséon 32, (Louvain, 1953).

Gribomont, J., 'Le monachisme au IVe siècle en Asie Mineur du Gangres au Messalianisme', *Studia Patristica* 3, ed. K. Aland and F. L. Cross (Berlin, 1957) pp. 400–15.

Griffith, S. H., 'Asceticism in the church of Syria: the hermeneutics of early Syrian monasticism', in *Asceticism*, ed. Wimbush and Valantasis, pp. 220–45.

Griggs, C. W., *Early Egyptian Christianity from its Origins to 451* CE (Leiden, 1990)

Guerout, J., 'Le testament de Ste. Fare', *RHE* 60 (1965) pp. 762–821.

Guillaumont, A., 'Le texte véritable des "Gnostica" d' Évagre le Pontique', *RHR* 142 (1952) pp. 156–205.

Guillaumont, A., 'Un philosophe au désert: Évagre le Pontique,' *RHR* 181 (1972) pp. 29–56.

Guillaumont, A., 'Histoire des moines aux Kellia', *Orientalia Lovanensia Periodica* 8 (1977) pp. 187–203.

Gussone, N., 'Adventus-Zeremoniell und Translatio von Reliquien: Victricius von Rouen *De Laude Sanctorum*', *Frühmittelalterliche Studien* 10 (1976) pp. 125–33.

Hallinger, K. 'Papst Gregor der Grosse und der heiliger Benedikt', *Commentationes in Regula Sancti Benedicti*, ed. B. Steidle, Studia Anselmiana 42 (Rome, 1957) pp. 231–319.

Hallinger, K., 'Das Wahlrecht der Benediktusregula', *ZKG* 76 (1965) pp. 233–45.

Hallinger, K., 'Regula Benedicti 64 und die Wahlgewohnheiten des 6–12 Jahrhunderts,' *Latinität und alte Kirche. Festschrift für Rudolf Hanslik zum 70 Geburtstag*, ed. H. Bannert and J. Divjak (Vienna–Cologne–Graz, 1977).

Hanson, R. P. C., *The Search for the Christian Doctrine of God: the Arian Controversy 318–381* (Edinburgh, 1988).

Harpham, G. G., *The Ascetic Imperative in Culture and Criticism* (Chicago and London, 1987).

Harrison, V. E. F., 'Male and female in Cappadocian theology', *JTS* NS, 41 (1990), pp. 441–71.

Häussling, A. A., *Mönchskonvent und Eucharistiefeier*, Liturgiewissenschaftliche Quellen und Forschungen 58 (Münster, 1973).

Heiming, O., 'Zum Monastischen Offizium von Kassianus bis Kolumbanus', *Archiv fur Liturgiewissenschaft 7* (1961–2), pp. 89–156.

Hen, Y., 'The Structure and Aims of the *Visio Baronti*', *JTS* n.s. 47 (1996) pp. 477–97.

Herbert, M. *Iona, Kells and Derry: the History and Hagiography of the Monastic 'Familia' of Columba* (Oxford, 1988).

Herity, M., 'Early Irish Hermitages in the Light of the *Lives* of Cuthbert', in *St Cuthbert*, eds Bonner, Rollason and Stancliffe pp. 45–63.

Heussi, K, *Der Ursprung des Mönchtums* (Tübingen, 1936).

Hill, P., *Whithorn and Saint Ninian. The Excavation of a Monastic Town* (Stroud, 1997).

Hilpisch, S., *Die Doppelklöster: Entstehung und Organisation* (Münster in Westphalia, 1928).

Hochstetler, D., 'The meaning of monastic cloister for women according to Cæsarius of Arles', in *Religion, Culture and Society in the Early Middle Ages*, ed. T. F. X. Noble and J. J. Contreni (Kalamazoo, 1987) pp. 27–40.

Hodgkin, T. *Italy and Her Invaders*, vols IV and V (Oxford, 1885).

Hollis, S., *Anglo-Saxon Women and the Church: Sharing a Common Fate* (Woodbridge, 1992).

Holzherr, G., *Regula Ferioli. Ein Beitrag zur Entwicklungsgeschicte und zur Sinndeutung der Benediktinerregel* (Einsiedlen, 1961).

Homes Dudden, F., *Gregory the Great: his Place in History and Thought* (2 vols, London, 1905).

Hughes, K., 'The changing theory and practice of Irish pilgrimage', *Journal of Ecclesiastical History* 11 (1960) pp. 143–51.

Hughes, K., *The Church in Early Irish Society* (London, 1966).

Hunter, D. G., Resistance to the virginal ideal in late fourth- century Rome: the case of Jovinian', *Theological Studies* 48 (1987) pp. 45–64.

Hunter, D. G., 'Helvidius, Jovinian and the virginity of Mary in late fourth-century Rome', *JECS* 1 (1993) pp. 47–71.

Hunter, D. G., 'Vigilantius of Calagurris and Victricius of Rouen: ascetics, relics and clerics in Late Roman Gaul', *JECS* 7 (1999) pp. 401–30.

Jacquet, J., 'L'adoption par les ermites d'un milieu naturel et ses consequences sur leur vie quotidienne', *Le site monastique copte des Kellia. Sources historiques et explorations archéologiques. Actes du Colloque de Genève 13 au 15 août 1984* (Geneva, 1986) pp. 21–9.

James, E., 'Archaeology and the Merovingian monastery', in Clarke and Brennan, eds, *Columbanus and Merovingian Monasticism*, pp. 33–56.

Jaspert, B., *Die Regula Benedicti – Regula Magistri Kontroverse* (2nd edn., Hildesheim, 1977).

Jay, P., 'Le purgatoire dans la prédication de saint Césaire d' Arles', *Revue de Théologie Ancienne et Médievale* 24 (1957), pp. 5–14.

Jenal, G., *Italia Ascetica atque Monastica. Das Asketen-und Mönchtum in Italien von den Anfängen bis zur Zeit den Langobarden (ca. 150/250–604)*. Monographien zur Geschichte des Mittelalters, 39, 2 vols (Stuttgart, 1995).

John, E., 'The social and political problems of the early English Church', *Journal of Agricultural History* 18 (1970) Supplement in Honour of G. Finsberg, ed. J. Thirsk, pp. 54–6.

Jones, A. H. M., *The Later Roman Empire*, vol. 2 (Oxford, 1964).

Judge, E. A, 'The earliest use of Monachos for "Monk" (P. Coll. Youtie 77) and the Origins of Monasticism', *Jahrbuch für Antike und Christentum* 20 (1977) pp. 77–89.

Karayannopoulos, I., 'Basil's Social Activity: Principles and Praxis', in *Basil of Caesarea*, ed. Fedwick, pp. 374–91.

Kardong, T. G., 'The monastic practices of Pachomius and the Pachomians', *SM* 32 (1990) pp. 58–78.

Kasper, C., *Theologie and Askese. Die Spiritualität des Inselmönchtum Lérins im 5. Jahrhundert* (Münster, 1991).

Keller, H., 'Mönchtum und Adel in den *Vitae patrum Jurensium* und in der *Vita Germani Abbatis Grandivalensis*', in K. Elm et al., eds, *Landesgeschichte und Geistesgeschichte: Festschrift für Otto Herdin zum 65 Geburtstag* (Stuttgart, 1977) pp. 1–23.

Kelly, J. N. D., *Jerome. His Life, Writings and Controversies* (London, 1975).

Kelsey, N., 'The body and the desert in the *Life of St. Antony*', *Semeia* 57 (1992) pp. 132–51.

Kirwan, C., *Augustine* (London, 1989).

Klingshirn, W., *Caesarius of Arles. The Making of a Christian Community in Late Antique Gaul* (Cambridge, 1994).

Kraemer, C., 'Le Saint-Mont: Première implantation monastique de Lorraine', *Archéologie Médiévale* 19 (1989) pp. 59–79.

Lapeyre, G., *Saint Fulgence de Ruspe. Un évieque catholique africain sous la domination vandale* (Paris, 1929).

Lapidge, M. and Dumville, D., *Gildas: New Approaches* (Woodbridge, 1986).

Lapidge, M. 'Gildas' education and the Latin culture of sub-Roman Britain', in Lapidge and Dumville, eds, *Gildas* pp. 27–50.

Laporte, J., 'Les origines du monachisme dans la province de Rouen', *RM* 31 (1941) pp. 1–13.

Laporte, J., *Le Penitentiel de saint Colomban* (Tournai–Paris–Rome–New York, 1958).

Lawless, G., *Augustine of Hippo and His Monastic Rule* (Oxford, 1987).

Le Goff, J., *La Naissance du Purgatoire* (Paris, 1981).

Leclercq, J., 'La Sainte Radegonde de Venance Fortunat et celle de Baudovinie. Essai d'hagiographie comparée,' *Fructus centesimus. Mélanges offerts à Gérard*

J. M. Bartelink à l'occasion de son soixante-cinquième anniversaire Instrumenta patristica 19, (Steenbrugge, 1989) pp. 207–16.

Leipoldt, J., *Schenute von Atripe* (Leipzig, 1903).

Lemariginer, J. -F., 'Quelques remarques sur l'organisation ecclésiasatique de la Gaule du VIIe à la fin di IXe siècle, principalement au nord de la Loire', *Settimane di Studio del Centro Italiano di Studi sull' Alto Medioevo* XIII (Spoleto, 1966) pp. 451–86.

Lesne, E., *Histoire de la propriété ecclésiastique en France*, Mémoires et Travaux des Facultés Catholiques de Lille VI, vol. I (Paris–Lille, 1910).

Leyser, C., ' "Let me speak": vulnerability and authority in Gregory's Homilies on Ezekiel', in *Gregorio Magno*, vol. II, pp. 169–82.

Liebeschuetz, W., 'Problems arising from the conversion of Syria', *The Church in Town and Countryside*, Studies in Church History 16 (Oxford, 1979) pp. 17–24.

Lienhard, J. T., *Paulinus of Nola and Early Western Monasticism* (Cologne–Bonn, 1977).

Lifshitz, F., 'Les femmes missionaires: l'exemple de la Gaule franque', *RHE* 83 (1988) pp. 5–33.

Linage Conde, A., 'El Monacato Betico del Sevillano San Isidoro', *SM* 32 (1990) pp. 131–8.

Lorenz, R., 'Die Anfänge des abendländischen Mönchtum im 4. Jarhundert', *ZKG* 77 (1986) pp. 1–61.

Löwe, H., ed., *Die Iren und Europa im Frühen Mittelalter*, 2 vols (Stuttgart, 1982).

MacDonald, A. D. S. 'Aspects of the monastery and monastic Life in Adomnan's Life of Columba', *Peritia* 3 (1984) pp. 271–302.

Macqueen, J., *Saint Nynia* (Edinburgh, 1990).

Malone, E. E, *The Monk and the Martyr* (Washington, D.C., 1950).

Markus, R., *The End of Ancient Christianity* (Cambridge, 1990).

Markus, R., *Gregory the Great and His World* (Cambridge, 1997).

Masai, F., 'La "Vita Patrum iurensium" et les debuts du monachisme a Saint-Maurice d'Agaune', in *Festschrift Bernard Bischoff, zu seinem 65 Geburtstag* (Stuttgart, 1971) pp. 43–69.

Mayr-Harting, H., *The Coming of Christianity to Anglo-Saxon England* (3rd edn, London 1991).

McCone, K., 'Brigit in the seventh century; a saint with three lives?', *Peritia* 1 (1982) pp. 107–45.

McCone, K., *Pagan past and Christian present in early Irish literature*, Maynooth Monographs iii (Maynooth, 1990).

McLaughlin, T. P., *Les Très Ancien Droit Monastique de l' Occident* Archives de la France Monastique, vol. XXXVIII (Ligugé–Paris, 1935).

McKitterick, R. 'Nuns' scriptoria in England and France in the Eighth Century', *Francia* 19 (1992) pp. 1–35.

McLynn, N. B., *Ambrose of Milan: Church and Court in a Christian Capital* (Berkeley, 1994).

McNamara, J. A., 'Living sermons: consecrated women and the conversion of Gaul', pp. 19–37 in L. T. Shank and J. A., Nichols eds, *Medieval Religious Women*, vol. II, *Peace Weavers* (Kalamazoo, 1987).

McNamara, J. A., Halborg, J. E. and Whatley, E. G., *Sainted Women of the Dark Ages* (Durham and London, 1992).

McNeil, J. T. and Gamer, H. M., *Medieval Handbooks of Penance: A Translation of the Principal Libri Poenitentiales* (New York, 1938, 1990).

Meredith, A., 'Asceticism–Christian and Greek', *JTS* n.s. 27 (1976) pp. 313–32.

Meyvaert, P., 'Peter the Deacon and the Tomb of St Benedict', *RB* 65 (1955) pp. 3–70.

Meyvaert, P., 'Towards a history of the textual transmission of the Regula S. Benedicti,' *Scriptorium* 17 (1963) pp. 83–111.

Meyvaert, P., 'The enigma of Gregory the Great's *Dialogues*: a response to Francis Clark', *JEH* 39 (1988) pp. 335–81.

Meyvaert, P., 'A comment on Francis Clark's Response', *JEH* 40 (1990) pp. 344–6.

Miller, P. C., 'The blazing body: ascetic desire in Jerome's Letter to Eustochium', *JECS* 1 (1993) pp. 21–45.

Miller, P. C. 'Jerome's Centaur: A hyper-icon of the Desert', *JECS* 4 (1996) pp. 209–33.

Moreira, I., '*Provisatrix optima*: St. Radegund of Poitiers' relic petitions to the East', *JMH* 19 (1993) pp. 285–305.

Morris, R., *Churches in the Landscape* (London, 1989).

Mundó, A., 'Les anciens synodes abbatiaux et les *Regula SS. Patrum*' *Studia Anselmiana* 44 (1959) pp. 107–25.

Muschiol, G., *Famula Dei. Zur Liturgie in merowingischen Frauenklöstern*, Beiträge zur Geschichte des Alten Mönchtums und des Benediktinertums 41 (Münster, 1994).

The Nag Hammadi Library in English, revised edn, gen. ed. J. Robinson, (Leiden, 1988).

Nelson, J., 'Queens as Jezebels: Brunhild and Balthild in Merovingian history', in *Medieval Women*, ed. D. Baker (Oxford, 1978) pp. 31–78.

Neufville, J. 'Sur le texte de la Règle des IV Pères', *RB* 75 (1965) pp. 47–95.

Neufville, J., 'Les Éditeurs des Regulae Patrum: Saint Benoît d' Aniane et Lukas Holste', *RB* 76 (1966) pp. 327–43

Neufville, J., 'Règle des Pères et Second Règles des Péres. Texte critique', *RB* 75 (1965) pp. 307–12.

Ní Cathain, P., and Richter, M., eds, *Ireland and Europe: the Early Church* (Stuttgart, 1984).

Nowack, P., 'Die Strukturelemente des Stundengebets der Regula Benedicti', *Archiv für Liturgiewissenschaft* XXVI (1984) pp. 253–304.

Ntedika, J., *L'evolution de la doctrine du purgatoire chez Saint Augustine* (Paris, 1966).

Ntedika, J., *L'évocation de l' au-delà dans la prière pour les morts* (Louvain, 1971).

Nussbaum, O., *Kloster, Priestermönch und Privatmesse; ihr Verhältnis im Westen von den Anfängen bis zum hohen Mittelalter*, Theophaneia 14 (Bonn, 1961).

Ó Carragáin, É, *The City of Rome and the World of Bede*, Jarrow Lecture 1994 (Jarrow, 1994).

Ó Corráin, D., 'Women in early Irish society', in M. MacCurtain and D., Ó Corráin, eds, *Women in Irish Society* (Westport, 1979) pp. 1–13.

Ó Corráin, D., 'The early Irish churches: some aspects of organization', in D., Ó Corráin ed., *Irish Antiquity: Essays and Studies presented to Professor M. J. O' Kelly* (Cork, 1981) pp. 327–41.

Ó Cróinín, D., *Early Medieval Ireland 400–1200* (London, 1995).

O'Donnell, J. J., *Cassiodorus* (Berkeley, 1979).

O'Neill, J. C., 'The origins of monasticism', in *The Making of Orthodoxy. Essays in Honour of Henry Chadwick*, ed. Rowan Williams (Cambridge, 1989) pp. 270–87.

Olson, L., *Early Monasteries in Cornwall* (Woodbridge, 1989).

Orlandi, T., 'Coptic Literature', in Pearson and Goehring, eds, *Roots of Egyptian Christianity*, pp. 51–81.

Orlandis, J., *Estudios sobre las institutiones monasticas medievales* (Pamplona, 1971).

Palliser, D. M., 'The "minster hypothesis": a case study', *Early Medieval Europe* 5 (2) (1996) pp. 207–14.

Pantoni, A., *L'Acropoli di Montecassino e il Primitivo Monastero di San Benedetto* (Montecassino, 1980).

Parsons, T., introduction to Weber M. *Sociology of Religion*, trans. E. Bischoff (Boston, 1963).

Patlagéan, E., 'L'histoire de la femme déguisée en moine et l'évolution de la sainteté féminine à Byzance', *Studi Medievali* 3rd ser. XVII (1976) pp. 597–623.

Percival, J., 'Villas and monasteries in later Roman Gaul', JEH 48 (1997) pp. 1–21.

Petersen, J. M., *The Dialogues of Gregory the Great in their Late Antique Cultural Background* (Toronto, 1984).

Porcel, O., 'San Gregorio Magno y el Monachato. Cuestiones controvertidas', *Monastica* I (Montserrat, 1960) pp. 1–95.

Poulin, J. C., 'Hagiographie et politique: la première Vie de St Samson de Dol', *Francia* V (1978) pp. 1–26.

Power, K., *Veiled Desire. Augustine's Writing on Women* (London, 1995).

Pricoco, S., *L'Isola dei Santi* (Rome, 1978).

Prinz, F., *Frühes Mönchtum im Frankenreich. Kultur und Gesellschaft in Gallen, den Rheinlanden und Bayern am Beispiel der monastischen Entwicklung (4. bis 8. Jahrhundert)* (Munich–Vienna, 1965).

Puech, H.-C, *Sur le manichéisme et autres essais* (Paris, 1979).

La Riche Personnalité de Sainte Radegonde. Conférences et homélies prononcées à Poitiers à l'occasion du XIVe centenaire de sa mort (587–1987) (Poitiers, 1988).

Riché, P., *Education et culture dans l'occident barbare 6e–8e siècle* (Paris, 1962).

Roberts, C. H., *Manuscript, Society and Belief in Early Christian Egypt* (1979).

Rollason, D., 'Hagiography and politics in Early Northumbria', in *Holy Men and Holy Women: Old English Prose Saints' Lives and Their Contexts*, ed. P. E. Szarmach (Albany, 1996) pp. 95–114.

Roper, M., 'Saint Wilfrid's landholdings in Northumbria' in *Saint Wilfrid at Hexham*, ed. D. P. Kirby (Newcastle, 1971) pp. 61–80.

Rouselle, A., *Porneia: On Desire and the Body in Antiquity*, trans. F. Pheasant (Oxford, 1988) pp. 172–8.

Rousseau, P., 'Cassian, contemplation and the cenobitic life', *JEH* 26 (1975) pp. 113–26.

Rousseau, P., *Ascetics, Authority and the Church in the Age of Jerome and Cassian* (Oxford, 1978).

Rousseau, P., *Pachomius. The Making of a Community in Fourth-Century Egypt* (Berkeley–Los Angeles–London (1985).

Rousseau, P., *Basil of Cæsarea* (Berkeley, 1994).

Rubenson, S., 'Christian asceticism and the emergence of the monastic tradition', in *Asceticism*, ed. Wimbush and Valantasis, pp. 49–57.

Rubenson, S., *The Letters of St. Antony. Monasticism and the Making of a Saint* (Minneapolis, 1995) originally published without translations of the letters themselves as *The Letters of St. Antony: Origenist Theology, Monastic Tradition and the Making of a Saint* (Lund, 1990).

Rudmann, R., *Mönchtum und kirchlicher Dienst in den Schriften Gregors des Grossen* (St Ottilien, 1956).

Ryan, J., *Irish Monasticism. Origins and Early Development* (Dublin and Cork, 1931, 2nd edn, 1972).

Saint Martin et Son Temps, Studia Anselmiana 46 (Rome, 1961)

Sainted Women of the Dark Ages, ed. and trans. J. A. McNamara and J. E. Halborg with E. G. Whatley (Durham and London, 1992).

Sansterre, J.-M., *Les Moines grecs et orientaux à Rome aux époques byzantine et carolingienne (milieu du VIe siècle-fin du Xe siècle)* 2 vols. (Brussels, 1983).

Schneider, D. B., *Anglo-Saxon Women in the Religious Life: a Study of the Status and Position of Women in an Early Medieval Society*, Ph.D thesis, Cambridge, 1985.

Schulenburg, J. T., 'Strict Active Enclosure and its Effects on Female Monastic Experience (ca. 500–1100)', in *Distant Echoes*, ed. L. T. Shank and J. A., Nichols, pp. 51–86.

Schulenburg, J. T., *Forgetful of their Sex. Female Sanctity and Society ca. 500–1100* (Chicago and London, 1998).

Seebass, O., 'Fragment einer Nonnenregel des 7 Jahrhunderts', *Zeitschrift für Kirchengeschichte* 16 (1896), pp. 465–70.

Shank, L. T. and Nichols, J. A. *Medieval Religious Women*, vol. I, *Distant Echoes*, Cistercian Studies 71 (Kalamazoo, 1984).

Shank, L. T. and Nichols, J. A. *Medieval Religious Women*, vol. II, *Peace Weavers* Cistcercian Studies 72 (Kalamazoo, 1987).

Sharpe, R., 'Some problems concerning the organisation of the early Irish church', *Peritia* 3 (1984) pp. 230–70.

Sharpe, R., 'Churches and communities in early medieval Ireland: towards a pastoral model', *Pastoral Care before the Parish* (Leicester, 1992) ed. J. Blair and R. Sharpe, pp 81–109.

Shaw, B., 'The age of Roman girls at marriage: a reconsideration', *JRS* 77 (1987) pp. 30–46.

Shaw, T. M., 'Creation, virginity and diet in fourth-century christianity: Basil of Ancyra's "On the True Purity of Virginity"', *Gender and History* 9 (1997) pp. 579–96.

Shaw, T. M., *The Burden of the Flesh. Fasting and Sexuality in Early Christianity* (Mimeapolis, 1998).

Shelton, J., Introduction to *Nag Hammadi Codices: Greek and Coptic Papyri from the Cartonnage of the Covers*, ed. J. W. B. Barns, G. M. Browne and J. C. Shelton (Leiden, 1981).

Sims-Williams, P., 'Varieties of Monasticism', *Religion and Literature in Medieval England 600–800* (Cambridge, 1990).

Smyth, A., *Warlords and Holy Men. Scotland AD 80–1000* (Edinburgh, 1984).

Spidlik, T., 'L' idéal du monachisme basilien', in *Basil of Cæsarea*, ed. Fedwick, pp. 361–74,

Stancliffe, C., *St Martin of Tours and his Hagiographer. History and Miracle in Sulpicius Severus* (Oxford, 1983).

Stancliffe, C., 'Cuthbert and the Polarity between Pastor and Solitary', in *St. Cuthbert, his Cult and his Community to AD 1200*, ed. G., Bonner, D., Rollason, and C. Stancliffe, (Woodbridge, 1989) pp. 22–42.

Stancliffe, C., 'The thirteen sermons attributed to Columbanus and the question of their authorship,', in *Columbanus*, ed. Lapidge, pp. 93–202.

Stancliffe, C., 'Venantius Fortunatus, Ireland, Jerome: the evidence of Precamur Patrem', *Peritia* 10 (1996) pp. 91–7.

Stenton, F. M., 'Medeshamstede and its colonies', in *Preparatory to Anglo Saxon England*, ed. D. M Stenton (Oxford, 1970)

Stewart, C., *Cassian the Monk* (Oxford, 1998).

Stramara, D. F., 'Double monasticism in the Greek East, fourth through eighth centuries', *JECS* 6 (1988) pp. 269–312.

Straw, C., *Gregory the Great. Perfection in Imperfection* (Berkeley and Los Angeles, 1988).

Stroumsa, G., 'The Manichaean challenge to Egyptian Christianity', in *The Roots of Egyptian Christianity*, ed. B. A. Pearson and J. E. Goehring (Philadelphia, 1986) pp. 307–19.

Stroumsa, G., 'Monachisme et marranisme chez les manichéens d'Égypte', *Numen* 29, (1982) pp. 184–201.

Taft, R., *The Liturgy of the Hours in East and West* (Collegeville, 1986).

Thacker, A., 'Memorializing Gregory the Great: the origin and transmission of a papal cult in the seventh and early eighth centuries', *Early Medieval Europe 7* (1998), pp. 59–84.

Thacker, A., 'Monks, preaching and pastoral care in England', *Pastoral Care before the Parish* eds Blair and Sharpe pp. 140–41.

Thomas, C., *Christianity in Roman Britain* (London, 1981).

Thomas, C., *And Shall These Mute Stones Speak? Post-Roman Inscriptions in Western Britain* (Cardiff, 1994).

Timbie, J., 'The state of research on the career of Shenoute of Atripe', in *The Roots of Egyptian Christianity* eds Pearson and Goehring pp. 258–70.

Tosi, M., 'La presenza della *Regula Benedicti* nel monasteri di S. Colombano', *Archivum Bobiense* III (1981) pp. 7–58.

Tosi, M., 'Arianesimo Tricapitolino norditaliano e penitenza privata Iroscozzese: due piste importante per riprendere la questione critica delle opere di Colombano', *Archivum Bobiense: Rivista degli Archivi Storici Bobiense* X–XI (1988/9) 9–118 and 12–13, pp. 5–144.

Tosi, M., 'I monaci colombaniani del secolo VII portano un rinnovamente agricolo-religioso nella fascia littorale Ligure', *Archivum Bobiense: Rivista degli Archivi Storici Bobiense* XIV (1992) pp. 5–106.

Trevett, C., *Montanism: gender, authority and the New Prophecy* (Cambridge, 1996).

Vagaggini, C., 'La posizione di San Benedetto nella questione semipelagiana', *Studia Anselmiana* 17–18 (1947) pp. 17–83.

Valantasis, R., 'Adam's body: uncovering esoteric traditions in the *Apocryphon of John* and Origen's *Dialogue With Heraclides*', *The Second Century* 7 (1989) pp. 150–62.

Valantasis, R., 'Daemons and the perfecting of the monk's body: monastic anthropology, daemonology and asceticism', *Semeia*, 58 (1992), pp. 47–79.

Valantasis, R., 'Constructions of power in asceticism', *Journal of the American Academy of Religion* 63 (1995) pp. 775–821.

Valantasis, R., 'Is the Gospel of Thomas ascetical? revisting an old problem with a new theory', *JECS* 7 (1999) pp. 55–81.

van Bavel, T. J., ' "Ante omnia" ' et "in Deum" dans la "Regula Sancti Augustini" ', *VC* 12 (1958) pp. 157–65.

van Dijk, S., 'The Urban and Papal Rites in Seventh and Eighth-Century Rome', *Sacris Erudiri* 12 (1961) pp. 411–87.

Veilleux, *La liturgie dans le cénobitisme pachômien au quatrième siècle*, Studia Anselmiana 57 (Rome, 1968).

Veilleux, A., 'Monasticism and Gnosis in Egypt', in Pearson and Goehring, *Roots of Egyptian Christianity*, pp. 271–306.

Verbraken, P.-P., 'Les Dialogues de saint Grégoire le Grand: sont-ils apocryphes? À propos d' un ouvrage récent', *RB* 98 (1988) pp. 272–7.

Verheijen, L., *Saint Augustine's Monasticism in the Light of Acts 4: 32–35* (Villanova, 1979).

Verheijen, L., *Nouvelles Approches à la Règle de saint Augustin* (Abbaye de Bellefontaine, 1980).

Veyne, P., 'The Roman Empire', in P. Ariès and G., Duby, *A History of Private Life*, vol. I (Cambridge, Mass., 1987) pp. 5–234.

Vieillard-Troiekouroff, M., *Les monuments religieux de la Gaule d'après les oeuvres de Grégoire de Tours* (Paris, 1976).

Vööbus, A. H., *History of Asceticism in the Syrian Orient*, vol. I (Louvain, 1958) pp. 66–78.

Walsh, J. R, and Bradley T., *A History of the Irish Church 400–700 AD* (Blackrock, 1991).

Walters, C. C. *Monastic Archaeology in Egypt* (Warminster, 1974).

Wansbrough, M., review of F. Clark, *The Pseudo-Gregorian Dialogues* in *Heythrop Journal* 30 (1989) pp. 356–7.

Ware, K, 'The way of the ascetics: negative or affirmative', in *Asceticism*, ed. Wimbush and Valantasis, pp. 3–15.

Weber, M., *Sociology of Religion*, trans E. Bischoff introduction by T. Parsons, (Boston, 1963).

Wemple, S. F., *Women in Frankish Society. Marriage and the Cloister 500–900* (Philadelphia, 1981).

Wemple, S. F. 'Female spirituality and mysticism in Frankish Monasteries: Radegund, Balthild and Aldegund', in *Peace Weavers*, ed. Shank and Nichols, pp. 39–53.

Whitelock, D., McKitterick., R., Dumville, D., eds, *Ireland in Early Medieval Europe* (Cambridge, 1982).

Wickham, C., *Early Medieval Italy* (London, 1981).

Wiesen, D. S., *St Jerome as a Satirist*, Cornell Studies in Classical Philology 34 (Ithaca, 1964).

Williams, M. A., *Rethinking 'Gnosticism'. An Argument for Dismantling a Dubious Category* (Princeton, 1997).

Wilmart, A., 'Les *Monita* de l' abbé Porcaire', *RB* 26 (1909), pp. 475–80.

Wimbush, V. I., *Ascetic Behavior in Greco-Roman Antiquity: A Sourcebook* (Minneapolis, 1990).

Wipszycka, E, 'Les terres de la congrégation pachômienne dans une list de payements pour les apora', in J. Bingen et al., eds, *Le monde grec. Pensée, litterature, histoire, documents: Hommages à Claire Preaux* (Brussels, 1975) pp. 623–36.

Wipszycka, E., 'Le monachisme égyptien et les villes' in *Travaux et Mémoires* 12 (1994) pp. 1–44.

Wisse, F., 'The Nag Hammadi Library and the heresiologists', *Vigiliae Christianae* 25 (1971) pp. 205–23.

Wisse, F., 'Gnosticism and early monasticism in Egypt' in *Gnosis, Festschrift für Hans Jonas*, ed. B. Aland (Gottingen, 1978).

Wisse, F. 'Language mysticism in the Nag Hammadi texts and in early Coptic monasticism. I: Cryptography', *Enchoria* 9 (1979) pp. 101–20.

Wollasch, J., 'Benedictus Abbas Romensis. Das römische Element in der frühen benediktinischer Tradition' in N. Kamp and J. Wollasch eds, *Tradition als Historischer Kraft. Interdisziplinäre Forschungen zur Geschichte des frühen Mittelalters* (Berlin and New York 1992) pp 119–37.

Wood, I., 'A prelude to Columbanus: the monastic achievement in the Burgundian territories', *Columbanus and Merovingian Monasticism*, eds Clarke and Brennan, pp. 3–32.

Wood, I., *The Merovingian Kingdoms 470–751* (London, 1994).

Wood, I., *The Most Holy Abbot Ceolfrid*, Jarrow Lecture, 1995 (Jarrow, 1995).

Workman, H. B., *The Evolution of the Monastic Ideal* (London, 1913).

Wormald, C. P., 'Bede and Benedict Biscop', in *Famulus Christi*, ed. G. Bonner (London, 1976) pp. 141–69.

Wormald, C. P., 'Bede and the conversion of England: the charter evidence', Jarrow Lecture (Jarrow, 1984).

Wormald, C. P., 'St Hilda, Saint and Scholar (614–80)' in *The St Hilda's College Centenary Symposium*, ed. J. Mellanby (Oxford, 1993).

Wyschogrod, E., *Saints and Postmodernism: Revisioning Moral Philosophy* (Chicago, 1990).

Yarborough, A., 'Christianisation in the fourth century: the example of Roman women', *Church History* 45 (1976) pp. 149–65.

Young, B. K., 'Exemple aristocratique et mode funeraire dans la Gaule Merovingienne', *Annales ESC* 41 (1986) pp. 370–407.

Zelzer, K., 'Der Rufinus-übersetzung der Basiliusregel im Spiegel ihrer ältesten Handschriften', *Latintät und Alte Kirche. Festschrift für Rudolf Hanslik zum 70 Geburtstag*, eds. H. Bannert and J. Divjak (Wien–Köln–Graz, 1977) pp. 341–50.

Zelzer, K., 'Von Benedikt zu Hildemar. Zur Textgestalt und Textgeschichte der Regula Benedicti auf ihrem Weg zur Alleingeltung', *Frühmittelalterliche Studien* 23 (1989) pp. 112–30.

Zelzer, K, 'Zur Frage der Observanz des Benedict Biscop', *Studia Patristica* 20 (1989) pp. 323–9.

Index

Lightning Source UK Ltd.
Milton Keynes UK
UKHW02f2245191217
314764UK00008B/152/P